MORE ABOUT
HOW TO WRITE A MI££ION

Also available

How to Write a Million
(includes *Plot, Characters & Viewpoint*, and *Dialogue*)

More About How to Write a Mi£££on

DESCRIPTION *by Monica Wood*
REVISION *by Kit Reed*
SETTING *by Jack Bickham*

ROBINSON

London

Robinson Publishing Ltd
7, Kensington Church Court
London W8 4SP

This collected edition first published in the UK by
Robinson Publishing Ltd 1996

A copy of the British Library Cataloguing in Publication Data
for this title is available from the British Library.

ISBN 1-85487-435-7

Printed and bound in the EC

10 9 8 7 6 5 4 3 2

FOREWORD

by Michael Ridpath

I enjoy thinking about how to write a good novel. It is a huge question, and one that is impossible to answer completely; perhaps that is its fascination. So much is required from a novelist: originality, imagination, dedication, skill with words, sharp observation, an understanding of people, the time and ability to work alone on one project for months or even years. It's daunting. It becomes even more daunting when you read Dostoevsky, Fitzgerald or Martin Amis. How could I, or you, or any ordinary human being write like them?

You need courage to begin writing. A mixture of humility, so you accept that you know little and have much to learn, and faith in yourself that one day you will produce something that other people will want to read. When measured against any author you admire your prose will at first seem lifeless, embarrassing even. At this point you can give up. Or you can try to become a better writer.

This process can be immensely rewarding. There is so much to learn, so many techniques to be tried. There is the joy of creation: a truly interesting character, an ingenious plot twist, or the evocation of a scene precisely as you remember it. I have been writing for five years now, and during that time I have been learning constantly, developing my skills, pushing myself towards new challenges. I still have much to learn, and I am looking forward to learning it.

There are a number of ways to go about this. The first is to read as widely and carefully as possible within the field that you want to write about. The second is to learn from your own mistakes, both through trying to pinpoint them yourself, and through persuading others to point them out to you. The third is to let someone else teach you.

This last is what the three books in *More About How to Write a Million* do. They look at the elements of writing fiction in detail, in a no-nonsense practical way. They can answer the sort of questions that can leave you staring at the ceiling for hours, questions like, 'How can I introduce this flashback subtly?', or 'How can I make this character more sympathetic?', or 'How can I make this small town come alive for the reader?' If we were all natural geniuses, we wouldn't need these books. But when I have spent an afternoon crossing out more words than I have written, I need all the help I can get.

The first of these books, *Description*, by Monica Wood, covers one of the most intimidating aspects of writing for a beginner. Fear of appearing awkward in my descriptions, or just plain silly, was almost enough to put me off writing in the first place. But over time, I have come to realize that good description is more about finding exactly the right detail in a scene, than about original or dazzling imagery and word-play. *Description* shows that to be a good writer, you need to be a sharp observer, rather than a walking thesaurus.

The book also has some excellent advice on wider issues of style. As Monica Wood writes: 'Style is not a set of authorial quirks! It is a set of deliberate decisions, made over a series of drafts, that becomes an integral part of the story's impact.' She takes you through these decisions, with practical advice on when to show and when to tell, point of view, dealing with flashbacks, the tag-lines for dialogue, and that most cringe-making activity to write as well as read, describing emotion. Refreshingly for a book about writing, it is well-written.

Revision is not boring. When writing a novel, I seem to spend 40 per cent of the time on planning and writing the first draft, and 60 per cent on revision. And the revision is as enjoyable as the initial writing. Honestly.

It is only when you stand back and look at your first draft that you can begin to think properly about issues such as pace, balance, which sub-plots are interesting and which are not. Only then do you begin to understand your characters properly, their nuances, their desires. This is when you can incorporate the clever twists, the subtle references, the precise descriptions. And as you polish and polish your story, it begins to shine. This applies especially to writers who have yet to see their novels published. I am convinced that it was only because I spent two years rewriting my first novel, *Free to Trade*, that it made its way to the top of the slush pile. Spending time revising gives you a chance to stand out from the crowd of other writers who have promise, but have not yet worked hard enough to fulfil it.

Revision, by Kit Reed, provides practical advice on this process. It highlights weaknesses to look out for in your plotting, dialogue, characterization and style. And it also discusses the pros and cons of writing a carefully crafted first draft, as opposed to dashing one off and saving careful thought for later efforts.

At first sight, *Setting*, by Jack Bickham, covers much of the same ground as *Description*. But whereas *Description* tells you how to describe a scene, *Setting* tells you how to observe it. This is a very useful skill. Much of my second novel, *Trading Reality*, was set in Fife, an area of Scotland I do not know well. Armed with *Setting*, I was able to observe and record a whole range of sights, smells and sounds which provided just the right details at the writing stage. Almost every story has a background; this book shows you how to infuse the characters and the plot with the feel of that background.

But these three books are more than handy tools to get you out of difficult situations. For any writer who has spent time thinking about how he can improve his work, they can be intriguing, even exciting. They suggest new ideas, new approaches to writing. They get your brain working.

I hope you enjoy reading these books. More importantly, I hope they help you enjoy writing your own.

Michael Ridpath

DESCRIPTION

MONICA WOOD

For Dan Abbott—teacher, craftsman, friend.

ABOUT THE AUTHOR

Monica Wood is the author of a novel, *Secret Language*, which is currently under option as a television motion picture. Her frequently anthologized short stories have appeared in such publications as *Redbook*, *The North American Review*, *Yankee*, *Tampa Review* and *Manoa*. Her stories have been read on public radio, nominated for the National Magazine Award, and given special mention in the Pushcart Prize. A native of western Maine, she now lives in Portland, Maine, where she freelances as a writing instructor and copy editor.

CONTENTS

INTRODUCTION

Description is not so much an element of fiction as its very essence; it is the creation of mental images that allow readers to fully experience a story. When you write a story, you offer an account of a chain of events, the characters that inhabit those events, and the places in which those events occur. How you describe those events, characters, and places affects your readers' perceptions.

Every technical decision you make during the writing of a new story—from the length of your sentences to your choice of point of view—becomes part of that story's description. The statement "John showed up with a gun" describes an event. "John arrived, pistol glinting in his hand" describes the same event with a little more pizazz. Your instinct for jazzing up a plain declarative sentence has repercussions, however, because the rewrite describes something beyond a simple action. For starters, the rewrite gives us a bit of atmosphere—"glinting" suggests light and gives the gun an aura of menace. Second, it tells us something about the observer, who uses the more accurate word "pistol," and is aware of the "glinting." Third, it suggests something about John's state of mind: a man with a glinting pistol must surely be aching to pull the trigger, whereas a man who simply shows up with a gun could have any number of intentions. The mental images in the rewrite are profoundly different from those in the original sentence. Even the smallest decisions about description can affect a story in countless subtle ways.

When you write, you create a fictional world. You may describe that world in lyrical prose fashioned around a central metaphor; you may opt for a stark, straightforward telling that uses few adjectives;

you may invent a first-person narrator who uses made-up words; you
may render a story entirely in dialogue, evoking characters through
the cadence of their voices. Good description takes many forms and
does not depend solely on adjectives and adverbs for impact. A statement as simple as "the man wept" may be all the description you
need for a particular scene. What makes one story more finished—
more "real" and alive—than another is not a matter of adjectives per
sentence; it is the *accuracy* and *relevance* of whatever description you
do use.

Describing a character as "a beautiful girl who made heads turn"
is not especially accurate: she could be Chinese or African, six feet
tall or four-foot-nine. Focussing on her "coppery hair" or "deeply
flecked eyes" creates a more accurate mental image. If the *fact* of her
beauty rather than a literal picture is what you want to convey, however, then a line of dialogue may make for the most accurate description: " 'Isn't she pretty?' Al said." Or you might write, in a one-line
paragraph:

She was a beautiful girl.

The sentence, like the character, stands alone. The placement of that
sentence accurately evokes the image of a character in a class by
herself.

In addition to being accurate, description must be relevant to
the story at hand. You need not describe the "old, scarred, rickety
maple table in the foyer" when a simple "table in the foyer" will
do. A string of adjectives like this—words with similar meaning and
impact—doesn't create much of a mental image and may even distract the readers from your fictional world. This is irrelevant description, description for its own sake. If the table is important, then describe it in a way that shows its relevance to the story. The same
table described as "a sentry burdened by weeks of unopened mail"
becomes an object with a purpose in the household. The description
also suggests something about the people in the household—why do
they let their mail go for weeks unopened? Remember, you are not
merely writing; you are writing a story! It is up to you to guide your
readers through the story's events and make sure they don't get lost
in a thicket of words and images along the way.

TYPES OF DESCRIPTION

The suggestions and guidelines contained in this book are not designed to alter your natural writing style. Description comes in many forms. The oft-maligned minimalists—many of them brilliant chroniclers of modern life—use spare, economical prose that, paradoxically, opens up a story. A few well-placed details (a half-smoked cigarette, a broken heel, a muddy sunset) can express the essence of a character or place. Other writers are more flamboyant, even rambunctious, with their descriptions: syntactical pyrotechnics spark from every page. Each of these extremes brings its own brand of delight to both writer and reader.

In *A Soldier of the Great War*, novelist Mark Helprin tells an epic tale of war in which descriptions of thunderstorms and moonrises take up pages at a time. Women's faces, the war's grisly battles, ice-laden cliffs, fields, houses, paintings—all are rendered in close, precise, lyrical detail time and again, to the consternation of some readers and the delight of others. Why this much detail? Why not simply tell the story? Because, as the happy reader gradually discovers, *A Soldier of the Great War* is not a tale about war but a tale about beauty. The protagonist is a professor of aesthetics and war veteran at the end of his life, and the story's lyrical descriptions are true to his view of the world. Beauty, we discover, is an affliction, a refuge, an absolute truth. In the final scene, the old soldier/professor watches a flock of swallows being taken down by a hunter. No matter how many are felled, more rise up, banking and fluttering in an exquisite sky. Just as the novel's protagonist has fallen and risen time and again, unable *not* to hope, the swallows keep rising because they know how to do nothing else. It is a memorable scene, a harrowing view of beauty, a metaphor for the novel itself:

> Alessandro turned again to the swallows. Though the sun backlighted them into hallucinatory streaks of silver, he neglected to shield his eyes, and he watched them fill the sky. As the hunter approached the base of the cloud, he made no effort to go quietly or to conceal himself.
>
> Alessandro followed the paths of single swallows in steep arcs rocketing upward or in descent. How quick they were to turn when turning was in order, or to roll and dart through

groups of birds fired at them, as if from a cannon, in an exploding star. This they did of their own volition, and they did it again and again.

For Alessandro they were the unification of risk and hope. It is hard to track them in violent winds high in the blue where they seem to disappear into the color itself, but as long as they take their great chances in the air, as long as they swoop in flights that bring them close to death, you cannot tell if, having risen, they will plummet, or, having plummeted, they will rise.

A story like this demands the lyricism with which Helprin infuses it; a stingier description would neither tell the same tale nor reveal the same character.

At the other end of the continuum are the short stories of Raymond Carver. His prose is quiet, stark, and studded with small, exquisitely chosen details—a descriptive style that matches his somber stories about the terror and pathos of ordinary lives. In "Nobody Said Anything," the narrator—whose irritable, exhausted parents are on the brink of splitting up—observes his mother leaving for work in her white blouse and black skirt:

> . . . Sometimes she called it her outfit, sometimes her uniform. For as long as I could remember, it was always hanging in the closet or hanging on the clothesline or getting washed out by hand at night or being ironed in the kitchen.

Not an adjective in the whole passage, and yet Carver paints an accurate, vibrant picture of the boy's mother, informing the readers about how the boy views her and what their life together is like.

In the novels of Anne Tyler you will find a descriptive style that falls somewhere between these two extremes. Tyler's characters are unusual, often eccentric, and yet utterly real. She makes them real through description that is, like all good description, accurate and relevant. In an early scene from *The Accidental Tourist*, Macon is observing Muriel, "hoping for flaws." The word "hoping" is key here, for Macon does not want to fall for Muriel, or anyone. He does find flaws, described this way:

> . . . a long, narrow nose, and sallow skin, and two freckled knobs of collarbone that promised an unluxurious body.

Macon's view of Muriel's nose and skin might lead readers to believe he is not attracted to her, but the "freckled knobs of collarbone" give him away, a detail that shows Muriel to be both vulnerable and endearing. This is an accurate portrayal of Muriel—she is indeed a bony woman—but also a relevant one, for Macon is exactly the person who could take a meticulous physical inventory of someone and not realize what he is really seeing.

Whether you fall on the baroque or puritan end of the description continuum or somewhere in between, remember that description is not a separate technique that decorates a story; it is a variety of techniques that combine to make a story. After the joyful rush of the first draft, these decisions must be consciously reviewed. Are my details accurate? Did I use the right point of view? Did I use too much narrative and not enough scene? Is my dialogue realistic? Does the flashback create a full enough portrait of the character's childhood? Is my style too ornate for this simple setting? Is the pace too slow or too fast? Are my metaphors overdone? All these questions go straight to the heart of description.

As you read through this book you will be reminded again and again that good description does not flow naturally from the pen. All writers, no matter how experienced, must consciously and purposefully attend to the techniques that make up description. In the following chapters I will explain these techniques—for example, the telling detail, dialogue, point of view, scene, narrative, and flashback—and offer you different ways to use them. By studying these techniques and applying them to your own work, you will come to understand how critical these techniques are for creating rich mental images, for turning a story from an account of something to a description of something. As every writer knows, writing can be by turns thrilling and delightful, discouraging and cheerless. What better antidote for those occasions of discouragement than the discovery of brand-new fiction-writing tools!

CHAPTER 1

DETAILS, DETAILS

DETAILS, AT LEAST THE KIND that make fiction live, can be as small as a well-placed adjective and as large as a central metaphor. Beginning students often scratch their heads when told their stories lack detail. Didn't they point out that the heroine possessed an "interesting personality"? Isn't that a detail? Well, yes and no. It's a detail, but not a useful one. A "calamitous personality," maybe; the "personality of a bee trapped in a mason jar"—now we're talking detail. A detail is a word or phrase or image that helps the readers "see." Don't tell your readers that Judy "looked sad," tell us about the shape of her mouth or the lifeless slats of her hair. Avoid details that call to mind *anybody* and use the ones that call to mind *somebody*.

THE TELLING DETAIL

Sometimes it takes only one or two details to light up a character for your readers. These precise, illuminating finds are the "telling" details of fiction, for they stretch beyond mere observation to give the readers a larger, richer sense of character or place. The old man's carefully parted hair suggests that he has not totally given up. The tinny clatter of cheap crockery implies that the restaurateur has fallen on hard times. The sullen teenager's one-shouldered shrug connotes indifference tinged with contempt.

This kind of detail makes fiction more than what-happens-next storytelling. It makes description more than an account. The right details, inserted at the right times, allow your readers access to a

6

character's inner landscape, to his or her peculiarities, fears, and compulsions that cannot be easily explained. It is one thing to explain to your readers that a character is fearful, quite another to describe the way she shrinks from human touch.

Imagine that you are writing a story about a shy, middle-aged man named Frankie. All his life Frankie has been sheltered by his mother, who has recently died. Your story is about Frankie's struggle to define a life for himself. Picking up the story about two weeks into Frankie's plight, you could begin this way:

> Everything was his now: the bank account, his mother's apartment on Lexington, the fake mantel on which her heart-breaking shepherdess figurines went about their work.

Notice how the telling details in this opening sentence work together. In the first part of the sentence, we are introduced to someone whose mother has died and left some conventional things—money and an apartment. With only these details, we don't know how Frankie feels about his loss; for all we know he could have killed the old lady himself. But the sentence goes on to describe the fake mantel and the shepherdess figurines, "telling" details that soften the harsh introduction of property and money. We get a sense of an orderly apartment in which life was gentle. We have all seen those figurines, in the parlors of our grandmothers or in the windows of the five-and-dime. The way those figurines are described gives us two insights. One: that the shepherdesses are "heartbreaking" implies that Frankie is himself heartbroken; two: that the shepherdesses are going "about their work" implies that Frankie understands, however unconsciously, that he, too, must go on. In one opening line you have given your readers a setting, a character, and an attitude. You have opened the door not to a story, but to an entire world.

Openings like this one depend on your attention to detail. This attention requires careful work that often means paring an entire paragraph to one sentence. After you delete all the mundane, irrelevant information, you might have very little left and have to start again from scratch. The lazy way into this story would read something like this:

> Frankie's mother had died two weeks ago, leaving him ev-

erything she owned. He was heartbroken and scared, knowing he would miss his mother and the gentle life he'd led inside the walls of her orderly little apartment on Lexington. Yet on some level he realized that life must go on.

Do you see how much vitality you've lost by offering information rather than detail?

HOW DETAILS DRIVE THE STORY

At certain junctures, especially in a first draft, you may stumble across a detail that is so telling to *you* that it changes the direction of your story. After giving the readers a bit more about Frankie and his circumstances, let's say you decide to send him to the library, where he sees Andrea, the assistant librarian whom he's long admired from afar. He selects a book from the stacks and prepares to take it to the circulation desk. Which book? Here is the next telling detail. What if he checks out *Oliver Twist?* What about *How to Plant a Flower Garden?* What about *Oriental Sex Secrets?* For reasons you don't fully recognize yet yourself, you decide that *How to Plant a Flower Garden* is Frankie's choice. At this point it simply *feels* right. This choice is important not only because it reveals something about Frankie, but because it dictates where the story is going next.

Recognizing the junctures at which the telling detail is important will help you not only to write in crisp, evocative prose, but also to define your story. How do you recognize these junctures? Unfortunately, there are no rules for intuition, but you might notice that telling details crop up most often when the description addresses itself to one of two areas: a character's immediate surroundings or a character's decision to do something. Certainly the description of Frankie's mother's apartment (the character's immediate surroundings) engages the readers not with a character named Frankie, but with a *certain kind* of character named Frankie. Similarly, Frankie's choice of books (the character's decision to do something) allows the story to take not only a turn, but a *certain kind* of turn. If Frankie puts the garden book back on the shelf and takes the sex book instead, then your story has to head down a different path altogether. And if the story had opened with a description of bars on the windows instead of shepherdesses on the mantel, you would have an entirely different Frankie to work with.

The Frankie you have to contend with now, however, is not concerned with bars on windows. He is nervous about checking the book out himself; his mother had always performed this task for him. You can describe his discomfort in many ways. For starters, you can come right out and tell the readers what Frankie is feeling:

> Frankie wasn't even sure how to go about checking out a book. Was his library card still current? How much would he have to say? Perhaps he could get away with smiling his way through it; his mother always said his smile was darling.

The interior monologue ("Was his library card still current . . .") is nice, and as good a way as any to describe what Frankie is feeling. It's not until the final line, however, that we get the jolt of recognition that comes with just the right detail. That Frankie, a middle-aged man, is comforted by remembering that his mother always thought his smile was "darling" tells us volumes about his helplessness, his dependency, and his too-close relationship with his mother. You might try a little of that same subtlety in the sentences leading up to that final revelation:

> Frankie took his place at the back of the line and set his eyes on the fellow in front of him. A nice-looking boy (college student, Frankie decided), shirt collar turned up, jeans ripped fashionably at the knee. His three books, held casually against one hip, seemed stylish somehow, part of the outfit. Frankie watched him with the precision of a cat as the line dwindled, bringing him nearer to Andrea. Finally it was the boy's turn; he exchanged a few pleasantries with Andrea, his words not so much spoken as poured. Frankie turned to the woman behind him and offered her his place, then waited once again at the line's end, squinting under the harsh fluorescent light. Maybe he could simply smile through the transaction. His mother always said his smile was darling.

This version is longer, but more precise. In the first version the details are few and all we know is that Frankie is generally worried about speaking to Andrea. In the second, you invent someone for Frankie to compare himself to, and the way Frankie views this boy is very telling. By describing how the college kid looks, you are also implying that Frankie must look exactly the opposite, and also that Frankie sees him as competition for Andrea's interest. Here's a twist you hadn't thought of until you began to describe the college boy in the kind of detail that reflects back on Frankie. Also, the observation that the boy's words seem "poured" lets us in on Frankie's fear of how his own words will sound. Perhaps Frankie has a good reason for not wanting to speak? An accent? A stutter? You're learning something about a character of your own invention as your careful details carry you forward. Revelations of this kind become more common as your powers of observation become more precise.

Like most writers, you probably begin a first draft with only a general idea of what is going to happen. The telling detail can be your compass, your way of navigating through a story, guiding your character down one path at the expense of another. Let's say you're writing a story about a lonely office worker who adopts a litter of puppies. While you're describing your main character, out pops a description of her hair, "so silver it looks cold." You like it—but you've got a problem: a woman with cold hair doesn't sound like the puppy-loving type. Therefore the litter of puppies you've left at her office door poses a dilemma quite different from the one you originally envisioned. The story was going to be about a woman's struggle to keep seven puppies; now the story is going to be about a woman's struggle to get rid of seven puppies. The telling detail is a joy to the appreciative reader, but to you, the writer, it is also a valuable doorway through which you enter the mysterious inner chambers of your own characters' lives.

ADDING DETAILS IN LATER DRAFTS

Telling details appear in two ways: suddenly, from your unconscious, to tell you what you need to know about your characters; and deliberately, from your conscious writing self, who already knows the character very well and must divine the most vivid way to convey that knowledge to the readers.

How do you deliberately create a telling detail? In our story about Frankie, many telling details came to us suddenly, and dictated the course of the story. This is what happens in first drafts. In later drafts, however, after we have a good idea of who the character is and the shape of the story in which we have placed him, we should look around for places where a telling detail could enrich the prose. Suppose the first draft contains a scene in the apartment just after Frankie has come home from the library. He gets a glass of milk and sits down at the kitchen table with the book. He begins to leaf through the book, marvelling at the magnificent floral specimens. The scene, as written, contains some rich imagery, including pictures of flowers that seem to furl out from the damp pages, and drops of milk sliding along the side of the glass as Frankie sets it down.

Very nice. But wrong, you decide, in retrospect. At this point in the story, Frankie is still in a cocoon; he has not yet decided to do anything about his life. He cannot yet see the possibilities in flowers. The imagery should be dry, not wet. Get rid of the milk. Put him in the parlor instead of the kitchen, and describe the dusty sunlight coming through the windows. Describe the chalky sound of his weight shifting in the chair. The pictures in the book are flat, not furled. Frankie doesn't yet have the imagination to see real flowers from these pictures. The pages are dry, not damp. Perhaps the sound of his fingers on the pages sounds a little like mice in the walls.

Telling detail is part inspiration and part determination. Keep reminding yourself (in the later drafts) what your story is really about, what phases of human understanding your character is passing through, and create the details accordingly.

ENGAGING THE SENSES

In your rush to get an early draft committed to paper, you could be relying too much on the visual aspects of description. Even your "telling" details are probably visual ones: a shard of mirror, a twisted lamppost, a blue eyelid. *Remember, you have four other senses to work with: taste, touch, smell, and sound.* What your character smells and hears may be even more important than what he sees. A festooned riverboat (a feast for the eyes) might be easy and fun to describe, but the metallic taste in the captain's mouth or the sulphurous odor of the water may be more important to the story.

Look again at the "lazy" beginning from our story about Frankie:

> Frankie's mother had died two weeks ago, leaving him everything she owned. He was heartbroken and scared, knowing he would miss his mother and the gentle life he'd led inside the walls of her orderly little apartment on Lexington. Yet on some level he realized that life must go on.

This passage suffers from more than just a lack of telling detail; did you notice that not *one* of the senses appears here? Frankie—and the reader—hears nothing, smells nothing, tastes nothing, feels nothing, and sees nothing, unless you count the general visual impression suggested by the "orderly" apartment.

Let's continue with Frankie's story as we explore ways of improving description by using sensory details. Frankie checks out his book on flower gardening without saying a word to Andrea. (Let's decide that he does have a stutter.) Humiliated, he slinks out of the library with the book tucked under his arm like something he has stolen.

As it turns out, Frankie *does* end up stealing the book, because he loves it so much and is too shy to return to the library to renew it. He ignores the overdue notices as he spends his spring and summer creating a garden on the patio of his mother's apartment. By August, there comes a moment when Frankie learns something about gardening:

> Frankie studied the bare spots in his garden, perplexed. Except for a stunning pair of day lilies that he'd been assured would grow anyplace, nothing was blooming. The bursts of magenta and blue he'd been counting on since April were nowhere to be found. The delphiniums and hollyhocks—whose show-stopping blossoms he'd been drawn to in the book—were pathetic little sprigs. He glanced up at the weak city sun and realized his mistake: The "full sun" described by the book had never shone on him.

The foregoing passage is adequate for describing Frankie's puzzlement, but a quick scan reveals a missed opportunity. The setting is a *garden*, for goodness sake, and yet the passage engages none of the senses except the sense of sight. Try this one again, using more sensory detail:

Frankie dug into the soil, breathing its damp aroma. He shaped his fingers around the delphiniums' stunted roots, then sat back, perplexed. Except for a pair of ordinary day lilies that rustled near the railing, nothing was blooming. The delphiniums that had caught his eye on the dry pages of his library book had grown only a few inches, a wizened row of sprigs. Below him, the clamor of the morning commute began in the street, exhaust fumes rising. Frankie squinted up at a weak strand of sunlight muscling its way through the grainy air, just enough of a glimmer to warm his balding head. Wiping his hands on his shirt, he realized his mistake: The "full sun" described by the book had never shone on him.

Notice how the sensory details enrich this passage. The competing sounds in this passage—rustling lilies and morning traffic—contain intimations of both hope and despair. Similarly, the garden's damp scent and the feel of sun on Frankie's forehead are signs of hope that offset the despair of the stunted plants and the city's grainy air. This passage is full of atmosphere that illuminates not only Frankie's bewilderment, but his fragile position. He can follow the promise of his garden (the lilies, the rich soil) or succumb to its failure (weak sunlight, exhaust fumes, pathetic sprigs). Instead of information about Frankie, we now have insights about Frankie, for sensory details are evocative, suggestive, telling. And because we've been seduced into sensing Frankie's world, we now have a stake in how he chooses to move through it. The final line presents a challenge: Will Frankie come down on the side of hope ("full sun") or despair ("never shone on him")?

Sensory details invite readers to take your character's side, to understand what is happening to him, to empathize with his every hope and fear. These details bring breadth and depth to character and setting, informing your readers in ways that are surprising, revealing, and a pleasure to read.

SIMILE AND METAPHOR

The strong imagery contained in simile and metaphor is the blood and guts of descriptive fiction. Without it you are working with a mere skeleton, telling rather than showing. Used well, simile and metaphor bring prose to life; paradoxically, however, its overuse can smother the prose and bury the story.

A simile is a figure of speech, usually introduced by *like* or *as*, that compares one thing to another:

> Emmett is as relentless as a wolverine.
> Jenny's eyes shine like chips of onyx.

Because a simile's sole function is comparison, it is not quite as evocative as a metaphor. A metaphor does not so much compare as *transform* one thing to another:

> Luanne was a dainty little bird of a woman, given to quick movements.
> Behind the house Feldman laid out four squadrons of flowers that sprouted, mute and soldierly, exactly where he had planted them.

Metaphor is subtler and more revealing than simile, evoking imagery beyond the original comparison. Luanne is transformed into a bird, with all the attendant (and unmentioned) fluff and chatter and skittishness that we associate with birds. Feldman's squadrons of flowers suggest something about Feldman himself, evoking military associations and the sense that Feldman always gets exactly what he demands.

With a simile, the comparison stops at the end of the sentence; with a metaphor, the reader's imagination goes on to include all the images and associations that the metaphor implies.

Sometimes you can convert a prosaic simile into a vivid metaphor:

> **Simile:** Emmett is as relentless as a wolverine.
> **Metaphor:** "Emmett?" Judy said. "Emmett is nothing but a wolverine, hateful and relentless. Sometimes at night I think I hear him out there, panting at the edge of the yard."

The metaphor transforms Emmett from a man who reminds somebody of a wolverine into a man who embodies the wolverine's terrifying qualities and who evokes the resulting fear and loathing.

A metaphor can resonate far beyond its original invocation; you can thread a metaphor all the way through a story if you want to. An insistent rain might fall through a story about a failed businesswoman trying to get back on her feet. This kind of recurring imagery is a story's *central metaphor*. For example, you could fashion a story around an ice-climbing expedition, using it to mirror and vivify the up-and-down emotions that the climber is experiencing in his crumbling marriage. Michelangelo's *Pietà* could be the central metaphor in a story about a woman artist tending her own dying son.

Writers often discover central metaphors by accident. A friend might exclaim, "I love the kite-flying as a metaphor for Kate's marriage," leaving us to nod wisely while secretly wondering how we ever missed it. Much of our writing comes from the subconscious, and we are all guided by our own personal metaphors, which is why some authors seem to write the same novels over and over. Make yourself aware of your own recurring metaphors, and be careful not to let them become stale.

Whether you discover a central metaphor by accident, or deliberately set out to create one, make sure to weave it subtly into the body of the story, and keep it free of cliché. For example, a five-page story about a young girl's coming of age may be smothered by too many images of springtime, making a simple story seem overblown and melodramatic: blooming flowers, blooming girl. Just because you find some recurring images while rereading a first draft does not mean you are obliged to turn those images into a central metaphor. You may even want to cut some of the images and let the story stand a little more by itself.

Let's return for the moment to our story about Frankie. Notice that a central metaphor is beginning to show itself: light. The harsh fluorescent light of the library; the weak strand of sunlight on his bald head; the observation that full sun has never shone on him. Once you discover a pattern like this, you have a decision to make: punch it up, or tone it down. In this case, the central metaphor of light suits your purpose for Frankie, and you can punch it up a bit by altering Frankie's appearance. Instead of a bald head, give him a stalk of unruly, flame-orange hair that embarrasses him almost as much as his stutter. When the sun shines on him he looks like a lighted match. The recurring image of light in this story is a metaphor for the darkness of Frankie's life, for he has never truly ventured out into the sun. The scene where he is kneeling in his garden with the sun shining on him is a powerful one, inviting the suggestion that Frankie is like the flowers he has planted. Will he blossom like the "ordinary" day lilies, or wither like the delphiniums, which were more promising on paper than in reality?

Let's give Frankie a break and write him a happy ending. He decides he isn't made for raising showy flowers; he doesn't have the right conditions (literally and metaphorically, of course). However, he knows he can grow easy flowers, as proved by the day lilies, so he fills his barren garden with them, discovering how beautiful they are when massed together. As a final act of faith, he gathers the most beautiful of the lilies and heads back to the library to return the book to Andrea. The story ends with Frankie standing in front of the library first thing in the morning, waiting for Andrea to unlock the door. This final moment cries out for a strong image; after all, Frankie has decided to allow the full sun to shine on him at last:

> Frankie stood at the library door, flowers in one hand and book in the other, his hair brushed into the red pompadour of a rooster about to announce the dawn.

This final metaphor (the rooster) illuminates Frankie's awkward confidence (his wild red hair has been turned into an asset) and his decision to begin anew. Moreover, "announcing the dawn" brings in a final, reassuring image of light.

THE VIRTUE OF RESTRAINT

Simile and metaphor are irresistible writing devices, but you must take care to control your impulses. We writers are always seeing things in terms of something else (it's called imagination) but imagery can become so burdensome that the readers can't find the story. Metaphors look obvious and simple-minded if rendered too directly and too frequently. Images like thunderclaps during the sex scene, or wolves howling on the evening before the execution are best left behind. And beware of mixed metaphors, in which imagery runs away with itself and ends up confusing the readers:

> Arianna shook back her mane of auburn hair. She began

to slink toward me, a lioness with the single-mindedness of a rattlesnake.

Are you comparing Arianna with a lion or a snake? Once you've begun with one image (the "mane of hair" already suggests a lion), don't mar it by adding something else. It can be fun, however, to allow your characters themselves to mix metaphors. The character who proclaims "You can't make a gift horse out of a sow's ear" makes for entertaining company.

WRAP-UP

The next time you set out to write a story, remember how versatile the telling detail can be. One well-placed detail can save you half a page of description. Telling details can be come upon accidentally in the rush of a first draft, or they can be deliberately crafted, puzzled over, and inserted into places where either your character or plot requires a certain kind of image: timidity (a fleeing mouse, half-drawn shades); corruption (broken-up asphalt, fishnet stockings); hope (apple orchards, new shingles). These details are the "way in" to the story, and the readers will appreciate them.

Details are not merely visual; remember to engage all the senses. The dryness of chalk on the fingers can be more arresting than the visual image of a character's whitened fingertips. Sounds and scents and tastes also add to a reader's engagement with the story.

Simile and metaphor make fiction breathe. Simile, which is a figure of speech comparing one thing with another, can help readers "see" what you're describing. Beware of its overuse, lest you be accused of trying too hard to be writerly. Metaphor is subtler than simile, because it does not compare so much as transform. A little girl becomes a kitten when described in terms of feline mewing and skittish motion. Metaphors can be contained in one sentence, or expanded to thread through an entire story as a central metaphor. A snowstorm, a railroad, or a pair of red shoes are images that could be expanded into metaphors for confusion, progress, or heedlessness.

The telling detail is where description begins. It is the device through which you introduce your readers—and sometimes yourself—to the true nature of your characters.

CHAPTER 2

SHOWING AND TELLING

SHOW-DON'T-TELL, SHOW-DON'T-TELL, show-don't-tell. Wherever you go—writing conferences, university classrooms, writers' groups—you hear this well-used writing maxim. "Showing" is generally thought of as using vivid details and engaging the senses, therefore painting a bright descriptive picture for the readers: the richness of a landscape, the shock of disappointment in a new marriage, the fireworks of rage between Character A and Character B. "Telling" is generally thought of as the absence of vivid detail—uninspired narrative that serves only to explain what is going on in the story: who is related to whom, where the town is located, how Character C got her nickname, and so on.

Neither of these characterizations is entirely correct. "Show, don't tell" is a *guideline*, not a rule! "Showing" can indeed reveal character and plot in a dynamic way. However, "telling" can often do the same thing as long as you find the right words. Showing and telling are equally powerful and important descriptive techniques. Before we explore their possibilities, let's review their differences.

WHAT'S THE DIFFERENCE?

Showing and telling are the heart and soul of description, but many inexperienced writers have trouble discerning the difference between them. The following example should give you a fair idea of how these techniques differ. Imagine you've created a mousy little character named Alice, whom you introduce through the technique of "telling":

> **Version One—Telling:** Alice was a timid young woman who looked like a mouse. She was short and skinny, with brown hair, small eyes, and a pointed face. She always peeked inside the doorway before entering a party, thus giving herself a chance to flee in case she saw no one she knew.

Now try this introduction again, this time using the technique of "showing":

> **Version Two—Showing:** Alice hovered at the door of Everett's apartment, chin lifted, tiny feet balanced on their toes. She peered inside, shrinking at the loudness of Everett's new stereo. She breathed quickly, her black eyes darting back and forth, as if keeping her face in motion might prevent her from toppling over. When she finally spotted the wide-grinning Everett approaching, she scurried to the punch bowl, her flat shoes making a scritching sound on the polished wood.

In Version One, you tell the readers that Alice looks and acts like a mouse; in Version Two, you show her in mouselike terms: black eyes, quivering face, tiptoed stance, scritching sound.

Each version is serviceable enough, but each also comes with potential problems. In Version One, the description of Alice is accurate but perfunctory: timid, short, brown hair, small eyes. The passage picks up a little with the image of her "peeking" inside the doorway, then loses steam again with a plodding explanation: "thus giving her a chance to flee . . ." The readers can't really "see" Alice here. You are pausing to tell them something about Alice in order for the next part of the story to make more sense. When Alice finally walks into the party and hides behind a potted plant, the readers understand that she's doing this because she is timid and mouselike. This explanation is fine, for now; you have not necessarily made a mistake in telling the readers what Alice looks like. But if subsequent descriptions take the same form (Reginald was tall and grim and looked like a goose; Evelyn looked like a plucked chicken and had a temperament to match), your prose is going to start seeming flat and expository. You're explaining too much up front, rather than letting the characters reveal themselves through their words and deeds. The readers will feel as if they're watching characters on a screen, or leafing through photographs of characters, rather than entering the story and inhabiting the characters' world.

In Version Two, on the other hand, you allow the readers into Alice's world. We can feel Alice's nervousness because of the motion and sound in the description: she darts and hovers and scritches and shrinks. Again, there is nothing wrong with this passage. In fact, it portrays Alice so vividly that we can easily imagine ourselves at the door of the party with her. The caution with this kind of showing is not to overdo it. Depending on what happens next in the story, you may be lingering too long at the door. Maybe Alice isn't the main character, and all this "showing" is taking the spotlight away from someone else who is more important. Besides, too much showing can start to seem self-conscious, as if you're brandishing your arsenal of similes and metaphors just for the heck of it. Your characters might even disappear in the process. Don't let your prose style overwhelm the story you want to tell.

Too much telling can flatten your story, too much showing can overwhelm it. What's a conscientious writer to do? A combination of showing and telling usually yields the best description:

> **Combination:** Alice stood at the door of Everett's apartment with all the self-possession of a field mouse. Hands clasped at the waist, she stood on tiptoe and peered inside to see who she might know.

The reason the combination works so much better is that a little bit of telling makes the showing seem less labored. By coming right out with the mouse analogy at the beginning, you can give Alice's mouselike qualities a more subtle turn; the phrase "all the self-possession of a field mouse" suggest lots of other mouselike qualities: skittishness, vigilance, furtiveness. You don't have to "show" every one of them. A couple of small touches—clasped hands, tiptoed stance—paints a nearly complete picture. Don't deny your readers the pleasure of filling in some details themselves.

Examine the work of your most cherished authors, and you will find that the show-tell combination permeates their best stories. To admonish writers to show and not tell is to rob them of the deep satisfaction of learning to balance these wonderful techniques.

SCENE AND NARRATIVE

The above examples illustrate showing and telling only in their most general application. In their most technical form, showing can be thought of as *scene*, telling as *narrative*. To properly balance scene and narrative so that a story takes on depth and insight and rhythm and shape, you must first understand the difference between scene and narrative and how they complement each other.

Scene serves a specific purpose; it usually contains dialogue; it has a beginning, middle, and end; and it moves the story forward. *Narrative* is the flow of prose—the string of sentences and paragraphs—that tell the story. A scene almost always contains some narrative, but the converse is not true; narrative does not have to contain scene.

Let's begin a story in two ways, first with a narrative passage and then with a short scene.

> **Narrative ("telling"):** Ms. Kendall was Middleton School's most popular teacher. She was always bringing in maps and atlases to brighten her classroom and motivate her fourth graders. The children adored her and ran to her aid every time they had a chance. Mrs. Brimley, the other fourth-grade teacher, watched this daily homage with a mixture of resentment and awe.

As you can see from the above passage, narrative allows you to make the point and do the informing yourself. You can give readers direct information about your characters' virtues, failings, and inner conflicts as well as the more mundane aspects of their lives: employment, appearance, or marital status, for example.

In a scene, on the other hand, the characters and setting can make the point for you:

> **Scene ("showing"):** Ms. Kendall paused at her classroom door and shifted her full-color maps of the NATO nations from one arm to the other. Spotting her, a small group of fourth graders dropped the books they were hauling and rushed to her aid, yipping like puppies, each clamoring to be the one to turn the knob.
>
> "Children! Children!" Ms. Kendall trilled, her musical laughter echoing down the dingy corridor. "One at a time, now. You can't all help at once."

> Mrs. Brimley, marooned at the far end of the hall amidst a splatter of upended math books, thinned her lips and sighed over the echo of stampeding feet.

This passage, though brief, can be considered a scene because it serves a purpose (to show that Ms. Kendall is popular with the children and that Mrs. Brimley resents it); it contains dialogue; it has a beginning (the pause at the door), a middle (the stampede), and an end (Mrs. Brimley's abandonment); and it moves the story forward (puts Mrs. Brimley in a position of reacting to what she has just experienced). Mini-scenes like this combine to create larger scenes, and the larger scenes combine to create a story. Scenes have to be relieved by spots of narrative, though, or your story will never end. For example, a narrative passage like this—"Mrs. Brimley marched the children through their multiplication drills, willing the clock's heavy hands to move"—saves you a long, unnecessary scene depicting Mrs. Brimley drilling her students. You can suggest the torpor of the long afternoon without subjecting the unfortunate readers to a torpid scene.

Most of us have been trained to think of narrative (telling) as "bad description" and scene (showing) as "good description." Certainly a case can be made that in the above examples, the scene is better than the narrative passage, but that's only because both passages are rendered in such extremes. The narrative passage is dull and expository—it doesn't vividly describe the Kendall-Brimley conflict. The verbs aren't particularly strong (was; motivate; ran; watched), and the picture being painted doesn't engage the senses. There is no sound or movement; again, we're watching characters on a screen. The scene, on the other hand, contains noise and movement and dialogue and marvelous verbs like "marooned" and "yipping." Does that mean you should begin this story with a scene? Not necessarily.

Perhaps you wish to paint only a brief (but potent) picture of the Brimley-Kendall relationship to get to the real story, which is about Mrs. Brimley. Perhaps you plan to portray Mrs. Brimley as a woman with numerous personal burdens—a dying mother, a divorce in progress, fading beauty, an ungrateful son—who becomes fascinated by Ms. Kendall, in whom she sees the girl she herself once was. In a rare impulsive moment Mrs. Brimley steals Ms. Kendall's classroom key. She begins to prowl Ms. Kendall's classroom at night, sifting through Ms. Kendall's button collection and cuddling the classroom hamster. In time she can't stop, for Ms. Kendall's possessions have become talismans of sorts, good-luck charms that fend off Mrs. Brimley's weariness and grief. If this is the story you decide to tell, then the above scene might not merit so much ado; you might want to deliver the initial information quickly, in order to get on with the real story. Back to narrative, then—but this time with more attention to the prose:

> **Narrative, second draft:** Mrs. Brimley envied Ms. Kendall's youth: her silky arms, her just-washed hair, her easy way with the thirty-five fourth graders they divided between them. The children preferred Ms. Kendall, every last one of them, and who could blame them? She had the voice of an angel; her laughter was a salve. *I love her,* Mrs. Brimley whispered dozens of times a day. *And I hate her.*

Do you see the difference? This is narrative that is every bit as effective as scene. Narrative does not have to be merely informational. This passage contains imagistic language ("silky arms" and laughter like a "salve") and a haunting bit of sound with the whispered "I love her . . . I hate her." The internal monologue (". . . who could blame them?") brings your readers deep inside Mrs. Brimley's experience.

Now you have an engaging story opening that introduces two contrasting characters and sets up a tense internal conflict in Mrs. Brimley. Technically, you have "shown" nothing, but by using imagistic language and a bit of internal monologue you have summarized the story's basic conflict and given your lucky readers a perfect point of entry: a character with some meat on her bones, and a story with a destination. You have revealed something about Mrs. Brimley that might have been diluted or lost in a full-blown scene.

If you forced yourself to "show" everything you've "told" in this passage, you'd be confronted with five pages instead of one paragraph. You'd have to begin with a scene that shows Ms. Kendall being the preferred teacher, then you'd have to show Mrs. Brimley in a situation where she loves Ms. Kendall, and another in which she hates her. You'd lose the immediacy of the dilemma, the mantra-like

I love her, I hate her, the tinge of mystery, and the intensity of Mrs. Brimley's sorrow. A scene-by-scene revelation would rob your readers of that exquisite, all-at-once wallop of insight—that Mrs. Brimley has suffered a long time with her conflicting emotions. Besides, your readers may become impatient with a story that takes too long to begin.

Of course, the happiest compromise in the scene-narrative dilemma is combination. This blending process is what good writing is all about. During revision you make continual decisions about scene and narrative, whether you realize it or not. You might throw out a line here, add a snippet of dialogue there, change an adjective or verb. You're balancing, balancing: scene and narrative, narrative and scene. Showing, telling, telling, showing. The combination often yields something like the following:

> **Combination narrative and scene:** Mrs. Brimley's 4A's, each with an armload of math books they were helping to transfer from the library to Room 3, spotted Ms. Kendall at the other end of the corridor. She was stalled at her classroom door, shifting her own bundle—full-color maps of the NATO nations—from one arm to the other. Dropping their books like so many bombs, the 4A's rushed to her aid, yipping like puppies, each clamoring to be the one to turn the knob.
>
> "Children! Children!" Ms. Kendall trilled, her musical laughter echoing down the dingy corridor. "One at a time, now. You can't all help at once."
>
> Mrs. Brimley, suddenly marooned amidst a splatter of upended books, thinned her lips and sighed over the echo of stampeding feet. She envied Ms. Kendall's youth: her silky arms, her just-washed hair, her easy way with the children. Who could blame them for adoring her? She had the voice of an angel; her laughter was a salve. Mrs. Brimley sighed, bending to retrieve the books. *I hate her*, she whispered, tucking back a ripped page. *And I love her.*

This blend of narrative and scene yields a meaty, intriguing opening for your story. Scene and narrative do not always have to be combined, however. You may have a stylistic preference for one over the other; your intentions for the story may require more narrative than scene, or vice versa. Some stories can successfully be rendered as scene alone—completely in dialogue and gesture, with no narrative at all. Other excellent stories are told entirely as narrative in which no dialogue intrudes and the prose flows smoothly from beginning to end. In general, though, a combination of scene and narrative makes for the most pleasing and traditional storytelling.

HOW TO "TELL"

Readers (and writing instructors) won't complain that you're "telling too much" as long as your prose sings. Whether you choose a folk song or an aria is up to you. Some telling can be downright showy and makes for splendid description. Look at the differences in the following simple, declarative sentences:

> Mrs. Brimley went into Ms. Kendall's classroom.
> Mrs. Brimley sneaked into Ms. Kendall's classroom.
> Mrs. Brimley lurched into Ms. Kendall's classroom.

All three sentences describe a person entering a room. Can you see how much less vivid the first one is than the others? Remember, no matter how small the action, you are *describing* it to the readers, not just informing them that it happened. You can add life to a sentence just by changing the verb. Verbs like "sneaked" or "lurched" suggest more than a mere action; they describe a character's state of mind. Embroider the sentence even further, with some strong images, and the prose springs to life:

> Mrs. Brimley sneaked into the darkened classroom, her breath stalled in her throat, her eyes caught on a slender thread of moonlight that defined the wire rungs of the hamster's cage.

This is a good example of a narrative passage that gets its energy from imagistic language. Not only are you telling your readers that Mrs. Brimley is entering the classroom on the sly, you are showing them her heightened sense of awareness by describing the light on the cage. You are also showing them that Mrs. Brimley's clandestine entry is at night without ever coming right out and saying "that night," or "long after dark." The thread of moonlight tells the tale. You can go on to describe the creases in Mrs. Brimley's face, the hair that's mashed down on one side, the glint of her mother's ring under the eerie light. Technically, you're still telling, but in a way that offers the readers a vivid picture of a woman who is not altogether grounded, at least not at the moment. Call it "show-telling" if you wish. Show-telling demonstrates your descriptive powers. No one will fault you for that. Readers complain, "It's too talky" or "Nothing's happened yet" only when the prose itself is flat.

Another way to get a "showy" quality into your narrative is to use internal monologue. Internal monologue is a narrative line that is intended to echo the character's own voice. It is a very effective way to bring the readers so close to the character's experience that they feel they are being "shown" the character's innermost thoughts. Look at the following narrative passage, which uses no internal monologue:

> **Straight narrative:** Mrs. Brimley skulked the perimeter of Ms. Kendall's classroom, allowing her eyes to adjust to the dark. Slowly the shapes of the classroom came clear: desks moved into groupings of four; a full-sized skeleton propped on its stand; silhouettes of posters and bookcases. The aquarium cast an eerie light across the back of the room, where Ms. Kendall's calico hamster ran round and round the wheel in its cage. Her heart seemed to beat in concert with that whirring wheel, for she felt guilty for leaving her mother alone and began to worry that something had happened in her absence. And yet she could not leave. Entering this classroom, this mysterious, underlit realm, made her feel so close to Ms. Kendall.

This is a perfectly functional "tell" passage that uses some good, imagistic language. Still, you are "telling" an awful lot: how Mrs. Brimley feels (guilty and worried), what the room looks like, why she won't leave (she feels close to Ms. Kendall). In the following revision, internal monologue enlivens the passage a bit, bringing readers so close to Mrs. Brimley's experience that the passage seems to "show" more than "tell," even though it retains its narrative character:

> **Internal monologue added:** Mrs. Brimley skulked the perimeter of Ms. Kendall's classroom, allowing her eyes to adjust to the dark. How beautifully the shapes appeared: desks in happy groupings, the classroom skeleton loitering on its stand; posters

and bookcases poised in silhouette! The aquarium cast an eerie light across the back of the room, where Ms. Kendall's calico hamster ran round and round the wheel in its cage. Like my heart, Mrs. Brimley thought, putting a hand on her chest. She felt it beating in concert with that whirring wheel. She had left her mother alone, but who could fault her? Who could blame her for lingering in this mysterious, underlit realm, this place that felt like the inside of her own soul?

Okay, maybe it gets a little melodramatic at the end, but can you see the way the internal monologue works to "show" what Mrs. Brimley is experiencing? It is as if Mrs. Brimley is speaking directly to us. Her voice emerges obscurely at first: *How beautifully the shapes appeared!* ; then more prominently: *Like my heart, Mrs. Brimley thought* ; and then we hear the echo of her literal voice: . . . *who could fault her? Who could blame her* . . . ? It's as if she is saying, Who could fault me? Who could blame me . . . ? Internal monologue, more than any other technique, blurs the line between scene and narrative, because the dialogue of a scene is implied within the narrative.

As you can see, telling doesn't exist in one box, showing in another. If the prose is rich and careful, showing and telling become inseparable.

HOW TO "SHOW"

Inexperienced writers often take "showing" to extremes. They believe that good description means showing everything right down to the polka-dots on the characters' underwear. They have been trained to believe that simply *informing* readers about something—a character's anger, say—is a failure of imagination. They believe they must "show" the anger in great detail to make the readers feel it:

> Maxwell's nostrils began to flare, and a wash of red began to rise from his neck upward, into his cheeks and forehead. He narrowed his eyes and his jowls quivered uncontrollably. Little gobs of spit formed at the corners of his mouth. Teeth bared, fists clenched, he spit the words into the public-address system.

This passage is a good example of trying too hard. This is a parody of rage, with nary a body part neglected. Showing and not telling can become a tiresome game: "50 Ways to Express Rage (or sorrow/love/ anxiety/bitterness/despair) Without Once Using the Word." Writers who play this game probably mean well; they believe their descriptive powers can be properly displayed only through one elaborate "show" after another. They become the victims of their own best intentions, for the writing becomes self-conscious and even ridiculous, with passages so loaded with detail that the readers can't find the story. Sometimes it's better to come right out and tell:

> Maxwell felt the full measure of his rage begin to rain down on him.

This description—which is a good example of show-telling (a rage so intense it seems to "rain down")—is terse enough to leave room for other elements of description—dialogue, for example—to complete the picture of Maxwell's anger:

> Maxwell felt the full measure of his rage begin to rain down on him. "You son of a bitch." He spat the words into the public-address system. "First Lester's will, and now this."

In other words, you have to *make decisions* about what to show. How you decide depends on the story. In the preceding example, Maxwell's rage is evidenced by what he says and not how his face looks. In a different story, Maxwell's face might be the better vehicle to "show" his rage.

Choosing What to "Show"

Imagine that your story contains a character named Eulalie, whose age and infirmity drive the storyline. You decide to spend some time "showing" her feebleness:

> Eulalie tottered across the street, her spotted hands curled around the glossy knob of her cane. Through her thin cloth coat you could see the stippled curve of her spine. Before her loomed the oaken doors of the Social Security Administration, stolid and heavy. She sighed. First she'd have to navigate what looked like five thousand granite steps, each of which would require a painful bend of the knee.

In this example, you don't "tell" the readers that Eulalie is old and infirm, and yet her fragility in the face of a hardy world is palpable. Her bent back implies burdens both physical and emotional; the thin coat implies modest means; the building is physically intimidating and promises pain, implying the same about the system it houses. These telling details evoke the readers' empathy, which is what showing is all about. By showing us Eulalie's physical state rather than telling us about it, you make her real, sympathetic, and understandable. This passage works so well because *you are not showing for its own sake*; the description contains important insights into Eulalie's life and character that shore up the story and make it more than a plot.

On the other hand, if you want to focus on Eulalie's considerable strengths *despite* her age, you might want to deliver the information about her age and physical state more directly, and save the "showing" to reveal her personality:

> **Version One:** Eulalie was 92 years old and ailing, but that wasn't going to stop her from marching right down to the Social Security Administration this very afternoon and giving those pink-cheeked little punks a piece of her mind.

In this version, Eulalie's age and infirmity are dispatched with at the outset ("92 years old and ailing"), leaving you free to concentrate on showing what's really important about her. Instead of wasting space "showing" her feebleness, you move instantly to the steel beneath the fragility. She is old enough and crotchety enough to view the clerks as "pink-cheeked little punks"; instead of walking or taking the bus, she plans on "marching right down" to confront them. The readers can imagine the whole story—a little old lady taking on a bureaucracy—from the language contained in that one sentence. And you've established character even further by using language that Eulalie would use, almost as if she were telling the story herself. You are not technically "showing" here; you are informing us that Character A is about to perform Action B. But if the language is rich enough, the story will shimmer whether you're "technically" showing or not. Look at the difference in the passage when you use an objective, expository style:

> **Version Two:** Eulalie, an old woman whose social-security checks had stopped coming since the death of her husband, was

angry. She decided to go to the Social Security Administration building, all the way across town, to find out what happened. She was feisty and crotchety and thought of the buttoned-down clerks as nothing more than pink-cheeked little punks.

The difference between Version One and Version Two is that Eulalie is not present in the second as she is in the first. Version One shows a picture of Eulalie and the possibilities contained in that frail shell. Version Two merely delivers information: Eulalie *is* A and *does* B and *feels* C. It is not showing; it is telling in the most pedantic sense. Again, we're looking at a character on a screen. We cannot enter Eulalie's world in Version Two the way we can in Version One. Instead of hearing echoes of Eulalie's own feisty, crotchety voice, we are *told* that she is feisty and crotchety.

WHEN TO USE NARRATIVE, WHEN TO USE SCENE

As a writer, you get to choose how to manage showing and telling. Jane Austen wrote entire novels in the "telling" style; Philip Roth's novel *Deception* is rendered wholly in dialogue, an extended "show." Reread some favorite stories or novels and identify the passages that tell, the ones that show, and the ones that combine the two. It can be an enlightening and inspiring exercise to see how admired authors handle the balance. Before you try imitating Roth or Austen, however, you should familiarize yourself with the practice of combining scene and narrative.

Generally speaking, when a story calls for some action, you write a scene. But some action is more important than other action. If you are writing a story about a woman who goes to the local butcher to buy some meat and finds the poor man bludgeoned to death behind the counter with his apron wrapped around his neck, you probably will render that action in scene rather than narrative. However, if the story is really about the woman herself and not the crime she witnessed, you might want to skip that scene altogether. Maybe the story depends more on how she describes the murder to others, over and over again. Witnessing the aftermath of a murder gives her an identity, a status in her family or town that she never dreamed of having.

You title the story "Witness," and begin by "telling":

> On Tuesday Ellen Kornbluth witnessed a murder. Or close enough. She saw the butcher, dead on his stained tile floor, the bloody apron wrapped around his poor pulverized head. Then she saw the orange tail of the murderer's coat, a whisk of movement through the back door.

With two lines of narrative you've introduced the witness and the murder as the *given* of the story; the actual story is revealed a few lines later, at the beginning of this scene:

> "I saw something," she said to her husband. "I saw a murder."
>
> Her husband looked up from his paper. "No, you didn't."
>
> Ellen felt a little flutter of triumph, a cool trilling through her veins. "Oh, but I did. And I've been to the police, and I sat in one of those interview chairs like you see on TV."
>
> He folded the paper once, twice. Set it down on the coffee table that still held the sheen of a special polish Ellen had bought from the hardware store two doors down from the butcher. The dead, murdered butcher. "You saw no such thing," he said, and she could see he was already jealous.
>
> She smoothed her sweater over her bosom, then again down each arm. "I stopped in for the polish, and then I picked up some bread at Mrs. Cutler's, and then I ran into Mrs. Doyle. She had herself a nice pork roast and asked me if I could give her my pineapple pork recipe from memory, which of course I could, and it took about ten, fifteen minutes what with the other things we found to talk about. Ten minutes at least, long enough for a man to do murder." She looked up slyly. "I thought to myself, I'll pick up a nice pork roast myself, since I'm right here in the neighborhood. That's what I thought to myself." She plucked a couple of cat hairs from her cuffs. "The murderer wore an orange coat." She could barely keep from dancing. "I'm the eye witness. That's how the police wrote me down."

Do you see how, in this story, a full-blown murder-discovery scene at the beginning would undercut the essence of the story? Ellen's triumph is not really in witnessing a murder but in being able to puff herself up later as an "eye witness." A scene that shows Ellen walking into town, stopping for furniture polish, stopping for bread, stopping to chat with her friend, entering the butcher shop, calling out for service, walking around the counter, discovering the body, catching sight of the orange coat, calling the police, and so on might be compelling in and of itself, but the story is not set up to support such a scene. That initial action is the not the important action; that's not where the story is. The story begins *after* the discovery of the murder: Ellen's smugness and glee over the butcher's unfortunate demise give the story its tension and drama, and expose the dullness of her life and marriage. The way she smiles slyly and plucks cat hairs off her sweater while trying to keep from dancing is the important action. A scene is entirely called for here: this is the location of the "real" story.

Most experienced writers develop a sixth sense about when a scene is called for to interrupt the narrative. A little voice appears at the back of their consciousness, saying "This is boring," or "The pace is slowing down." The only way to develop this sixth sense is to write a lot (dozens and dozens of stories) and learn by trial and error. In the meantime, though, keep asking yourself *where* the story is, and place your scenes there.

As another example, let's try a story about a wife who has an affair with her husband's boss. Is the dramatic tension of this story contained in the husband-wife relationship, or in the emotional tug-of-war between the wife and the lover? Try the story both ways. You might find that the story interests you most when the husband and wife are having an ostensibly normal dinner at home. The phone rings. She answers. It's the boss (her lover), wanting some information from the husband about an important account. He can't come to the phone because he's in the happy process of feeding their small son, whom he adores, so she relays messages back and forth, having her own illicit conversation with her lover at the same time. Good scene. Great descriptive possibilities, loaded with nuance. This is where a scene belongs, where the real story (the husband-wife relationship) occurs. The wife-lover part of the story, which is less important, can be delivered through narrative—

She saw him twice a week, at the same hotel. For two hours she would pretend to be a character from a movie, charming

and irresistible and living a life far from the cereal-stained coun-
tertops of their too-small apartment.

A full-blown scene showing the wife-lover liaison and what they say
to each other and how they conduct their hello and goodbye would
feel like extra weight in the story, a sluggish spot in need of cutting,
because the affair is almost irrelevant to the real story.

On the other hand (in fiction there is always another hand),
the wife-lover relationship may be the part that interests you most.
Suppose the woman meets the lover in the hotel at the usual time,
but because she can't find a babysitter she brings the boy along. The
lover is miffed; the woman is hurt that after all this time the lover
isn't content to "just talk" for a few hours, and also that he doesn't
seem interested at all in her adored little boy. The scene could follow
their desultory conversation, the arrival of room service (which the
rambunctious boy accidentally knocks over) and an argument which
the woman comes to realize is their breaking up. On the way home
she is surprised to realize that she's looking forward to seeing her
husband because of the way his face lights up whenever he sees the
boy. In this version of the story, wife-lover is more important than
wife-husband: the story is about a woman leaving her lover, not about
whom she is leaving him for. The child is the key to the breakup,
not the husband. In this case it's the husband-wife part that can be
dispatched through narrative:

> Mark was the dependable sort, always on time. He was the
> one who remembered to send birthday cards to the various
> members of the family. And he was more mother than she was.
> He was the one who liked to read bedtime stories and wrap their
> son's peach-colored body in a thick towel after a bath.

This narrative serves the proper purpose of describing the wife more
than the husband. We get a sense of what she *isn't* (maternal, depend-
able) by reading a description of what he *is*. You don't need a scene
to show the father's devotion, because that's not where the story is.

One more story. This one is about a man named Ethan who,
deserted six months ago by his wife, is struggling to forge a relationship with his seven-year-old son:

> In July, six months after Jackie had left him and his son to

fend for themselves, Ethan decided to give the boy a party. He was seven, a difficult age, Ethan thought, always whining about something. The party would be something new, a fresh start for both of them. A celebration.

The children arrived in several clusters, according to what street they lived on. Ethan forced his son to stand at the door and hand out a pointy hat to each child that entered the house. The afternoon was a disaster, ending with a couple of bloody noses and a wedge of cake stuffed through the wire bars of the bird cage. One little boy was taken with cramps so severe Ethan began to wonder if he'd paid enough attention to what he'd mixed into the cake. Gamely he'd hosted a round of "Pin the Tail on the Donkey" and then a treasure hunt, only to discover that most seven-year-olds were jaded old men, even the girls, unaffected by the wide-eyed wonder he remembered from his own youth. The giddy celebration of life that Ethan had anticipated had not come to pass, and he sat amongst the wreckage of damp streamers and crazy glue wondering why.

This is a good example of a first draft that shows a writer in search of a story. The narrative is part summary, part imagery, and jams a lot of action—an entire afternoon's worth, in fact—into a very small space. This paragraph could serve as an outline for a fifteen-page story. We have a setup (father giving party to "start fresh"); a conflict (son won't cooperate except by force); a rising action (the events of the party); a climax (the party goes out of control); and a resolution (father left among wreckage). What we don't have, however, are the subtle descriptions that reveal the "real" story, the subtext: How do Ethan's feelings change over the course of the story? What else is happening in Ethan's life that makes the success of the party so important to him? How does he really feel about his son? In other words, we haven't located the story yet.

How do you "find" the story? Begin by slowing down. Take one moment of the narrative that interests you and expand that moment into a scene to see if you can discover what's going on:

Ethan closed his hands over his son's knobby shoulders. "You're going to stand here and pass out hats if I have to hold you here myself."

"I don't want a party," Billy whined. "I don't like those kids." He whipped around, wrenching his shoulders from Ethan's grasp, and gave him that straight-line mouth that reminded him of Jackie before she left them. He was going to be just like her, the glass half empty, always half empty.

"You're just going to have to learn to get along, Billy," Ethan said. He could hear the soft wheedling he had often used with Jackie. "Parties are nice. It's what nice people do. It's part of the social intercourse." He sighed, listening to himself. "It's a good world out there. No one's out to get you." He smiled extravagantly, pointing out the door. "There's Timmy. You like Timmy. Now, aren't you glad we did this?"

Billy frowned deeply, and Ethan could see the word *No* forming on the bow-shaped mouth he'd inherited from his mother. The boy took a breath, and before Ethan knew what he was doing he'd slapped the word from Billy's face with the flat of his hand.

Ironically, the scene gives you far more insight into your characters than did the original narrative, which was packed solid with information. When you compare the boy to the mother early in the scene ("that straight-line mouth"), you discover something: everything that happens between Ethan and Billy will echo the relationship between Ethan and Jackie. Ethan's repressed rage will be acted out on Billy. The original narrative—though full of practical information (length of the separation, Ethan's hope for the party, the individual events of the party)—could never give you these insights. Through scene, you "found" the story.

For describing something wildly disappointing or moving or confounding, a scene almost always does the trick better than narrative. The complexities of human behavior are best described by what the characters themselves say and do, rather than through a narrative interpretation of what they say and do. In the above examples, the difference between

Ethan forced his son to stand at the door and hand out a pointy hat to each child that entered the house. The afternoon was a disaster. . . .

and

> Ethan closed his hands over his son's knobby shoulders. "You're going to stand here and pass out hats if I have to hold you here myself."
>
> . . . [Billy] whipped around, wrenching his shoulders from Ethan's grasp, and gave him that straight-line mouth that reminded him of Jackie before she left them.

is about five shades of meaning. The scene offers an instant reading of the father-mother-son triangle. If you find yourself confounded by one human entanglement after another in pages of straight narrative, stop and ask yourself if a scene would help light your way.

Another time when scene can rescue a story is when you are working with a character that could be easily labeled a "type." The following line— "Cindy was a flirt"—can be improved with some showier telling—"Cindy was a green-eyed blond who could spot a Yalie from the distance of, say, a dance floor." But it still doesn't do much but lie on the page. A flirt is a cliché. Green-eyed blonds are the stuff of TV cop shows. A scene does the trick much more effectively:

> Cindy racketed into the room, wearing her roommate's tiny spangled dress. "Eldon," she cooed, offering her one bare hand. "Hasn't it been ages?" She slid a finger gingerly along the inside of his lapel and smiled.

Of course, this passage isn't long enough to be technically considered a scene, but it does have scenic properties. It serves a purpose (to show Cindy's flirtatious character); it contains dialogue; it has a beginning (her entrance), a middle (her dialogue) and an end (her gesture); and it moves the story forward (someone has to react to her action).

By showing Cindy's flirtatiousness through scene rather than telling the readers that she's a flirt, you are giving her some individuality and stretching the limitations of stereotype. The sleaze, the goody-goody, the bitter old man, the blushing bride—all these cardboard cutouts can be brought to life through scene. An elderly character described as "a bitter old man" is little more than a cliché. This same old man shown tearing up his address book or disconnecting his phone becomes a unique character that breaks stereotype.

WRAP-UP

"Show, don't tell" is merely a guideline for beginning writers, not a rule. A good story can be "told" as well as "shown," and usually a combination of the two techniques yields the most satisfying descriptions. Generally speaking, you show through scene and tell through narrative.

Scenes are most effective when you are trying to reveal the complex interplay between characters, or between a character and himself. Instead of telling the readers that a character is painfully shy, you might shape a scene around that shyness: for instance, somebody could challenge the shy character's religious beliefs while she's minding her own business in the grocery line.

Narrative is most effective when you are trying to fill in background information or move quickly through time to connect two scenes. Instead of writing a full-scale scene in which a young couple worries about how to tell their folks about their recent elopement, you could dispatch the information through a line or two of narrative: "On the way home they decided to tell her parents, who were the soft-spoken ones, and leave his blustering parents in the dark."

Too much scene can make a story seem drawn out, even endless; too much narrative can make a story feel dry and expository. A story takes on so much life—not to mention a pleasing shape—when you move back and forth between scene and narrative. Using the techniques together offers you the most opportunity to vary your descriptions, to give readers an accurate mental picture of the story you wish to tell.

Showing and telling both have a place in good fiction. You may have been taught that "showing" is good and "telling" is bad: if so, rethink your position! With care and attention to language, you can write a beautiful story through showing alone, telling alone, or through a pleasing combination.

CHAPTER 3

DESCRIPTION AND FORWARD MOTION

GOOD STORIES MOVE. They start at the beginning, move through the middle, and end at the end. This is not as simple as it sounds.

Without forward movement, even good characters can find themselves in dull stories. Characters can't just sit around ruminating; they have to do things, say things, go places, interact with people and institutions and their own impulses. A man thinking about death is not a story; a man building his own coffin is. Be wary of stories in which your characters reflect and remember and wonder a lot. Is all that wondering getting them from point A to point B?

Don't ask who your character is; ask what your character does. Trust that she will reveal herself to you through her words and deeds. You might think you know exactly who she is at the outset—she is your creation, after all—but until you take her through at least one draft of the story, until you undertake the burden of describing her in various circumstances, you don't know for certain how she'll react. She may do or say things you didn't plan for; you may have to make alterations in plot (sometimes major ones) to accommodate her emerging personality and motivations. This sense of adventure is what makes writing so much fun.

Good stories are often psychological in nature—character-driven as opposed to plot-driven. Even so, when people ask, "What's the story about?" we tend to describe the plot: A woman loses her child in a store. A man blows up his father's car. A child catches his parents making love. In a very real sense, this physical information is what the story is "about."

What turns plot into story, however, is the *emotional* information

that we convey to the readers. (Some writers prefer the word "psychological" to "emotional." I prefer "emotional" because it implies conflicts of the heart as well as the mind.) Emotional information reflects
a character's inner landscape: A woman discovers the melancholy of
her marriage. A man discovers his hatred for his father. A child discovers his separateness from his parents. These are the same emotional discoveries that make real life so interesting and horrifying
and beautiful and compelling. Gather some characters together, give
them something to react to, and you've got the ingredients of a story
that can move, like life, on two levels: physical and emotional.

HOW STORIES MOVE

Forward movement in fiction is twofold: physical and emotional. *Physical movement* is the movement of the plot from beginning to end:

1. In a department store, mother berates child for swiping several stuffed animals from toy department; now in the hardware department, she "looks away" for a few moments; child
   disappears.
2. Father makes a scene, begins ordering everyone around; entire store engages in search for child.
3. Mother searches Home section of the store, where beautiful
   furnishings are arranged in idealized "rooms."
4. Mother finds child asleep on canopy bed in store display, toy
   animals gathered tightly around her. Mother lies down next
   to child.

Physical movement, as you can see, follows a plot line. First A happens, then B, then C. When your plot stalls on you, the story stops
moving.

The other kind of forward movement, *emotional movement*, follows
the development of character rather than plot:

1. Mother's irritation with child stems from a succession of in-
   consequential fights with her husband. He's with her now
   because he can't "trust her" to pick out the right kind of

porch light by herself. Mother's inattention occurs when she becomes fascinated with another couple and their child. She contemplates their beauty and peacefulness. When she turns around, her own child is missing.

2. Father's tirade makes mother feel eerily calm. She begins her own search, awed by her composure. She thinks of it as "competence."

3. Mother searches among home furnishings. The beauty and implied family harmony of the displays devastate her. She imagines her husband raging through a different part of the store, and begins to imagine all the ways he will blame her when the child is found. She refuses to imagine a scenario in which the child is not found.

4. Mother finds child in bed display; recognizes her own need for refuge from her husband's harsh judgment. Succumbs to the temptation of the beautiful canopy bed and all the peace and safety it implies.

In this example, plot and character are inextricable: the physical content moves with the emotional. One can exist without the other, but both are enriched by the other's presence. A story that featured this same character standing in a store longing for an idealized family life would not be very interesting; a story that featured only the action of a couple searching a store for their lost child might be interesting but not very rich.

Stories move forward most seamlessly when plot and character mesh. As you move the mother through the physical line (plot) of the story, you can illuminate her emotional progress (character) through her observations. At the beginning, before the child is gone, she observes things somewhat coldly:

The store was high-ceilinged and bright, punctuated by straight lines: long corridors laid out like streets; grids of steel that held the harsh overhead lights; upright black shelves that housed the switchboxes her husband was pawing through. His own straight lines were turned away from her—his shoulders and back and the grim bottom edge of his hairline.

Notice how this description is all lines and edges; notice also the hardness of the language: *punctuated, harsh, grim, edge.* Later, during

the search for the child, her observations become gentler, even surreal, suggestive of longing:

> She searched through a grouping of stuffed chairs gathered
> like a roomful of uncles after Thanksgiving dinner.

Or:

> She saw a succession of porcelain vases, round and con-
> stant, set on the honeyed tables as if waiting for the flowers
> the husband has just brought home.

Notice how the words change; something is happening inside her.
The same store that a moment ago had "harsh light" is now full
of comfortable chairs and domestic-looking vases. Emotional
movement is contained in subtle descriptions that take the character
through the motion of the plot toward some discovery or revelation
or turning point. A plot is critical, but *which* plot is almost irrelevant. This woman's turning point could have come during a car
crash or a visit to a museum or a bout with illness—any scenario
that could accommodate themes of refuge. The lost child is one of
a thousand possibilities for this particular character's emotional
development.

You don't want your story to move at the same rate from start to
finish. A story's pace is controlled by the physical and emotional
goings-on in the story, and those goings-on are controlled by description. In this story about the lost child, the pace should probably
quicken as the search expands, creating tension (will the child be
found?) that reflects the character's increasing panic. At the beginning of the search, the description could be almost leisurely; after
all, the child is probably right around the corner, or obscured behind
a store display:

> She walked to the end of the aisle, past a brilliantly colored
> pyramid of paint cans. She could imagine the brazen colors
> catching her little girl's interest. Each can resembled the torso
> of a brand-new crayon. She peered around the jagged shape
> and saw nothing but more cans of paint, their chrome handles
> glinting under the light.

Notice the calm, unworried quality of this narrative. The mother is allowing herself time to imagine herself in her child's place, and is herself noticing, if not admiring, little details about the store: the shape of the paint display, the appearance of the cans, the play of light. She is also "walking," not running or lurching, and "peering," not scanning or checking or glancing. In other words, the mother, like the description, is not yet moving very fast.

When the mother does not find the child within the first couple of minutes, though, the stakes suddenly rise. The child could indeed be lost, or worse, abducted. Both the physical and emotional pace of the story are affected. The mother's heart speeds up, and so does the description:

> Aisle six, wrenches. Nothing. She rounded the corner and fled down aisle seven. Screws, wedges, hinges, bolts, nothing. Aisle eight, nine, ten. Nothing but hubcaps and headlights. "Mitzi!" she called, her voice jarring against all that steel and chrome. "Mitzi, answer me, damn it, can you hear me?"

Do you see how you've quickened the pace by using short, staccato sentences? Neither you nor your character can afford to linger over details here. You are giving bare-bones information, for the character is no longer capable of becoming distracted by what she *can* see; she is too preoccupied with what she cannot see: her daughter. The emotional content of the story at this point cannot support a physically slow description.

By the time we approach the end of the story, the search has gone on for a while and erupted into a full-blown family crisis. The father's been yelling at everybody in the store, especially the mother. The mother's initial burst of energy has been dulled by her husband's cruelty and the futility of her search. She is now wandering blindly through the Home section, broken down by fatigue and sadness, not only because of the lost child but because of what she has come to see as a lost chance for a happy family life, whether or not the child is found. Here, you can slow the pace again, for the story is about to end, and the mother is beginning to give up:

> She wandered into a rounded, windowed section of the store that was dressed up to resemble a succession of bedrooms, each more sumptuous than the next. Yards of canopy. Eyelet lace. Sugar-colored pillows she wanted to disappear into. Was

everything white, or was she only imagining it? Had the day's revelations bled the color from her eyes? White, everything white: sheets and towels folded into pearly mounds, doilies and ruffles and washcloths scattered like snowdrifts against cloth-covered tables. And there, sleeping like a pixie on a fresh expanse of cotton, lay her daughter, her white-blond hair dissolving against a lace coverlet.

The mother is so exhausted that her surroundings become surreal, and the frothy description reinforces everything she's experiencing emotionally. The story's physical description has kept perfect pace with its emotional content.

CREATING CONTEXT

Sometimes a story demands more than just a plot to move its emotional content forward. When a story becomes very complicated, or a little too crowded with characters, or stretched over a long period of time, you may want to create a *context*. Context is the descriptive background in a story that sheds light on its meaning. Context is larger than plot; it gives the characters a larger arena in which to hate or love each other, to discover or destroy themselves, to fall under or triumph over adversity.

Contexts can be large: World War II, the Catholic Church, death. Contexts can also be small: winter, a wedding, a hometown. Context provides forward motion at the emotional level, using symbols and metaphors that reinforce emerging themes in a story. It also can serve the practical purpose of organizing the physical movement of a story into beginning, middle, and end. For example, a story told in the context of weather can follow a season or seasons for its beginning, middle, and end: the beginning unfolds during planting, the middle during harvesting, the end during the dormant winter. At the same time, the context reinforces developments character: a woman's suntanned face gives way to winter-bitten skin that reflects her gathering bitterness.

In Edith Wharton's *Ethan Frome*, the plot follows Ethan's doomed affair of the heart with Mattie Silver, the "companion" of Ethan's sickly and querulous wife. It is a dark story told in the context of the

cruel New England winter. After a brief prologue, the story opens
this way:

> The village lay under two feet of snow, with drifts at the
> windy corners. In a sky of iron the points of the Dipper hung
> like icicles and Orion flashed his cold fires. The moon had set,
> but the night was so transparent that the white house-fronts
> between the elms looked gray against the snow, clumps of
> bushes made black stains on it, and the basement windows of
> the church sent shafts of yellow light far across the endless undu-
> lations.

This descriptive passage sets up a context that will be carried through
the novel—the characters cannot escape the literal and metaphorical
cold. And yet the shafts of yellow light sent undulating over the snow
deliver a hint that warmth is possible even in this unforgiving place.
The love that develops between Ethan and Mattie is that drop of
warmth, but the landscape literally and figuratively becomes their
doom. As the story progresses, Wharton softens the landscape a bit
when Ethan begins to imagine himself and Mattie together:

> They finished supper, and while Mattie cleared the table
> Ethan went to look at the cows and then took a last turn about
> the house. The earth lay dark under a muffled sky and the air
> was so still that now and then he heard a lump of snow come
> thumping down from a tree far off on the edge of the wood-lot.

Even though the landscape is softened here—the domestic quiet implied by the cows and the muffled sky—Wharton preserves an unre-
lenting sense of foreboding with that disquieting, far-off thumping
of snow. The context remains steady throughout, with repeated images of sterility and starkness and frozen ground, as the physical and
emotional lines of the story culminate in a toboggan accident that
destroys Mattie and Ethan in different ways.

The plot of Jane Smiley's novel *A Thousand Acres* unfolds in the
huge context of land—the family-owned, generations-old "thousand
acres" of the title. The land is something that must be reckoned with
at every turn in the book, for the land is the characters' livelihood
and also their prison. It is both beautiful and menacing. The context
provides an irony that resonates throughout this story of a multitude
of family betrayals set into motion by the patriarch's dividing of the

land. (It's a retelling of *King Lear*.) Because the land must be tended to in all its seasons, the context provides a blueprint for moving the plot along. Ginny, the narrator, begins and ends her story by describing the land:

> ... you could see our buildings, a mile distant, at the southern edge of the farm. A mile to the east, you could see three silos that marked the northeastern corner, and if you raked your gaze from the silos to the house and barn, then back again, you would take in the immensity of the piece of land my father owned, six hundred forty acres, a whole section, paid for, no encumbrances, as flat and fertile, black, friable, and exposed as any piece of land on the face of the earth. ...
>
> ... I thought it appropriate and desirable that the great circle of the flat earth spreading out from the T intersection of County Road 686 and Cabot Street Road be ours. A thousand acres. It was that simple.

The ensuing story is anything but simple, and ends with another view of the same land:

> Let us say that each vanished person left me something, and that I feel my inheritance when I am reminded of one of them. When I am reminded of Jess, I think of the loop of poison we drank from, the water running down through the soil, into the drainage wells, into the lightless mysterious underground chemical sea, then being drawn up, cold and appetizing, from the drinking well into Rose's faucet, my faucet. I am reminded of Jess when I drive in the country, and see the anhydrous trucks in the distance, or the herbicide incorporators, or the farmers plowing their fields in the fall, or hills that are ringed with black earth and crowned with soil so pale that the corn only stands in it, as in gravel, because there are no nutrients to draw from it.

The poison beneath the land echoes the poison beneath the family relationships. The context of land reinforces every lie and betrayal the characters inflict on one another.

Not all contexts are this large. The breadth of the story should dictate the breadth of the context. A story about a marriage breaking up would work quite well in a small context: the story takes place over the course of an exceptionally dry summer, say, its attendant images of burnt lawns and dead flowers reinforcing the story's emotional content. A story about the dissolution of an entire family might work well in a larger context such as a five-year drought or a civil war.

Let's start small, with a story about a middle-aged woman named Harriet who comes to realize that she has squandered her life. That's the "story," the emotional content; the plot, however, takes her through the machinations of her first dinner party in twenty years. Her model for this party is a wine ad she saw in a magazine. The ad depicts a genteel, dress-up dinner party—an image so vivid in Harriet's mind that it becomes the context for the story. This context contains symbols of an elegant, upper-crust lifestyle which contrasts nicely with Harriet's middle-class limitations. It also has the potential for illuminating themes like falseness and self-deception. Also, the dinner party gives you a blueprint for moving the plot forward: appetizers, main course, dessert.

Suppose you begin the story by showing Harriet getting the appetizers ready in the kitchen. As in all the previous examples, careful description heightens context and connects the story's physical and emotional forward movement:

> She put one bright canapé after another onto a silver tray, fretting over each rose-shaped radish, each olive-topped cream-cheese cracker, each polished cherry, each frilly spray of parsley. She frowned. The props that had suggested whimsy in the magazine photograph took on an air of desperate excess when crowded onto her grandmother's silver platter. She tried to imagine the wine-blushed faces in that ad, all of them frantically happy. What, exactly, were they looking at? The food? Each other? Their own fabulousness? Harriet sighed. It was too late now. The menu was set, the table decorated, the guests invited and arrived. Whatever she had overlooked would have to wait.

By describing the tray of hors d'oeuvres so vividly and then revealing Harriet's disappointment, you imply that this is more than just a dinner party to Harriet, and that she's beginning to suspect that her lavish expectations may not be met. The context begins to form, for what reader has not longed to step into the midst of an ad like the one Harriet is remembering? Because you render Harriet's reaction to the ad in such precise detail ("wine-blushed," "frantically happy"), your readers have no choice but to measure Harriet's party against the wine-ad party.

What's next? Suppose Harriet glances out the kitchen door and spots her husband, Marty, looking stiff and unyielding among the drift of guests, whom she realizes are all *her* friends:

> She let the door fall closed, picked up her burgeoning tray and practiced moving with it in the clean privacy of her kitchen. She stopped, listening once again to the light-hearted weave of voices, and suddenly remembered certain old friends—all those laughing girls!—who had gone off to work or traveled out of state or otherwise drifted away.
>
> "Hors d'oeuvres," she called cheerily, brandishing her tray. Everyone looked up. The women were dressed in skirts and pantsuits, the men in ordinary shirts, as though they had arrived here straight from the office.

In this passage, you move the story forward emotionally, and that emotional movement is made richer by the context. Notice how even small contextual details reveal character: Harriet's "burgeoning tray" harkens back to the wine-ad party in all its bounty, but the phrase also reminds us of Harriet's burgeoning expectations, and her dim sense of her own "desperate excess." Because we recognize that Harriet's hope is for the wine-ad party, we understand without being told that Harriet is disappointed to see the "skirts and pantsuits" and "ordinary shirts."

In the next scene, Harriet circulates through her living room with the tray, realizing that she doesn't actually know any of her guests very well. She makes little stabs at small talk, remembering her earlier expectations:

> She had imagined herself glancing around gaily, discussing things topical and stimulating. She had imagined glasses raised in convivial gladness. How extravagant the women's dresses, how smooth and muscular their exposed shoulders. And the men! Leaning forward, listening to her opinions, relaxed and genial, stretching in their beautiful silk shirts.

Even though Harriet is remembering past thoughts in a brief flashback, the emotional content of the story is moving forward because you are revealing even more about Harriet's self-delusion. The passage is full of Harriet's foolishness—convivial gladness and beautiful silk shirts, indeed!—almost as if she is remembering the wine ad as something she actually experienced. The wine-ad image of "... men leaning forward, listening to her opinions, relaxed and genial ..." suggests this lonely woman's desperate hope for something that will never happen.

Using the context as a story organizer, you can enter the story's middle through the vehicle of a main course. The action accelerates and the stakes rise. Harriet tries vainly to strike up some "topical" conversation with the increasingly taciturn guests; Marty picks a fight with the man sitting across from him; Harriet takes the man's side, which triggers another argument between her and Marty; finally, the guests one by one remember other appointments or babysitters at home and drift off.

The end of the story is signalled by the end of the party. Marty stalks upstairs without a word, leaving Harriet alone to preside over the half-eaten remains of her elaborate dinner:

> Harriet drew herself up and collected the dirty plates and took them to the kitchen. She could see traces of the delicate pattern—little blue flowers—between gobs of sauce and bits of meat and the frayed heads of asparagus. Marty was moving through their bedroom overhead, his steps heavy and grave. Along the counter twelve cuts of cheesecake were lined up on filigreed dessert plates, one perfect cherry atop each slice. She looked closer: the cherries had begun to bleed, leaving uneven drizzles along the lovely white wedges. Harriet shook her head, clucking to herself. She had left them out too long. She had not paid enough attention. Not that it mattered; there was nobody here to eat them.

Notice how the physical and emotional endings coincide. Harriet rues her bleeding cheesecakes, and the nature of that observation (the marred appearance of the white cake) gives your readers to understand what Harriet now realizes: Not only has the party been a dismal failure, but so has her life. She has left *herself* "out [of life] too long," and is only now feeling the enormity of her exile.

Ethan Frome draws its power from the similarity between the story and its context—the hopeless people and the hopeless weather. This little story about Harriet draws its power from the *contrast* between the story and its context—the real party and the wine-ad party. Context can work with or against a story with equally satisfying results.

FORWARD MOTION AND PHYSICAL DESCRIPTION

There is no greater (nor annoying) motion-stopper than immobile chunks of physical description. A head-to-toe tour of a character's appearance, clothing, etc., before we know anything else about him, is at best ineffective and at worst counterproductive. Not only is this technique clunky and amateurish, it stops the natural flow of the story. The inexperienced writer often introduces characters this way:

> At the knock on the door, Alan looked up from his desk. Walter Clayton ambled across the carpet, holding out one hand. "I've been looking forward," he said.
>
> Walter Clayton was thirty-five years old, dark-haired, with blue eyes that looked forced open. He liked basketball, but at five-feet-two wasn't tall enough to play. His feet were small and square. His graying hair was parted severely to one side and his ears were pinned close to his head. The only thing big about him was his hands: large and meaty, with thick, calloused fingers and curiously shellacked nails. He wore a suit of blended silk, and his cuffs protruded an elegant half-inch below the sleeves. As he sat down his pant legs rode up, revealing an extraordinary pair of chartreuse wool socks.

This is not bad description; in fact, it is good description. The details are precise and interesting. The problem is that the descriptive information is given all at once. We are left to drum our fingers until the writer gets back to the plot. I recently read a good novel, a well-written psychological thriller, in which *every single character* was introduced this way. It became distracting, then mildly amusing ("I wonder if he knows he's doing this?"), and finally infuriating. You don't want to tamper this way with your readers' good graces.

Lack of movement is not the only problem with this kind of "chunk" description. As I discovered from reading the aforementioned novel, when readers are introduced to a character in this way, they will not remember what the character looks like later on. Despite your heroic efforts at description, readers tend to accept chunks of physical description as "snapshots" that they look at once and then forget. The characters get short shrift! Descriptions should guide readers to the most telling, characterizing details; when all the details are lumped together they take on equal weight. Reading a long, detailed physical description is like looking at a painting from a distance of two inches: it becomes a big blob that's hard to keep in perspective. Deliver physical characteristics a few at a time, and the character in question becomes much more seeable:

> At the knock on the door, Alan looked up from his desk. Walter Clayton ambled across the carpet, holding out one meaty hand. "I've been looking forward," he said.
> Alan shook Walter's hand. "Have a seat."
> As Walter Clayton sat, the cuff of his immaculate silk pants rode up to reveal a pair of chartreuse socks. "Abby sent me," he said. "But of course you know that."
> Alan stared at the small round face, the blue eyes that looked forced open. "You have information for me, Mr. Clayton?" he said, glancing down at the preposterous socks.
> "I do," Walter Clayton said. He patted the sides of his graying hair. "Yes, indeed." He gave out a thin-lipped grin. "Oh, I do, indeed."

Do you see how this one-detail-at-a-time description turns Walter Clayton from a mannequin in a storefront to a full-blooded character? We discover the eccentric details of Walter's physical appearance at the same time he is being revealed as a character, and therefore each detail takes on added significance. The details *mean* something. If details emerge one by one in increasing significance, the character encroaches on our consciousness in a way that makes him real, and the story rolls along without missing a beat.

FLASHBACKS AND THEIR PROBLEMS

Used judiciously, the flashback is a magnificent descriptive tool. Flashbacks move a story back in time, giving us insights about characters we don't know well.

Imagine you're writing a story about Marcus, a ruthless inside trader who seems to have no conscience. Your descriptions are as deliberately dispassionate as his life: he goes to work early in the morning, when the sky is a "low, steely ceiling"; his office is "fluorescent and silent," and his apartment is furnished with "chrome and leather, with a high-tech kitchen as clean as a space station." After Marcus tells his fiancee that her clothes aren't right for the party he wants to take her to, you insert a brief flashback that shows Marcus as a boy on a dirt-poor Iowa farm, putting on a handed-down suit for his father's funeral.

The descriptions in the flashback, which suggest humiliation and despair, contrast with the hard, unemotional imagery of the present-time story. Paradoxically, flashbacks can move stories backward and forward at the same time. This story takes a leap forward as we gain a fuller understanding of Marcus. We can suddenly see why he is ashamed of his fiancee's clothing and why he might want to live the way he does. Flashbacks can flesh out your characters, add to the readers' perceptions, and change the mood or direction of a story.

Flashbacks are not always brief, nor do they always move stories forward. This is not to say that long flashbacks are bad. They can be badly handled, however, and often are. They may feature awkward transitions; they may take too long; they may contain flashbacks within flashbacks; they may deliver chunks of information that stop the action and therefore have a dry, expository quality. All of these drawbacks affect the natural movement that good stories require.

Used effectively, flashbacks enhance the emotional movement of a story, deepen the story's imagery (an image that figures prominently in a flashback takes on extra meaning when used again in the main body of the story), and organize a story by weaving information into the narrative at critical times. Most important, they can enhance the descriptive nature of a story by shoring up some of the more elusive aspects of a character. Like scenes (many flashbacks *are* scenes, in fact), flashbacks can help you locate your story. That Iowa farm may be the key to understanding Marcus's present motives; the story's heart is not on Wall Street but back in Iowa.

Even well-written flashbacks pose risks. One, readers may become impatient to return to the present action; two, they may become so engrossed in the flashback that they're disappointed to get back to the present action; three, they may feel they've been absented so long from the present action that they can't very easily pick up the thread of the original story. My own rule of thumb about flashbacks is that they are such a bother and so hard to make seamless that they should be used only when you have no other workable descriptive choices.

Transitions

The most common problem with flashbacks is getting into and out of them. When introducing flashbacks, inexperienced writers often resort to devices like the following:

> I opened the drawer to my mother's desk and discovered the emerald ring. The sight of it brought me back to that day nearly thirty years ago when she gathered us into the living room to tell us she was leaving.
> "Boys," she said. "Come here. Mama has something to tell you."

Or:

> Roland slipped the letter through the gold-painted mail slot and paused. Something about the deeply cut design of the door reminded him of another door, another life, another time . . .
> It was 1955 when he had first gone to the lumberyard to get some wood for a new door. His father took him down in the truck, and he loved the rough sounds that rattled up through the seat as they moved over the pocked road.

These transitions are burdensome and somewhat awkward, and take away from the nice flashbacks that they introduce. Never use ellipses (. . .) to telegraph a passage back in time. It looks amateurish and usually makes your opening line seem like a voice-over in a B movie. Also, avoid phrases like "it brought me back to" or "suddenly I remembered." Forget the fanfare and enter the flashback directly:

> I opened the drawer to my mother's desk and discovered the emerald ring she had been wearing the night she told us

she was leaving. I was six. "Boys," she said. "Come here. Mama has something to tell you."

Or:

> Roland slipped the letter through the gold-painted mail slot and paused. The deep cut of the door was similar to the one he and his father had once designed for the house in Cutler. His father had driven him down to the lumber yard in Grandad's 1955 Chevy pickup, and he loved the rough sounds that rattled up through the seat as they moved over the pocked road.

Do you see the difference? Here, you enter the flashback with no "I remember" prologue of any kind. The transition in time barely makes a ripple in the story's forward motion.

Coming back out of flashbacks can be tricky as well. The shorter the flashback, the easier the return:

> Holly turned the key and held her breath. Last week at this time it had been Alfred on the other side of the door, lounging in her favorite chair, drinking her good sherry, his fingers coiling around the stem of the glass as he smiled up at her. "Hello, Sweetheart," he said, his upper lip curling. Maybe she should have given him the money. She pushed open the door, half expecting to see him again, but the only living creature was the cat slumbering on the sofa.

The character's transition from remembering last-week Alfred to pushing open today's door is seamless, because you haven't diverted the readers from the present action long enough for them to forget anything. Only three sentences of flashback intrude on the present-time story.

Transition problems usually crop up when you try to return to the main story after a flashback of several paragraphs, or several pages, or, in some cases, several chapters. In case the readers have forgotten the present-time story, you announce its return with a drum roll:

> . . . She waved goodbye to the birds that eddied above the sea-green fields of her grandmother's saltwater farm.
>
> The sound of bells brought her back to the present.

Or:

> . . . The sight of his wife's fingers moving over the piano's shiny keys would forever remain a memory he kept to himself.
>
> But that was all in the past; Mr. Goldberg rubbed his eyes and turned again to his papers, which suddenly looked thin and pale.

In these returns, you might as well be holding up a cue card: AND NOW, BACK TO OUR STORY IN PROGRESS. To avoid this awkwardness when moving out of flashbacks, use the same direct approach that you would in moving *into* a flashback:

> . . . She waved goodbye to the birds that eddied over the sea-green fields of her grandmother's saltwater farm.
>
> Bells sounded outside her window. She rose from her desk to look down at the street.

Or:

> . . . The sight of his wife's fingers moving over the piano's shiny keys would forever remain a memory he kept to himself.
>
> Mr. Goldberg rubbed his eyes. The papers spread on his desk looked thin and pale.

Easy in, easy out. Delete phrases like "brought her back to the present" or "that was in the past" or "suddenly he realized he'd been daydreaming." They are almost never necessary. With longer flashbacks you may want to use asterisks or white space—that is, several blank lines on the page—to signify a major leap from past to present:

> . . . defeated and bereft, Mark staggered over the sidewalk. He wanted only to be alone. He stood in the shelter of a urine-soaked doorway, clutching the gritty lapel of his cousin's jacket.
>
> * * * *
>
> The clock tower struck four as Mark stepped out of the arched doorway of the bank lobby. He stood on the street, squinting up at the sky, hands thrust deep into his pockets.

These physical cues give readers a moment to get their bearings and prepare to re-enter the present-time part of the story. White space in a short story is similar to a chapter break in a novel. It is the author's polite way of telling readers that the scene is changing.

The more unassuming your transitions in and out of flashbacks, the less your story will have an "assembled" quality: *this* part (e.g., the flashback to the Vietnam War) goes here, and *that* part (e.g., the therapy session in 1995) goes there. Assembly is the opposite of flow. To maintain a sense of forward motion and descriptive cohesiveness, make your transitions in and out of flashbacks as invisible as possible. You want your story to feel like an inevitable whole, not a collection of parts.

"Frame" Stories

For some reason inexperienced writers have a penchant for "frame" stories, in which the present-day action frames an extended flashback. For example, the story may open with a man's description of his mother's burial, which triggers in him an extended flashback of the summer his dog died, and how his mother's practical strength helped him accept the death of his beloved pet. Then the story returns to the present-day gravesite where the man is saying his final goodbye to Mom, and the readers are now supposed to have a deeper understanding of his grief. This structure stops motions cold, for the readers spend the bulk of the story wondering when he's going to get back to present action, and what on earth the present action has to do with the extended flashback. The result is just as awful as you'd suspect. Stories like this begin this way:

> I walked the long dirt path to the open gravesite under a white, curiously cold sun. Friends and colleagues murmured their condolences; their voices blended into a quiet, indecipherable stirring in the air. My wife leaned her cheek against my arm as we listened to the minister's bland intonations. When finally they lowered my mother's coffin into the ground, the strong scent of earth brought me back to one unforgettable summer over twenty years ago.
>
> Sparky, our family dog, turned nineteen that summer, a day after I turned nine. My mother thought it would be fun to have a birthday party to which we invited both boys and dogs.

After this awkward introduction to the flashback, the narrator goes

on to describe that fateful summer. On the last page he returns to
the present in another awkward transition:

> I buried Sparky at the back of my mother's garden with a
> spade she kept in her tool shed. I stayed there, sitting on the
> upturned grass, until she came down long after supper to help
> me pick some flowers to lay on his grave.
>
> Now, twenty years later, as I toss some flowers from that
> same garden on her grave, I can thank my mother for all she
> taught me about remembering the dead.

Frame stories almost always have transition problems, because the
frame, unbeknownst to the author, is usually unnecessary. The extended flashback usually can stand as a story all by itself. Notice also
that the frame makes the story's other problems—principally the sentimental descriptions—much more glaring than they should be.
Framing a flashback points a thousand red arrows at it. The most
innocent description sags under the burden of momentousness. ("A
cherry-red barn?" we ask. "Cherries must be really significant!")
Don't do this to yourself. Unless the flashback and the frame are
critically, unequivocally interdependent and *there is no other way to
merge the past and present*, the frame is irrelevant. A frame like the one
in the above example begs the questions: Why not make the flashback
the story? Isn't the story about that transforming summer, not about
the mother's funeral? Whether or not the mother dies twenty years
later, isn't the lesson she taught him during that summer the point of
the story? The line that comes after the introduction to the flashback
would, with minor adjusting, make a great opening for a story all by
itself:

> The summer I turned nine, my dog turned nineteen. My
> mother gave us both a party.

Bingo, you're moving again! You have dropped the readers into the
midst of a story, one that has wonderful descriptive potential. Gone
is the clumsy introduction, not to mention the wet blanket of sentimentality that dear old Mom's burial provides. Without the lead-in,
the flashback no longer has to support a present-day story that isn't
really a story. Instead, the flashback stands alone as a memoir-style

narrative told by a reminiscent narrator. No introduction or grand finale required.

In rare cases, a frame *is* necessary. You probably should keep the frame *if the frame part of the story is the direct result of the flashback*: A man is hiding his true identity from his wife and kids, because he's a fugitive from a 20-year-old crime. Also, you should keep the frame *if the frame is more important than the flashback*: A woman's children ask her to tell about the baby she lost fifteen years ago; in the telling, they all realize that the lost baby is the only one the mother ever loved. If you must keep the frame, then avoid pitfalls by relying on the transition rules: easy in, easy out. Use white space if you have to. Don't belabor the "that was then and this is now" point. If you're writing a very long story, or a novel, transitions back and forth are often necessary and can be elegant and subtle as long as you don't introduce them with a drum roll.

Expository Flashbacks

When you have a lot of background information to account for, flashbacks are enticing. In the interest of expediency, you might be tempted to bunch all the background information together like this:

> Kit flung open the door. "Betty!" she cried, enfolding the bony form of her only cousin.
>
> "Wait." Betty stiffened. "I have something to tell you first."
>
> Kit looked at her cousin, whom she hadn't seen in years. They had been each other's best friend back on the farm in Montana, young girls who had sat night after night on their grandfather's porch counting fireflies and following the magnificent arcing path of the bats that lived across the road in their uncle Cyrus's barn. Their childhood had been one of loss and redemption. They lost their parents in the same spectacular crash on the Monson Road that people still talked of twenty years later. Earlier that summer they had been shuttled off to their grandmother's farm in Shapleigh where their uncles had identical farms all the way up and down the River Road. Their fathers, the youngest of the eight Harding brothers, were deep into some business deal that required travel and, it seemed, the corralling company of their wives. The girls didn't mind; they

loved their uncles, each other, and that string of verdant farms. It was there they had found solace from their grief, in the blond fields of wheat and the borders of stooped trees and the magical, female comfort of each other.

"The farm burned down," Betty said.

Informational flashbacks like this knock a story flat. You open a door to the readers (literally, in this case), then shut it while you fill in the background. In the meantime, we're itching to find out what Betty wants to tell Kit. Their shared childhood may be critical to the story, but it does not have to be described at this particular time, nor all at once. Blocks of information tend to be short on specifics, anyway; the descriptive details start to fall away and get replaced by dull exposition. You'll notice that the above flashback, though it contains a few nice phrases and some pretty images, delivers information that feels irrelevant, at least at this point in the story. Who cares, *right now*, that their parents died? What difference do Uncle Cyrus's bats make, *right now*, when we haven't even heard Betty speak? Background details are best given in the present flow of the story, on a need-to-know basis. Give your description a chance to breathe, instead of choking it into one thick chunk. Move your story forward by dispensing description little by little in a series of brief, delicate flashbacks:

"What do you mean, the farm burned down?" Kit asked. She sat on the plump sofa, pulling Betty down next to her. "You don't mean Grandma's farm."

"I'm sorry," Betty murmured. "There's nothing left. The barn, the outbuildings, the house, nothing. Burned." She looked at Kit. "Nothing to show but a couple of charred porch rails."

Kit put a hand to her mouth, stunned by an image of that beautiful old porch. She and Betty had spent hours there, especially at night, watching the bats dip over the road that separated their grandmother's farm from their uncle's. The night their parents died they had sat all night in the sloped shelter of its roof, their thin arms twined together, watching the empty road.

"I don't believe it," Kit said, shaking her head. "How can a place so beautiful be gone?"

You can continue to fill in details like this as the story progresses. Then, when you must stop to flash back, the flashback becomes a forward-moving narrative in itself, one that concentrates on the important things because the chaff has been weeded out:

> "Sometimes I think God hates us," Betty said. "Seems like heartache has followed us all our lives."
>
> Kit nodded. The night their parents died had been hot and starless. The two girls had spent the entire day in Uncle Arden's barn, petting the horses, making little forts out of hay. When they made their way back to the house it was long past supper and no one had thought to call them. From far down the road she could hear the frantic blue whine of the sheriff's siren. The driveway was jammed with uncles' cars, every light in the house was blazing, and someone was shouting into the kitchen phone.

This flashback, which could easily go on to describe the rest of the night's events, works well because it comes at a point in the story where the readers are willing to stop a moment to delve into the characters. We have already met Kit and Betty and gotten several hints about their closeness and shared experience through snippets of flashback. Because you've planted the relevant details, we are now ready for the full story. The flashback provides that full story in the nicest sense of the word: it is a *story*, with a beginning, middle, and end, containing its own forward motion.

The Past Perfect

A cautionary note on the use of flashbacks: Beware the past perfect! The past perfect can get you into a flashback, but sometimes you can't find your way out. In the following flashback, the past perfect is in italics:

> He *had been* a good worker in those days. He *had had* his own truck and a crew of two. Every morning he *had gone* down to the post office and waited around for the first stirrings of village life, and by nine o'clock he *had always had* a job. He *had gone* home every night with money in his pocket . . .

Well, you get the idea. For some reason inexperienced writers slip into a deer-in-headlights relationship with the past perfect when writing flashbacks. Once they latch on, they can't move away. But the continued use of "he had done" and "he had said" serves only to remind readers again and again that this is a flashback and not the real story, which makes the movement of the story sluggish and uninteresting.

Don't be afraid to move out of the past perfect quickly, even immediately. In the following example, the simple past tense provides the flashback with a forward movement of its own. (The introductory past-perfect verb is in italics.)

> He *had been* a good worker in those days. He had his own truck and a crew of two. Every morning he went down to the post office and waited around for the first stirrings of village life, and by nine o'clock he had a job. He went home every night with money in his pocket . . .

In most flashbacks the past perfect is required only briefly—for the first one or two verbs—to establish a movement back in time. After that, let the simple past tense pull the flashback forward, especially in flashbacks with a lot of dialogue—nothing is more distracting than "he had said" and "she had answered."

FLASH-FORWARDS

The flash-forward, a little-used fiction technique, gives your readers a glimpse of the future:

> Alison wanders through her new house, wondering how she will possibly fill it. Her sofa and coffee table look like doll furniture under the cavernous ceilings. Even the light switches look foolishly small against the broad white expanses of wall. Twenty years from now, missing the husband and children she does not yet know she will have, she will wander through this same house wondering how she will possibly empty it.

A flash-forward hurtles your readers ahead in the story, sometimes too fast. Flash-forwards can add poignancy and weight to a character's situation, but if you have no compelling reason to telegraph future events you risk being (rightfully) accused of gimmickry. In the preceding example, Alison is a character who is always looking on the other side of the fence, so the brief description of her future is probably appropriate.

Ironically, flash-forwards do not have to be rendered exclusively in future tense. In my novel, *Secret Language*, I use one flash-forward, during the present-tense wedding of Faith, the main character. Faith is remote and wary, terrified of life's ordinary joys. At her wedding, she "steps out of her body" to watch from a safe distance:

> . . . Heat bears down on her from all sides but she cannot warm herself. She's gone cold with the fear of love and the knowledge of her unbelonging, so cold she can barely stand, and so she removes herself from this joyful gathering, steps away from them all while her chilled body stays.
>
> She watches Joe slip the ring over her knuckle. She watches herself murmur "I do," all the faces tensing forward because they cannot hear her.
>
> She will remember this moment many, many times. Remembering, she will believe that if she had only been able to warm herself, if she had only stayed inside her body as she pledged forever and true, she might have learned to live with a man like Joe, a man who loved her.

The movement of tense in this passage is deliberate. First, I move from present tense to the future tense of the flash-forward ("She will remember this moment . . ."). Then the flash-forward itself becomes a passage in which a mini-flashback takes place ("if she had only been able to warm herself. . . ."). This is tricky; I am telegraphing, through flash-forward, a scene in which Faith will look back. Why did I complicate the passage like this? Because the novel is about Faith's journey toward an emotional place where she can finally "warm herself" and indeed "learn to love a man like Joe." Faith is a woman who refuses to live in either the past or the future, only the present, and to place her in both the past and future in this passage serves as a pivot point in the novel. It was the best device I could think of to describe this paradoxical, elusive character. At this point, where flash-forward and flashback converge, the book takes a sudden emotional leap forward.

In our story about Sparky the dog, the flashback became the story because the frame (the mother's funeral) was less important or interesting than the flashback. If you insisted on using the mother's eventual death as a way of adding weight to the story of the boy's ninth summer, a flash-forward would do nicely:

By morning the dog was dead. He was lighter than I expected, his fur still smooth. I followed my mother to the section
of our land that looked down over Blue Creek. Tearless and
solemn, we buried Sparky next to a growth of mustard flower.
My mother let me fill the hole and mound the iron-red earth.
The spade was one she sheltered at the back of the toolshed,
for it was little-used and almost beautiful: sharp and solid, with
a thick handle fashioned out of a light, burled wood; the very
spade I would use ten years later at an occasion no less solemn
but marked by many tears.

Flashbacks and flash-forwards are satisfying descriptive devices, but
beware of using them unless you can articulate your reasons. "To fill
in information" is not good enough. You can fill in information a
little at a time during the natural forward course of the story. Ask
yourself every time: Why am I flashing back? To endear the readers
to a not-yet-met character? Fine. To contrast a character's present
husband with the former husband? Sure. To create a context that
will resonate in a reader's mind as the story progresses? Sounds good.
You can probably name a dozen good reasons for using flashback,
but if you can accomplish your goal without one, why not save yourself
the aggravation?

A WORD ON THE SET PIECE

A set piece is a detour in the path your story takes. It is a fixed descriptive diversion executed with great care: an elaborate description of a
horse farm, for example, or a brick-by-brick account of the building
of a museum.

Digressions are fun. You're writing about a character in a terrible
emotional crisis, and all of a sudden the circus comes to town and
you find yourself devoting four and a half pages to the elephant act.
Such a set piece can be brilliant and beautiful and a pleasure to read,
even if it appears to have only a marginal connection with the rest of
the story. If you're going to stop the story's present action, then stop
it big! Like a well-crafted flashback, the set piece can take on its own
momentum.

A good set piece only *seems* irrelevant to the story at hand. A two-page description of the way rain moves across the prairies may seem like a mere literary detour, but in fact it telegraphs the swift changes that are about to befall the character in the story. A set piece about the building of a skyscraper may be entirely appropriate in a story about a woman building a medical practice, or a parent building a relationship with a difficult child. Also, a set piece may suggest how a character thinks, what a character's moral limits are, and so on. In a story about a retired nurse longing for a more interesting life, the set piece about the circus might highlight the fanfare and theater of the trapeze act. In a story about an ex-con, the same set piece might address the cruelty of forcing animals into cages.

If you find yourself caught up in a set piece, make it count. The description should be delectable, with lots of little-known facts and details that will dazzle your readers. A tour of your grandmother's living room (unless she lives in an igloo or a culvert) probably wouldn't make much of a set piece, but a description of wine-making in Napa Valley might. Readers aren't too cranky about diversions as long as they learn something in the process—something delivered with a descriptive flair, that is.

Finally, be sure the story—or novella, or novel—can support the weight of the digression. A ten-page story can't support a four-page set piece. A ninety-page novella can. A novel, of course, is the roomiest place to peer down those roads not taken.

WRAP-UP

A good story depends on forward motion, and forward motion depends on many aspects of description technique. Stories move on two levels, physical and emotional; when delivering details, you must attend to the emotional as well as the physical content of the story. A character's view of a snowstorm may be lean or sumptuous, depending on his state of mind. Sometimes you have to create a wider descriptive framework—a *context*—in order to handle the emotional complexity of certain stories. A story about a recently widowed man may need the context of a crime-ravaged neighborhood to adequately deliver the sense of caprice and futility that often accompany loss.

The head-to-toe physical description of a character, although a wonderful test of your descriptive powers, can stop a story cold if rendered in large chunks. Try delivering physical details one or two at a time, allowing your readers to get to know a character within the natural forward flow of the story. The characters will be more memorable that way, and you won't have to test your readers' patience by stopping the story every time you want to introduce somebody.

The flashback is another descriptive device that helps your readers get to know a character. Paradoxically, a flashback can move a story forward even though it literally moves backward. As long as the information in the flashback is relevant and interesting—containing the kind of description that engages a reader and illuminates a character—the story will gain momentum. To give flashbacks the best chance of working without stopping forward motion, you must watch for familiar pitfalls. Transitions in and out of flashbacks should be direct and seamless; the flashback should be *part* of a present-action story, and not vice-versa (if the flashback begins to take over the story, then it probably *is* the story); the flashback should contain its own descriptive flow and not be used as a repository for background information; and the past-perfect tense should be replaced by the simple past tense as soon as possible in a flashback (the past perfect serves only to remind readers that the flashback is a diversion from the "real" story).

The flash-forward, on the other hand, is a literal movement forward—a description that announces a future event. Use it sparingly or not at all, for the direct telegraphing of events ruins a story's tension much more often than it adds weight or poignancy.

The set piece is another motion-stopper that can test even the most forgiving reader's good nature. The set piece is a descriptive detour that usually comes from the author's fascination with a subject: how an airplane works; what Monet's gardens at Giverny look like in winter; the history of the Micmac Indians in northern Maine. A successful set piece contains illuminative description and enchanting information. Even if it has only a marginal relationship to the other events of the story, the set piece should suggest something about the way a character thinks or how the events in the story are about to unfold. The story or novel in which the set piece resides must be long enough to contain it; a five-page set piece will burden a short story and brighten a novel.

If forward movement is a problem you struggle with in your fiction, analyze your description techniques. Check for blocky, inert descriptive passages. Check your transitions back and forth in time. Make sure the details enhance both the physical and emotional content. Description is so much more than reportage; it is invention, imagination, and re-creation.

CHAPTER 4

DESCRIPTION AND DIALOGUE

DESCRIPTION AND DIALOGUE are usually discussed as entirely separate techniques. In practice, however, description and dialogue often become inextricable and always have similar functions: to enrich the readers' understanding of a story, to move the story forward, and to help the readers "see" a character. Good dialogue *is* good description.

When a character proclaims, "I'm fed up with you, Arnold. I'm clearing out of here right now," her anger is just as evident as it would be if described through narrative. On the other hand, a long and pointless dialogue sequence in which two characters drink coffee and chat aimlessly about dog grooming stops the motion of a story as effectively as a long and pointless narrative description of dog-grooming.

How you describe a field or a person's anger or a parade or a dying wish depends on your personal preferences and the story's general "feel." Sometimes dialogue is the right choice; sometimes narrative description is the right choice. Often, a combination of dialogue and narrative works best. In any case, the language should be precise, the metaphors apt, the details relevant. All good description, whether in dialogue or narrative form, should follow the rules of good writing.

TYPES OF DIALOGUE

Describing through dialogue is a challenge well worth the trouble. Different characters see things differently, and the kinds of descriptions they make tell a lot about them. Some dialogue lends itself to description better than others. *Direct dialogue*, which is the direct back-and-forth conversation between two or more characters, is not a natural vehicle for description, because many characters don't have the powers of observation necessary for conveying strong images to the readers. In the following example, Patti, an ordinary woman who works in a bakery, sounds too much like a writer to be convincing as a baker:

"You work all night?" Gus said, surprised.

"Bread doesn't bake itself," Patti said. "How do you think it gets to the shelves by six in the morning?"

Gus considered this. "I'd hate working at night. It must be kind of creepy being back there all by yourself."

"No, it's wonderful," Patti said. "The solitude, the pristine quiet, the aromas of yeast and flour. When I first come in I wait before turning on the lights. In that half-light I can just make out the marvelous shapes of the equipment, the subtle glint of chrome and steel, the vats of frosting arranged like sentries against the far window."

Patti sounds too self-consciously poetic here, especially after her first line of dialogue ("Bread doesn't bake itself. How do you think it gets to the shelves by six in the morning?"), which establishes her as no-nonsense and practical, not the reflective poet type who delivers the soliloquy on aromas and half-light. If you really want Patti's description of the bakery to stay in the story, consider *indirect dialogue*. Indirect dialogue paraphrases a character's words:

"You work all night?" Gus said, surprised.

"You think bread bakes itself?" Patti said. "How do you think it gets to the shelves by six in the morning?"

Gus considered this. "I'd hate working at night. It must be kind of creepy being back there all by yourself."

"No, it's wonderful," Patti said. She sat down and took a breath, then proceeded to describe the beauty of a bakery at night: the solitude, the pristine quiet, the aromas of yeast and flour. Even the dimness of the light seemed to charm her, for she described the shapes of the equipment, the subtle glint of chrome and steel, the vats of frosting arranged like sentries against the far window.

In this version, the poetic description is easier to swallow because Patti doesn't say the words directly. Readers won't stop to wonder whether Patti is the type who would wax poetic about "the subtle glint of chrome and steel," because the description, though attributed to Patti, belongs more to the narrative than the character. For this particular passage, indirect dialogue offers your readers the information that the bakery is, at least to Patti, a magical place. And yet you don't have to give Patti dialogue that seems too magical for her character.

Direct dialogue works best with less poetic descriptions. For example, a character named Rowe, who is describing the injuries his brother received in an accident, can do the job very well all by himself:

> "So, how's Gordon?" I asked.
> "Great," Rowe said, "if you don't mind sewed-shut eyes."
> "They sewed his eyes shut?"
> "It's temporary." Rowe shrugged. "Just as well, really. This way he can't see his face."
> I didn't want to hear it, but Rowe wasn't one to skimp on detail. "His teeth are a mess," he continued. "You ever see a whale's mouth? All the teeth look kind of chewed up and stashed back in, every which way? That's Rowe. Make you sick to look at him. The skin's all gone on the left side, nothing but raw meat."

This is a case where indirect dialogue would only dilute the impact of the raw description contained in the direct dialogue:

> I was sorry I'd asked. Rowe gave me a description of Gordon's new face—chewed-up teeth and the skin torn away, exposing raw meat. They'd sewn his eyes shut. Rowe said it was enough to make a person sick.

The indirect dialogue here robs your readers of Rowe's personality and the sense that he relishes delivering the gory details. The information seems sanitized and less immediate, because we can't hear Rowe's voice, only a third-party rendition of Rowe's voice. It's the difference between witnessing a three-alarm fire and reading about it in the paper.

Perhaps you want to tone down the gory details. You prefer a gentler rendition of the injuries. In that case, indirect dialogue is a good choice after all:

> According to Rowe, Gordon's teeth had been broken out, his eyes stitched shut, and his skin rubbed raw, as if slapped over and over by a mighty, invisible hand.

You can also combine direct and indirect dialogue as a way of enhancing certain kinds of description:

> "Look at this place," Sally said. "You're forty years old and still living in what can only be referred to as a *pad*."
> "What's wrong with it?"
> "Beaded curtains, for starters. And this album collection. Nobody collects albums. It's so retro."
> "Hey, this is a valuable collection," he said. "My Jimi Hendrix stuff alone is worth plenty." But she wouldn't quit. She recited a list of his beloved possessions as if they were character flaws: aloe plant; lava lamp; Grateful Dead poster; Indian-print slipcover; waterbed. "Are you finished?" he asked.
> She shook her head. "Honey, I'm just getting started."

In this passage, you give your readers just enough direct dialogue to show how the two characters argue. Then, in indirect dialogue (*She recited a list of his beloved possessions. . . .*) you suggest the flavor of the rest of the argument without boring everybody with a blow-by-blow. If you were to write the scene in direct dialogue from start to finish, you would dilute Sally's power, making her sound too strident or whiny:

> "Look at this place," Sally said. "You're forty years old and still living in what can only be referred to as a *pad*."
> "What's wrong with it?"
> "Beaded curtains, for starters. And this album collection. Nobody collects albums. It's so retro."
> "Hey, this is a valuable collection," he said. "My Jimi Hendrix stuff alone is worth plenty."
> "Maybe so, but look at the rest of this stuff. This lava lamp, for instance. Lava lamps went out with love beads."
> "They're back," he protested. "You see them all the time now."

"And this silly Grateful Dead poster. The Grateful Dead weren't any good twenty years ago and they're even worse now."

"Says you."

"That's right. And I say this Indian-print slipcover should take a trip to Goodwill. Maybe some needy homeless person could cut it up and use it for handkerchiefs."

"Hey, leave that alone."

"And another thing," Sally said. "This aloe plant is the stupidest thing I've ever seen. Natural medicine, my foot."

Et cetera, et cetera. Not only does Sally lose her verve, but the scene begins to bog down with too many lines of dialogue that are similar. The original passage was tighter and snappier thanks to the succinct description of the indirect dialogue.

CONVERSATIONS IN SPACE

When writing dialogue, keep in mind that readers appreciate being able to "see" where the conversation is taking place. Conversations do not occur in a vacuum; the speakers are usually doing something else—ironing clothes, starting a car, arranging flowers—while they are speaking. Also, physical surroundings can influence what characters say; a conversation held in a church might be a little more subdued than the same conversation held in a deli. To make a scene come alive, you must attend to the context of the conversation. In other words, most dialogue needs some descriptive interruption in order to make its full impact. Descriptive interruptions can take the form of a narrative break—a full-paragraph (or longer) description of a tent site in the middle of a conversation between two campers, for example—but more often these interruptions are brief and intermittent, taking the form of *dialogue tags* and *gestural pauses.*

Simple dialogue tags are the "he said/she said"'s of a dialogue sequence:

"Henry," Elizabeth said. "Tell me more."

Or:

"The car is gone!" Elmore shouted.

Or:

> "Not now," I told him. "I'll explain later."

Simple dialogue tags are for identifying the speaker or implying a pause. They do not offer any description.

Dialogue tags *can* be descriptive as well as functional, however. *Descriptive dialogue tags* are tags with modifiers or modifying phrases attached:

> "Those are my flowers," he said, crossly.

Or:

> "Let me get it," she said, reaching for the phone.

Or:

> "Just who do you think you are?" I asked, looking up.

These tags offer more than speaker identification. They describe an action or a state of mind. As a general rule, though, don't use adverbs to describe the speaker's mood. Avoid the trap of "he said, cautiously" or "she said, flirtatiously"; caution and flirtatiousness should be implied by the dialogue:

> "Wait a minute," he said. "Okay, now you can light the fuse." [words imply caution]

Or:

> "Why, Ricky," she said. "I do believe you're flirting with me." [words imply flirtatiousness]

The occasional, well-placed adverb is probably okay. You find them in dialogue tags written by our best writers. But you don't find them often, which makes their impact that much stronger when they do occur.

Adverbs work best in dialogue tags when the state of mind is contrary to the speaker's words:

> "I got all A's," he said, glumly.

Or:

> "You wrecked my car!" she said, happily.

Or:

> "Why, you little creep," she said, sweetly.

Modifying phrases ("he said, reaching for the phone"; "she said, looking up") added to a tag help advance the story or provide clues about the characters' motives:

> "Emily, how nice to see you again," Abner said, clenching his fists.

Or:

> "Here goes nothing," Mary said, raising the sledgehammer over her head.

In the first instance, Abner's clenched fists tell us something about his feelings toward Emily. In the second instance, Mary's raising of the sledgehammer moves the story's action along.

Gestural pauses are descriptive, full-sentence interruptions that enhance or replace dialogue tags. They are similar in function to descriptive dialogue tags in that they can reveal a character's motives and move the story forward.

> "Henry," Elizabeth said. She pulled her chair up close. "Tell me more."

Or:

> Elmore came tearing down the street. "The car is gone!"

Or:

> "Not now," I told him. I slid into the booth and ordered a beer.

How important is adding description to dialogue in the form of tags and gestural pauses? Extremely. Tags and pauses can cast a conversation in many different ways. The following conversation contains no description:

"Sally."

"I can't hear you."

"Come on, Sal, talk to me."

"I saw your mother this morning. She had some very interesting news about you."

"My mother's nuts, okay? She's off on one of her little trips to the moon. Everything that comes out of her mouth is a complete lie. It's not her fault, she can't help herself."

"Really? She seems to think she's helping you and Abby Ross plan your June wedding."

"Abby Ross? I don't even know Abby Ross. I've never even met Abby Ross. Abby Ross lives on the Foreside, for heaven's sake, what would she want with a schlup like me?"

"How long have you been seeing her?"

"Listen, I can show you the papers. I had her committed for six weeks last year. She's a pathological liar. You have to forgive them because they don't really understand all the damage they're doing."

This is direct dialogue that describes a man trying to weasel out of a tight situation. However, you can change the characters' personalities one way or another by adding description to the dialogue in the form of descriptive dialogue tags and gestural pauses:

Hank opened the screen door gingerly. "Sally."

She looked up from the flowers she was arranging. "I can't hear you," she said. She set her chin and went back to work. Dozens of roses lay in a heap at her elbow.

"Come on, Sal, talk to me."

She picked up a pair of shears and began to snip the stems. "I saw your mother this morning. She had some very interesting news about you."

"My mother's nuts, okay?" Hank said. He sidled to the far side of the kitchen, far from the sound of stems being snapped off. "She's off on one of her little trips to the moon. Everything that comes out of her mouth is a complete lie. It's not her fault, she can't help herself."

"Really?" Sally said, pointing the shears. "She seems to think she's helping you and Abby Ross plan your June wedding."

"Abby Ross? I don't even know Abby Ross. I've never even

met Abby Ross. Abby Ross lives on the Foreside, for heaven's sake, what would she want with a schlup like me?"

"How long have you been seeing her?" She held up the shears and began making little snips at the air. He moved a little farther, putting a table and a couple of chairs between them.

"Listen," he said. "I can show you the papers. I had her committed for six weeks last year. She's a pathological liar. You have to forgive them because they don't really understand all the damage they're doing."

No matter how we might have read the original dialogue, in this version we are compelled to view Sally as the one with the upper hand. She's the one with the scissors, and Hank "sidles" out of their reach. The heap of roses presents a vague impression of dead bodies, given the circumstances of her wielding the shears as a weapon. Hank shrinks from the sound of "stems being snapped off." Clearly he mistrusts his own safety in the presence of this angry woman. The dialogue becomes a cat-and-mouse game in which Hank is clearly the mouse. The description is what gives the dialogue sequence its comedic turn.

Different description choices, however, can quickly turn the mouse into a very menacing cat:

Hank burst into the kitchen and planted himself behind her. "Sally."

She looked into the sinkful of dishes. "I can't hear you."

"Come on, Sal," he said, yanking her arm. "Talk to me."

She waited a very long time, her eyes on the water, until he released her. He relaxed a little, retreated to the refrigerator to rummage for a beer. "I saw your mother this morning," she murmured. "She had some very interesting news about you."

He slammed the refrigerator door. "My mother's nuts, okay? She's off on one of her little trips to the moon. Everything that comes out of her mouth is a complete lie. It's not her fault, she can't help herself."

Sally turned, folded her arms as if steeling herself against his anger. "Really? She seems to think she's helping you and Abby Ross plan your June wedding."

Hank began to redden. "Abby Ross?" The long cords of his neck began to pulse. "I don't even know Abby Ross. I've never even met Abby Ross. Abby Ross lives on the Foreside, for heaven's sake, what would she want with a schlup like me?"

She let out a breath. "How long have you been seeing her?"

He advanced on her then, spots of sweat beginning to darken the front of his shirt. "Listen, I can show you the papers. I had her committed for six weeks last year. She's a pathological liar." She flattened herself against the sink as he lumbered over the slick linoleum. "You have to forgive them," he said, his voice dropping eerily. "They don't really understand all the damage they're doing."

In this version, the description surrounding the dialogue gives the scene a sinister twist, *even though the dialogue is exactly the same.* Notice how the descriptions control the pace of the scene, and how that pace implies danger. If you want to slow the pace of a dialogue sequence, add descriptive interruptions. If you want to quicken the pace, use description sparingly or not at all. The first version of the preceding dialogue sequence reads at a fast, breezy clip that makes the scene feel almost lighthearted, and the last version reads slowly, with pauses implied by descriptive interruptions like "He advanced on her . . ." or "She waited a very long time. . . ." The result is two dramatically different scenes.

OVERDESCRIBING DIALOGUE

Be careful not to overdo it, though. Too much description in a dialogue sequence can "flood" your dialogue:

"Here's the envelope," Stanley said. He held the envelope out, his eyes fixed on the ludicrous embossed return address with the pink-tinged logo of his uncle's company.

Eleanor hesitated. She squinted up at the fluorescent lights, considering. Then she plucked the envelope from Stanley's hands, her lacquered nails gleaming. "This will be our little secret, Stanley," she said, stuffing the envelope into her purse. "I promise you, no one will ever know." She ran one deft hand across her hair.

Stanley laughed. A flat, disdainful sound. "As long as the money keeps flowing?"

Eleanor's lips parted into a thin smile. "You don't mind so much, do you?" she said soothingly. "It's Uncle's money, after all." She drew her purse closer to her coat as if daring him to take the money back.

Stanley hung his head like a bad dog. "You don't understand, Eleanor," he said, clenching his weak fists. "That's what makes it so humiliating."

She pursed her lips, inching closer to him, taking arrogant little baby steps. "Poor dear."

He shook his head, steeling himself against his own stupid tears. "I can't pay my rent," he said. He sucked in his breath and let it out slowly, his cheeks deflating. "I can't meet my child support payments. I can't even pay off a blackmailer with my own money."

Under all the hesitating and squinting and handing over and smiling and head-hanging and head-shaking and breath-taking, your dialogue is struggling to be heard. Unfortunately, the constant descriptive interruptions force your readers more than once to backtrack a line or two to figure out what question or comment the speaker is responding to. Description interruptions are most effective when inserted sparingly:

"Here's the envelope," Stanley said.

Eleanor plucked the envelope from Stanley's hands. "This will be our little secret, Stanley," she said, stuffing the envelope into her purse. "I promise you, no one will ever know."

"As long as the money keeps flowing?"

"You don't mind so much, do you?" Eleanor said. "It's Uncle's money, after all."

"You don't understand, Eleanor. That's exactly what makes it so humiliating."

She pursed her lips. "Poor dear."

"I can't pay my rent," he said. "I can't meet my child support payments. I can't even pay off a blackmailer with my own money."

See how much more dramatic this scene is without that blanket of description? In the first version you gave the readers too much guidance. Ironically, by clearing out the guideposts you made the conversation easier to follow. Your readers don't have to backtrack. And the description still delivers the crucial information—that Stanley is at Eleanor's mercy—without overwhelming the scene.

Be careful, also, about making your descriptive additions to dialogue too similar. In this first sequence, a modifying phrase follows each line of dialogue; the sequence feels rote and wooden:

> "Over here," Alan called, waving his glove.
> "Did I miss the game?" she asked, picking her way over the grass.
> "It rained. We're just now getting started," he said, giving her a kiss.
> "Do you expect me to stay for the whole thing?" she asked, scanning the bleachers.

In this second version, a gestural pause precedes each line of dialogue:

> Alan waved his glove. "Over here."
> She picked her way over the grass. "Did I miss the game?"
> He gave her a kiss. "It rained. We're just now getting started.
> She scanned the bleachers. "Do you expect me to stay for the whole thing?"

The second version is as wooden as the first, because the gestural pauses one after another seem to be following a predetermined pattern. Your best option is to combine several kinds of descriptive interruptions in the same sequence:

> "Over here."
> "Did I miss the game?" she asked, picking her way over the grass.
> "It rained," Alan said. "We're just now getting started."
> She scanned the bleachers. "Do you expect me to stay for the whole thing?"

In this final version, the dialogue takes center stage. The descriptive interruptions, because they are varied and therefore unobtrusive, lend shape and rhythm to the dialogue.

IMPLYING SETTING

Let's say you want to write a story in which plot and character are revealed chiefly through dialogue. Instead of explaining the setting through a descriptive interruption ("the woods were dark"), you can imply setting through dialogue:

> "These trees are beginning to suffocate me," April said. "You'd have to hold a gun to my head before I'd live here."
>
> Carrie looked around. "It's not so bad. Aunt Jean says country air's supposed to be good for you."
>
> "Air? How can air get through all these trees?" She looked up. "Your aunt must have double-sized lungs and a hell of a lot of fortitude. How can she tell day from night?"
>
> Carrie kept walking. "I think the house is at the end of this path, if I'm remembering right."
>
> "I hope she has electricity," April said. "I feel like I'm walking in the bottom of a well."

The setting implied through this dialogue is a thick woods with a house nestled somewhere therein. The beauty of implying setting through dialogue is that you allow your readers to "see" the characters—the histrionic April and tranquil Carrie—at the same time they are seeing the setting.

Make sure the characters' descriptions sound natural, and not staged for the readers' benefit. Precise description of setting shouldn't come at the expense of the characters:

> "Carrie, I'm really getting tired of walking through Ten Acre Woods looking for your Aunt Jean's house."
>
> "I think the turnoff is at the end of this path," Carrie said. "We'll just keep following it, even though it's overgrown with blackberry bushes in full bloom."
>
> April looked up. "The trees are so thick and dark. I don't like the deep Maine woods."

Both versions describe a similar circumstance: Carrie and April are walking through thick woods on a path that will eventually lead to Aunt Jean's house. The first version sounds like two people talking, and the second sounds like two people announcing. What went wrong? In the second version, the characters are describing a setting that they are too familiar with to speak of in so formal a way. So they sound like stick figures. People never make reference to what they already know. If you and a friend are walking through Ten Acre Woods, you refer to it as "here," or "this godforsaken place"—anything but Ten Acre Woods; you both already know where you are. Similarly, if you and your friend are looking for your aunt's house, you don't say, "I'm tired of looking for Aunt Jean's house," you say something like "When will we get there?" or "Do you see the house yet?" That the house in question belongs to Aunt Jean is already known to you both, so you wouldn't normally identify it any further than "the house." Similarly, the fact that the blackberry bushes are in full bloom is too obvious for Carrie to mention so precisely. She might say, "Let's get some berries" or "I just scratched my leg on that bramble," but she would not say "blackberry bushes in full bloom."

If you have to fully describe your setting early in the story, then do it through narrative:

> They were hiking through Ten Acre Woods in search of the small bungalow that belonged to Carrie's aunt Jean. It was mid-morning, but the sun was all but missing for the depth and breadth and height of the stern, ancient trees. Their path was nearly invisible, thick with blackberry bushes in full bloom, and given to false trails that forced the two women to continually double back on their tracks.
>
> "These trees are beginning to suffocate me," April said. "You'd have to hold a gun to my head before I'd live here."
>
> Carrie looked around. "It's not so bad. Aunt Jean says country air's supposed to be good for you."

The logistical details of setting are best delivered through narrative. If the interaction between characters is your main concern at the moment, you can give a general impression of the setting through dialogue and fill in the specific details a few at a time as the story progresses.

DESCRIPTION BY OMISSION

Remember the 1988 Vice-Presidential debate in which Lloyd Bentsen said to Dan Quayle, "You're no Jack Kennedy"? Everybody watching

understood that Bentsen had deeply insulted Quayle, and yet he had
not maligned his character or accused Quayle of anything untoward.
What he did was describe a man in terms of what he wasn't. This
verbal skulduggery works as well in fictional dialogue as in the real
thing.

Let's say you want a character to describe his hotel room:

> "Where did you stay?" Bernice asked.
> Izzy closed his eyes and shuddered. "You wouldn't believe
> it. The sheets were gray, the windows were gray. Even the water
> was gray. The TV didn't work and the blinds wouldn't stay down.
> I stayed awake all night squashing cockroaches."

In this description, you give your readers a vivid picture of the hotel
poor Izzy stayed in. You can conjure an equally memorable picture
by describing the place in terms of what it wasn't:

> "Where did you stay?" Bernice asked.
> Izzy closed his eyes and shuddered. "Let's just say it wasn't
> the Hilton."
> Bernice waved him away. "The Hilton's overrated, in my
> opinion."
> "At least they fumigate once in a while," Izzy said. "And
> you don't get rashes from the shower, last time I checked."

In the revision, you invite your readers to imagine much more than
the specific details of the first version. The fact that Izzy's hotel "isn't
the Hilton" evokes opposite images: rude personnel instead of polite,
wrinkled sheets instead of ironed, and so on. Also, Izzy's contention
that at the Hilton "they fumigate once in a while" and "you don't
get rashes from the shower" creates images at least as horrible as the
ones in the first version. We can picture armies of bugs marching
over a soggy, balding carpet, and a shower with inches of mildew and
who-knows-what-else clinging to the walls. All this, and Izzy hasn't
actually said one word about the place; he's talking about the Hilton.

This technique works well when a character is describing people, too:

> Mac watched my daughter make her way from one end of
> the pool to the other. "Not exactly Esther Williams," he said,

"but then again she's only nine."

Or:

"Who's our new boss?" I asked.
"Remember Arthur?"
"Yeah," I said. "The man was an angel."
"Let me make this clear," Alice said, leaning close to my face. "Our new boss is not Arthur. Not even close."

The unsaid is a powerful tool. It can be used in narrative description as well ("Linden Island was not the tropical paradise the group had been led to expect from the travel guide . . ."), but direct dialogue is its most natural venue. After all, people are prone to use description by omission, whether they are sipping tea in a restaurant or participating in a nationally televised debate.

WRAP-UP

Description and dialogue often overlap. Your characters can describe in four lines of dialogue something that might take you two paragraphs of narrative to convey. Neither dialogue nor narrative description is an inherently better technique; which choice you make depends on the individual scene. If you want a breezy, fast-paced scene, then use a lot of dialogue and a little description. If you want to slow the pace of a scene, then add descriptive interruptions to your dialogue. Descriptive interruptions can add comedy or suspense or poignancy to a scene, because they guide the readers' perceptions in a way straight dialogue—which can be interpreted in many ways—cannot.

Dialogue can be direct—

"I'm pregnant, everybody!" Kristen announced

—or indirect:

Kristen announced that she was pregnant.

Direct dialogue generally delivers a better sense of a character's personality, but indirect dialogue can give you more room to use your own language for description:

> Holding on to her blossoming belly, Kristen announced her pregnancy in a voice loud enough to fell a moose.

A combination of direct and indirect dialogue usually makes for a natural-sounding exchange between two characters, especially if the scene is long and filled with details that don't warrant their own lines of dialogue:

> "I hate your mother," he said, "because she's Polish." Then he went on to malign my Italian grandfather, my Jewish brother-in-law, and my English aunts.

Descriptive interruptions almost always enhance a dialogue sequence, because conversations do not take place in a vacuum. People talk while shaving, moving furniture, scaling mountains, and mailing letters. These descriptive interruptions sometimes come as full narrative breaks, but more often take the briefer form of *dialogue tags* and *gestural pauses.*

Simple dialogue tags ("he said/she said") identify speakers and imply pauses. *Descriptive dialogue tags* describe a character's actions and/or state of mind:

> "Not in this lifetime," he said, heaving the body overboard.

Descriptive tags like this keep the action going while the characters are conversing. Avoid adding single adverbs to dialogue tags ("he said, angrily"; "she said, sadly"); the state of mind should be implied in the dialogue itself or in the ensuing action. You shouldn't have to explain the meaning of a line by adding crossly/avidly/sadly/happily.

Gestural pauses are full-sentence interruptions in dialogue that enhance or replace dialogue tags:

> "I heard you, Ivan," Millicent said. She waved him away. "But you'll have to wait."

These pauses usually describe a gesture that delivers information about a character's mood or motives.

Dialogue tags and gestural pauses can control the pace and even the meaning of a dialogue sequence, but they can also smother the dialogue if used too frequently. Also, be sure not to use the same kind of tag or pause with each line of dialogue—the conversation will appear wooden. Look up an author whose use of dialogue you admire. Chances are you'll find some lines tagged, some modified with a phrase or full-sentence pause, and many others left to stand alone.

You can use dialogue to imply setting without having to make a full-scale description of a place or event. A line like

"My God, this place looks like the dark side of the moon," Henrietta said,

can replace a whole paragraph of narrative description. You can also imply setting by what a character doesn't say about it. A line like

"It's not exactly Sesame Street," Brenda murmured,

can describe the mean streets of a large city without mention of broken windows and bloodstained concrete. Be careful not to "stage" dialogue only for the readers' benefit, though. "Let's climb the glass-strewn stairs of my three-story apartment building" sounds more like an announcement to the readers than part of a conversation. People never make mention of what they already know; if the broken glass and three stories are important, you'll have to find another way to reveal them.

Think of dialogue as a description technique. Good dialogue, like all good description, should help you move your story forward, illuminate your characters, and enrich your readers' perceptions of the story.

CHAPTER 5

DESCRIPTION AND POINT OF VIEW

POINT OF VIEW IS THE PERSPECTIVE from which a story is told. It is the single most important choice you make for your story. More than any other technique, point of view influences how readers perceive the story you are trying to tell.

Which character is my main character? Which character do I want readers to empathize with and understand? How do I want readers to view the setting? All these questions can be answered by your choice of point of view.

When point of view is well chosen and firmly in place, the story hums along, seemingly all by itself. When point of view falters, the story loses its focus, its momentum, its reason for being. Point of view is the glue that holds a story together; it also dictates what kind of description you may use and which characters get to do the describing.

Imagine the story of Cinderella in the wicked stepmother's point of view, or Dickens's *A Christmas Carol* narrated by one of the ghosts. The wicked stepmother wouldn't be able to see her own wickedness or Cinderella's smudged beauty, and the Ghost of Christmas Yet to Come wouldn't give a hoot about the parlor games in the home of Scrooge's nephew. Point of view heavily influences description; different perspectives bring out vastly different aspects of a story.

For beginning writers especially, point of view can be difficult to grasp; it requires constant attention. Point of view becomes less intimidating with experience, but its problems haunt every writer at one time or another, no matter how accomplished or experienced he or she may be.

Point of view comes in three forms: first person, second person, and third person. You have a few other choices within these three categories.

FIRST-PERSON POINT OF VIEW

Beginning story writers love to employ the first-person narrator, a common and useful technique for creating immediate, seductive, captivating fiction. The trouble comes when the story's narrator is too closely based on the author. A reader pauses: Is this fiction, or an essay, or what? It's true that most of us began writing by writing about ourselves, and that an author's life often yields engaging and even powerful writing. But fiction is its own discipline; you might even say it's more challenging than non-fiction, because you have to invent a life before you can begin to interpret it.

The Narrator Is Not You

To make the first person work effectively, keep one thought in mind: *The narrator is not you.* An essay is not a short story. A memoir is not a novel. In fiction, the first-person narrator is a *character you create.* Since you have created him and decided to let him tell the story, it is your duty to remember that he is no one but himself. Allow him his own voice, his own beliefs, his own eccentricities, however distant they may be from your own. Think of the first-person narrator as your chance to be somebody else for a while, like an actor playing a role.

The problem of author-as-narrator is only compounded when the events being described in the story "actually happened." Real-life events rendered as fiction almost always fail, because our editing radar doesn't work very well with stories too close to our own experience. We end up putting everything in, because everything that happened to us in this particular scenario is remembered as important. The softies among us may also take out key scenes so as not to hurt Mom's or Uncle Bill's feelings. If you must fictionalize an actual event, then take the point of view of someone else involved in the event and use him or her as your narrator. Take a key item and change it dramatically—a lost love becomes a lost job, a plane crash becomes a fender-bender, a pet dog becomes a herd of sheep. You can mine the emotional territory that interests you while inventing fiction that is fresh and new.

The worst defense for a failed story is "It really happened."

You may not like your first-person narrator, and that's fine. Let her talk. She has a story to tell in her own way; the worst thing you can do to her story is impose yourself on it. Don't be afraid your son will think you had a short career as a loan shark. Or, worse, that your readers will think you're a bigot, with a mouth like the one on the narrator you've created. This is one of a writer's occupational hazards. Don't censor your narrators! (Mom will understand.) If a reader insists that your narrator is you, then score one for your descriptive powers.

Once you've established a proper distance between the first-person narrator and yourself, and between yourself and the events being narrated, your challenge isn't over. In fact, it's just beginning. First-person narration comes with problems—some enjoyable, some aggravating, all of them approachable. Let's begin with the problem of observation.

The First-Person Narrator As Observer

The first-person narrator is, above all else, an observer. A first-person narrative has a distinctive "voice"; voice becomes character, character becomes story. But what makes that voice worth listening to? Sometimes it is the grammatical miscues and syntactical detours that define a voice—regional idioms, occupational buzz words, grammatical pyrotechnics—but even a narrator with a quirky voice is not interesting unless he or she has a good story to tell. Celie, the narrator (by way of letters to God and her sister) of Alice Walker's *The Color Purple*, has a distinctive grammar, but what makes her so compelling is the way she observes her world:

> Us dress Squeak like she a white woman, only her clothes patch. She got on a starch and iron dress, high heel shoes with scuffs, and a old hat somebody give Shug. Us give her a old pocketbook look like a quilt and a little black bible. Us wash her hair and git all the grease out, then I put it up in two plaits

that cross over her head. Us bathe her so clean she smell like a good clean floor.

This passage is breathtaking not simply because of the "accent" of the speaker, but because of her acute and telling observations. What she chooses to observe tells us a lot about her world. Her similes make use of the homely objects within her own grasp. The pocketbook looks like a quilt; the clean smells like a floor.

Holden Caulfield, narrator of J.D. Salinger's *The Catcher in the Rye*, reveals himself similarly:

This family that you could tell just came out of some church were walking right in front of me—a father, a mother, and a little kid about six years old. They looked sort of poor. The father had on one of those pearl-gray hats that poor guys wear a lot when they want to look sharp. He and his wife were just walking along, talking, not paying any attention to their kid. The kid was swell. He was walking in the street, instead of on the sidewalk, but right next to the curb. He was making out like he was walking a very straight line, the way kids do, and the whole time he kept singing and humming.

Holden's slang, which is a delight to listen to, pins him to a certain age and era, but what makes him real is his series of heartbreaking observations. He finds sorrow and poignancy and pathos everywhere, especially in children. "Kids' notebooks kill me," he tells us after reading his little sister's. Describing a boy who fell out a window, he says,

Finally, what he did, instead of taking back what he said, he jumped out the window. I was in the *shower* and all, and even *I* could hear him land outside. But I just thought something fell out the window, a radio or a desk or something, not a *boy* or anything.

Through his distinctive observations, Holden reveals his own alienation and despair.

The trick of making a first-person narrator's observations authentic is to make sure that the narrator speaks from his own experience. Holden's use of the phrase "poor guys" clues us to the fact that he is one of the "rich guys." Celie's "clean floor" shows us something about her unadorned world. A different kind of narrator might compare that clean smell to newly printed money. A narrator other than Holden might not have noticed the child's walking in a straight line, but rather the cut of the child's coat. Consider the differences in the following line delivered by different narrators:

> Sandra's son reminded me of a prince, only more imperious.

Or:

> Sandra's kid looked kind of like my cousin Gino, only loads cuter.

Or:

> Sandra's little boy reminded me of that boy in the shelter, only fatter, and a cleaner face.

Or:

> Sandra's boy reminded me of a hush puppy, only stupider and higher strung.

All of these narrators have a set of experiences and prejudices and obsessions that is unique to them. As their author you must allow them their own visions.

Lest you become too discouraged, remember that the "right" observations don't come in the first and second drafts. It takes almost as long to get to know a fictional person as it does a real person. For example, you may not know how your narrator would observe a flooded basement until you have seen her in other situations. In the first draft, she would probably see the flooded basement in more or less the way you would see it:

> I stuttered down the steps, groping for the light. I grabbed the pull-chain and cursed out loud at what the light revealed. Two feet of water, enough to unloose my books from their shelves. They drifted languidly on the water's surface, darkening horribly as the grainy water crept up their innocent spines.

This is the observation of a narrator who loves books. Clearly, she is pained to see the books in such a state. The word "spines," though it obviously refers to book spines, feels strangely human, as if the narrator were imagining herself in the creeping water. The books seem to have a life of their own, drifting "languidly." Through this keenly observed moment, you show your readers something about the narrator. But this is only a first draft; you have no idea who this person really is. What if it turns out, by the end of the story, that the floating books is the only suggestion that this woman has an intellectual life? Perhaps the story is all about her compulsion to keep this flooded house in the best possible condition so that she can sell it out from under her two-timing husband. Three or four drafts later, this woman has become much more solid in your mind. Her single-minded vindictiveness fascinates you. You go back through the scenes, scouring the piece for false notes, and the flooded basement is the first alarm. Books? This woman, you suddenly realize, hasn't read a book since she was sixteen. Even if there were books floating around down there, she wouldn't see them in this panicky way. She would have a completely different view from yours:

> I stuttered down the stairs, groping for the light. I grabbed the pull-chain and nearly laughed out loud at what the light revealed. Books. A little marina of books floating on at least two feet of grimy water, some of them sinking already, some of them light enough to float forever. There must have been a hundred of them, all Barry's silly books he'd kept from college, bobbing like mini ice floes in the basement of the house I resolved right then and there would be sold before summer. I kicked one with my foot. Getting to the sump pump was going to be a problem.

In this revision, the narrator doesn't have any feeling for the books except as a hindrance to her action. In the first draft you had no way of knowing this, so you "filled in" with observations of your own. Now you have no choice but to muster the fortitude to *go back and erase yourself from the first-person narrator's experience,* to allow the story to be hers and hers alone.

Good first-person observation rests on imagination—your ability to envision how one particular character might perceive the world around him. To observe through another's eyes takes practice, and this is one area in which writing exercises actually help. Try describing a car wreck from the perspective of five different passers-by: one might notice the blood, another the dented hood ornament, another the stunned face of the driver. Imagine how each of them might be standing, or breathing; what inaudible words might be escaping their lips? Imagine where they might just have come from, or where they are on their way to. A funeral? A playground? Put on their clothes, take up their space on the sidewalk, and then, looking through their eyes, write what you see.

First Person and the Child Narrator

Creating a first-person narrator is a special joy as long as you remember that every sprig of description, every observation, belongs to that narrator alone. This "ownership" becomes a particular challenge when your narrator is a child. Sometimes it seems as if your only choice is between some Dickensian orphan and the precocious little brother on a television sitcom. Don't despair; your choices are actually endless, as varied as the number of children in the world. The challenge is to find one child's unique voice, a voice readers are willing to believe.

If you are in the habit of listening to real-life children, however, you see your problem. Who, really, wants to listen to a 10-year-old (unless he's yours) tell a story of any considerable length, with his pauses and detours, faulty logic, limited insight and vocabulary, and self-absorbed world view? The trick is to make the child seem ten (good luck working with a first-person narrator any younger than that) while giving him the gifts a good storyteller needs. Remember the fundamentals—the telling detail, simile and metaphor, use of the senses—and keep the language simple:

> For a second I wasn't sure it was really Grandma in that bed. At first I thought maybe she was a ghost, but the hissing turned out to be her trying to breathe. There was something wrong with her skin, little cracks all over, like somebody dipped a spider's feet in red paint and let him walk on her. Her mouth left a wrinkled little hole where her teeth were supposed to be. "Hey, Grandma," I said. "It's me, Freddy!" She looked right at me with grandma eyes and that's when I knew it was her.

The passage is descriptive in several ways. You convey a physical picture of the dying woman; you suggest the child's fear (the hissing) that eventually gives way to his natural enthusiasm (the sudden dialogue); and you add a poignant little punch when he recognizes "grandma eyes." This is a sophisticated picture rendered in language that befits a ten-year-old.

You want to avoid fancy vocabulary, of course, but don't underestimate your narrator, either. Some child narrators end up sounding like this:

> I looked in the bed but I wasn't sure it was Grandma. She sounded just like a big, scary ghost 'cause it was hard to breathe. Boy was I scared. Her face was marked all over with little red lines that looked just like spider legs. And she didn't have her teeth in, so her mouth was real tiny and wrinkly. "Hey, Grandma," I said. "It's me, Freddy!" She looked at me real slow. Her eyes were just like Grandma's, so I knew it was her.

This second example probably sounds more like a "real life" 10-year-old, but "real life" dialogue rarely translates well. You have to manipulate it to make it sound real on the page. Don't shortchange your child narrator. He can manage complex sentences and good rhythms as well as any adult. Keep the vocabulary simple, don't skimp on metaphor (he can handle that, too), and let him talk.

First Person and the Reminiscent Narrator

The reminiscent narrator is an adult looking back on a turning-point experience, usually one from childhood or early adulthood. Your challenge and responsibility as the writer is to make sure the description doesn't get too mushy. Reminiscence is dangerous stuff; the reminiscent narrator treads the fine line between sentiment and sentimentality. In the following example the adult narrator tells the story of his father's dying, back when the narrator was ten years old:

> I was sadder than I had ever been before, looking out the window of the room where my father lay dying. He was trying to sing my song, but he was so sick by then he couldn't bring it off. My heart sank and I fought back tears as I listened. Finally I ran to him and threw myself on the bed and hugged him as hard as I could, fighting back a river of tears.

This narrative manipulates readers into feeling sad, because it takes a pretty hard heart not to be moved by these circumstances. But the passage is nothing more than cheap melodrama, with the clichés of sinking hearts and rivers of tears. And notice that the passage contains not one concrete image: it is simply an explanation of how the narrator felt, in abstractions. Compare this to the following passage, which is from the end of "Leo," a short story by Sharon Sheehe Stark:

> From behind me came a thin strand of sound, low and broken. I thought he was moaning and, frozen, I could not turn to him at first. Minutes passed, the rain drummed down, and in the same instant I recognized the tune, it came to me, like shocking news, that on this day of measured time I, Jeremiah, was still a child. I left the window and went to him, driving myself tight against the bony harp that was my father's body. He went on humming my song, stopping often for breath, until we both went to sleep.

In this profoundly moving passage, specific detail summons our deepest emotions. The "thin strand of sound," the "bony harp," the "stopping often for breath" are things we see and hear and feel. This narrator never tells us that he still faces a well of grief over a long-ago death; rather, he leads us through his experience as if it were our own, and this is what makes the story so unforgettable. When treading deeply emotional material, your reminiscent narrator must rely not on easy abstractions ("I was sadder than I had ever been") but on fresh, specific, and relevant details. By embracing the specific you can usually keep yourself clear of melodrama. Tears and heartaches are a dime a dozen and touch us only briefly; the image of a "bony harp" is unique and touches us forever. Don't aim to make your readers cry. Aim to make them remember.

First Person and Physical Description

How the first-person narrator observes the world is one matter; how he observes himself is another, much thornier matter that has flummoxed inexperienced writers since forever. How does a first-person narrator describe herself? Let's say a character named Julia is a physically beautiful woman, for reasons that are important to your story.

In the third person, you can describe Julia as thoroughly as you wish without sounding self-conscious:

> Julia fidgeted at the study carrel on the third floor of the library, winding a strand of auburn hair around her finger. She had the look of a Botticelli maiden, her wide, flat face composed and pale, delicate blue veins pulsing under the translucent skin of her brow.

Try converting the above passage to first person and see what happens. What you get is a cloying, self-indulgent passage that begins, "I fidgeted at the study carrel" and goes on to say, "I had the look of a Botticelli maiden," ending with, ". . . the translucent skin of my brow." What a drastically different character from the ingenuous young woman reading in the library!

The physical description of a first-person narrator presents a perplexing problem that has more than one solution. Try some of the following solutions to see which techniques best fit the purposes of your story.

Let the narrator describe herself outright. A first-person narrator can sometimes describe herself without resorting to the self-indulgence of the preceding example. It's up to you to find a descriptive tone that fits the narrator's personality. How direct you allow the narrator to be depends on what kind of character you wish to create.

A wry, self-confident Julia might describe herself this way:

> Because I'm red-haired and grey-eyed and fond of tight clothes, men keep mistaking me for their old girlfriends. "Wanda!" they'll holler, charging across the street, against the light. "Marlene? Is that you?" they'll ask, scanning my chest as if looking for a name tag.

A narrator like this one reveals not only her appearance, but her personality. We expect an unsentimental story from a self-confident woman. Although she hasn't come right out and said it, she obviously appreciates her own good looks. She doesn't tell us that "some men" or "most men" look at her. "Men" look at her; in fact, they risk life and limb to get to her side of the street! A narrator like this is a true challenge—she demands a linguistic flair that you must sustain over the dozen or so pages of a short story. You have to give this version of Julia a rollicking syntax and quick wit in order to do justice to her *joie de vivre*. She's got pizazz, so the writing's got to have a little extra fizz, too.

A less confident Julia might sound more like this:

> At the finishing school I attended in my nineteenth year, Jessica Lange was the rage. Meryl Streep, Kathleen Turner. Blonde was in. My hair was a blemish they were too polite to mention, like a scar or leg brace. I was the only girl in my dorm who didn't have call-waiting. "Redhead," my roommate would whisper mournfully when describing me to a potential blind date.

Here we have the beginnings of a physical description from a different kind of storyteller. In this version of Julia, her wryness is tempered by a certain restraint. She sounds reserved (". . . in my nineteenth year . . ."); indeed, she sounds like the product of a finishing school. We may expect a bit of self-deprecating humor (the last line could be tongue-in-cheek, we don't quite know yet), but that humor will exist only in the context of longing or reflection.

Self-description does not have to contain wryness or irony to sound natural. As long as there is a logical reason for self-description, even the most self-effacing character can get away with it. Let's reinvent Julia yet again. This time she is just beginning to emerge from a shut-away life:

> After my father died I lost one hundred and twenty pounds—a whole person—and my true face began to appear: the high cheekbones I remembered from my youth, the grey eyes larger somehow in so much less flesh. Even my hair seemed more prominent—red and curly—now that my extra face was gone.

Here Julia is solemn and reflective; we don't expect pizazz. We expect a more thoughtful, even meandering story, something that matches Julia's reflective tone. Her self-description, though direct, has a chilling subtext, because Julia is really talking about an emotional metamorphosis, not a physical one.

Use description by association. If your first-person narrator is not the type to describe herself at all, then you've got to get sneaky. How about letting her compare herself to someone else? In the following example, Julia is shy and confiding; you can let her speak of her beauty this way:

> I have my mother's hair, thick and red. She used to braid it for me, her trembly fingers sifting the strands as I stood before her, paying attention. I have her eyes, too, grey and wide set, and her pinked lips. I inherited her face when what I wanted was her spirit.

In this version, we infer Julia's beauty from the unusual coloring and the fact that she's comparing herself with her mother, who has "spirit," which is a form of beauty all by itself. Because she is speaking of her appearance in terms of inherited traits, the self-description seems neither too self-conscious nor too self-congratulatory. After all, she has nothing to do with her looks, she got them from her mother. Do you see how you have slipped Julia's appearance into her own narrative while offering your readers some clues to her personality? She remembers her mother lovingly, and looks back on her childhood with benevolence.

Notice also how you've woven in the phrase "paying attention"; it's an evocative phrasing that probably has something to do with the emotional content of the story. Maybe Julia missed something after all: she didn't pay *enough* attention. Or, maybe something she did pay attention to at her mother's knee is now coming back to help or hinder her. Remember, always: *Description is rarely used for its own sake, but to present a story in a certain way.* If Julia had been "wriggling and writhing" instead of "paying attention," then you would have yet another version of Julia on your hands.

You needn't stick with family members to make associative descriptions. Consider this example:

> Bobby was Irish, I was Italian. Though our appearance was a study in contrasts (his hair was flame orange, mine so black it looked blue), we were both poor and in need of longer pants, so our teachers often took us for brothers.

Notice that the narrator's description draws on ethnic proclivities that paint a vivid picture. Because their hair color is described in such extremes, we know that Bobby looks not just Irish, but very Irish, and that the narrator looks not just Italian, but very Italian. Doesn't it go without saying that Bobby's eyes are blue, his skin pale? That the narrator's skin is dark, his eyes brown, maybe even black?

Besides giving your readers a physical description of the narrator, you give your story a powerful context. Ethnic differences contrasted with economic similarities is evocative and intriguing, hinting at a rich and complex story.

Use your plot. If a certain physical feature—a scar, a limp, baldness, obesity—is important to the plot, then your best bet is to introduce it in context:

> Because I had always been the biggest kid in the class, I was accustomed to being last in line.

Or:

> I boarded the bus (jammed as usual) and scanned the faces. Usually there was at least one—a wizened grandmother or a good-natured child—who didn't mind sharing space with a white man.

Or:

> "One life jacket," Jamie murmured. "Only one of us can jump."
> Frank's eyes flew open. "But we'll die on board. The boat is sinking!"
> "We have ten minutes, tops," Jamie said evenly. "Who's it going to be?"
> Each of them slid a resentful little glance my way, and I leaned on my crutches with a thrill of defiance.

In the first example, the narrator is a loser who attributes his bad luck to his large size. In the second, the narrator is a stranger in a strange land, whose color is the heart of the story. In the third example, the narrator's handicap will become his triumph as he uses it to manipulate his comrades into saving his life. In each example, the physical characteristic contributes to the story: *because* he's big, he's always last; *because* he's white, he encounters hostility; *because* he's on crutches, he is resented but saved. The physical description feels natural because it is essential to the plot.

The observant second party. Let another character do the narrator's work for her. Observant second parties can point out a bad dye job or a club foot more naturally than the narrator can— they are on the outside looking in. The observer can describe directly, or the narrator can report what the observer says. Careful here. A report like "He told me I was the most exotic, breathtaking beauty he had ever seen" makes the narrator look bad, unless she is being ironic or naive. Consider the following examples, which use second parties who are in a position to observe Julia:

> My mother was always telling me how pretty I was, how grey my eyes, how red my hair, the color of rusted fall leaves, she said. I carried myself like a queen, she said, over and over, like a preemptive strike against the neighborhood boys who might not share her enthusiasm. To my sister, whose beauty went without saying, she offered nothing at all.

Or:

> "Where did you get those pretty grey eyes?" Mrs. Lawson cooed, her plump and dimpled self bent over to look me in the face. Her own eyes loomed large, blue and full of questions. I backed up, not knowing what to say. Where did eyes come from? I retreated to my playhouse, away from Mrs. Lawson and all the other adults who pelted me daily with questions to which I didn't know the answers.

Or:

> "I wish I had your hair," my sister sighed. "Red is all the rage right now." She laughed. "You're finally in style, Julia."
> "Imagine that," I said dully. I knew what she was up to.
> "Of course we'll have to cut it. It's too long the way it is now. Too heavy." She lifted the front of my hair as if parting a curtain.

In each of these examples the physical description is parceled out only as it belongs to and illuminates the story. The first example reveals a daughter's remembrance of her own appearance, but more important, her mother's indulgence; the second example reveals a child's appearance, but more important, that child's terror of the ordinary adult world; the third example reveals a woman's appearance, but more important, her combative relationship with her sister.

You may have your own solutions for describing a first-person narrator, or you may use a combination of the above solutions, which overlap anyway. Be careful, however, of solutions that seem too easy. In the rush to get a story down, you might be tempted to resort to hackneyed devices, which do nothing for your story except mark it as a beginner's. The following suggestions should keep you out of trouble.

Avoid the mirror. In the mirror technique, the narrator is passing by a hall mirror, or shaving in front of the bathroom mirror, or catching a glimpse of himself in a storefront just about the time a physical description is in order. "A haunted face stared back at me." "I saw a woman with grey eyes and red hair." "I realized I still had blood on my face." This device isn't always bad—sometimes a character can be effectively startled by his own appearance—but often it feels too obvious, and besides, it's been done to death. Unless the mirror is an integral part of the story, such as a magic mirror, a vain narrator, avoid using it.

Avoid the overly observant second party. This solution is what you get when you try too hard. "But you're so beautiful!" the *overly* observant second party might say. "Those lovely grey eyes, and that thick, auburn hair you inherited from your mother. Your slim waist and delicate hands. How can you think you're plain?" Unless the observant friend has an urgent reason to be going on like this, the description looks staged, calls attention to itself, turns the observer into a nitwit, and robs the narrator of her own voice. You must constantly remind yourself how people really speak. "You're so beautiful!" a second party might reasonably say, but would she include the color, texture, and origin of the hair, the color of the eyes, the look of the hands and waist? Not likely. Let the observant second party gush over Julia's beauty if she must, but slip in the specific details with a subtler stroke, using the aforementioned solutions.

Avoid staged details. We've discussed this already, but it bears repeating: Don't stage details for the readers. Details of physical appearance should appear *naturally* in the story, not like this:

> Joe drew his gun. I backed up, clutching at the loose strands of my ash-blond hair.

Goodness, your readers ask, this woman's about to die and she's telling us what her hair looks like? First-person narrators almost never "just happen" to think of their hair or eye color, or their height or girth or anything else. Usually they are fixed *outward*, on what they themselves are seeing, not what others are seeing in them. If you find yourself placing physical details at illogical spots in your story, go back to the above "good" solutions for physical description.

FIRST-PERSON POINT OF VIEW

- An "I" narrator tells the story himself or herself.
- The "I" narrator is not the author; you must erase yourself from your narrator's experience!
- Allow the "I" narrator his own quirks, prejudices, and vocabulary.
- Make sure the "I" narrator's observations fit with her world. A professional skater might call the night sky "black as ice"; a printer might call the same sky "black as ink."
- When the narrator is a child, simplify the vocabulary but don't necessarily drop all imagery from the prose. A child sees in simile, too: "The dog was big as a bear."
- When the narrator is an adult looking back (a reminiscent narrator), watch for sentimentality. Avoid cliché. Use the specific in place of the abstract. Replace indistinct feelings ("I felt nervous") with something the reader can see or feel or hear: "Every tick of the clock sounded like a gunshot."
- If you want the reader to get a physical picture of the narrator, be careful about letting the narrator describe himself. Don't use mirrors, ponds, or storefronts to let the narrator see himself and relay what he sees to the reader.
- The "I" narrator should describe himself only if the descrip-

tion also reveals his personality: "I admit I was a handsome devil." Otherwise, try the following techniques:

1. Describe by association: "I'm husky like my sister."
2. Use the plot: "Because I was tall she put me last in line."
3. Use an observant second party: "I thought you'd look much older," he said.

SECOND-PERSON POINT OF VIEW

The second-person point of view isn't used much, probably because it's a bit strange—not the way readers are used to having stories presented to them. Also, second person can begin to feel cloying or gimmicky over the space of a long story or a novel. Not that it can't be done: Jay McInerney uncovered the full potential of second-person point of view in his novel *Bright Lights, Big City*. Lorrie Moore used second person to great advantage in her story collection *Self-Help*.

Second person is often used as a glorified first person, as if the first-person narrator were talking to herself:

> Because you're red-haired and grey-eyed and fond of tight clothes, men keep mistaking you for their old girlfriends. "Wanda!" they'll holler, charging across the street, against the light. "Marlene? Is that you?" they'll ask, scanning your chest as if looking for a name tag.

Notice that the descriptive style is exactly the same as in the first-person point of view. You can't inject your own comments or observations; the story belongs entirely to the second-person narrator.

The second-person narrator has a bit more leeway than the first-person narrator when it comes to physical description. For one thing, the confident second-person tone implies a certain degree of chutzpa: the narrator is almost always infused with self-confidence:

> You sidle up to the teller's window and run a hand through your thick black curls. She's yours already. She likes the dimple

in your chin, even the creases that have lately turned up near your eyes when you smile.

If you transpose the above passage to first person, the character sounds unacceptably obnoxious. Second person gives the readers just enough distance to accept this kind of self-description from a character.

The second-person point of view is usually rendered in present tense, perhaps because present tense reinforces that second-person sense of urgency. Ordinary observations seem weightier somehow when transposed from first to second person. The smallest details take on extra gravity, and you can add tiny descriptive touches that you can't get away with in first person:

> **First person:** I peer into my husband's musty study. The clock I stole from Mr. Bloom is still ticking, its square and gloomy face revealing nothing.
> **Second person:** You peer into your dead husband's study. The clock you stole from Mr. Bloom is still ticking, its square and gloomy face revealing nothing.

In second person the description of the clock takes on more ominousness, and you are also free to add the adjective "dead." The word "dead" in the first-person version of this passage would have seemed too staged, as if you had planted it there only for the readers' information. In the second-person version, it fits right in with the weighty feel of that point of view.

SECOND-PERSON POINT OF VIEW

- "You" is the stand-in for the "I" narrator: "You walked into your cozy little house and some blond had eaten all your porridge."
- The story belongs to the "you" character just as if he were a first-person narrator. Keep the details true to the "you" character's experience.
- Careful not to let the "you" character sound like an outtake from a Humphrey Bogart movie. The second-person tone can

easily slip into hard-boiled-detective mode: "You approach the door. You knock. You turn the knob. You hold your breath." Vary your sentence constructions to avoid this pitfall. Don't start every sentence with "you," any more than you'd start every sentence with "I" in a first-person story.

- Physical description is easy to bring off with a "you" character, because second person strikes a confident tone: "You decide to wear the red raincoat because it makes you look like Liza Minelli on a good day."

THIRD PERSON OMNISCIENT POINT OF VIEW

Third-person narration can take various forms, depending on how close you want your readers to get to your characters. Third-person narrative is traditionally divided into two broad categories: *omniscient* point of view and *third-person-limited* point of view. In *omniscient narrative*, a (usually) disembodied, all-knowing "voice" tells the story. Some omniscient voices have so much personality that they seem to be characters themselves:

> Our darling heroine's words, spoken in a frail tremor that could turn the blackest heart inside out, resonated through the choir loft like the final notes of a hymn.

The momentary dip into first person ("our darling heroine") is a nineteenth-century convention that is little used today. Nevertheless, omniscient narrators can be fully present even when they do not announce themselves so overtly:

> Angel Callahan, a plump, silly woman with a thicket of graying hair, lumbered across the lane like one of the sloe-eyed sheep she was so fond of herding.

Other omniscient narrators are nearly invisible; the story seems to have appeared fully formed on the page, unaided by hand or voice:

> Randall pressed the envelope closed, the tips of his fingers

whitening as he mashed them against the gluey flap. His siblings watched, their eyes glittering darkly.

The omniscient narrator may enter the mind of all the characters, in a "God's eye view":

> The contents of Randall's envelope scared Jill, intrigued Marty, and disgusted Joan.

Or, the narrator may remain objective—a mere "camera eye view" that reports events without entering the characters' heads:

> Randall sealed the envelope as his siblings watched. All the faces in the room reflected varying degrees of anger.

Or, the narrator may confine omniscience to one character, in a "focused omniscience":

> Randall Gardner was a shrewd, unfeeling man with a flair for the dramatic. The morning shadows slatted across his back as he bent languorously over the writing table. He sealed the envelope with a theatrical flick of the fingers, aware of the dark glow of his siblings' glittering eyes. That he had no idea what they were thinking was his first failure of the day.

As you can see from these examples, the omniscient narrator has great latitude. The omniscient "eye" may roam all over a story, from character to character, place to place, past to present to future. The omniscient "voice" may interpret events or merely record them. And, unlike the first-person narrator or third-person-limited narrator, the omniscient narrator has the entire English language at his disposal. (I use "he" for simplicity's sake, though the narrator is more of an "it" that a "he" or "she.") The omniscient narrator can use language as formal or casual as he wishes, regardless of the characters whose story he is telling.

These point-of-view choices affect the readers' mental image in different ways. The omniscient narrator may give us a perception of the events and also a feeling or attitude about those events. Or, the omniscient narrator may be so invisible as to grant us only the barest information that we must then make our own judgments about. What we perceive depends on the nature of the omniscient narrator.

Omniscience is tricky business; the trick is finding the narrative style and tone that fit the story and then keeping that style and tone consistent. As the preceding examples show, omniscient narrators don't all sound the same. It is up to you to find the omniscient voice that fits the story's purpose. Consider the following first lines:

> **Example One:** Once upon a time . . .
> **Example Two:** Upstate New York.
> August 1906.
> Half-moon and a wrack of gray clouds.
> Church windows and thirty nuns singing the Night Office in Gregorian chant. Matins. Lauds. And then silence.
> **Example Three:** Who that cares much to know the history of man, and how the mysterious mixture behaves under the varying experiments of Time, has not dwelt, at least briefly, on the life of Saint Theresa, has not smiled with some gentleness at the thought of the little girl walking forth one morning hand-in-hand with her still smaller brother, to go and seek martyrdom in the country of the Moors?

The first example is the opening line of countless fairy tales; the second is the opening of Ron Hansen's short novel *Mariette in Ecstasy*; the third is the first line of George Eliot's great novel *Middlemarch*. From these first lines, we understand something about the type of story we are about to hear. The omniscient narrator makes a pact with readers from the outset: Settle in; listen; I know everything and will relate it in a certain way and in due course. The omniscient voice—that is, the descriptive style—is established immediately and profoundly affects the way we perceive the story.

The omniscient narrator often has a perspective—sometimes subtle, sometimes overt—on the story being related. He may even insert opinions from time to time. In *The Portrait of a Lady*, Henry James describes his main character this way:

> Isabel Archer was a young person of many theories; her imagination was remarkably active. It had been her fortune to possess a finer mind than most of the persons among whom her lot was cast; to have a larger perception of surrounding facts, and to care for knowledge that was tinged with the unfamiliar.

It is clear that this omniscient narrator (who in the opening of the novel even refers to himself as "I" and then disappears gradually as the story unfolds and Isabel becomes the primary focus) has opinions about all kinds of things, including Isabel's qualities and those of her contemporaries. The omniscient narrator must, above all, carry an air of authority. This is true whether you choose a fully present omniscient narrator or an invisible one. Readers must feel they are in the hands of the expert, the one who knows everything there is to know about the story in question, and who plans to relate the story in exactly the order, style, and method it was intended to be told.

The Omniscient Tone

Assuming this authority is a great challenge to the writer. Because the omniscient narrator has access to every character's background, disposition, and inner thoughts, and may choose to reveal any or all of these things at any given time, a writer can become overwhelmed with too much choice. Keep reminding yourself that what unifies the omniscient narrative (or any narrative, for that matter) is consistency of descriptive style. Beginning writers often believe they are writing in the omniscient point of view, but a lack of consistency mars the overall tone so vital to a convincing omniscient narrative. For example, if you present the daughter in your story as "juked on quaaludes, tippy-tappin' her painted toes, and singin' man-oh-man like a cat in heat" and two pages later describe the father as "a midwestern gentleman of portly stature and possessed of a heart burdened by melancholy," the unlucky readers are left to puzzle over a host of characters in search of an narrator.

The following examples illustrate how the right descriptive style can unify tone. This is the opening of a story about Anna Tremblay, a spoiled debutante who has just returned from a charity mission in Central America.

Anna's welcome-back party was just getting started. Her mouth dried when she saw Ralph walk in. She slunk behind one of the beaded curtains to look him over. His puppylike features were crossed with misgiving. He was worried about seeming too eager or too casual—he still couldn't believe that Anna had spent six weeks helping to build a health clinic in God-Knows-Where. Evelyn had filled him in on the tantalizing details, though he made a point of believing only a quarter of anything

Evelyn had to say. Marcus, standing by the punch bowl and
clutching his wife's silk purse, squinted at the party-goers with
disdain. "These people don't give a hoot about Anna," he told
his wife. "They're just hoping for some virtue by association."
His wife nodded; she agreed with everything her husband said
not because she loved him but because she was afraid of him.

Whoa! Whose party is this, anyway? Beginning writers, thinking they
are telling a story with an "objective" (i.e., omniscient) narrator,
make the mistake of jumping from character to character because an
omniscient narrator is allowed to. (A little like climbing a mountain
because it is there.) The problem is, the above passage *has* no omniscient narrator. In fact, there is no narrator at all, just a bunch of
characters clamoring for center stage. There isn't much description,
either, you'll notice. A narrator doesn't simply *relate* a story, he or she
describes a story. The omniscient narrator should assume a certain
perspective and stay with it—think of omniscience as the same music
playing in the background from beginning to end. Let's try this party
again, this time with an omniscient narrator who, while not a character himself, lends a definite perspective to the story.

> Because they liked to be seen every four or five weeks, every-
> one on Park Place Drive turned out for Anna Tremblay's wel-
> come-home party. Anna, determined to appear a free spirit, had
> her father's drawing room cleared of furniture and decorated
> with eight hundred tiny straw dolls strung on wire so thin they
> appeared to be dancing on air. The effect was frivolous and
> frightening all at the same time, much like the pastel facades of
> the Park Place houses.
>   At eight-thirty Ralph Plunkett arrived, the imperious rustle
> of his trenchcoat vibrating strangely in the cavernous, empty
> room. Anna offered her hand—ringless, sunburned, slivered
> from six selfless weeks of hammer-and-nails in Guatemala—like
> some exotic hors d'oeuvre; Ralph hesitated only a moment be-
> fore he impulsively kissed it. "Welcome back," he said, then
> looked up as a flurry of other guests appeared at the door. The
> Stillwaters, the Coopers, the Smythes, the Jernigans, coiffed and
> bejewelled, their tinkling laughter swirling around a subtle core
> of malice. Anna greeted them all, extending that same unpol-
> ished hand, that naked, exotic thing, her prize.

In this second version of the party, the prose is unified by a central voice, an omniscient presence that sees the entire neighborhood and describes the events with a pointedly arched eyebrow. Although we don't yet know who the central character is going to be (by the third or fourth paragraph, we *should* know, however), what *is* clear is that the story contains themes of class, pretension, deception, and that the storyteller has an opinion about them. The details are more specific and meaningful than those in the first version, and every word seems to flow from the same consciousness. The piece is so convincingly unified by perspective and tone that the word "selfless" has to be taken as condescension and nothing else.

An omniscient narrator may love or hate his characters, but he is rarely neutral. The pathos or ridicule or humor in a story lies in the way the omniscient narrator chooses to describe events. The tone may be casual or formal, humorous or grave, admiring or condescending. These perspectives are revealed through such innocent devices as adjectives, verbs, adverbs, syntax, even punctuation.

The omniscient narrator above describes Anna as "*determined to appear* a free spirit," which alerts the readers to Anna's smugness and self-delusion. How differently would we perceive Anna had the narrator observed, "Anna *was* a free spirit"? Why, we might actually believe that her Guatemalan trip was selfless. To strengthen the notion of Anna's self-delusion, the narrator describes the party decor not as "lots of South American decorations" but, rather, as the specific "eight hundred tiny straw dolls strung on wire. . . ." This accuracy of detail not only gives us a better sense of the absurd decor (and the personality of Anna and the whole neighborhood), but also gives Anna away by revealing the number of dolls as if she had counted them herself. Some free spirit! It is clear that Anna has thrown much time and thought into this party, that she wants to be perceived in a certain way. The narrator tells us that her efforts are "frivolous and frightening all at the same time, much like the pastel facades of the Park Place houses." We understand immediately that the story will be about more than a neighborhood party, because a certain tone has been set. The final line, which refers to Anna's scarred hand as her "prize," gives away the narrator's perspective: Anna is a rich girl who thinks six weeks of work is a badge of courage, and she's going to milk it for all it's worth.

Notice, too, the imagery that the omniscient narrator uses; it is loaded with meaning. The room is "cavernous, empty," much like the characters' lives. Ralph's coat makes an "imperious rustle," which calls to mind the very rich and the presumption of power. The image of the straw dolls seeming to dance on air is powerful in the context of Anna's artifice—is she any more substantial than one of those dolls? The description here is careful, relevant, accurate, and consistent in tone—this is how omniscient narrators are created. This narrator doesn't miss a thing, and the story he is handing to the readers is deftly layered with his interpretation of events.

Omniscience and Physical Description

In the omniscient narrative, physical description of characters is not very restrictive. Knock yourself out. Compare the main character to Jack Ruby or a burrowing mole or Princess Grace. It's your show. The omniscient narrator sees everything however he wishes to see it. You needn't worry about violating a character's point of view, because the point of view does not belong to the character in an omniscient narrative; it belongs to the voice or presence that is telling the tale. What you do need to watch for, however, is the omniscient narrative's consistency with itself. The above story would strike a false note if Anna Tremblay were compared to a "beauty-parlor groupie, all hair goop and Mary Kay." The references to "goop" and "Mary Kay" would be out of step with this omniscient narrator's arch, sophisticated vocabulary. You could use the same comparison with slightly different wording:

> Her excellent address notwithstanding, Anna always looked as if she'd just stepped out of a beauty parlor down on Third Avenue, in full violation of the unspoken rule that a sophisticated woman's hair should not be as wide as it is high.

Obviously Anna herself would never offer such a description; nor would Ralph or the other guests at the party. The omniscient narrator has a wonderful freedom with physical description that can be a lot of fun for the writer. This freedom of description is an omniscient narrative's best virtue, making its other challenges well worth the trouble.

Omniscience and Child Characters

Child narrators can be effective storytellers (see the section on first-person point of view), but what if you don't want your child character to tell her own story? She might not have the language to express her complicated situation; perhaps something takes place in the story (a secret adoption, or a plot to kidnap her) that the child can't know about; or maybe the story must be told in an arch tone that is contrary to the child's nature. A switch to omniscience will instantly solve all problems of child voice and child tone and child perception; what you sacrifice, however, is proximity to the child.

When you convert a first-person narrative to an omniscient narrative, you begin to write a different story altogether, whether you want to or not. You sacrifice the child's wide-eyed descriptions for a more sophisticated (but often more lyrical, more satisfying) description from an omniscient narrator. Look at the following examples:

> **First person:** Momma's going away today. I know because Auntie Rita told me. I was sitting on Momma's big trunk and Auntie Rita scooched down to look at me. I smelled lipstick on her mouth, and little sparkles of powder showed on her face when she smiled. . . .
>
> **Omniscient:** It was Rita who had to tell the child that her mother was going away. The child sat on the lip of the great packing trunk, her spindly legs hanging over the edge, the heels of her Mary Janes tick-ticking against the lock. Rita squatted awkwardly on the balding carpet and looked into the child's light-filled eyes. Rita smiled. "Honey . . ." she began. But that was all. Aunt and niece remained still in the buttery light, their mouths locked against questions they dared not ask or answer.

If you are willing to forego the first-person immediacy of the child's experience, you often end up with a richer story with more shades of meaning in the descriptions. In the second version the child's perspective is gone, and yet the heartbreak of the scene remains, aided by buttery light and locked mouths and ticking shoes. The "tick-ticking" shoes suggest not only a child's fidgety demeanor but the excruciating passage of time: the child has only a few more moments before her mother leaves. Similarly, their "locked" mouths suggest not only an inability to speak at the present moment, but a sense that this moment itself will be "locked"—locked into the child's memory, locked out of future conversations. A child narrator cannot convincingly deliver this kind of description herself.

Sometimes a story demands an intimacy with the character that omniscience cannot provide. Without resorting to first-person narration, you want to draw your readers deep into the character's experience. This is where third-person-limited point of view comes in.

THIRD-PERSON-LIMITED POINT OF VIEW

The other type of third-person narrative is the *third-person-limited consciousness* (some call it *third-person central intelligence*, or *third-person central consciousness*). This point of view, which we'll call *third-person-limited*, has a somewhat omniscient feel, but breaks from omniscience in that it works from *inside* the character. The story must follow the point-of-view character's version of events.

Omniscience works from the outside in; even if the omniscient narrator concerns himself with only one character, he is still free to rove around and observe things that the character can't see. In third-person-limited, however, *the readers are not allowed to perceive or observe anything that the main character cannot perceive or observe*, which somewhat limits the kinds of description you may use.

Look again at this example from the section on omniscient point of view:

> Randall Gardner was a shrewd, unfeeling man with a flair for the dramatic. The morning shadows slatted across his back as he bent languorously over the writing table. He sealed the envelope with a theatrical flick of the fingers, aware of the dark glow of his siblings' glittering eyes. That he had no idea what they were thinking was his first failure of the day.

In order to convert this passage from omniscient to third-person-limited point of view, we must alter it considerably:

> Randall liked to use his flair for the dramatic. He bent languorously over the writing table and sealed the envelope with a theatrical flick of the fingers, aware of the dark glow of his

siblings' glittering eyes. That he had no idea what they were
thinking was his first failure of the day.

The third-person-limited narrator *inhabits the character's body*. Randall
has no way of seeing slats of light on his own back, so we cannot put
those slats of light into the description. Ralph docs not think of himself as shrewd and unfeeling, so we must find other ways to suggest
these character flaws. These limitations can be pesky, but they're well
worth the trouble if your goal is to give readers an intimate bond
with the character.

Because the third-person-limited narrative confines itself to the
consciousness of only one character, its style has certain limits. The
description—the similes and adjectives and metaphors—must contain imagery that exists in the realm of the character whose story is
being told. Remember, in omniscience you're working from the outside in—"Emily's rain-soaked hair stuck to her bare back in gummy,
webbed tendrils"—and in third-person-limited you're working from
the inside out—"Emily's rain-soaked hair felt like cold snakes on her
back."

In third-person-limited point of view, the readers are not *looking*
at a character, they are *inhabiting* a character. For this reason, it's a
good choice for short fiction, bringing the readers immediately into
a character's world and holding them there until the last word. Take
a look at a recent issue of fiction magazines like *Story* or *Glimmer Train*;
chances are you'll find a preponderance of third-person-limited point
of view.

Degree of Intimacy in Third-Person-Limited

The omniscient point of view comes with choices: God's eye view,
camera eye view, and focused omniscience. Third-person-limited also
contains choices, though fewer of them. There is only one category
of choice, really: degree of intimacy (John Gardner called it "psychic
distance"). For example, you may choose a very intimate third-person-limited point of view, in which the descriptions match the character's vocabulary, ethnicity, socio-economic status, prejudices, and
world view. The third-person-limited narrative voice sounds almost
as confiding as a first-person narrator, as if you were merely repeating

what the point-of-view character would have said herself. The degree of intimacy with the character, in this case, is great. In a less intimate third-person-limited point of view, you still remain inside that character's experience, taking care that the readers see or hear nothing that the character can't see or hear, but the language you use to convey that experience is more sophisticated or lyrical. In this case, the degree of intimacy is distant.

Let's experiment with varying degrees of intimacy in the following passage about an undereducated Oklahoma teenager who is witness to her father's arrest for car theft:

> **First person:** I couldn't believe they was coming for Daddy. I set to hollering my head off and banging my feet so hard on the porch you could see sparks flying off the heels of my shoes. I thought maybe I could scare them police away, but it didn't work, they come for him anyway; when Daddy held out those poor bony wrists I had to shut my eyes against the sunlight screeching off those big steel cuffs.
>
> **Third-person-limited (intimate):** Emmy couldn't believe they were coming for Daddy. She set to hollering her head off and banging her feet so hard on the porch you could see sparks flying off the heels of her shoes. She thought maybe she could scare the police away, but it didn't work, they came for him anyway; when Daddy held out those poor bony wrists she had to shut her eyes against the sunlight screeching off those big steel cuffs.
>
> [*Notice that the grammar is corrected, but the description is exactly the same and her father is still referred to as "Daddy."*]
>
> **Third-person-limited (less intimate):** Emmy couldn't believe they were coming for her father. She began hollering her head off and banging her feet so hard on the porch you could see sparks flying off the heels of her shoes. She thought maybe she could scare the police away, but it didn't work, they came for him anyway; when her father held out those poor bony wrists she had to shut her eyes against the sunlight screeching off those big steel cuffs.
>
> [*Notice that the father is now "her father" instead of "Daddy," and "set to" is changed to "began." The character's actual voice is beginning to disappear, though the readers are still experiencing the story from inside the character.*]

Third-person-limited (distanced): Emmy couldn't believe they were coming for her father. She began to shout and holler, stamping her feet so hard that sparks appeared between her shoes and the floorboards. She was hoping she could scare the police away, but they came for him anyway; when her father held out his poor bony wrists she had to shut her eyes against the sunlight glancing off the officer's cruel-looking handcuffs.

[*Notice how the language has gone more formal, though we are still inside Emmy's experience. One more step away and we'd be looking at her from the outside, that is, with an omniscient narrator.*]

The above examples show you the restrictions of language in third-person-limited. You can work close in or far away, but the perspective must be the character's and not the narrator's. If you wanted to make the above passage a little more descriptive by adding a simile, be careful how you choose. You might end up making a mistake like this:

. . . the light glanced off the steel cuffs with the unbearable brightness of an African desert.

Oh, really? And where might Emmy, a farm kid from Oklahoma, have seen this African desert? Okay, on TV maybe, but your readers might stop to wonder. What you have done here is announce your presence as the author by violating the readers' intimate connection to Emmy's mind and heart. An image so foreign to Emmy's experience forces us to suddenly look at Emmy from the outside in. Emmy might compare the glare of the handcuffs to sunlight on waves of grain, or a shimmer of heat lightning, or the morning sun glancing off the silo. But African deserts are too far out of her realm to be plausible; it violates our belief that we are moving through Emmy's world.

Each character, no matter what her circumstances, has a store of imagery at her disposal. It's up to you to root it out. The third-person-limited narrator must remain invisible; the character is the only presence. You may take liberties with grammar and style, but the way the character sees the world is the way you must see the world, for now. (Save your own visions for an omniscient narrator.) Far from enriching the story, description that is foreign to the character's life merely calls attention to itself.

Physical Description in Third-Person-Limited

The problems of physical description in third-person-limited are almost identical to those in first person. Remember, in third-person-limited you must keep the readers inside the body of the character; therefore, you cannot allow a description like this:

> Patty watched the elevator doors groan open. Alan was standing inside, smirking, the manuscript he'd stolen from her tucked into a leather binder. She watched with disbelief as he lifted one manicured finger to beckon her inside. She felt her breath escape in small stutters through her closing throat. "You," she said, but the word dried on her tongue. Blood swirled in her head and her pulse banged against her temples. "Going up?" he asked. Her brown eyes blackened with rage.

Up until the last line, "Her brown eyes blackened with rage," you have your readers firmly planted inside Patty's consciousness. Then, suddenly, you ask them to jump outside Patty's perspective for just long enough to look at her brown eyes. The readers may not be able to identify just why, but they will feel momentarily distanced from the story. Do you see how the description falters with that one line? You've moved us from the inside to the outside. If you *must* provide a physical description of Patty, then go back to the beginning of this chapter and try some of the physical-description techniques for first-person narrators. Some of those techniques work beautifully in third-person-limited. For instance, in this scene you have access to an *observant second party*:

> The elevator doors opened. "Hello, Brown Eyes," Alan said.

Or, you could use *description by association*:

> She studied him carefully. His hair was a vague no-color, his skin dull and cold. Prison pallor, they'd laughingly called it when she worked here. Too many fluorescent lights. She liked to think she no longer looked like that. She liked to think her skin had recovered its Italian glow, that the blue highlights had returned to the dark of her hair.

Or, you could *use your plot*:

> They got off at the fifteenth floor, where a platoon of blonde secretaries marched in and out of glass-fronted offices. Patty sighed. How had she ever fit into this place, where being a brunette was considered a handicap?

When writing in third-person-limited point of view, remember, always, to *work from the inside out, not the outside in.*

Third-Person-Limited and Child Characters

The old theater maxim "Never work with children or animals" could also be applied to writing fiction. Children and animals register on the melodrama meter almost before you've written a word. They turn out too cute or too smart or too forlorn or too mischievous or too something. In the section on first-person point of view, we explored ways to allow child narrators to tell their own stories convincingly. In the section on omniscient point of view, we saw that omniscient narrators can more fully tell a child's story, but the downside is the readers' loss of intimacy with the child. Third-person-limited gives you the best of both: you allow your readers to experience the child's world without having to shackle yourself to the child's language.

Let's look again at Freddy, the first-person narrator we heard from in the section on first-person point of view. Freddy is ten years old, looking in on his dying grandmother:

> For a second I wasn't sure it was really Grandma in that bed. At first I thought maybe she was a ghost, but the hissing turned out to be her trying to breathe. There was something wrong with her skin, little cracks all over, like somebody dipped a spider's feet in red paint and let him walk on her. . . .

First-person narration works quite well for this character, but a third-person-limited narration would grant you more leeway with language:

> Freddy stole up the steps, his heart thump-thumping against his ears. The door before him seemed achingly large, thick with paint. Grandma's sick, they had told him, but what did they mean? He held out one palm—the fingers still stained

with blueberry juice—and pushed. The door groaned open and there she was, white and weightless as a feather. The skin over her temple was webbed and pulsing, nearly translucent. "Hey, Grandma," he whispered. "It's me, Freddy." She turned to look at him. Freddy nearly cried out with relief to see those familiar Grandma eyes, blue as ice. She moved her lips but he couldn't hear her over the sound of his hammering heart.

In the above passage the language is sophisticated and lyrical, not language Freddy himself would use, and yet the description is true to Freddy's experience and vision. The similes—using feathers and ice—are taken from objects in Freddy's world. The readers see nothing that Freddy does not see, hear nothing that Freddy does not hear; the passage is filtered through Freddy's consciousness and his alone. And yet the storyteller is someone other than Freddy, a nearly invisible vehicle that presents Freddy's story to the readers. You as the author have preserved Freddy's child-ness without sacrificing your natural descriptive style. This freedom of language is what makes the third-person-limited point of view so satisfying.

Of course, you may decide to limit your description to a more intimate third-person-limited view, and come up with something like this:

> Freddy looked into the bed but he wasn't sure it was Grandma. She sounded just like a big, scary ghost because it was hard for her to breathe. He was so scared! Grandma's face was marked all over with little red lines that looked just like spider legs. . . .

However, why use Freddy's language when you don't have to? If you're going to restrict the language of the story to a ten-year-old's abilities, then you might as well leave the story in the first person.

THIRD-PERSON POINT OF VIEW

Third-person point of view takes two forms: *omniscient point of view* and *third-person-limited point of view*.

Omniscient point of view comes in three styles:

- GOD'S EYE VIEW
  1. The storyteller sees all the action—even action that the characters can't see—and sometimes expresses opinions about it.
  2. The storyteller knows all the characters' thoughts and feelings, and can move from one character's "head" to another's.
  3. The omniscient narration is always in third person, unless the narrator is God, or a magic dog, or a ghost, all of which are problematic, to say the least.
  4. The narrative contains a tone of authority that unifies the story. ("Once upon a time there were three bears....") Readers feel they are in the hands of a reliable storyteller who will deliver all the relevant aspects of the story in the proper order.

- CAMERA EYE VIEW
  1. The storyteller sees all the action, but does not know the characters' thoughts and feelings.
  2. The storyteller has no opinions about characters or events. The story is reported but not interpreted.
  3. The camera-eye view makes for a distanced narrative, and can become frustrating to the reader if the story is a long one.

- FOCUSED OMNISCIENCE
  1. The omniscient storyteller sees all the action, but enters only one character's thoughts and feelings.

Third-person-limited is the other kind of third-person point of view.

- The story is told in third person, but through only ONE character's point of view.
- The reader is not privy to anything that is outside this one character's sight or hearing. The reader knows only what this character knows.
- In third-person-limited, the reader experiences the character from the inside out: "The rain made Emily's hair feel like cold snakes on her back." The reader is made to feel he or she is inhabiting the point-of-view character's body.

WRAP-UP

Good description flows from point of view, and vice versa. When determining point of view for your next story, remember your choices: first person, second person, and third person. The first-person point of view requires an engaging and convincing narrator. The second-person narrative has a distinctive tone and offers you slightly more descriptive latitude than first person. The third-person point of view offers you the most descriptive freedom. You may use an omniscient narrator who has access to any and all characters, who may or may not express opinions, and who may reveal as much or as little of a character, or characters, as he likes. The third-person-limited narrator, on the other hand, has access to only one character, and may not venture outside that character's perspective or reveal anything that the point-of-view character does not see, feel, or know.

Once you have a good grasp of the limits and freedoms of the various points of view, be sure to match the descriptive style to the point of view you have chosen. Children see the world differently from adults; old people have a different vocabulary than young people. An invisible omniscient narrator adopts a more formal tone than a fully present omniscient narrator. An educated first-person narrator has a different speaking style than an uneducated one. A third-person-limited narrative can be so distant as to feel nearly omniscient, or so intimate as to feel a half-step removed from first person.

Physical descriptions of your characters should not violate point of view. These details must emerge as a natural part of the story and not simply as information for the readers' benefit. Be careful also to separate yourself from your narrators, whether or not they are in first person. The "I" or "Eye" telling the story is not really you, it is a character you create.

Don't be discouraged if you have to refer back to this chapter many times before point of view becomes second nature. It is a problem of craft that even the most experienced writers grapple with again and again.

CHAPTER 6

DESCRIPTION AND STYLE

A WRITER'S STYLE IS COMPOSED of hundreds of choices big and small, from point of view to sentence length to word choice. As you work through the first drafts of a story, you should be struggling with certain questions: Is the main character the right one? Am I using the best point of view? Does the structure enhance or hinder the story's progress? Do I need more scenes and less narrative? Should I change tense? Are the paragraphs too long or too short or too similar? Am I using too many modifiers or too few? These questions help you form your descriptive style.

If you have already "found your style," however, and always write in a certain way, these questions become moot. If you always write in present tense with nineteen-year-old narrators who favor compound sentences, your stories may eventually run out of energy and start sounding alike. Examine any writer's body of work and you will find stylistic changes (some of them dramatic) between the early work and the later. Try to stay open to changes in your own style, to keep yourself interested in and challenged by your own writing.

Many inexperienced writers overlook the fact that style evolves as much from the characters as from their creator. A style that suits the first novel may wreck the second, because the characters in the second novel see the world differently from the characters in the first novel. Wedding yourself too soon to a writing style can squelch your natural instincts for adventure and experimentation. Think of the hundreds of characters you might never meet!

CHOOSING DESCRIPTIVE STYLE

In a first draft we don't yet know our characters or fully understand the situation we have placed them in. The first draft of a story usually has a vague shape, an approximation of a beginning, middle, and end, and a theme that is barely discernible. The only thing we can literally "see" in a first draft is the writing style. Florid or bare-bones, it is there on the page. Perhaps because we are so grateful at this stage to have *something* we can see, we are reluctant to alter the style that brought us the gift of a first draft. In subsequent drafts we may change the main character, manipulate the plot, alter the sequence of events, add scenes and jettison others—but the original style we leave alone. Why? Doesn't it stand to reason that changes in plot or character should affect style? Writers often forget to go back and check for stylistic harmony, and yet that harmony is the very thing that gives a story its final polish.

Let's analyze descriptive style through some examples. A first-draft passage set in a rural backwater might sound like this:

> **Version One:** Franny sat on the porch, cracking one knuckle after another, squinting out at the ragged, dusty stretch of asphalt that passed for a road. Tuckered and heat-weary, she hissed a ribbon of air through her lips. Her brother Emmett was on his way, so they told her, but she'd believe it when she saw his mud-ugly face and not one minute before.

This descriptive style is peppered with imagery in keeping with a rural setting. But what if you decided, midway through the fifth draft, that your story about this estranged brother and sister would be better served in a more suburban setting? Fine, you say, let's move the story from Rural Route 1 to a Cape Cod-style house on Maple Street:

> **Version Two:** Franny sat in the breezeway of her mother's neat white Cape, cracking one knuckle after another, squinting out at the sedate blacktop of Maple Street. Tuckered and heat-weary, she hissed a ribbon of air through her lips. Her brother Emmett was on his way, so they told her, but she'd believe it when she saw his mud-ugly face and not one minute before.

Something is suddenly wrong with this picture. The stylistic flourishes don't work in a non-rural setting. Phrases like "tuckered and heat-weary" and "mud-ugly" clang against the ears. Down-home phraseology doesn't sound right unless the setting is down-home.

It is nearly impossible to change a story without altering style at least a little; even if the characters are essentially the same, they have a different address now. The story requires a different descriptive tack:

> **Version Three:** Franny sat in the breezeway of her mother's neat white Cape, cracking one knuckle after another, squinting out at the sedate blacktop of Maple Street. The trees, fully leafed, seemed vaguely military, lined up and staring. She cast her eyes down, letting a noisy ribbon of air escape her lips. Her brother Emmett was on his way, so they told her, but she'd believe it when she saw his unwelcome face and not one minute before.

Can you see the style evolving into something else as the story changes? The first version, with its dust and heat, conjures expectations of ancient family feuds set amidst the unforgiving southern landscape. The second version, with its suburban setting and down-home phrasings, conjures a variety of expectations that don't go together very well. The third version suggests a subtler, more tightly controlled family conflict, with its military imagery and sophisticated language.

By the fifteenth draft you may decide that the rural setting is more in keeping with the story's intentions after all. By this time, however, you've developed a style that feels comfortable to you: a present-tense omniscient narrator with a "writerly" vocabulary. The lyricism feels true to the story's lofty theme of betrayal and forgiveness. Do you have to alter the style again in order to go back to the original setting? Probably not, if this is indeed your fifteenth draft. The style is solid enough by now that it can withstand a change in setting:

> **Final Version:** Franny sits on the splintered porch rail, draping her bare legs over the edge. They dangle like ropes: long, delicately knotted, burnished by the sun. Her fingers, too, are long, and she works one hand over the other, her knuckles making chips of sound in the hot, empty day . . .

This passage seems more whole, more finished, than any of the other examples. The down-home phraseology is gone, but the poetic language that replaces it evokes a hot country day just as effectively. The prose is delicate and strong at the same time, like the character you are describing. The individual images are gentle—"draping her legs," "delicately knotted," "chips of sound." And yet the resulting picture—the actual thing being described by these images—is a strong, knuckle-cracking, sunburned young woman. Here is a person of limited prospects who has the potential to do something extraordinary when faced with a family conflict. Style and content harmonize, and the story feels finished.

As you can see by the number of examples here, stylistic harmony rarely happens by accident. You have to play with different kinds of description, over a great number of drafts, before you discover the right notes. This is not a matter of "hitting" the right style, like turning a roulette wheel and hoping for a black seven. Style develops, little by little, as you work a story through its paces. So, don't be in too much of a hurry. Your goal, after all, is not to make the writing effortless, but to make it seem effortless. That marvelous fraud is achieved only one way—through relentless hard work.

WHEN CONTENT AND STYLE CONTRAST

Style does not always have to match a story's content. You can describe ragged people in tidy prose. You can describe a corporate takeover in the comfortable slang of a night watchman. Sometimes, a contrast between style and content works to a story's advantage. The opening of *A Wrestling Season*, a novel by Sharon Sheehe Stark, presents a simple situation. Trover, a middle-aged lawyer, does not want to go to his father's funeral. His wife makes him go anyway:

> In the end, of course, they all went, as Trover knew they would from the start. He knew as much even as he addled and deviled and danced his dances. . . . What was he if not a hostage, as always, in the heart of his own family? As they peeled out between the two large fields, he noted dimly the plucked and stubbled landscape and that their man Sprecher was out in the cold, mowing yellow grass. Wasn't this November? Wasn't it

going to snow? And how suddenly open the land was, haze in the distance, the horizon revoked and nothing, *nothing*, mediating between him and the unopposable outwardness of things. He closed his eyes.

The surface of this situation is ordinary enough, but the author's lyrical style infuses this ordinary character with an almost mystical quality. We understand that Trover is a man capable of depth and feeling no matter what his outward appearance may show.

Marlene Buono, in her short story "Offerings," does something similar, only in reverse. The situation in the story is mystical, but prose is simple. The two-page story gives us a woman who collects apologies, placing them in her pockets, sewing them into her hems, fashioning them into paper birds. The story ends with a visit to her husband's grave:

> She opened the hatbox she had brought along and lifted out an apology that she had meant to give her husband before he died. It was an awkward shape and she rarely looked at it because it filled her with shame. She deftly folded the edges until the perimeter of the regret was smooth. Emily studied the apology before each fold, carefully coaxing it to forget its graceless form and accept her design.
>
> She took an hour to give it the wingspan it needed. When she placed the finished apology on the tombstone she watched it unfold its wings and fly.

In the first example, an ordinary situation is made magical with lyrical description. Here, a surreal situation is made accessible by direct, unadorned description. We understand that Emily has an ordinary person's regrets and sorrows, no matter how extraordinary her actions seem on the surface. In each case, the story's heart is revealed through contrast.

Whether to contrast content and style depends on your intention for the story. Suppose you are writing about a vivacious, successful actress who will discover, over the course of the story, that she has lived life only through her stage roles and that her real life is little more than empty gesture. A bubbling, florid style would match her outward appearance, but a pared-down style would honor the subtext, which is the emptiness of her soul. Let's try the pared-down style first:

Version One: Esmerelda stood outside the theater, studying her own image. The poster was finely printed and resembled the old-fashioned movie posters her friends were fond of framing for their living rooms. Her hair in the poster was blonder than in real life. Her smile was broader. Her fingers were longer. The poster was no mirror. She could not see herself there.

This style creates an intriguing narrative tension. Something is just slightly askew here; the character does not quite fit the spare prose that describes her. You're implying a seriousness, even a foreboding—a hint that the journey of this story will turn inward, perhaps in ways that Esmerelda is not ready for. Even her extravagant name is made more ordinary in the context of these simple sentences and everyday words. This descriptive contrast invites the readers to peer behind Esmerelda's glitzy facade.

A more flamboyant description, one that is more in keeping with Esmerelda's outward exuberance, delivers a somewhat different expectation:

Version Two: Esmerelda skittered over the dirty Forty-fourth Street sidewalk in shapely black stiletto heels, listening to the sparks of sound that followed her like an echo. She stopped just below the lighted marquee, the sequins on her dress making shimmering tracks along her body as she moved under the light. She gazed at the poster that bore her own image. Blonder, longer-limbed, infinitely happier, her poster self smiled into the night with the arrogance of a Park Avenue pigeon. *Go around me,* her poster self seemed to say, glinting strands of hair flying away from her head like molting feathers. *Just try to make me move.* The other Esmerelda, the flesh-and-blood Esmerelda, the Esmerelda who had spent four tumultuous hours deciding on a dress, lifted her face to the marquee and fixed her eyes straight into the icy light of a hundred tiny moons.

In this version, which features long, looping sentences and lots of imagery, there is not much contrast between who Esmerelda is and how you present her. This already flamboyant character becomes larger than life, promising a big, bright story. Careful, though: an oversized character combined with oversized prose might be too much for the readers to swallow. Esmerelda might end up looking like a character in a soap opera.

Let's make another try at contrasting style and content in this story about an ordinary supermarket clerk:

> **Version One:** Abigail dragged a box of cornflakes across the scanner and let it float down the stainless-steel chute. Spreading her fingers, she palmed a dappled cantaloupe and swept it twice over the tiny window until she heard the beep. She watched the cantaloupe roll down behind the box, squat and graceless and yet possessed of a liquid slow motion. Next, she hefted a can of peas, its multicolored label pulsing with images of nature's bounty. Everything today was color and shape: the dangerous red of the Cortlands, the tidy domes of the egg cartons.

Here, a lyrical style contrasts with a mundane setting. Readers get a sense that something extraordinary might happen to a girl who sees beauty in a can of peas. Notice how much movement you've built into the description: the box "floats"; the label "pulses"; the cantaloupe is "possessed of a liquid motion." Notice also the colors and shapes: "squat and graceless"; "dappled cantaloupe"; "dangerous red"; "tidy domes." What a feast for the senses! The readers prepare for a story in which something interesting is going to happen, no matter how little potential the character, an ordinary check-out clerk, seems to have.

What happens if you match style and content here?

> **Version Two:** Abigail scanned several items: a box of cornflakes, a can of peas, two cartons of eggs. Then she scanned a pound of fish, a bottle of bleach, and a bag of apples. She watched the scanner light up with each pass of her hand.

This pared-down style dulls an already dull situation. What happened to Abigail, who had so much promise just a moment ago? She disappeared along with the descriptive flourishes. This passage contains no adjectives, no adverbs, no color, no sound. Content and style match too well: the result is a monochromatic description, the literary equivalent of a one-color painting.

A CASE FOR MINIMALISM

Never has a descriptive style been revered and maligned as much as minimalism. Minimalism, which is currently out of fashion due to overexposure, has never been satisfactorily defined. To most writers, minimalism means short and spare. The story is barely told; the readers are supposed to read between the lines. A minimalist story requires strong details and a compelling main character. The characters are usually ordinary working stiffs dealing with life's ordinary slings and arrows. Some critics dubbed these stories "Kmart fiction" because of some minimalists' tendency to use brand names of places and products as a shorthand for characterization. (A character's use of Aqua Velva is supposed to suggest his age, income, and value system, for example.) The best of these writers, however—Raymond Carver, Ann Beattie, Mary Robison, Amy Hempill—do indeed paint complex pictures with only a few strokes. They dig in and find exactly the right details to reveal character without resorting to brand-name characterizations.

Minimalism suits many beginning writers because it fares well with simple, one- or two-character stories. This is not to say that writing minimally is easy. It only *looks* easy. In fact, minimalist stories are hard to write and easy to parody. The second version of our story about Abigail the grocery clerk, for instance, is a parody of minimalism. The readers are supposed to "read between the lines" to find meaning in a list of grocery items. Many short-story writers of the seventies and eighties adopted this no-frills descriptive style in an attempt to imitate the great minimalist writers, most notably Raymond Carver. (I wrote some imitations myself, I'm sorry to say.) What we forgot—in our rush to flatter our elders in the sincerest form possible—is that for a story to hold up under this style it must be *inherently interesting*. When prose is this minimal, you have no place to hide.

If your natural writing style tends toward minimalism, do not despair. Attention to descriptive style can turn a monochromatic story into minimalism at its best. The smallest adjustments in the grocery-item passage, for example, can infuse even a spare story with a sense of expectation:

Version Three: Abigail scanned several items: a box of corn-flakes, a can of peas, two cartons of eggs. Bleach. Fish. Apples. With every pass of her hand, the scanner made a sound like a heart hooked to a machine.

Notice how the syntax changes the rhythm of the passage. The long opening sentence followed by three one-word sentences creates a little dance of words. The final sentence begins with a prepositional phrase rather than the conventional subject-verb-object, and includes a simile that suggests something about the character's life. Does Abigail herself feel like a heart hooked to a machine? Already the story seems to promise a character's transition from one state to another. Varied sentence constructions, telling details, evocative images— these small descriptive choices help even the slimmest stories crackle with life.

If your stories are small and your style unadorned, take care to vary your construction and include a relevant image every so often. The life of your story depends on it.

A CASE FOR MAXIMALISM

"Maximalism" is not a literary term, exactly. John Barth used it to describe large, sweeping novels that present entire worlds, such as Pynchon's *Gravity's Rainbow*. Nowadays the term accurately describes the backlash against minimalism. Suddenly, editors are receiving truckloads of stories that would delight a Victorian: elaborate settings, lush descriptions, event piled upon event, casts of thousands. Loquacious narrators are telling the stories of their lives and including everybody else's stories while they're at it. Many of these stories are wonderfully literary, beguiling, and hugely entertaining. Before you rush to pad your stories with outtakes, however, remember that although less isn't always more, *more* isn't always more, either. Every word counts, whether the story is long and lush or short and spare. Take that detour if you must, but make sure it winds back to the main road.

You could "maximalize" the story about Abigail the grocery clerk by exploring some past events or people from her life: A rock concert at which she met a roadie who gave her drugs and broke her heart; her father's last day at home before he left with another woman; a teacher who changed her grade after she pretended to cry. These detours—lengthy and complicated as they may be—make sense because they relate to Abigail's present-day story, which involves a man who claims to be auditioning women for a movie. He's probably lying, but Abigail can't afford not to believe him. The remembered events (rock concert; Dad's last day; grade change) are important because they remind her of her acting ability (crying for the teacher), and of men who lie (Dad and the roadie).

One way to manage a "maximal" story is to keep a *strong stylistic focus*. The prose style focuses the story. In her novel *The Shipping News*, E. Annie Proulx focuses an episodic story about a newsman in Newfoundland by using deliberately eccentric prose. Peppered with the foreign-sounding vocabulary of Newfoundland, the prose style reminds us at all times that the main character is a stranger in a strange land. Also, Proulx often begins sentences with the verb rather than the subject, giving her prose the clipped, imperative feel of newspaper headlines, a stylistic quirk that keeps the newsman central to our experience.

Perhaps we could find a similar stylistic focus in our story about Abigail the grocery clerk. Perhaps Abigail is remembering incidents from her life—the roadie, her father, and the teacher—as if they had occurred in a movie she once saw. Why not incorporate movie-style language into the prose? The first digression could begin like this:

> The last time she had taken a man at his word was in May, on the day of the annular eclipse of the sun. She burst out the sliding doors at the end of her shift to find the day eerily still, the chatty spring birds gone silent. A shadow passed over the parking lot with the sepia tone of an old movie. Cut to evening. A rock concert in progress. Girl, late teens, appears at the door, waving the backstage passes she won by being the fifteenth caller. She is allowed in, only to find a thicket of roadies shielding the fleeing band.
> She: Your hair's too long.
> He: Who the hell are you?
> She: Your hair's too long. I can't see your eyes.
> He offers her a shot of tequila, and an unfiltered cigar-

ette, and some pretty pink pills she can never remember the name of.

She slid a pound of ground turkey over the scanner and winced at the sound. *Cut to present,* she thought grimly.

The other digression could have a similar movie-reel format. No matter how many times Abigail digresses from the present, the readers will not be left wondering what happened to the girl in the grocery store, because every stylistic flourish that suggests a movie will also suggest the present-action story about the movie maker. All the extra characters and story lines will be unified by style.

If Abigail's story is about something that doesn't lend itself to stylistic innovation, you might want to focus the narrative by using a *central image.* A house. A color. A pet. A dress. Let's say the story is about Abigail's being burdened by a family pattern of heroism. She works double shifts to support her mother and grandmother, lovely yet sickly women who are beyond reproach. People seem to think it should be a privilege for Abigail to waste her youth caring for them; all the women in the family, from Eve on down, have made selflessness their *raison d'être.* Abigail's great-great aunt once saved a hypothermic baby by ripping off the beaded skirt of her wedding dress and wrapping the child in it, scandalizing onlookers and saving the child. Abigail tells this story to one of her customers, then remembers another story, one about her grandmother:

> Of course, there was a war on. She rationed salt. She rationed sugar. She rationed butter. She rationed her deepest wants, waiting for her man—Abigail's grandfather—to come home. She had a dress in her closet, a soft cotton sheath with real brass buttons. She had Uncle Geoffrey take her picture and send it to Grampa in the Philippines. A beautiful blonde woman in a sky-blue dress.

The story goes on to tell about the progress of the war and the toll on the women back home. Shortages become crises, and the grandmother ends up cutting the brass buttons from the dress as a donation to the war effort. The dress is simply not the same dress now, so she remakes it into a bunting for the baby who will turn out to be Abigail's mother.

Then Abigail remembers a third dress story, this one involving her mother, who once hand-sewed an Easter dress and left it on the doorstep of an impoverished playmate of Abigail's. By this time Abigail is tired and cranky from what is becoming a thunderous noise from the grocery scanner. She tears off her smock—a tacky polyester thing with her name stitched in orange letters. She leaves work, goes straight to a store, and wastes a week's pay on a new dress, something tight and trashy, a dress that couldn't possibly become a prop in yet another story about selflessness. Abigail's story incorporates several generations of stories, and yet it feels unified because of the common detail of the dress.

Another way to focus an expansive narrative is to use a *strong setting*. George Eliot used a place—the fictitious Middlemarch—to weave many separate story lines in her novel of the same name. Alice Munro often uses place to unify her delightfully meandering stories. *Strong first-person narrators* can focus a story, too. Narrators with quirky observations and charming voices can wander far off the path with barely a whimper from the readers, who feel tethered to the story by way of the narrator's voice.

Unifying a narrative with any number of these stylistic strategies offers you a chance to expand your story's horizons while retaining the illusion that it is being told with exactly the right number of words.

AVOIDING SENTIMENTALITY AND MELODRAMA

One of the pitfalls of generous description is sentimentality and melodrama. The more you love your characters, the more you must watch out for overblown descriptions. Oh, how tempting it is to wring our damp hands when our beloved characters are suffering!

Our personal feelings about our characters' plights are directly related to the number of modifiers we use. Mr. Smith becomes "lonely old Mr. Smith"; a drowned mouse becomes a "poor little mouse"; a virtuous young boy becomes a "sincere young sprite with clear blue eyes." Consider the following description of a man reaching the summit of a mountain:

He wiped the beads of sweat from his feverish brow, hoisted himself over the last, excruciating outcropping, and gasped victoriously at the triumph of nature that lay before him in all its dewy beauty. A magnificent blue sky hung silently above him, velvety blue valleys lay below him, and all around him the snow-capped peaks gleamed in the sun. He sat down, exhausted and happy, as the sweet blue tundra flowers danced with vicarious joy.

All right, already! the readers cry. You want to *move* your readers, not steamroll them. Note the number of adjectives and adverbs here: "feverish"; "victoriously"; "last, excruciating"; "dewy"; "magnificent blue"; "silently"; and on and on. Over ten modifiers within three sentences. To compound the problem, the modifiers are ordinary words used in the ordinary way. Where are the surprises in this passage, the fresh turns of phrase? *Remedy Number One: Edit your adverbs, count your adjectives.*

Compounding the problem of too many modifiers is the use of cliché: "fevered brow"; "triumph of nature"; "blue valleys"; "snow-capped peaks." These hackneyed phrases add nothing new to the readers' perceptions and serve to make the prose embarrassingly sentimental. *Remedy Number Two: Avoid cliché.*

Next, note the use of the pathetic fallacy in the last line. Pathetic fallacy is a term that describes the bad habit of ascribing human emotions or qualities to nature or inanimate objects. Those tundra flowers can no more feel vicarious joy than they can fry an egg. Sometimes the pathetic fallacy *can* be used effectively:

The house was obscured by a fence of cruel spikes.

Or:

The orchard trees, bowed and halfhearted, had been twisted into submission by Mr. Abel's hacksaw.

Images like these can work as metaphors in the appropriate story. But when you resort to grateful daisies or happy hydrangeas you've probably crossed the line. *Remedy Number Three: Avoid the pathetic fallacy.*

WRAP-UP

A writer's style is not immutable; style often changes to suit a given story. Although certain writers can be said to have a "practical" style and others a "lyrical" style, individual novels and stories by the same writer will demonstrate his or her so-called style to varying degrees. Even the most famous stylists vary their prose depending on the story at hand. Certain stories by James Joyce are more "Joycean" than others, for example. Ann Beattie is more "Beattian" in *Falling in Place* than she is in *Picturing Will.* Style evolves as much from the creation as it does from the creator.

Sometimes descriptive style matches the content of a story, and sometimes style and content contrast. Either way, the descriptive style can enrich the story you want to tell. Plain prose and simple constructions may reinforce the theme of simplicity you want in a story about a cloistered nun; a more lyrical style, on the other hand, may suggest the complexity of the nun's inner life. Wait until you have a few drafts on paper before you make a final decision. Style evolves over the course of many drafts, and you should allow it to change as you come to know your characters better.

Certain descriptive styles come in and out of vogue, and it's hard to resist their pull. Minimalism, which came into fashion during the seventies with the stories of Raymond Carver, made a big splash and was copiously imitated. Poorly executed minimalist stories have a dull, monochromatic feel that comes from a style that is intended to be simple but comes out simply flat. Minimalism requires exquisite telling detail and an inherently interesting situation.

As a backlash against the ubiquitous minimalism, stories are now getting bigger, sprawlier, and more lushly described. Big, multi-parted stories require stylistic unity in order to feel whole. A strong stylistic focus, a central image, a strong setting, or an unusual first-person narrator are stylistic techniques that can help you shape an overgrown story.

Maximalism, like minimalism, is a trend. Fiction fashions come and go, and the only way to survive these waves is to ignore them. Write your stories however they demand to be written—in vogue or out.

One descriptive style that is never in vogue, however, is sentimentality and melodrama. You can avoid this snakepit by scrupulously editing your prose. Measure your modifiers to avoid overwriting; weed out all clichés; and never commit the pathetic fallacy, which is ascribing human emotions to natural phenomena or inanimate objects.

Descriptive style profoundly shapes your readers' experience. Style is not a set of authorial quirks! It is a set of deliberate decisions, made over a series of drafts, that becomes an integral part of the story's impact.

CHAPTER 7

DESCRIPTION AND SETTING

DESCRIPTION OF SETTING is probably what Elmore Leonard meant when he said (possibly apocryphally), "I try not to write the parts people skip." It is true that pages-long accounts of the vineyards of France or the houses of San Francisco or the mustard fields of Virginia or the streets of Greenwich Village have the dangerous potential to put readers to sleep, but only if the description seems like an after-thought, or a writer's self-indulgence. When you take care to make a description of setting integral to the story—that is, if it sets a tone or mood, foreshadows future events, or suggests the characters' motives or desires—then you will be able to keep your readers engaged.

DETAILS THAT TELL A STORY

If Edith Wharton had set *Ethan Frome* in the Deep South instead of New England, she would have been compelled to write a different book. The lugubrious heat of southern Mississippi could not rein-force the frigidity of her characters' loveless existence—Wharton needed the brittle winter landscape of Vermont to fulfill her novel's purpose. Setting is as important to certain stories as the characters who inhabit that setting. Can you imagine *The Great Gatsby* set in Minneapolis, or *Oliver Twist* set on a farm in southern Italy?

Not all stories require a strong sense of place. Many successful novels and stories take place in nameless cities or anonymous yards or on unidentifiable stretches of road. Their energy and atmosphere come not from setting, but from the complexities of character, the intricacies of plot, the quality of language. If setting *is* part of a story, however, it should have a function other than to create atmosphere or background. Descriptions of place are like snapshots—they record a setting. Unfortunately, some snapshots, like some descriptions, are more involving than others.

Imagine looking at your uncle Simon's photographs of his trip to Wyoming. You sift through view after view of dark mountain ranges, cloud-filled sky, red sunsets, and long shots of prairie dogs, trying to keep your eyes open. Why does magnificence always seem so dull in reproduction? Probably because most people aren't good photographers: they snap their cameras with no eye for composition. Nothing stands out. Still, you come upon a happy accident occasionally: a moment before Uncle Simon snapped Mount Rushmore, his hat blew off his head and began rolling end over end into the middle of his shot. The result is a picture of Uncle Simon's fishing cap floating like an offering before the stony likenesses of four American presidents. Not only do you suddenly have an image you can remember, you have a way of understanding why Uncle Simon was so awed by his trip, and you know what he means when he tells you, "I felt small."

Descriptions of setting should provide that same click of understanding. You can go on for pages about the white cliffs of Dover, but until you throw in the equivalent of Uncle Simon's fishing cap, the yawning readers are reading (or, more likely, skipping) the equivalent of a dimestore postcard. The purpose of place description is not to provide a general background or atmosphere, but a *specific* background or atmosphere. Telling the readers that the sunset is beautiful or that the town was built in 1723 is fine; but if the sunset turns out to be the last thing the character sees in the living world, and 1723 is the birthdate of the character's earliest known ancestor, then the setting takes on added weight.

Every description of place should have a memorable quality that hints at the story's meaning. Otherwise, you're just filling up space. Let's take as an example a story about a woman visiting Quebec City, Canada:

Version One: Maxine walked along the Dufferin Terrace, a walled promenade that surrounded the upper part of Quebec

City. The sky above her was a lovely blue, and below her the St. Lawrence River ruffled along, busy with boats. As she approached the end of the Terrace, she could see the Chateau Frontenac, its turrets gleaming in the afternoon light.

This description is not bad, but neither is it breathtaking or even useful. Nothing in it gives the slightest clue as to the reason for Maxine's presence in this city. The turrets are nice, and the "ruffling" river is mildly interesting, but the description is too generic to allow the readers to "see" the city in any particular way.

Benign descriptions of setting add nothing to a story's purpose. If the setting is static and perfunctory, existing only as an introduction to other events, then it serves merely as a way into the story, and that's not good enough. In the example of Maxine in Quebec, you should give your readers some small indication about what the setting means to her. Is it intimidating? liberating? scary? exciting? Maxine could be local, a tourist, a travel guide on her lunch hour, or a thief on the lam. Right now she isn't much more than another landmark in the setting.

Let's try this description again, with an eye toward giving place description a purpose:

> **Version Two:** Maxine walked along the Dufferin Terrace, practicing her French. She whispered the words for *please* and *thank you* and *how much*, occasionally glancing over the wall at the cliff's dizzying drop into the blue-black water of the St. Lawrence River. A half-mile ahead of her the Chateau Frontenac already appeared to loom—frothy and ridiculous against the modest jumble of buildings that surrounded it. She stopped to stare, trying to pick out her room from the hundreds of tiny curtained windows. Slices of sky appeared through the hotel's dozens of turrets, making greener the ancient hotel's rusting copper rooftops.

This revised description gives your readers a much stronger sense of a woman in a foreign place. The walk on the terrace takes place in the context of her practicing her French, which immediately sets her up as a stranger. The proximity of the cliff lends a mild sense of danger or disequilibrium to her experience. The "hundreds of tiny, curtained windows" suggest the hotel's enormity, but also suggests the anonymity Maxine must feel as she looks for her room. At the same time, the great chateau looks "frothy and ridiculous," rather than imposing or intimidating. Maxine may be alone in a large and foreign place, but the whimsical description of the hotel suggests that she is not frightened at the prospect. These details are the equivalent of Uncle Simon's fishing hat, for they place Maxine in Quebec City in a way that allows us to "see" both her and the city.

Relative Details

Besides making the story itself more evident, the revised version improves on the original in another way. The various parts of the setting—the sky, the hotel, the terrace—are rendered in relationship to each other.

One way to make a setting come alive is to describe one thing in relationship to something else. The size of a tree becomes more vivid if you describe the bird's nest wedged into the end of one of the branches, or the nuthatch working its way down miles of trunk. A river can look black against a blue sky, or blue against a backdrop of pale buildings.

In Version One of the above description, each detail is independent of every other detail. First we see the terrace, then the river, then the chateau. We don't know how big one thing is compared to another, or how far apart the things are, how impressive they are to Maxine, or even what anything actually looks like, except that the chateau has turrets. In Version Two, however, the chateau becomes a focal point because of its contrast with the "modest jumble of buildings" that surrounds it. We assume that the chateau must then be "immodest" and that it stands apart from or above the "jumble." We "see" the city through that one contrasting detail, and understand why the chateau "already seems to loom" when Maxine is a half mile away. Similarly, the sky is not simply a sky, but a detail that visually shapes and colors the rusted copper rooftops of the chateau. Relating details to each other in this way adds depth and accuracy to a setting, inviting readers into the world of the story.

Sensory Details

As in any good description, sensory details can help shape the readers' experience. Consider the following descriptions of the same pond:

> **Version One:** Belle turned off Lucas Street to where the gravel path wound around the pond. The sky was blue, the day warm, the ground solid under her feet. She walked down the path to where the reeds began, and looked across the water to where some water lilies floated over the brackish surface. A family of ducks made their way through the lilies, quacking softly. A wind disturbed the water, and she closed her eyes. She loved this place; she could get away from her family here. It was peaceful and calm.

> **Version Two:** Belle held to the path until it crooked around the south end of the pond. She stopped for a few moments simply to listen, then followed the trail she had matted into the grass over the past two weeks. It wound through the reeds and ended at the edge of the water. She sat down, pressing her hands into the spongy earth, listening hard, dissecting the confusion of sound: an oriole's mournful piping, the rustle of grass, the white noise of insects, the slap of muskrats diving from the banks, the intimate quavering of mallards steering through snags of water lily. By now she could identify each note of the pond's great teeming. Behind her, on the other side of the trees, whined the morning commute on Lucas Street, high and insistent and inescapable. Farther still, she could (she imagined) hear the clash of words—ugly, staccato, incomprehensible—in the cluttered kitchen she had come here to escape.
>
> A gust of wind moved the water, making the world reflected there—tree, cloud, sky—seem to explode, then calmly reassemble itself. She looked to the far bank. A blot of yellow moved through the brushy tangle of the pond's far side, a warbler looking for nesting material. It was the time of year for making homes.

Version One introduces any old character looking at any old pond. Version Two introduces a troubled woman coming to a unique place that she has chosen for its restorative qualities. What's the difference? Look at the sensory quality of the detail. In Version Two, Belle is taking in this place very specifically, through her senses. The generic description of the first version—reeds, ducks, and water lilies—gives way in the second version to more specific detail (the sound of orioles, mallards, muskrats) and the occasional visual surprise, like "blots of yellow [moving] through the brushy tangle."

Notice, too, that in Version One the details are almost exclusively visual, and in Version Two the details are almost exclusively aural. Describing the pond through sound rather than sight works in two ways. One, sound makes the pond much more sensually alive, more a real place than a snapshot in which "the sky was blue, the day warm." When we experience a place, we often tune in through sound as much as sight. Here, we "see" everything even more clearly through the vehicle of sound, because sound connotes movement: the mallards' quavering brings to mind a raft of birds moving over the water; the insects' "white noise" brings to mind harmless swarms of nearly invisible bugs; the sound of the muskrats brings to mind their disappearing backs and dripping tails; even the "whine of traffic" conjures images of incessantly moving cars.

The focus on sound suggests that Belle can dissect the "confusion of sound" in the pond in a way she cannot dissect the "incomprehensible" sounds in the "cluttered kitchen she had come here to escape." The pond is not simply fill-in or background or atmosphere: Belle's presence there is purposeful and gives us information about her. Every noise and color in that pond has a counterpoint in the house that Belle is escaping. Even as she marvels at the "intimate quavering of the mallards," she can hear the "whine of traffic just over the ridge of trees, high and insistent and inescapable." The conflict in the story is beginning to suggest itself through the description of place.

It's easy to get lost in the beauty of your own prose when describing setting, but you can't afford to forget for one moment that you are *writing a story*. Every beat of the prose must have some bearing on the story you wish to reveal.

THE SETTING'S HISTORY

Another way to reinforce conflict in a story is to use the historical significance of certain settings. Suppose you decide to set a story in

Boston's North End. You know the area well, and you believe its rich history will add interest and atmosphere to a story about a brother and sister. You're right—the setting does have potential, as long as you include its history in a way that naturally fits the story. Avoid presenting historical details for their own sake:

> Tom snaked his way through the winding streets of Boston's North End, his throat constricting with the news he had yet to deliver. He couldn't remember where Audrey lived; perhaps if he kept driving something would begin to look familiar. He made another turn. The tidy buildings—vestiges of a Puritan vision that began in 1630 with John Winthrop—gave the now prosperous state capital the look of a little village.

The history here detracts from your story. Just as your readers begin to wonder about the news Tom has to deliver, you subject them to a travel-book aside about Colonial America. It feels like an interruption. What if you used the history to magnify something that's going on inside the character?

> Tom snaked his way through the winding streets of Boston's North End, his throat constricting with undelivered news. He leaned against the steering wheel, peering around and through the tidy Colonial buildings, searching for a landmark. He knew only that she lived near the Old North Church, where Paul Revere had once ridden frantically over these same crooked streets, sounding the alarm.

Here, Paul Revere's "frantic" ride gives an outer shape to Tom's inner turmoil. By evoking Paul Revere's famous ride, you imply that the news Tom has yet to deliver is bad, or at least calamitous in some way. We also get the feeling that Tom would like to be able to shout out his news the way Paul Revere did, but his constricted throat shows us that for some reason he can't. History works beautifully here, giving us not only an interesting glimpse of historical Boston, but an insightful glimpse into the main character.

A historical setting can reinforce a story by illuminating theme, revealing character, enriching plot. A famous battlefield might enrich a story about a cutthroat business deal or a cracking marriage; the town of Bethlehem could add humor or pathos to a story about a carpenter's wife on her first bus tour. If you choose a setting that readers readily recognize as a historical landmark, you have more or less obligated yourself to use the history of that place to illuminate parts of your story.

SETTINGS LARGE AND SMALL

Some descriptions of setting are big and sweeping, some minute and compact. You have to decide which kind works best for a particular story. Do you need the whole forest, or just one tree? In a story about a young boy feeling dwarfed by his boisterous family, the mountain setting should probably be large:

> He lay in his bed, staring out at the malevolent sweep of mountain that ringed the valley.

If the boy feels strong and powerful, the same setting might take on a more accessible quality:

> From here he imagined he could make out the starry shapes of wild azaleas that blazed along the slope.

Almost any large setting can be made small—that is, readily accessible to the readers—if you attend to detail. The pebbly shingles of the town's black roofs. The green bottle floating in the middle of the ocean. The *Bloomingdale's* bag tangled in a Central Park tree. With these details, you guide the readers' eyes to the specific and away from the general landscape.

PROBLEMS WITH "ACTUAL" PLACES

When my first novel, *Secret Language,* came out early in 1993, I was asked by a local deejay to come in for a radio interview. The novel is set in Portland, Maine, where I live, and contains occasional references to streets and landmarks in the city. One of the first questions the disc jockey (who had read and liked the book) asked was this: "About your main character, Faith—is her house the one at the end of Norwood Street?" When I told him that Faith's house existed only in my imagination, he seemed disappointed, for he was sure he had located exactly the house in the novel. Everything fit, he insisted: the shape of the lawn, the bird feeders hanging from the trees, the porch and walk. Of course I was pleased that my invented place seemed so real to him, but I was also bemused by the problem of putting fictional people in real places.

Beware the Locals

One problem with describing a setting that is real is that reality changes. In the interest of authenticity, you might move to Seattle for a year and write an entire novel there, meticulously recording street names and architectural styles and common surnames and typical weather. By the time the book appears two or three (or ten) years later, however, the Good Times Deli on Washington Street has been torn down and turned into Tom's Texaco. Carver Avenue, the scene of a head-on collision that begins Part II of the book, is now a one-way street. There is no overestimating the glee some readers experience when coming upon geographical glitches in their home turf. "Your book was wonderful," they write. "However, there are no middle schools in Greenfield. We go from elementary to junior high." Your admirable impulse to create accurate descriptions has blind-sided you by delivering exactly the opposite effect you intended. Instead of wowing your readers with accuracy, you've made them fretful and petty.

Fictionalizing Reality

Why not fictionalize an actual setting? You can make up a neighbor-hood and place it "near" a familiar landmark:

> Vernon's house on Drake Street was a ten-minute walk from Harvard University. The proximity of that famous institution was evident in Vernon's neighborhood only by the occasional plastic bag from the Harvard Coop that got caught in the stiff tentacles of the naked, spindly trees or mashed into soggy, un-recognizable lumps between the sidewalks' yawning cracks.

Notice that the neighborhood is meticulously described with no mention of its exact location. (Be sure to check a map to make sure there is no "real" Drake Street anywhere near Harvard.) Your readers don't know whether the Drake Street neighborhood is ten minutes north, south, east, or west of Harvard; they understand that even though Harvard exists in real life, you are making up the rest of the map. They may even assume that the fictional neighborhood is based on an area they know, but because the street names aren't real, they can't check your facts against a city map. The familiar landmark lends authenticity to your setting, but the rest of the place is yours to do with as you wish.

You can do this in reverse, too: fictionalize the landmark but make everything else accurate. This technique is useful if the landmark in question—a university, a museum, a church, a branch of government—is going to be used in the story. The main character might be the college chancellor, for example, or the pastor of the church, or the curator of the museum. To avoid dragging actual persons into your fiction, you might try something like the following:

> From her top-floor apartment on Morning Street, she could see all the way down Munjoy Hill, a ziggurat of rooftops that ended with the commanding spire of St. Mary's rising from the foot of the hill into the bleak winter sky.

This setting is familiar to anyone who lives in Portland, Maine, except that the church at the foot of Munjoy Hill is not "St. Mary's," it is the Cathedral of the Immaculate Conception. Why bother to change the name? Let's assume this is the beginning of a story that involves characters who work in and around the church and school. You certainly don't want to confuse actual persons—the president of the parish council, for example—with fictional characters. And you don't want people chiding you for getting the number of windows wrong, or putting the altar at the wrong end of the church, or abolishing the 10 a.m. mass for one that begins at 9:30. The solution is to fictionalize a local landmark simply by changing its name. By doing so, you make a pact with your readers: *I'm borrowing the church for a little while, okay?* Readers are more than happy to make the loan, and if you're lucky, the fictionalized landmark will become as real to them as the actual one.

WRAP-UP

Long descriptions of setting that function merely as backdrop or atmosphere can quickly wear a reader's patience. When describing the city or vacant lot or mountain range or fire escape that serves as your story's setting, keep in mind, always, that you are telling a story. How does this particular setting bear on the characters' actions? How do the characters perceive this setting? Does anything about this setting—its colors or odors or sounds—suggest the characters' inner conflicts and desires? The story's setting should be an integral part of the story you wish to tell.

Settings shouldn't be "the parts people skip." You must add details that remind readers that the setting has a purpose. An abandoned fishing line at the shore of a river, a pile of books on the library floor, a badminton net tangled on the church spire—these details keep the readers aware that a story is being unmasked even as it is being "set."

To get the most out of a description of setting, make the details relative to each other rather than important only to themselves. A thatched hut is made small by a description of the giant palm trees that shelter it; a crumbling brick sidewalk is made luminous by a description of the sun's path over its chipped surface. Remember, too, to engage all the senses: a place can be "seen" through sound and scent and touch and taste.

Sometimes the history of a place can be used to the story's advantage. An orphanage restored into a hotel might make a good setting for a story about a couple on vacation, hoping to get pregnant. A construction site might enhance a story about a friendship in need of repair.

Descriptions of setting can be majestic or modest, depending on the story's needs. The broad view—the vast rippled surface of a lake—can bring grandeur to your setting, and the specific details—the silvery eye of a fish—can bring to your setting a cozy smallness.

Real places present special description problems. A place you describe today with dogged accuracy may have been razed by the time your book or story gets into print. Also, when you try too hard to be accurate you risk the fretful reader's complaint that getting from Main to Broad requires two left turns, not three. On the other hand, real places lend authenticity to stories. You might experiment a little with blending fact and fiction. For example, you might set a story in a real city, then make up a neighborhood within that city. Or, you might use the actual neighborhood of that city, then change the name of the church or school or monument that defines it. Readers are very forgiving as long as they recognize the rules.

Setting can be as important to a story as character or plot, and requires as much descriptive attention as any other element of fiction. Give it the care it deserves—your reward will be a story that feels authentic and unified.

CHAPTER 8

SPECIAL
DESCRIPTION
PROBLEMS

NO MATTER HOW GOOD OUR WRITING BECOMES, certain description problems are bound to crop up again and again. How do we describe an animal without making it seem like an illustration in a Peterson guide, or, even worse, a character in a Disney movie? How do we describe weather without resorting to cliché? How do we make a reader "hear" sound? The following strategies may help you solve these reoccurring problems of description.

DESCRIBING ANIMALS

If you include animals in your stories you are probably an animal lover. If you are an animal lover you probably share quarters with the world's smartest dog, the world's prettiest cat, or the world's most talented parakeet. Perhaps you talk to your animals as if they understand you. And, who knows, maybe they do. Please remember, though, that what works in life doesn't always work in fiction. Your eight-year-old Siamese might fetch your slippers, but a reader might not believe this of a fictional cat. So, as you are booting up your computer or sharpening your pencil or looking for your lucky pen, remind yourself that animals are not furry people, no matter how much you adore yours.

That said, how do you handle animals once you decide they do belong in your story? Like human characters, animals deserve to be rendered accurately, interestingly, and truthfully. If you err too much on the furry-person side, your animals end up looking like

Cinderella's sidekicks; too much on the field-guide side, your animals look like something mounted in a taxidermist's window.

Describing animals accurately is difficult, because all individual animals of a species, with few exceptions, look exactly the same. It is difficult to tell squirrels apart, for example, or rose-breasted grosbeaks, or caribou, or grizzly bears. Therefore, if you describe an animal accurately you offer a perfectly serviceable picture of a certain species of animal:

> Lisa's Saint Bernard followed her into the living room. It had a huge rounded head, a massive body, and loose jowls. "Sit, Chuckles," Lisa demanded, and the dog obeyed.

What you don't offer, however, is a picture of any *particular* animal of that species. Like human characters, each animal, closely observed, is unique:

> Lisa walked into the living room, her Saint Bernard lumbering behind her. It moved like a stevedore, barrel-chested and full of purpose. "Sit, Chuckles," Lisa demanded, and the dog obeyed, its wide and mournful face listing downward.

Here, you describe the dog as a Saint Bernard like any other—don't they all have mournful faces and barrel chests?—and yet you suggest the uniqueness of this particular animal through muscular verbs ("lumbering") and good use of simile ("like a stevedore") and intimations of personality ("full of purpose") that don't go so far as to make the animal a furry person. The vivid presentation has an added bonus: the name "Chuckles" is quite funny when applied to this serious, "mournful" creature.

Descriptions like this can so easily go wrong, of course. Language must be precise. Replacing a phrase like "his mournful face listing downward" with "he hung his head sadly" would violate the dog's animalness. In the first phrase, you are merely observing what the dog looks like, and in the second you are attributing emotion to a dog. Attributing human characteristics, emotions, or motivations to animals is called *anthropomorphism*—a major culprit in sentimental writing. The phrase "full of purpose" flirts with anthropomorphism, but it doesn't cross the line because it describes the dog's way of moving, not his moral integrity. Only if the passage were stuffed with

other, similar phrases (describing, say, the dog's loyalty or bewilderment or fear or guilt) would the phrase "full of purpose" feel sentimental or corny.

My favorite animal description of all time is from Ralph Lombreglia's story "One-Woman Blues Revival":

> It was a mammoth raccoon on the windowsill, looking at
> her with his broad masked face. He was moving his pointy nose
> all around, smelling the pantry smells. His long, black claws
> hung over the edge of the sill.
>
> You couldn't live in Vermont without seeing lots of rac-
> coons, but she'd never seen one this close up, so trusting and
> calm. She felt, after all these unsatisfactory years of adult-
> hood, that she might finally be in a fairy tale. "Who the hell are
> you?" she said. "Do you talk?" To her great disappointment,
> he did not.

In this delightful passage, Lombreglia weds Disney to Peterson. The
raccoon has a fanciful, cartoonish demeanor, "moving his pointy
nose all around, smelling the pantry smells," but the description
is accurate: "broad, masked face"; "long, black claws." Raccoons,
perhaps more than any other animal, make fools of humans, because
they're so darned cute we want to turn them into friends. Lombreglia
acknowledges this impulse by revealing the woman's hope that "she
might finally be in a fairy tale." He then yanks away any potential for
sentimentality by having her ask, "Who the hell are you?" instead of
saying something gluey like "Why, hello, little fellow." It's a brilliant
passage because it acknowledges all our projections and (understandable) silliness about animals while reminding us that a raccoon is
nothing more than, well, a raccoon.

Even if you stick to the most basic animal descriptions, you can
jazz up the prose by paying attention to shades of color, thicknesses
of coat, shapes of tails or paws or snouts. Consider different words
for common features, or fresh similes that describe those features.
A spotted leopard becomes a dappled cat. The shell of a tortoise
might remind you of the sun-leathered surface of your grandfather's
hands. The tail of a dog can resemble a hose or a bottle brush or an
ostrich feather. You can make your animal characters seem unique

or intelligent or charming or menacing by celebrating the very features and qualities that make them animals.

DESCRIBING WEATHER

Weather is part of our experience as human beings in this world, and references to weather are as impossible to avoid in literature as they are in casual conversation. Our awareness of weather is not awfully precise, however, unless we are barricading against a hurricane or shoveling out from a two-foot snowfall. The daily pleasantries we utter to each other—"Nice day, isn't it?"; "Think it'll rain?"; "Cold enough for you?"—are not really as much about weather as they are about our desire to connect with one another in a safe and superficial way. Safe and superficial is great for casual human relationships but deadly in fiction. Your literary descriptions of weather should be fresh and necessary rather than banal and irrelevant.

Direct and Indirect Description of Weather

Most readers like to know what the weather is like in a story they're reading—nothing elaborate, just a quick glimpse to determine whether it's winter or summer, raining or snowing. If you are using weather only to inform the readers—that is, if the weather actually has nothing to do with the events of the story—then your best bet is to keep the description as simple as possible:

> It had been raining for three days.

Or:

> When Tuesday finally came, the weather was clear and cold.

Or:

> By the time Harold reached his aunt's house, it was snowing.

These examples provide a quick scan, the literary equivalent of sticking your finger into the wind or your head out the window. By providing direct, literal description, you allow readers to take note of the weather and get on with the story. However, if the weather is going to have some effect on the events of the story or provide a certain kind of atmosphere that the story requires, you should try to make your account of the weather more memorable.

One way to do that is to describe the weather indirectly, by closely observing how certain kinds of weather make the world look. For example, instead of describing a day as frigid, you might have a character observe a frozen field. In Jack Holland's "The Yard," a story about a man remembering his boyhood experience of his grandfather's death, the raw and dreary day is revealed to us through the character's physical surroundings:

> The rain was standing in puddles between the cobblestones and in shallow little pools on the tops of the big barrels that were marshaled against the wall near the horse trough, row upon row, like great, dumpy soldiers. The puddles rippled in the cold February wind, which drove before it the little bits of straw floating on the stale water. The carts were covered with tarpaulin, their shafts lowered. My heart ached.

Note how little time the author spends on a direct account of the weather. He uses the words "rain" and "cold . . . wind," and that's it. Everything else is a *reflection* of the weather, from the "shallow . . . pools . . . on the barrels" to the "rippled" puddles to the "floating" straw to the carts "covered in tarpaulin." We get the impression of a very, very wet day after an extremely heavy rain, for water is everywhere. We can also imagine a grey sky, a bone-chilling cold, and a general dreariness, though the author does not describe these things directly.

Indirect description has two benefits. One, it delivers you from resorting to tired descriptions: rainy days, heavy snows, blue skies. Two, indirectness does three jobs at once. In the story excerpt above, the carefully observed reflections of weather give us the condition of the weather (rainy), the condition of the setting (a simple Irish village), and the condition of the observer (heartbroken). Here, the weather becomes a poignant reflection of a young boy's bewilderment and sorrow.

Engaging the Senses when Describing Weather

Weather is one of the most satisfying subjects for engaging all the senses. Weather can be *seen*, as in hailstones or snowflakes; weather can be *heard*, as in the drumming of rain on a tin roof; weather can be *felt* as moisture or heat or cold; weather can even be *tasted*, as in the sulphur tang of a steel mill on very hot days; and weather can be *smelled*, as in the scent of earth that comes with the first warm days after winter. Your senses give you a myriad of new ways to describe the familiar. Each sense describes a different aspect of the same weather.

Let's take a hot summer night and render it through all five senses:

> **Sight:** Defeated and exhausted, Alice and I watched the August steam rising from the sidewalks.
> **Sound:** We sat on the back porch, the hot night punctuated only by the click of ice in our glasses and the occasional snap of the neighbor's screen door.
> **Touch:** The air was so thick on my arms it felt like sleeves.
> **Taste:** My first sip of mint julep on Emma's steamy veranda meant summer was here at last.
> **Smell:** The night was so hot and clear I could smell the lilacs from Jack's garden a half mile down the road.

Notice how the use of the senses transforms weather from reportage to experience. If your story depends on weather for a certain kind of atmosphere or insight into the characters' situation, then it is not enough to merely *report* the weather; it is your obligation to *evoke* the weather. The sensory details in the preceding examples turn weather into part of the story rather than a mere backdrop. Steam rising from the sidewalks makes the characters' defeat even more unbearable. The sound of ice in glasses and screen doors banging evoke all of summer, not just one hot night. The feeling of air as "sleeves" puts us, quite literally (and uncomfortably), inside the character's skin. The taste of mint julep evokes a certain lifestyle as well as the advent of summer. The scent of lilacs infuses the story with a small-town neighborliness.

When describing weather, try to forget about the exact condition of the weather and instead explore the ways in which certain weather makes the world look and smell and feel.

DESCRIBING EMOTION

Because some writers fear being seen as melodramatic or sentimental, they avoid emotion-filled passages in their writing. Their characters can't afford to be deliriously happy or ferociously angry or desperately sad; they move through an emotionally neutral narrative in which their inner state is merely hinted at. The steel-gray sky serves as a metaphor for despair; a snippet of dialogue reveals a well of pain; a muted action—stirring sugar into a cup of tea, or pruning a hedge—suggests anger, or loneliness, or joy. All of these techniques are useful, even admirable, but sometimes we can get so worried about being caught in the act of sentimentality that our fiction suffers an even worse fate: It becomes bloodless. After a while the readers begin to cry out for a character to, well, cry out.

How your characters cry out marks the difference between heartfelt prose and schlock. Take a character with a broken heart (please!)—how do you describe this all-too-common feeling? The heart in question can break, or ache, or constrict; the owner of the heart can weep or sigh or sob; he or she can verbally express heartbrokenness by saying "I'm heartbroken" or "I'm sad" or "I want to die." These descriptions are true enough, but they don't move us in any specific way. It's a challenge to convey common, cliché, yet very human emotions without sounding melodramatic. You know you're in trouble if the expression of emotion is all cerebral:

> She was heartbroken. Bill had left her and now she was all alone with her tears, her aching heart and her sorrowful memories of a happier time. She felt she would never smile again. "I want to die," she said aloud.

Okay, we know this is awful. Why? There is not one concrete image in the entire passage, that's why. It's all *thoughts*. The character sounds like a self-pitying blubberpuss instead of a woman who is genuinely and rightfully sad. By transforming her fuzzy thoughts into concrete images, you can turn melodrama into poignancy:

That night, lying in her damp sheets, she listened to her
heart. Across the room his face stared out of the photograph
that seemed already to be yellowing. She stared into the dark,
imagining she could see dust gathering on the frame. He was
gone.

In this revision you employ strong, accessible images to invite your
readers into the character's world. Damp sheets, yellow photograph,
dust—these things are real. We can see and feel them. They allow us
to experience what the character experiences. We understand why
her heart is broken because we can see her transformed room.

The following example works in the same way, by avoiding the
cerebral and embracing the physical. A man is visiting his dying
mother. They are on the back porch, watching the sunset:

He watched the last red strand of sky fade to dark. "That's
that," his mother said. Then his heart broke.

Again, you give us specific images rather than thoughts or feelings.
The direct information—"his heart broke"—comes only after we
have been outside the character for a few beats. First we watch the
end of the sunset, then we hear the mother's cryptic comment. Only
then do you inform us that the character's heart is breaking. You
return us to the character with a jolt, so that we recognize his sorrow
at the same moment he does.

In the following two examples, the emotion is fortified not by
an outside image, but by the *behavior* of the characters:

Sarah leaned against the trellis, stricken with longing.
Henry crossed his hands over his chest, first one and then
the other. He held them there, protecting his heart.

The act of leaning against a trellis gives weight and credibility to the
information that Sarah is filled with longing. The measured act of
crossing his hands over his chest emphasizes Henry's fragile emotional state. Cerebral prose like "Sarah was filled with a sudden, inde-
scribable longing" or "Henry was overcome with grief" cannot by
itself tell the tale; you need the characters' bodies—their arms and
fingers and eyelids and knees—to fully convey to the readers that the
character is a human being who is suffering or savoring or fleeing or
fuming. The difference between cerebral and physical prose is the

difference between reading about an accident in the paper and pulling your own father from a crumpled car.

When managing emotional moments in your fiction, remember that the emotional moment itself—the sorrow, the joy, the shame, the rage—depends mightily on the prose that leads up to it. Overblown, melodramatic lead-ins only diminish the emotional moment. Conversely, stingy descriptions might leave readers ill-prepared for a dramatic emotional display. Strong, concrete images in place of abstract thought should carry the day.

The best build-up to an emotional moment I know of in recent fiction is in Kazuo Ishiguro's deeply affecting novel *The Remains of the Day*. The first-person narrator is Mr. Stevens, the aging butler of Darlington Hall, who embarks on a "motoring trip" during which he looks back on his life, trying to reassure himself that he has served humanity by serving a "great gentleman." His doubts about Lord Darlington's true nature—and therefore his own worth—slowly take shape as the narrative progresses. The final stop on his trip brings him face to face with Miss Kenton, who was once the housekeeper at Darlington Hall. Her crackling spirit was the one (unadmitted) bright spot in Stevens's life, until his excessive reserve drove her away. They meet. They talk. And, finally, Miss Kenton confesses her feelings:

> "But that doesn't mean to say, of course, there aren't occasions now and then—extremely desolate occasions—when you think to yourself: 'What a terrible mistake I've made with my life.' And you get to thinking about a different life, a *better* life you might have had. For instance, I get to thinking about a life I may have had with you, Mr. Stevens. And I suppose that's when I get angry over some trivial little thing and leave. But each time I do so, I realize before long—my rightful place is with my husband. After all, there's no turning back the clock now. One can't be forever dwelling on what might have been. One should realize one has as good as most, perhaps better, and be grateful."

> I do not think I responded immediately, for it took me a moment or two to fully digest these words of Miss Kenton. Moreover, as you might appreciate, their implications were such as to provoke a certain degree of sorrow within me. Indeed—

why should I not admit it?—at that moment, my heart was
breaking.

From a man whose life has been dedicated to submerging his emotions, the simple words "my heart was breaking" are enough to break
our own hearts. We understand that the entire book has been a preparation for Mr. Stevens's ordinary human admission. The hapless
aside—"why should I not admit it?"—makes his admission all the
more poignant, for had he been able to admit such things twenty
years ago, he would be telling a different story now. Straight-laced
words like "moreover" and "implications" only heighten the emotional impact by contrasting his proper outside with his disheveled
inside. What an unforgettable moment!

   Good fiction is about human interaction, and human interaction
takes place in the realm of emotion. Let your characters' hearts break,
let their laughter ripple, let their shame consume them. Beware the
critics, though. Several years ago a certain old, well-regarded magazine ran a short story by a certain young, well-regarded writer. The
story was about a former child movie star, now an old man, who visits
a dying little girl in the hospital. Granted, the story's premise is a
minefield for a writer wanting to avoid sentimentality and melodrama, but this particular writer's gorgeous prose rescued the problematic premise; the story became a brief, moving account of a moment between a man with his best years behind him and a child with
her best years never to come. Still, this story was listed in another
magazine as the "worst short story of the year."

   No matter how you decide to depict emotion in your fiction, you
run the risk of a bloodless critic looking down the long slope of his
nose and pronouncing your story a bowl of mush. Take the risk.

DESCRIBING SOUND

At various points in this book we have discussed the virtue of "engaging the senses" in fiction, including the sense of sound. The aural
aspects of description can be the most compelling and inviting
to readers, and yet many writers overlook sound, probably because
it can be so difficult to convey accurately. Sure, we can write of the

"splash" of water or the "rustle" of leaves or the "roll" of thunder or the "squish" of mud; these sound-words are familiar to readers, easily heard. It's the subtler sounds—a cat walking over gravel, a basketball banking off the backboard—that challenge our powers of description. Can we duplicate those sounds without writing gibberish?

Well, sure. We can even make up words if we have to. Get up and go to the nearest door. Open it and close it a few times. What does the door moving back and forth over the carpet *really* sound like? The sound is probably something like a *huff* or a *shuff* or a *hoof* or a *thuff*. If you're in a cavernous room with no rugs, the sound might be brighter and sharper: *clack* or *crick* or *crock* or *quick*. Are all these words suitable for describing the sound your character hears when his sister-in-law enters his study? Probably not. It depends on the prose that precedes the sound.

If you've written this story in straightforward, traditional prose, then a made-up word to describe a sound might feel false. For example:

> Lyndon leaned over his papers, staring out the window into the dark. He worried about Annabelle. She didn't trust him; he could see it in the narrow blue eyes, the suspicious curl of her lips whenever she condescended to speak to him. He spread his hands over the papers, protecting them. Then he heard her step in the hall, and the shuff of the door as she pushed it open.

In this passage the word "shuff" is at best puzzling and at worst confusing. The prose is too straight-laced (which is not to say bad) to support the sudden entrance of a made-up word. But what if the sound of the door is important to the scene? Perhaps you could find a more conventional word:

> . . . She didn't trust him; he could see it in the narrow blue eyes, the suspicious curl of her lips whenever she condescended to speak to him. He spread his hands over the papers, protecting them. Then he heard her step in the hall, and the door whispering open.

In revision the sound of the door opening is a "whispering," which is a conventional, accessible sound-word that describes not only the opening door (probably swinging open over a carpet) but the general unease of the main character, who is deep in thought, and worried. The "whisper" is perfect, the "shuff" distracting.

What if you were to write the same passage in more inventive, imagistic prose? Now the word *shuff* feels natural:

> Lyndon leaned over his papers. Night covered the open windows like a grainy cloth: impenetrable, opaque, vaguely dirty. He worried about Annabelle. She didn't trust him; he could see it in the hooded slits of her eyes, the suspicious slope of her lips whenever she condescended to speak to him. He spread his hands over the papers, protecting them. Then he heard her step in the hall, and the shuff of the door as she pushed it open.

In this version the prose leading up to the word *shuff* is plumped with simile ("like a grainy cloth") and various other images ("hooded slits," "slope of her lips," "impenetrable, opaque"), allowing the made-up word to stand unprotested. Although one style is no better than the other, each has its own intrinsic rules. You don't wear a tweed blazer with a chiffon dress, and you don't use words like *shuff* in conventional prose.

And what of those other, simpler sound-words—those splashes and rustles and squishes? Good prose includes familiar sounds: the crack of a bat, the flutter of wings, the roar of the wind, the shatter of glass. Horses neigh and nicker, cats yowl and mew, dogs bark and whine, birds twitter and cheep. Fires crackle, bombs explode, cars roar, houses creak. This is the way ordinary people describe the world, and there is nothing wrong with these ordinary sound-words. They belong in good prose, just as the ordinary but necessary verbs *to be* and *to have* belong there. You'll find great satisfaction, though, in periodically replacing these conventional sound-words with something a little more inventive, just as you sometimes replace familiar verbs. One entertaining way to transform sound is to literally mix up conventional sound associations. Horses neigh and houses creak— can these sounds work in reverse?

> Harriet lay in her great-grandmother's bed, exhausted. How many crates of knick-knacks and dishes and doilies had they packed today? Twenty? Fifty? She had long lost count. She

stared up at the ceiling and saw her childhood as clearly as a
scene revealed in a flash of lightning: the way she used to follow
the cracks in the ceiling, waiting for sleep, soothed by the soft
neighing of this ancient house.

And:

The next day they checked out the barns, and were astonished to find a horse tethered to a fence post, a heap of bur-
nished hay piled up beside him. "Who's this?" Harriet asked,
and the horse seemed to respond, unhorselike, with an odd
creaking that came from the back of its throat.

Reversing the sounds in these two passages is quite effective. The
house takes on a personality of its own, and the horse becomes something more than a horse—a creature with something to say. Is the
horse ill? Lonesome? Hostile? That "odd creaking" could mean a lot
of things, and the readers are suddenly standing at attention.

One last thing: Don't worry about getting kicked out of the writers' union for using a thesaurus. A thesaurus is a wonderful (striking;
marvelous; fabulous; wondrous; etc.) resource for finding new ways
to describe sound (or anything else, for that matter). Suppose you
want to describe a bird's nest falling out of a tree during a windstorm,
and the only word you can think of for the sound of impact is
"thump." The word doesn't seem quite right; the nest is too delicate
to make a thump. In the thesaurus under "thump" you find the
following synonyms: beat; pulse; throb; flutter; hit; slap; poke. Not
quite. You look up the synonyms for the synonyms. Under "throb,"
for example, you find these possibilities: tick; flutter; tremble; tingle;
thrill; twitter. Nothing there, either, except that the word "twitter"
reminds you that the nest is full of twittering baby birds. Now you
want a word to describe two sounds at once: the falling nest and the
agitated birds. Look up "twitter": tremble; thrill; quaver; quiver. Nice
word, "quiver." You decide that maybe the thump is right after all,
as long as you add other nuances of sound to the description of the
falling nest:

John braced for the worst gust of the morning. He looked
up just as the air began to roil. High in the willow, a burgeoning
nest quivered briefly in the wind, then twittered to the ground
and landed with a thump at his feet.

"Twitter" as a verb for motion rather than sound ("the nest ... twittered to the ground ...") is apt, for it accurately describes the visual teetering motion of the nest while suggesting the sound of the birds. "Twittered" (rather than "plummeted" or "fell") suggests the lightness of the nest in the windy air, leaving the word "thump" as an entirely appropriate sound-word to describe its final drop to the ground.

Sound-words are best used sparingly. Most of the time a simple description of the source of the sound is enough: "She heard the cat outside, walking over the gravel." No sound-word needed—and each reader hears something different.

WRAP-UP

Descriptions can be problematic, some more than others. Whenever you run into trouble, remember the fundamentals: telling detail, simile and metaphor, engaging the senses. By applying these fundamentals to all descriptive situations, you can describe virtually anything in a way that readers can hear, feel, and see. Animals require the same range of color and shape that you would give to a description of people. Sensory details are as important to describing weather as they are to describing landscapes. Finding just the right word for a sound is not much different from finding just the right word for a character's hair. Describing an emotion by identifying the right gesture is not much different from describing a fence by identifying the shape of the pickets.

Good description is only partly a mystery. Mostly, it is the wise application of a few sensible rules. With a little patience and determination, you can find exactly the right words to describe a snow leopard or a snow job or a snowstorm. This search is what makes writing such a continual and satisfying surprise.

CHAPTER 9

TIPS AND TRICKS

A COMPENDIUM OF ADVICE THAT SUMMARIZES some of the concepts already discussed in the book, this chapter looks a little like a workbench: if you pick and sort long enough, you'll find exactly the tool you didn't realize you were looking for. Some of the tips are new—random offerings that did not fit logically into any particular chapter but were worth noting anyway.

I hope you will use this chapter to rummage around for ideas and inspiration when you're struggling with a scene or having trouble getting from one part of a story to another. Suggestions given out of context can sometimes strike the right chord in a way an entire chapter devoted to one problem cannot. So, when you're stuck, or daydreaming, or otherwise not writing, scan the following tips and tricks to get you back on your way.

Expand your field of vision. Experienced bird-watchers know that different species of warblers feed at different heights on a tree. They look to the top for Blackburnians, across the middle for Magnolias, and in the lower branches for Black-and-Whites. Experienced writers follow the same instinct when observing people or nature. Don't get so focused on the sky that you miss the ground. A person's kneecaps might be as defining as his nose. The squeak of a person's shoes could be as telling as the squeak of his voice. Look up, down, all around for the details that best capture the thing you are describing.

Go beyond red, white, and blue. Don't be afraid to liven up your descriptions by getting creative with color. Cerulean is not exactly blue, russet is not exactly red. Describe the color of things with familiar objects: a jacket can be the color of eggplant, hair can be the color of hay. Mustard-colored, storm-colored, cabbage-colored, money-colored—all these colors say something not only about the object being described, but about the observer, too.

Circle your adverbs. Too many adverbs is a sign that you aren't working hard enough to let language transfer a scene from your eyes to the readers'. When reviewing your work, watch for unnecessary, irrelevant, or extraneous adverbs (especially the ones that end in "ly"). If you describe a main character as one who behaves "lovingly" and works "tirelessly" only to come home to a family that treats her "terribly," which causes her to speak to them "bitterly"—you have a description problem. You are describing things in the abstract rather than in the particular. Instead of telling us that the heroine works tirelessly, describe the callouses on her hands or her slow and heavy walk. Examine your adverbs to make sure you aren't forcing them to do the hard work of observation for you. They can't.

And while you're at it, circle your adjectives. Good description is not defined by the number of adjectives per sentence. When in the editing phase of writing you might try literally counting adjectives in any given paragraph. Paradoxically, a string of adjectives (no matter how bright and punchy) can diminish the descriptive power of a moment. For example, a sentence like "He turned his slack, reddened face to the white-hot, midday sun" is made flabby and unnoticeable by too many adjectives. "He turned his face to the white-hot sun" is direct and more dramatic.

Turn a bland simile into a vivid adjective. Similes can sometimes seem like a writer's desperate attempt to depict a vivid world. Turning similes into adjectives can help you vary your descriptive style and still retain the comparisons that help readers see what you see. "He had a face like a cabbage" can be converted to "his cabbage-like face." "She moved like a duck" becomes "her ducklike walk." "James dropped from roof to balcony, quick as a cat" becomes "his feline leap." Similarly, a description like "When George laughed he seemed to roar like a lion" can be made more effective with adjectives: "George unleashed a leonine [or lionlike] roar of a laugh." Or, you could skip both simile and adjective and simplify the description this way: "George roared."

Don't mix metaphors. The mixed metaphor gets first prize for exposing beginning writers. Metaphor disasters abound in most writers' early (and mercifully unpublished) work, whether they care to admit it or not. To wit: "Without her, he was a bird shot from the sky, his very foundation crumbling under the rotting timbers of his widowhood." This sentence looks amateurish and overwritten because conflicting metaphors are crowding each other off the page. Go with the bird or the house, but don't include them both. Birds don't have foundations or rotting timbers, and houses don't get shot out of the sky. You might try something like ". . . he was a bird shot out of the sky, suddenly wingless, crying out in disbelief" or ". . . he was no more stable than the house across the road, his foundation crumbling under the rotting timbers of his widowhood." In any case, don't make metaphors too obvious, as both of these are.

Tone down your metaphors. In the above tip, the metaphors are so heavy-handed as to be amateurish even once they've been unmixed. If you want to compare the poor guy to a wingless bird, you might lay out the *suggestion* of a bird instead of coming at us full-tilt with "he *was* a bird. . . ." For example, he could be sitting in his garden noticing that all the birds are showing up in pairs for the nesting season, or perhaps he could remember shooting birds when he was a child and *then* be reminded of their "crying out in disbelief." Metaphors that begin with "he *was* a lion" ("he was a lion of a man" is better) or "she *was* a cat" are usually too loaded at the outset to work. If you write, "She curled into the chair, catlike, and brushed the lint carefully off one sleeve, then the other," you give the character over to the metaphor of a cat without actually calling her a cat. Her deliberate movements ("first one sleeve, then the other") are reminiscent of the way cats groom themselves; the mere suggestion is enough to paint the picture.

Use the impersonal pronoun for animals. To avoid sentimentality, describe animals as "it" rather than "he" or "she." "The cat fetched its kittens one by one and carried them into the other closet" sounds less sentimental than "The cat carried her kittens . . ." The impersonal pronoun allows animals to remain animals. Leave the personal pronouns for the characters themselves to use. "She bit me twice," a first-person narrator might say of his dog, but a third-person narrative would read "The dog bit its master twice."

Jazz up your prose by engaging the senses. When a descriptive passage fails for no reason that you can easily discern, take a good look at your sensory details. Are they all visual? Add a sound or a scent to get the prose moving again.

Don't rely on brand names. If you present a character who wakes up on a Beautyrest mattress, eats a bowl of Cheerios cereal, laces up her Reebok sneakers, and grabs her Gucci briefcase before bicycling to work on her Bianchi mountain bike, you run the risk of creating an annoyed reader rather than a "real" character. Use brand names only when they serve to illuminate something about character or story. The Cheerios might be important if the character has been fighting with her kids over their crummy eating habits; the Reeboks might be important if the character spent a week deciding whether or not to take up jogging. It's hard to imagine any reason to include a Gucci briefcase in a description of anything except a briefcase store.

Don't use "telling" names. Who can forget Snidley Whiplash or Cruella DeVille, cartoon villains we loved to hate? Names like that work great in cartoons. Unfortunately, unless you're Charles Dickens, giving characters descriptive names only diminishes serious fiction. A track star named Bea Swift is going to seem like a cartoon character, no matter what your intentions. If you're writing humor or satire, then by all means name away—but for serious fiction, "telling" names won't do the job.

You can work with sounds when naming characters, however. A heartless surgeon might be made more vivid with a name like "Dr. Crutchfield" or "Dr. Hatch"—sounds that are reminiscent of ripping or tearing. The association isn't Snidley-Whiplash obvious, but does add just a dash of menace to the character. A kind old woman might be well served by a name like "Polly": the sound is round and soft.

The right name can make a character come into focus not only for your readers, but for you.

Don't use alien names. The above advice can be reversed: You shouldn't give your characters names that are too obviously meant to reveal their character, but neither should you give them names that are too alien to their character. For example, if you invent a wealthy, upper-crust English landowner with a name like Luther Johnson, you'd better be prepared to explain how he came by that name (it could be the heart of the story). On the other hand, if you write about an American sharecropper named Neville Windsor, a similar explanation is in order. (I, for one, would love to hear it.)

Don't pile on the details. Too many details in a passage of prose can obscure its meaning. For example, the story of a social worker visiting the house of a notoriously recalcitrant family could begin this way:

> The mud in the grassless yard was about two inches thick, at first spongy and yielding under her feet. She moved through the litter-strewn pathway to the house, through the spare parts of long-forgotten cars, sun-bleached Popsicle wrappers, coils of rope, tatters of ink-smeared junk mail, various and colorful plastic parts from several generations of children's toys, junked wood that had once been part of several decent but inexpensive discount-store furniture, clay pots with jagged cracks, and an inexplicable assortment of kites in various stages of decay. Alice picked her way through the obstacle course, aware of the low and glowering sky above her that carried the tang of sulphur from the mill downriver. She shifted her briefcase from one arm to the other, aware of its weight and heft and how it must make her look—like a bureaucrat from the state come to torture some unsuspecting family. She looked up to find the lady of the house, a massive woman in a calico apron, staring like an owl from behind the screen door. Alice smiled and waved as the mud began to pull at her shoes, making each step forward like a leap through time and space.

This is a lot of detail, and in the right story it could work just fine. Know, however, that you always have the option of weeding out details so the readers can see the forest for the trees. You don't have to set up a scene by describing everything from the weather to the buttons on the character's blouse. Keep in mind the central image you yourself can see when entering your character's world:

> Alice picked her way through the pulling mud, her eye on the massive woman behind the screen door. Each step was harder than the first—besides the mud she had to watch for discarded car parts and broken toys—and she began to believe she was moving in great, agonizing leaps through time and space.

More detail is not always better. Every once in a while you have to remember to let your prose breathe!

Use adjectives in surprising ways. Try to write description that contains verbal surprises. An adjective like "sweet" does not always have to describe sugar, or a kitten, or a baby. How about a sweet tractor, or a sweet hurricane? Flex those adjectives! In the right story, seemingly unrelated adjective-noun combinations—frightful goodness, ferocious necklace, barnlike body—can strike exactly the descriptive note you want.

Don't use unusual adjectives twice. Common adjectives like "small," "large," "brown," or "wet" can be repeated in a story, sometimes three or four times, without drawing attention to themselves. Less common adjectives, however—"lissome," "electrifying," "fractious," "sinister"—should be used only once per story. A good adjective repeated becomes a bad word choice.

Check for descriptive consistency. If Dorothy has blue eyes on page two, then she'd better have blue eyes on page nine. You'd be surprised how often inconsistencies crop up. If you write only on weekends, or are rewriting a story you began five years ago, you are especially prone to having descriptive inconsistencies.

Don't mix up point of view. Any description of a character or place or event takes on a particular perspective. That perspective may be your own, or a first-person narrator's, or a third-person narrator's—whatever point of view you choose, stay consistent. The third-person narrator might see the clear blue sky as ominous; the main character might see the same sky as a sign of good luck; the "camera eye" would objectively record the sky as blue. Don't call the sky ominous on page one and lucky on page five unless you've clearly and deliberately shifted point of view. Decide who's calling the descriptive shots right at the beginning.

Don't enslave yourself to "showing." "Show, don't tell" is a guideline, not a rule. Sometimes telling is more effective than showing. A brief statement—"Helen was a cheat. It was that simple"—may be far more effective than a two-page scene showing Helen at work as a cheat. Telling can be just as thrilling as showing as long as the prose is interesting and engaging.

Elevate the mundane with some lyricism. When describing things that are inherently dull—a pig farm, for example—inject some fresh imagery and lyrical phraseology into the description. The pigs might resemble failed dictators, say; the hoof-marked mud might be hardened in spots and reminiscent of an elegant, pressed-tin ceiling; the setting sun might cast ribbons of color over the sagging fences. Beauty and ugliness exist in everything we see if we're willing to look hard enough.

Avoid sentimentality and melodrama. Sentimentality runs rampant when we write in abstractions: "She was wracked with grief." "His happiness knew no bounds." Avoid melodrama by sticking to accessible, concrete images: "She covered her face with her hands." "He ran down the green slope of lawn, his long hair spraying out like a fireworks." Describe the things we can see or hear; we can't see or hear "wracked" any more than we can see or hear "no bounds." We can, however, see a woman's hands on her face or a man's hair spraying out as he runs.

Avoid "realistic" details that alienate the readers. Say you're writing a story about an ornithologist. You don't know much about birds yourself, so you flee to the library to research the science of birds. That's fine. Drink it in. Learn all you can until your ornithologist's motivations and passions are as familiar as your own. When you finally sit down to write the story, though, don't treat your readers to the fruits of your labors. *You* should know the difference between *altricial* and *precocial*, but your readers don't necessarily have to. People love to learn new things through fiction, but only if the story itself remains center stage. Introduce unfamiliar words or facts as part of the story's natural unfolding. Resist the temptation to show off; your hard work should be invisible by the time it gets to the page. The only purpose of all your bird research is to make your character, the ornithologist, believable to the readers. Jargon words like *passerine* and *syrinx* will alienate your readers, while the lay terms—*perching bird* and *voicebox*—will allow them into the fascinating world of birds. The paradox of fiercely researched stories is that the more technical terms you throw in, the more the readers figure you don't really know what you're talking about. It looks like overcompensation. If you're such an expert on the migratory pattern of scissor-tailed flycatchers, then why can't you explain it in plain English? If you *must* use jargon (perhaps that's the way the character talks), then take care to explain in some other way what the words mean:

> "Here's where the damage is," Dr. Hendrix said. He examined the cardinal's orange beak, working it open and closed with his fingers. "Do you see how the upper and lower mandibles aren't closing properly?"

Certain unfamiliar words can be worked into context, of course—you don't want to insult your readers by going too far in the direction of simplicity. Just remember that you're writing a story, not a textbook, and that the character himself should be more interesting than the work he does.

Don't abuse your thesaurus. Thesauruses are life-savers, but they can't turn bad prose into good. If you find yourself running to the thesaurus every five minutes then you aren't working hard enough. If you want just the right word to describe your mother's garden, don't expect the thesaurus to provide it. You're better off sitting in your mother's garden for half an hour and taking in the experience of what you would like to describe.

Use description to place dialogue in context. Conversations don't take place in a vacuum. People talk while eating, cleaning house, shoveling snow, appraising jewelry, committing murder. A descriptive tag as simple as " . . . she said, giving the cement mixer another turn" can remind your readers that the characters are not talking heads and that a story is in progress.

Above all, enjoy yourself! We all have something to say. We all have joys and sorrows and magical moments in our past that shape our unique view of the human condition. Sharing our view through the written word should be the easiest thing in the world. It isn't, though; sometimes it's the hardest thing in the world. Writing is tough work. It requires time, and concentration, and self-confidence, and extraordinary patience. This is true whether you're writing your first story or your hundredth. Because the writing process requires so much from us, we often get frustrated or discouraged or just plain furious about the whole thing. When this happens, remind yourself that writing is supposed to be fun. Don't take yourself so seriously. If the story you're writing now never sees publication, so what? I can look back on dozens of my own unpublished stories and see them as the steps that led to the published ones. Nothing you write is ever wasted! Like the basketball player who spends every morning shooting nothing but free throws, you have to practice to get better. On those days when you feel like a tongue-tied hack, remind yourself why you write. Remind yourself of the joy your own words can bring you. Remind yourself how good it feels to finish a first draft. Remind yourself how satisfying it is to finally send a story out with hope and a prayer. It's the process, not the product, that brings the most satisfaction. Not all of us will see the product—a published story—but the process is ours for the taking. No entry fee, no prerequisites— just a pencil and an idea.

INDEX

REVISION

KIT REED

for Lois Gould

ABOUT THE AUTHOR

Kit Reed is a novelist who teaches student writers at Wesleyan University in Connecticut. Her short stories have appeared in magazines ranging from *Cosmopolitan* and *Missouri Review* to *The Magazine of Fantasy and Science Fiction*. In addition to her eleven novels and four short story collections, she has published *Story First: The Writer as Insider*, a widely used text for writers of fiction. Her most recent novel, *Catholic Girls*, is now in paperback. A member of the National Book Critics Circle, Kit Reed is a frequent reviewer of fiction for publications, including *The New York Times Book Review*.

CONTENTS

Preface

If you could buy a document or a piece of magic that would enable you to write successful fiction, if you could learn one thing that would make you able to write successful stories and novels, how much would you be willing to pay? Ten dollars? A hundred? A thousand?

How far would you be willing to go to get it?

Most of us who make a life in fiction would spend every penny we have and call it cheap at the price. We would travel to Katmandu or China to find the key.

Now for the trick question.

What if the secret to success in this case turned out to be not a matter of parting with dollars and cents, but of expenditure of time? How many hours would you be willing to spend? Ten? A hundred? A thousand?

If most of us would happily spend thousands for the secret to success, then it makes sense for us to spend as many hours as it takes to find it.

Surprisingly, many writers—particularly beginning writers—are skinflints here.

They're ready to give everything but the time.

Many of us get so committed to what we already have on the page that we will do anything to avoid rewriting. Yet it's the extra time that makes the difference.

Fledgling writers are often so excited by what they are doing that they never get past the first draft. There's nothing like that first flush of accomplishment. Look what I did! The sense of pleasure and wonder often outstrips what's on the page. So do expectations. Many beginners think a piece of work is wonderful not because of what it is, but because they wrote it. One adult class I taught at Wesleyan University turned in their first exercises convinced they were going to sell them to the magazines immediately and thus recoup the cost of tuition.

Their first lesson turned out to be a hard one: *everything you write is not perfect*.

The second was easier: *But you can make it better*. How? Through revision.

An important first step, then, is *keeping an open mind*. This means being willing to reconsider. Many student writers would rather argue than think through something they have written, going to any lengths to defend rather than rewrite what's already on the page. The best ones understand that no matter how hard they've worked or how pleased they are, what they have is probably only a beginning. Some discover that they're draft writers. That "story" they handed in turns out to be not a story but rather raw material which they will cut, shape, expand and reorganize over several weeks until it becomes a finished story. Others, who revise as they go, word for word, sentence for sentence, page for page, learn that even though the work may be polished, it isn't finished. It may need cutting here, expansion there—the kind of dramatic development that makes it more accessible to the reader.

Writing "The End" does not necessarily mean you are finished. It means you are finished with *this draft*. For the time being. Until it becomes clear what you need to do next.

Nobody enjoys this moment of truth. Professionals who have given their all to a story or a novel only to run into editorial criticism feel most of the same things beginning writers do: commitment to the vision that made them begin the work in the first place, distress at the idea that *after all that work* it's still not ready.

We don't necessarily expect praise when we turn in a piece of work we are proud of, but we are brought up short by anything less than acceptance. Remember, professionals revise as part of the process of composition. We've already spent tens or hundreds or thousands of hours writing and rewriting to create what we think is the final version.

Then our first reader doesn't get it. Or our agent or an editor doesn't get it. Or one or the other thinks it's going to be good as soon as we make revisions.

Our first instinct may be to argue. Some of us go through all the classic stages — rage, denial, depression, bargaining and acceptance. In the end we're going to listen to editorial comments, dig in and rewrite. Again. Again. Revising, we close the distance between the work at hand and publication. Until it's published, we can't hope to reach more than a handful of readers.

If we cared enough to write the work in the first place, we certainly care enough about it to rewrite it.

We know it's the only way to reach our audience.

Working writers know that there are no tricks, no special documents that automatically entitle a writer to success, but there is a way. This book is designed to help you find it.

It is revision.

It takes guts, persistence and a heart of steel for beginning writers to turn revision into an organic part of their working equipment, but it can be done, and once you begin, you're going to see immediate payoffs. Those of us who have been around for a while can tell you that revision is far easier than inventing something in the first place. It goes faster and it makes your work better.

Forget about money for the time being.

Be willing to spend the time.

CHAPTER 1

NOTHING YOU WRITE IS CARVED IN STONE

I'M TOLD THAT NOT EVERYBODY out there resists the idea of revision — that there are, in fact, beginning writers who plunge in joyfully without having to be encouraged. Those of you who are already happily engaged in revision as a way of life are encouraged to move on to the later chapters — Chapter Three and everything that follows.

I do, however, want to point out that I've learned through working with undergraduate writers that a great many beginning writers *think* they're revising when they've made a few superficial changes. Even attitudes sometimes need revision.

As for those of you who revise endlessly as a way of putting off the inevitable moment of judgment — or, in fact, beginning something new — I have words for you, which will come in Chapter Twelve: Knowing When to Quit.

In the meantime I'm going to assume that many of you have picked up this book precisely because you know there's something you ought to be doing but you need encouragement because you can't quite bring yourself to do it. For you, I offer a cautionary tale, in hopes that I can help you shortcut a few hard lessons.

ONE WRITER'S STORY

Like you, I was interested in audience — I wanted one. Unfortunately, I used to think everything I wrote was wonderful even before I finished it. Like so many beginning writers I was hung up on the amateur's concept of inspiration. I transferred the voices I heard directly to the page—too fast. The fact that the words came so easily convinced me they must be right—whether or not they were. I thought each story was wonderful just because I wrote it.

Since then, I've made a number of painful discoveries, which I've organized here in hopes they may help you.

Rule One: Your First Thoughts Are Not Necessarily Your Best Thoughts.

I remember thinking if readers didn't get what I was trying to do the first time I wrote a story, it was because they were stupid, not because there might be a problem with the story. In spite of negative signals from the outside world—teachers' comments on my papers, and later, printed rejection slips in droves—I believed in myself as a writer. In order to believe in myself as a writer, I thought, I had to believe in everything I wrote. I wrote it, which meant it must be right . . .—Didn't it?

It took me three years of hard work and heavy losses to learn that getting it right involved more than just getting it written.

Rule Two: Nothing You Write Is Carved in Stone.

Well, who knew? Encouraged by an easy first sale, I had decided that not only could I write, I could be a good writer without much effort. By the time I learned that I wasn't good every time, and I wasn't necessarily good on a first draft, I had written some twenty-two stories a year for three years and not sold any of them. I had a hit-or-miss attitude toward what I was doing, thinking that if I fired enough rounds of buckshot out into the world, sooner or later I was going to hit my market.

I see now that it would have made more sense for me to spend all the time it took to perfect a single guided missile designed to hit its target the first time out.

But I was only a beginner, hung up on pride. In spite of the kindness of an agent who read and said she could not sell any of these stories, I pinned her responses on bad judgment. If she said a story wasn't right for the marketplace, I thought it must be because I was committing *art* while she was, after all, in business. Unfortunately, I wasn't enough of a grownup about my writing to learn by revising. Getting a story back from my disappointed reader at the agency, I never reread it and I certainly never rewrote it. Instead I would write another and fire it off.

Perhaps because we need it to survive in a world which is not necessarily crying out for our stories, most writers of fiction are born with a protective sense of self-confidence. We have to believe in ourselves before anybody else will. Unfortunately, there is a thin line between healthy self-confidence and blind vanity, and it's all too easy for us to slip across it.

Even when these early stories I wrote boomeranged, coming back almost by return mail, I was too blind—and deaf to criticism—to get the message.

In a way, you could say that during this miserable period I was teaching myself to write, but there were problems. Of the stories I wrote in those three years not one was published. I have little memory of them. Not even the manuscripts survive, which is probably just as well, given my slapdash attitude. If I still had them I'd be embarrassed to look at them—the flashes of talent, thin ideas, the serious problems with narrative.

All those hours of work! All those wasted words! All that blasted hope!

What if I had paid the two dollars, driven the five miles, gone the rest of the way around the block?

At the time, I couldn't bring myself to do it.

I remember thinking that if I didn't get a story right the first time, I didn't want to spend any more time on it. This accounts for all the abandoned efforts, mailed out three or four times to magazines, returned rejected, and after a brief period of mourning, put away forever.

I remember thinking I'd rather scrub floors or write a whole new story than rewrite an old one. Remember, I was a beginning writer.

As a writer who's survived, I hope you'll learn from my mistakes—and my all-too-gradual discovery that revision is a part of every successful writer's working equipment.

Rule Three: It Takes Revision to Turn a Loss into a Win.

At the time, pride stood between me and what I wanted. I needed to go the rest of the distance to become a professional. It was a hard lesson for an undisciplined beginning writer.

It took years for me to learn how to step outside the work—how to distance myself so I could see clearly exactly what I was doing. We'll talk about this at length in Chapter Four: How to Find Out Whether You're Finished When You Think You're Finished.

Rule Four: Shortstop Criticism—Be Your Own Toughest Critic.

Sometimes even before I'd mailed a story, I suspected there might be a problem with it. But with the false optimism of certain medical patients, I mailed it anyway, in hopes nobody would notice. It was like going to the doctor and failing to mention a specific symptom: if the doctor doesn't notice this symptom that's bothering me, then my problem is not serious.

I mailed my flawed stories thinking, If they don't notice there is a problem, then there's nothing the matter with these stories.

Who did I think *they* were? Who did I think I was, imagining I might be able to fool them?

They turned out to be the audience these stories never reached, the audience I would not reach until I learned to identify problems with each piece of work and solve them by rewriting.

In baseball, the shortstop catches the ball before it reaches the outfield or goes over the fence and loses the game for you. As I learned—on the job, and over a period of years—revision fulfills some of the same functions. It helps writers catch story flaws before they lose the reader.

Rule Five: If It's Worth Doing at All, It's Worth Doing Right.

Some writers are lucky enough to learn this on the job at the very beginning. Their early work is good enough to attract the attention of an editor who may want to publish it if they are willing to do the necessary revision. Such writers begin getting short notes at the bottom of those printed rejection slips from magazines, suggestions for revision that may lead to a sale. A publisher is interested in doing a novel—if the writer is willing to develop and perfect this scene, answer those questions, cut this section or expand that.

Others develop a healthy respect for revision in graduate writing programs all over the country, where battle-scarred professionals teach by example, or they may learn in the give-and-take of workshops in which fellow students criticize from the craftsman's point of view. Looking at student work in several drafts, they talk in detail about how to close the distance between what the student has in mind and what is on the page.

The rest of us have to learn on our own, working alone, with nobody to let us know how we're doing except those disembodied editors who keep sending rejection slips.

I'd like to say that for me the light dawned all at once, that I was converted overnight from careless pride to careful craftsmanship, but it seems I was a slow learner.

In time I figured out that if I had written sixty-six stories in three years and failed to place *even one of them*, maybe this was not the fault of doltish readers or the result of cruel fate.

It was not their problem.

It was my problem.

There just might be something the matter with the work.

Knowing there is a problem and doing something about it are two different things. I was fortunate enough to be belted along by three things: 1. editorial feedback in the form of one splendid reader at home and a market-minded reader in a literary agency, 2. increasingly lengthy editorial notes on rejection slips and 3. habits learned in the newsrooms of two city newspapers.

It's clear that sooner or later I was going to figure out that I had to start rewriting my fiction in order to make it do what I wanted. Techniques learned in the newsroom helped me go about it. I will talk about this at length in Chapter Three: Kinds of Revision.

What fascinates me now, looking back, is the fact that it never crossed my mind to object to revising in the newsroom. It was part of my job. Since I already thought of myself as a novelist-in-hiding, I was clearly less protective of my nonfiction. It seemed more important to get it into acceptable form to go into the paper than to stand around defending what I had already written.

A competent craftsman, I wrote and rewrote cheerfully, preparing news and feature stories for city editors in Florida and Connecticut. Because I had to recast the news lead—the opening of each story—as many times as it took me to get everything in and get it *right*, I got used to proceeding in exactly the same way every time I sat down to write. I composed and rewrote sentence by sentence, cutting where necessary to come up with a tight and well-organized story, to forestall complaints from city desk and questions from the copy editors. I was shortstopping criticism—in the newsroom, at least.

If the desk wasn't satisfied, I had to rewrite.

As a reporter I grew more and more careful about perfecting what I turned in because in the best of all possible worlds I would be corrected, or yelled at; in the worst, there was the outside possibility that I might get fired. Instead I ended up winning prizes for reporting.

Yet when I quit and began writing fiction full time, it was as if I had learned nothing. I can't now explain why I imagined writing fiction would be any different, but I did. It was, after all, fiction. Maybe I thought writing news and committing *art* were not the same things, but I can't for the life of me understand why I thought that unlike news writing, fiction could sprout in an untended garden.

After five years in a newsroom, I may have felt somehow released. Maybe I had the illusion that since this was fiction I could do anything I wanted and expect it to work out right the first time. After all, I thought, wasn't I inspired?

But there were those sixty-six unpublishable short stories.

It was only when I began applying newsroom techniques to fiction — typing and retyping sentence by sentence, paragraph by paragraph, page by page until I got something *right* — that my fiction turned into anything better than the hasty efforts of a gifted amateur.

Digging my feet in, moving reluctantly, I found my way into revision. I can't pinpoint the moment at which I began that first revision, but I remember what I felt:

1. Oh wow, this isn't so bad.
2. Hey, *this story is getting better*.

And I remember what happened. *I began selling more stories.*

Learning hard, I learned well. I can't think of any other way to write.

Rule Six: Extra Effort Closes the Distance between You and Your Audience.

In my time I have done up to five revisions of a novel I thought was finished before it left my hands on its first submission; I do so many sentence and page drafts that I counted seventeen attempts at the first page of my sixth novel, and those were only the ones I could manage to round up for a text on writing, *Story First: The Writer as Insider*. They went into an appendix titled, *Once More Through the Typewriter*.

The title bears some discussion. A Pulitzer Prizewinning friend who wishes to remain nameless at one point showed my resident critic and me a draft of a novel which, as it turned out, was not published until ten years later, at which time it earned him a quarter of a million dollars.

Both of us felt this early draft by a prizewinning author was not quite right but my resident critic found precisely the way to say it: "I think this ought to go once more through the typewriter."

An established professional, our friend took this in precisely the way it was intended. He put his new novel through the type-writer not once more but seven times. The seventh draft reached an enormous audience in hardcover, through book clubs and in paperback.

Then there's my eleventh novel. Remember this is a novel I wrote in sentence and page drafts in the first version, shaping, discarding, trying my best *at every stage* to make it as good as I could make it. The working papers for the first draft fill a sizable carton. Attacking a second draft, I entered the novel into my computer. I'll talk more about this later. I have gangs of these cartons in the attic, representing all the false starts and develop-mental stages of what is turning out to be a long career in fiction.

As time passed, it became clear that there was still more work to do if I expected my novel ever to be published.

I felt all the usual things — pride, anger that others didn't see what I saw in the work, reluctance to work on it one more time after I thought it was finished — but I move through these stages faster now, and without histrionics.

If there was more work to do then I was going to have to do it, and for a compelling reason.

I had to revise to reach my audience.

If I cared enough to spend an enormous chunk of psychic energy and four-plus years on this particular novel in the first place, I certainly cared enough to put in the time and effort necessary to take it the rest of the way — in this case to publica-tion, good reviews and paperback auction. It's clear to me that it's worth whatever it takes to move a manuscript from my desk to the readers who give it life outside my office.

Rule Seven: Revision Means Survival.

Remember those twenty-two stories a year I wrote for three years without ever once turning my hand to a revision?

It's as if they were written by a different person. It's also clear to me that the different person who launched those stories like faulty kites and watched them crash was still an amateur.

Yes I learned to write while I was turning out three years' worth of flawed stories with no changes, no looking back and no time for second thoughts, but those sixty-six stories are forgotten. I can't help but wonder what I could have made of them if I had been willing and able to make myself spend the time to take them the rest of the way to an audience.

What if I had reread them before I mailed them in the first place? Gone back and put them once more through the typewriter? Twice? Three times?

What if I had listened to criticism, instead of wasting energy on arguing?

Revision might have turned some of those early losses into wins for me. It's clear that revision has worked for me again and again in the years since. An editor says: we may want to go ahead and publish this if you're willing to talk about revisions.

I don't waste time arguing. In many cases editors see what I can't—what the piece of work looks like to an outsider.

Editors and publishers can do something else I can't do for myself, unless I want to spend my life supporting vanity presses. They can buy my work and get it published. They take it to an audience.

I've told my embarrassing but all too common story at length in hopes it will speed you toward revision. Try to make revision part of your natural working equipment—a tool of the trade as essential as the instrument or machine you write with.

At this stage you should also know that once you've broken the sound barrier—cut through the beginner's initial resistance to reconsider and rework a story—you'll be amazed by results.

No, you haven't wrecked your story.

You've made it better.

What's more, since you've written it once, you already know how it comes out, which means you've developed second sight. Within the framework of the piece you're revising, you've acquired *the ability to see the future*. You can go back to the beginning and make all the signs point in the right direction.

Now, let's look at your own attitudes toward revision. Try to answer these questions honestly.

1. Do you ever rewrite?
   a. If so, when and why?
   b. If not, why not? Be a strict judge here.
2. Do you ever reread a piece after you think it's ready for submission?
3. Do you ever reread after you get negative criticism?
4. If you do reread, are you pleased or do you have misgivings?
5. If you're pleased with your work, do you care if readers agree with you?
6. Do you try to see whether readers are going to be just as pleased as you are? or:
7. Do you think criticism means not that you have a problem with the story, but that there's something the matter with the reader?
8. Do you make too many assumptions about your reader? Do you ever think:
   a. Any smart reader is going to "get" this.
   b. Anybody who doesn't get it doesn't deserve to get it.
   c. If it isn't quite right, readers are never going to notice.
9. If you reread a "finished" work and have misgivings, do you:
   a. Rework the story?
   b. Send it out anyway?
10. Do you ever think, I'll make revisions only if an editor/publisher promises to buy it.
11. If you think you already revise quite enough, thank you, do you really? Does revision for you mean more than:
   a. Making a clean copy of the story you just wrote?
   b. Making a few superficial word changes?
12. Have you ever:
   a. Made significant cuts in a "finished" story?
   b. Reworked entire sentences, paragraphs or pages to complete your thinking?
   c. Found it necessary to reorganize a story so that everything points in the right direction?
   d. Revised to make certain scenes more dramatic?
   e. Further developed sections to make your intentions clear to the reader?

Now look at your answers, especially to the last two questions. Even if you honestly think you already revise—and like it— you're going to learn something.

If you've stopped at occasional word changes or called making a clean copy "revision," you have more work to do. If you are anything less than wholehearted in your desire to reconsider and rewrite—and do your utmost to complete your thinking and reach your reader—then it's time to make some changes.

And keep in mind my cautionary tale. I've confessed for a reason. If I can save you a year, or even ten days, then maybe those three years of busted short stories I wrote will have earned their keep. I want to help you cut through some of the painful stages of denial that cost me so much wasted time and effort.

By being willing to spend the extra time before a story leaves your desk, you're going to save time in the long run—the time it takes to reach an audience.

CHAPTER 2

HOW REVISION WORKS FOR YOU

I JUST GOT OFF THE PHONE with one of the denizens of the downtown Writers' Room, a place where New Yorkers who are professional writers rent space and move in with typewriters, computers or copy pencils. They like the Writers' Room because they work better in an office situation than they do at home. These include well-known novelists, biographers and writers of other nonfiction.

I called to ask my friend for a manuscript page to demonstrate how one established novelist goes about revision. She offered an early draft and finished page from her new novel, and her interest in the project sparked an exhibition about revision at the Writers' Room. Examples of rough drafts and finished pages filled the hall and drew national attention. You'll find them included in this book in the Appendix.

Everybody in the Writers' Room had something to contribute, because among professionals, everybody revises as part of the process. Except perhaps for Harlan Ellison, who says he completes revision in his head before he ever sits down at the typewriter, most established writers see their work through more than one version.

Without spelling out all the reasons we revise, most of us know we have to do it. It's part of our life. Although we may not be able to identify results before we reach the end of the road, we know there is a payoff. Revising, we are learning what we have to say while we figure out the best possible way to say it.

Some start by writing by hand and at a certain point convert to typewriter or computer. Others type or print a draft and then make pen or pencil changes between drafts, and still others make multiple changes as they go along, perfecting each sentence before they move on to the next one. We understand that we get even more from revision than we put into it. Sometimes, we're revising for immediate publication. At other times, with no immediate or specific market in prospect, we revise with even greater intensity because it helps us clarify and focus what we are doing.

In the case of some writers, a faithful exhibition of all the stages of even one paragraph revision would take up several display cases. No two first and last drafts look the same because no two writers work in exactly the same way, but one thing remains constant: everybody revises. A look at a couple of manuscripts will give you an idea what's going on.

We'll begin with a piece of student work because the gap or distance between first and later drafts is usually more pronounced in works by beginning writers. The immediate and obvious payoff makes revision particularly rewarding. Problems are more apparent and results are easier to see. Here is a passage from a student short story, reprinted with the author's permission.

I've duplicated his first version as it looked after I had read and put notes on it. Although they protest that they have rewritten their work before they turn it in, most undergraduate beginners are talking about one or two minor word changes. When we get together they admit this more or less cheerfully and, if we're going to work well together, they move on into more serious consideration of revision. Usually they're astounded by the results. Willingness to revise is perhaps the most important thing I have to teach them.

If my notes seem harsh here, remember, I am trying to do two things: to find out what this writer has to say and help him to say it better, and to get him used to bringing his work up to standard *before* it ever leaves his hands, even in the classroom.

The student and I talked through my notes on this passage, after which he sat down at my computer and arrived at the second version. He found his own way of solving the problems I had pointed out. He also had some ideas about how to tell the rest of his story.

One of the things we discussed at length was the fact that in the original passage he was so busy *describing* things that he had forgotten the need to *demonstrate*. The revision indicates placement of a scene that will show what it is about Nyla that fascinates the narrator. As things *happen* to the characters in a living scene, the author — and readers — will get to know Nyla considerably better.

Nyla was so secure in her self-love that her sense of self simply transcended all other things. She was so comfortable with loving herself, that her self-love was in no way compromised by loving someone else. She would tell you she loved you, if she actually did; but never could you expect that her love for you would influence the way that she might act. Nyla's behavior was solely the function of her first priority - Nyla. This is not to say that Nyla's ego was so pure that she was void of any vanity -- such would be a lie: However, Nyla's vanity was more an indiscretion than a flaw. I mean by this, that her vanities could no more compromise her happiness than could anything else. The green girl was the type of person who could tell you straight out and directly to your face that she was going to hurt you and that she was going to end up screwing you; the type of person who meant it; and the type of person that you believed when they said

18

[handwritten margin notes: "USE ACTIVE VOICE in FICTION ALWAYS" and various editing marks]

[handwritten: EBB your PROSE]

it. She was the one person out of a hundred for whom the ultra serious worked; speeches that would have seemed melodramatic coming from the other ninety-nine, sounded serious when they were spoken by Nyla. And when she would tell you that she was going to end up hurting you - and you wouldn't for a moment doubt her and you would in fact begin to fear the moment as she spoke of it - you wouldn't be repelled from her. With an hypnotic type of aura that only a vampire should possess, she would effortlessly suck you into your own doom as though it were your God given fate.

2 - A

As we sat down together so he could work on this passage, my student watched the prose change for the better. As he worked on perfecting the way he said what he had to say, it became clearer to him and to the reader what he was doing. Cleaning up his prose, trying to make it more precise and direct, he made his meaning clearer. Rewriting, he kept the best of what he had done, tightened and gave it direction.

Now let's look at his revision, the result of a single session.

Nyla was so secure in her self-love that her sense of self simply transcended everything else. She was so comfortable with it that loving someone else was not a compromise. She would tell you she loved you, if she actually did, but you couldn't expect her love for you to influence the way she acted. Nyla's acts were the function of what was most important to her—Nyla. This is not to say that she was without vanity—that would be a lie; it was more of an indiscretion than a flaw.

Here, the author leaves space for a scene. He knows he's going to have to DRAMATIZE and DEMONSTRATE to bring Nyla to the reader.

He's already simplified the prose—and in the process, focused on what he's trying to say about Nyla.

She was the one person out of a hundred for whom the ultra serious worked; speeches that would have seemed melodramatic coming from the other 99, sounded serious when she made them. And when she would tell you that she was going to end up hurting you—and you wouldn't for a moment doubt her and you would in fact begin to fear the moment as she spoke of it—you wouldn't be repelled. With an hypnotic aura that only a vampire should possess, she would effortlessly suck you into your own doom as though it was your God-given fate.

This piece has a few more yards to go, but the difference between the author's first and second drafts is dramatic. He's on the right road; if he keeps working, he's going to find a way to interest an audience in his story.

In a way, starting work on a new draft is easier for beginners than for established writers, because:

1. A professional's first version is likely to look fine, even when the author or editor thinks it's off the mark.
2. Most professionals release only work that has already been through several revisions.

Going back to the drawing board can often be painful, but essential. Approached about this book, novelist and critic Thomas M. Disch (*Camp Concentration*, *The Businessman: A Tale of Terror*) was in the process of quitting two jobs in order to get to the revision of a new novel—work he has to do before it's ready to be published. He confessed that he'd been putting off this revision for two years—taking on extra reviewing chores, teaching, writing an interactive computer game—anything to avoid doing what he knew needed doing. Now he's getting down to it.

The knowledge that revision has worked for him before—and will work again—will keep him going. He knows he has to go the last mile to reach his audience. In the process, he will complete the work to his own satisfaction because the best writers are their own harshest critics.

Disch's notebook pages—and final copy of a published story—demonstrate that professionals don't think they're finished even when the work looks finished. Unlike student work, in which flaws are often apparent, his rough draft looks perfectly acceptable. Only the writer knows there's more to be done here. Disch is editing himself even in the first draft, scrawled into a notebook. In the final draft, he has expanded and developed in some cases, cutting back dialogue for effect in some places and in others, punching it up for emphasis.

A look at Disch's manuscript and other samples included in the Appendix demonstrates what a number of working professionals go through on the way to completing a work of fiction.

For the moment, so you can see how the process looks, let's examine just one writer's manuscript pages. Unlike some writers, who use notebooks only when they're away from home, novelist Lois Gould leaves home in order to work in notebooks. She composed her newest novel, *Subject to Change*, in notebooks.

Gould says an early editor quoted the poet, Valery, on revision: "No work of art is ever completed, it is only abandoned."

For her, as for so many other successful writers, revision is part of composition. It is slow, thorough and rewarding. Gould wrote her new novel and made heavy revisions in one set of notebooks. Then she copied the text into another set, revising as she went. This necessitated a third handwritten copy, which then went to a typist. Gould did another revision on the typescript, which was then corrected and sent to her publisher. She admits that she did further revision in galleys, and has made one or two essential word changes in page proofs, the final stage the author sees before receiving bound copies.

She says, "A publisher once said I would end up revising in some bookstore, snatching the last copy out of a customer's hand, muttering, 'Excuse me, sir, I just thought of a better word. Or two . . .?' "

Attached are a notebook page *from the second draft*, along with corresponding page proofs.

He will test it now, upon his own
body. The screw can be controlled; a
gentle push sliding, a flowering within.

feels his body resist
with it, but does not fall.

Cornelius unwrapped his magical plant-root; in an excellent
now he sits gazing at it, touching it with a trembling finger. Invulnerable
in battle, deadly assurity in the use of weapons, yet the shape of it has
disturbed him; it seems to twist like a woman writhing in pain, in ecstasy,
its color, more corpse-like than brow, by the candlelight of his candle —
then when he first understood it? It sweats, or his palms have made it slippery —
He draws the thing in. Twisting; as it
in the dark folds of his wardrobe he gazed — the root shine
I see him instead a playing thing: the here he's
pear, the petals of the shaker a soothing murmur escapes his throat,
surprising him. He must test it, yet all his
gleams up at him, as though it would speak. He tests it with
light fingers; it springs open. Silent + powerful, power of open
listening to his own breath; the smaller pear will do for another
test, in the morning, he will share it with the king before the jousting
he will spread a salve.

Brother to brother. Flowering
asked innocent right to sire within
when the B. had guarding its treasury
last examined

the queen's precious
Catherine's bedspread, strewn with pearls like
a sunlit sky, lies in a tattered heap upon the floor. Pearls roll
everywhere, the soven is
a forest of frightened animals. False! all false! the queen's
velvet sleeps like the Panther
killed on cushion, within a golden coated serpent
a worthless forgery. This day Catherine has cramidded her treasures
the woman commanded a counting + a reckoning
catalogs, counted her treasures, counted, recounted
a weighing + a balancing
there is no doubt
all
the thievery. The woman has been questioned
the treasurer a hundred servants, guards, grooms
Catherine
cannot deny a certain image, the sound of a pearl crashing
upon a marble floor; Cornelius
hovering over the queen, his hands rigid, holding
as though they held a casket of magical air, of holy spirit, over her entranced
body. how came it there, why falling whence? Cornelius smiled
look, the Cassandra will to dispel the moment.
Now she reflects upon the crowd of messengers, armourers, magnificient
Cornelius + Henry

gician, he must not know the truth of the contest until after he wins it.

SAFE IN HIS ROOMS, Cornelius has unwrapped his magical plant-root, bathed it in an excellent wine, fed it with hearty rough bread. Now he sits gazing at it, touching it with a lover's trembling fingertip. Invulnerable in battle, deadly aim in the use of weapons ... yet the shape of it disturbs him still, arousing a feeling of dread, like a sickness. It is the way its limbs seem to twist, like the limbs of a woman, grotesque, writhing. In pain or ecstasy? Are they one and the same, in a woman? Is the peculiar yellow color of the thing more corpse-like now, by the light of his candle, than when he first unearthed it? Does it sweat, or do his own moist palms make it slip in his grasp? Quaking now, he wraps the hideous thing in its finery, his fingers fumbling with the strips of cloth, leaving it half exposed. He flings open his wardrobe, thrusts the root deep within it, gropes for a safer plaything to occupy his restless hand, and finds it. Hard, cool to the touch, polished: an iron pear. It is a torture instrument of remarkable beauty. He strokes its rounded flanks; a soothing moan escapes his throat, surprising him. He must rest from this agitation he suffers, yet his senses rise. The black pear gleams up at him, as though it would speak. He tests its stem, within which lies the concealed screw; he turns it; the fruit springs open at his command, its perfect crescents silent and powerful, capable of shattering a mouth, teeth, jaws; or the inmost parts of a man or woman. He

it, but does not fall. Why not test the pear, now, upon his own body? The screw can be easily controlled, a gentle insertion of the pear, a sliding, a flowering within; no harm done. If all goes well he will share this fruit with the king. He prepares an unguent now, a salve. Yes. If all goes well, he will share this fruit with the king. Before the jousting. Brother to brother. Knight to sire. Flowering within.

THE QUEEN'S PRECIOUS BEDSPREAD, strewn with pearls like the night sky, lies in a tattered heap upon the floor. Pearls roll and scatter in all directions, white eyes darting into dark corners, until the hushed chamber is a forest filled with frightened animals. False! All false! The queen's fabled rope, coiled upon its velvet cushion, sleeps within its golden casket, guarding its treachery like the serpent in Paradise. A worthless forgery. This day a trusted serving woman, inspired by the lady Diane, inquired, all innocent, when the queen had last examined her treasures; when summoned the catalogues, the records! At once the queen commanded a counting, a recounting, a weighing and a balancing of every relic, every jewel.

There is no doubt of the thievery. The serving woman has been interrogated; all the serving women. The treasurers themselves; a hundred guards and grooms. Catherine cannot dispel a certain image, the sound of a single pearl crashing, rolling upon a marble floor; Cornelius the necromancer hovers over the queen, his white hands poised, rigid, as though they held a priceless gift of magical air,

Yes the notebook pages are hard — almost impossible — to read. For this author, recopying to make her changes legible on a new version is part of the revision process. Every time she does this, something changes and the work develops further. Revising, the author is refining word choices, becoming more precise about objects used by the character; she is furthering the development of the scene as she forges the language to create it. Like Disch, Gould is a stylist, whose choice of language fits and creates her subject.

Novelist, historian and biographer Paul Horgan talks compellingly about revision in his book, *Approaches to Writing* (Farrar, Straus and Giroux, 1974; Wesleyan University Press, 1988). The author, who has won two Pulitzer prizes, threw away five novels before he published *Fault of Angels*, which won the Harper Prize. He is a meticulous craftsman, who composes on the typewriter and revises in pencil, moving on to another typescript and yet another revision. He writes:

> Revision word by word and sentence does follow, for me, not once, but many times, each for different values.
>
> *These embrace precision in meaning*; as between two words of equal precision, choice, then, of that one which calls up image more vividly through color or sound or association; rhythm, the great key to readability, in small units of the text, such as the phrase and the sentence, rhythm in larger developments of the text, such as paragraph and the chapter, and finally rhythm in the work as a whole. In fiction, revision pursues each character of the story in a separate reading to feel the consistency, the living presence of each. Another complete revision is devoted to an examination to improve atmosphere and background. And so on, paying attention to each of the elements, including the humble mechanics, which combine to make a finished work — such matters as simple correctness in spelling, punctuation, grammar, syntax — the technical fabric by which the rich English language, with all its tributaries, is given its primary power of communication.
>
> . . . Such elements as I speak of are the structural fibers of writing, and not to respect them for their own sake, and

to love their purposes and their powers, is to have little promise as a writer..

The italics are mine. They demonstrate an important point about both writing and revision: *We find out what we have to say as we decide how to say it.*

As he reads for rhythm and precision, Horgan's revision develops and organizes what he has to say — *as he works on the way in which he says it.*

If words are the stuff out of which fiction is made, writers need — even in the early stages — to find THE RIGHT ONES. Having completed a draft *the best way we know how, using the best possible materials* from the very beginning, we still need to be careful, critical readers. There is more to be done.

I believe something profound happens to us when we begin revising. Two recent studies of manuscripts and working papers of famous American writers demonstrate.

In his introduction to *Faulkner's Revision of Absalom, Absalom!* Gerald Langford writes:

> As one of the major achievements in twentieth-century fiction, William Faulkner's *Absalom, Absalom!* would be an instructive work in which to study the writer's revisions even if these were confined to matters of word choice and sentence structure. Some of the revisions, however, are structural, and it is particularly interesting to learn that, while writing and reworking the novel, Faulkner altered in several ways his original design. . . . To trace the process of such revision is to experience a sharp focusing of the dominant theme of the novel, and to witness a demonstration of how the meaning of a fictional work can shape its structure and thus stand revealed by what has become the outward and visible sign, or form, of that meaning.

By making a close study of all the working papers of this famous American author, Langford has hit upon and demonstrated the truth of revision. Writers who have the time and patience would do well to look up this University of Texas Press book, which walks the reader through all the stages of Faulkner's struggle with his material. You see the novel develop under the author's hands *as he revises*.

Beginning *The Great Gatsby*, F. Scott Fitzgerald wrote:

"I want to write something *new* — something extraordinary and beautiful and simple + intricately patterned."

He did it at last, but not before throwing out one version of what he was trying to say and starting over from a "new angle." Completing a new draft, he then wrote: "Hard work sets in." He was talking about revision. Once a typist had taken over, he made more changes on what scholar/biographer Matthew J. Bruccoli believes were multiple typescripts.

Bruccoli examines the process in his introduction to a book containing photocopies of Fitzgerald's heavily revised original manuscript (*The Great Gatsby, A Facsimile of the Manuscript*, Micro-card Editions Books). In those days of cheaper composition costs, Fitzgerald made further revisions for editor Maxwell Perkins in the final typescript and completed them in galley proofs. He later wrote: "Max, it amuses me when praise comes in on the 'structure' of the book — because it was you who fixed up the structure, not me." What "fixed up" the structure was Fitzgerald's willingness to continue revision even after the book had been contracted for.

The book he is talking about is his acknowledged masterpiece.

These established writers' drafts demonstrate what to me seems the most important aspect of the process of revision, which cannot be separated from the process of composition. Again, we need to remember, because it is essential to everything we as writers do: *We find out what we have to say even as we are perfecting our ways of saying it.*

This dramatic strengthening of the writer's powers of DE-VELOPMENT and ORGANIZATION is the magical gift revision brings to the writer who has the wits and courage to spend the time on it.

This, then, is the hidden payoff of revision, and the strongest single reason I can think of for anybody who hopes to be a writer to write fiction with the idea that the first version is only the first step on what may be a long, hard road with success at the end.

Knowing what you do now about how established professionals think about their work, ask yourself:

1. When I write, do I try to say exactly what I mean?

2. Am I trying to put down the best thing I have to say in *the best way I can say it*?

3. Do I do this every time, or am I sometimes hasty or careless?

Asking yourself this question, remember that if you don't care about what you're doing, there's no reason any reader should. Your readers are going to get out of this work *only what you put into it*.

4. Am I heading in the right direction?

Remember, a wrong turn is a wrong turn, whether you take it at the very beginning of a story or in the later stages. A wrong choice made early in a piece of work can throw the entire mechanism out of kilter. Ask yourself: *Even in a first draft* can I try harder to find:

    a. The right name for the person or object I'm naming?
    b. The exact verb?
    c. The fresh and accurate adjective?

5. Am I willing to slow down enough to do these things in order to make my intentions clear to my reader?

You may already think you're trying hard in all these categories, and doing pretty well—you probably are. This book is designed to help you do even better.

Once you're committed to doing your absolute best *from the moment you sit down to write*, you're ready for a more detailed approach to revision.

CHAPTER 3

KINDS OF REVISION

YOU MAY BE RELIEVED TO KNOW that there is no right way or wrong way to write or revise fiction. Manuscript samples in the preceding chapter and in the Appendix demonstrate this.

Even moving by at high speeds, you can see that there are almost as many ways of going at revision as there are writers. Every good writer reads for style, character, truth of dialogue and accuracy of detail. These organic parts of the process of revision follow naturally from what I think of as the first two major kinds of revision:

1. *Draft writing, draft revision*. The draft writer gets out a first draft without stopping to look back and make changes. Revision comes in subsequent drafts.

2. *Block construction,* or: *revising as you go*. The writer using block construction revises sentence by sentence, progressing slowly through a story or novel to what is essentially a polished version.

Add to these first two major kinds of revision, a third. This one takes place after the story or novel exists in more or less complete form. It is:

3. *Revision to strengthen structure and story*. Reading for story, character, shape and what to put in and what to leave out, you may think you've already done this. Then it's time to read the work one more time—and do it again, if you have to. This involves an overall look at what appears to be a finished manuscript. It comes after all those considerations of style, character,

truth of dialogue and accuracy of detail are completed. This third kind of revision comes *after you think you're finished*.

Because they're part of the process of composition, we'll begin with the first two methods of revision.

Most writers use a combination of these first two methods. Draft writers are making word choices and phrase selections even as they move through the first draft, finding story and establishing structure. Sentence draft writers will perfect each sentence and each paragraph as they move on to the end of what looks like a finished and completely polished version, but then go back to do fine-tuning and in some cases find themselves making a structural revision.

Whichever method you use, you need to remember: AMONG PROFESSIONALS, REVISION IS PART AND PAR-CEL OF COMPOSING.

I. DRAFT WRITING, DRAFT REVISION

Some writers get their stories down *fast*, writing a rough draft while the idea is hot. They do their revising and fine-tuning on their second draft, their third, their eighth. They want to see the whole story so they can work with it.

Novelist and short story writer C.E. Poverman, whose first collection won the Iowa School of Letters Award for Short Fiction, quotes William Saroyan on this: "Something is better than nothing." Even if it's imperfect by nature, the first draft is a beginning.

A rough draft gives you a place to start.

It's far more productive to have a draft to work with—however faulty—than to sit staring at a blank page or a blank screen because our self-confidence is shaky, or because we're determined that the first sentence of the first page we write must be perfect.

This is particularly important to writers who can't get started because they can't bear to put down anything that isn't perfect. We all know so-called perfectionists who brood endlessly over a pocket full of ideas or the same handful of pages, letting us know that they are sitting on the greatest work on earth—if it ever gets finished. They may think they are perfectionists but they're only fooling themselves; they're putting off getting started.

Until you have something on the page, you aren't really writing fiction, you're only talking about it.

Remember, *nothing you write is carved in stone*. Draft writers know better than anybody that a faulty version of a story or novel is better than no version at all, and they know better than anybody that the first draft gives them something concrete that will improve as they work on it. They get down their ideas in a draft that from the beginning is designed to be rewritten. Thus: *first draft*.

A first draft is a starting place. *Once it's out there, we can do anything we want with it.*

Humorist James Thurber put it another way: "Don't get it right, get it written."

Survival Tactics

Some draft writers like to make a distinction between drafts by the methods they use to put their work on paper. It gives them the sense that they are making progress. Some will start with a notebook, composing by hand. When the notebook gets too hard to read, they let a typist make a clean copy so they can enter further changes by hand.

It cheers them up to see the first hesitant pages with scrawled notes and crossings-out replaced by a clean typescript. The progression to each new stage is a big milestone.

Others begin writing by hand and for the second draft, go directly to the typewriter or the computer. People who compose on typewriter or computer will choose different kinds of ink or paper to mark the progress from one draft to the next, or move from dot matrix to letter quality printer—anything to mark progress.

Advancing to a second draft, the draft writer goes back to correct the first and sometimes sketchy version, and to expand on it. Suggested descriptions take a fuller form. Hastily sketched scenes develop into full-blown dramatic moments. New scenes develop. The story organizes itself.

Advantages of Draft Writing

1. The psychological trick — thinking "it's only a draft" — makes it easier to get started. Think of a runner or a swimmer warming up. We've all got to write that first page sometime, and for many draft writers, the first draft is a warmup.

2. First drafts are often like first loves — vivid and passionate. The draft writer manages to enjoy all of the pleasure and excitement that come with a new idea, the delight that comes with invention. They are at the very beginning of the long road between first thought and finished product. The skilled draft writer manages to keep a sense of this first energy and passion in subsequent, more detailed and more fully developed versions.

3. A draft is an efficient way to find out where the story is going. Once the first draft is finished, you have the entire story in front of you. There are the bare bones of the idea more or less outlined, along with some of those inspired moments — the paragraphs or scenes that make it directly from the world of inspiration and onto the page without running out of control in the process.

4. The writer with a finished first draft knows where the story has been and where it's going. The first draft lets you see the entire story, from beginning to end — how it starts and what happens. *Because you know how the story comes out*, it's possible to go back to the beginning and make everything point toward the inevitable ending. Revising, you have the advantage of foresight and hindsight.

5. Early drafts by a true draft writer are the place for experiments and adventures, hits and easily forgiven misses. The investment of time is not as great as it will be when you reach the "final" draft, and rewrites are not as daunting. This is, after all, only a draft you are working on.

Writing in *The New York Times Book Review*, short story writer

David Huddle underlines the importance of recognizing a draft for what it is—something written on the way to what you are really writing. He talks about esthetic luck, suggesting that, like athletes, writers have good days and bad days:

> Esthetic luck is the major argument in favor of working through a process of revising a piece of writing though many drafts. If you're a supremely talented artist and you hit a very lucky day, then maybe you can write a poem or story or chapter of a novel that needs no revision. If you're a regular writer with your appointed portion of esthetic luck, you'll need to come at the piece again and again. I like to think of revision as a form of self-forgiveness; you can allow yourself mistakes and shortcomings in your writing because you know you're coming back later to improve it. Revision is the way you cope with the bad luck that made your writing less than brilliant this morning. Revision is the hope you hold out for yourself to make something beautiful tomorrow though you didn't quite manage it today.

6. The time scheme—how long it takes between writing the first page of one draft and beginning the next one—allows leeway for second thoughts, further development. You can think about changes, make further notes. Many draft writers make large organizational changes between drafts. Others discover that the story develops more fully and sometimes changes significantly between drafts. Think of time-lapse photographs of a child—at infancy, three, five, eight. It's the same child, but bigger and more fully developed. A child grows and changes. So will your manuscript.

II. BLOCK CONSTRUCTION: REVISING AS YOU GO

Having said all that about the advantages of draft writing, I wonder why I proceed the way I do—the way so many other writers do—perfecting each sentence, each paragraph and each page before going on to the next one.

I'll call what we do *block construction*.

I happened into block construction because I'm an essentially lazy person. Remember those sixty-six busted stories. The idea of writing a first draft *and then writing the whole thing all over* seemed horrible to me. Think of all that trouble! Think of all that time spent on making a new draft, copying the thing over in order to make changes. I used to think of it as time wasted.

If I could only get a story right the first time, I thought, I wouldn't have to rewrite it. I could spend my life avoiding revision.

Impatient by nature, I was never meant to be a draft writer. Instead, drawing on the experience of my newspaper days, I decided to shortstop criticism by making my first draft as right as I could make it. Composing on the typewriter, I was willing to type and retype and keep retyping my beginning *until I had it absolutely right*.

Clever me. No rewrites for me, I thought. My first draft is my only draft. Never mind how long it takes me to reach the end of it. Remember, this was the act of a lazy person.

Because I was convinced I was avoiding work by taking more pains at the beginning, I was happy to type and retype and retype a page *of my only draft*; I was willing to spend just as long on it as I had to spend to make it right, just as long as I thought when I wrote "the end" I was really going to be finished.

It's only now, as I remember the cartons upon cartons of working papers I piled up that I see how I managed to fool myself. Thinking I was taking the easy way out, I moved naturally into the essential habit of hard work. Discarded sentence and page drafts show me exactly how hard I worked then — how hard I'm still working. At the time it seemed natural and logical. It still does. Perhaps the key to the success of block construction is logic.

Sentence Draft Writers Begin at the Beginning

Reporters say that once you have your lead, your story is written. It seemed to me that if I could get my first sentence right, I would have my story in hand. I wrote and rewrote the first sentence until the second unrolled more or less naturally. I worked on the first paragraph until I had it right before moving on to the second. I perfected the first page before moving on to the next.

Something interesting happened along the way. If I made a word change or even a typing error on a page I would pull it out of the typewriter and start retyping it. Every time I did this, something happened. Sometimes I ended up reorganizing a paragraph I hadn't even realized needed it; other times I would find the story had taken its next logical turn, or a character would demonstrate depths I hadn't known were there the first time I wrote the scene. In the course of rewriting and re-rewriting (who was I fooling? I was never just retyping), in the course of improving the way I told my story, I made discoveries about it. My story developed as I forged the telling.

I was figuring out what I had to say as I found the right way to say it. From character names to setting details to precise nouns and exact verbs, word choices determine the course of fiction. Let me give you some idea how this happens.

Computer freaks play a game called *Zork*, the granddaddy of interactive computer games. The first screen gives minimal information. You are standing in a field. There is a mailbox next to you; in one direction there is a house; in another, a forest. You must decide which way to go. The next stage of the story reveals itself as you make your initial choices.

At every stage, making a choice uncovers more story and reveals a new batch of options.

If you choose the house, and find the trap door under the rug in the living room, you are let into a vast underground labyrinth. At each step you are presented with new choices. Go one way and you may be killed by the troll. Go another and you are on your way to discovering uncounted underground treasures. You must consider each choice carefully because each offers a different set of options.

Move slowly, choose carefully and you'll discover the extent of the underground kingdom. You may even survive to come back aboveground with all those treasures.

In a way, as writers, we are all exploring unknown territory.

Choose this narrative point of view and those characters and you've already decided a number of things about your story. You are developing narrative options. Block construction makes us make these choices *in order* and slows the rate at which we make them. Perfecting sentence by sentence, building block by block narrows the margin for error, as you choose among your options. Correct choices will lead you to the right ending for the piece of fiction you are writing.

I'm not the only writer who works this way. If you look at the drafts reproduced in the Appendix, you'll see that each of these writers is in an individual way refining and improving on what is on the page before moving on. And in each case the payoff is developmental.

Advantages to Block Construction

1. In some ways, commitment to sentence drafts is liberating. It allows us to play psychological tricks on ourselves in some of the ways draft writers do when they establish milestones by changing from pen or pencil to keyboard, or from one to another kind of paper.

a. It's easy to get to work because I don't have to write the whole story or chapter today. I don't even have to write a whole page. All I have to do is get one or two good sentences. If things don't go well today, I won't die because I also know there's some kind of buildup of energy. Ideas develop overnight. As long as I have something on the page, it's going to get better tomorrow.

b. This isn't a draft. Revision isn't daunting because it doesn't seem so much like revision. We're not talking about recasting a whole novel here, or even a whole story. I'm only rewriting a sentence. Never mind all those cartons of working papers. Perfecting one sentence at a time seems easy because after all, a sentence is only a sentence.

c. I have the advantage of the running head start. If things aren't going well I can always go back and tinker with the last few pages I wrote yesterday. By the time I've done the last bits of housekeeping on yesterday's work, refining this string of words, expanding that one, making narrative decisions as I go, I have a running head start into today's work. I've found out what's going to happen next.

2. Block construction makes writers begin at the beginning. Perfecting a first page, the writer is setting the style and the tone, pace and point of view of what is going to follow. By the time I have written a first page to my satisfaction, I know who is telling or observing the story, what the rhythms are. I am beginning to understand how to write what happens next.

3. As I suggest above, block construction is developmental. Not all of us start with a story completely formed in our heads, just waiting to be transferred to the page. Most of us who write longer fiction are like those computer freaks, playing *Zork*. We have to make choices in order to find out what we know, discovering details about our characters, listening closely to what they have to say to each other. Once we know who these people really *are*, we can find out what's going to happen to them. We know exactly how they're going to respond or react in any given situation.

The work develops naturally, limiting the possibility for characters to act out of character and protecting us from making hasty, sometimes wrong, narrative choices.

4. Block construction gives us time to solve problems as they come up, instead of putting them off for a later draft. All writers are doing work in their heads even when they look as if they aren't working. We walk around carrying unsolved problems in our heads, with our subconscious hard at work on unanswered questions. Building page by page, those of us who work by block construction move on to the next scene only after this one is solid.

5. We're discovering what we have to say. Advancing at the rate of a few paragraphs or a couple of pages a day, we find that much of our work is done in our heads in the hours between the time when we get up from work and the next day when we go back to it. Sometimes this means walking away from a story problem, letting it sit overnight. More often than not, we come back the next day to discover that the problem has solved itself. At other times, notes present themselves in batches. Ideas that were barely hatched on one day are all grown up by the next one.

6. Because we started at the beginning and are building block by block, things happen in order. This gives narrative control: events proceed logically and characters are true to themselves.

Looking at what I've done after a scene has developed, I may have to go back to expand or to cut, to change the shadings in a certain section or to explain a little more. What I don't have to do is go back and change what's happened, or try to wrench characters back on track. Characters who develop naturally behave that way.

REVISION AS A WAY OF LIFE

I said I began to compose this way, revising as I went, because I am an essentially lazy person who hated the idea of revision. This is particularly interesting to me now in view of all those cartons of working papers, in view of the fact that I can't number the hundreds of changes and corrections I've made even in the process of writing this chapter. It's clear that by trying to second-guess critics and get things right the first time, I backed into revision as a way of life. It is part and parcel of every paragraph I write.

The cold truth, however, is that in spite of all the dozens of stages I go through in composition, I am no better off than draft writers. Like them, when I write "the end," I'm not necessarily finished.

There are questions all of us need to ask ourselves, whether we're sitting down to read a first draft or a manuscript we think is essentially finished:
- Is it a story?
- Does something really happen? Is it going to be clear to the reader?
- If this is a story, is it as good as I can make it? Is it all here or are there key scenes or details missing? Do I need to cut or expand to enhance organization?
- Even though I think it's all here, are the scenes just sketched, or are they fully developed, so the reader will see what I see?

- Does everything unfold in the right order?
- Am I describing, or TELLING, more than I am demonstrating through scenes; i.e., SHOWING?
- Is it too long for what it does?
- If so, where does it need cutting?
- What about the tone? Does the whole thing sound as if it's written by the same person?

Whether you compose through several drafts or work mainly by block construction, so that your first attempt *looks* finished, you need to sit down, *read carefully* and ask yourself all these questions.

WHAT'S NEXT

As I suggested at the beginning of this chapter, there is no right or wrong way to write or revise fiction. Most of us find the way that's most comfortable for us, and it's likely to be a combination of draft and block writing and revision. No matter which mehod we choose, sooner or later we come up against that moment when we have written "the end" and discover we still need to consider one more reading, for that third major kind of revision: revision to strengthen structure and story.

This raises an important point. *There are things you have to do even after you think you are finished.*

Reading for Revision to Strengthen Structure and Story

All of us who write for a living take a work as far as we can take it before it leaves our hands. If we are draft writers we've worked through as many drafts as it takes us to arrive at a finished product. If we work by block construction, we've considered and reconsidered at every stage to make our story as good as we can make it. In some cases everything is fine. In others, we're too close to what we've written to see it from the outside.

We need help moving on to the next stage—what I think of as the third major kind of revision. I'm talking about reading with the idea that we may need to make further revisions to strengthen structure and story. This is the final judgment, shaping and in some cases reordering that makes a story or a novel move in a straight line from beginning to end. Whether we compose by draft or put our fiction together block by block, many of us think we've finished a story or a novel when, in fact, it's still not quite right. It may be too long in some places, or underdeveloped in others, or the major sections may be out of order.

We're reading for:

1. Truth of action
2. Accessibility
3. Completeness
4. Time scheme
5. Point of view
6. Length (with an eye to possible cutting)
7. Organization
8. And, once again, balance of showing versus telling.

I'll give you a special checklist and talk about this third major kind of revision at length in Chapter Eight: Reading for Story and Structure.

Finding Out Whether You're Finished

Meanwhile, it's important to note that most of us need help reaching the point where we're able to make this kind of judgment about a recently finished work. Some of us need to know when to persist. Others need to be told when to quit.

As writers, we've lived inside our story or novel on a day-to-day basis for so long that we're like construction workers with a complete set of blueprints who see only the immediate details of what they're building: how things are put together, what materials they're using. We're too close to our work to be able to see it clearly.

Whether we need to be told to stop or ordered to persist, we all need outside readers. It's time to get away from our work — to walk out of the house of words we have been building so we can stand back and get a good look at it.

This is the only way we're ever going to be able to see what it looks like to others.

We need distance.

CHAPTER 4

HOW TO FIND OUT WHETHER YOU'RE FINISHED WHEN YOU THINK YOU'RE FINISHED

YOU'VE JUST FINISHED a story.

How do you feel about it?

Because you've just finished, you may feel all those good things about finishing this piece of work: happy it's over, proud of it, hopeful for its future. You may also feel some not-so-good things — uncertainty as to whether your judgment is objective, that nagging suspicion that readers aren't going to see what you see, that your piece may not be all there yet.

You recognize the need for revision in an abstract way, but remember, you've just finished this story you're so proud of. How are you supposed to know whether it needs revision?

You may think it's the best thing you've done so far and it may be, but is it as good as you think it is? Is it as good as you can make it? Some wit pointed out that even a skunk smells like a gardenia to its mother.

Remember, some writers need to be told to persist, while others need to be told when to quit.

If you'd rather start something new than improve what you have, you belong in the first category.

If you'd rather go back than go forward, you belong in the second. Many beginning writers get so committed to process that they forget they're on the way to a finished manuscript — a piece of work they can walk away from with a sense of pride and

41

accomplishment. They'd rather brood over a manuscript, cherish it and fuss with tiny changes than begin something new or find out what other people think of what they've written. Compulsive tinkering helps them maintain the illusion that they're writers without ever having to do what professionals do:

1. Finish.
2. Lay it on the line and have it judged by others.

They tell themselves and others that they're *on the way to something perfect* when in fact they're not going anywhere.

They're protecting their sensitive feelings and putting off the inevitable hard work that comes with starting something new. These compulsive revisers make endless insignificant changes because it gives them the illusion that they're working while protecting them from the moment of truth.

If you are inclined to tinker, you may need to be ruthless with yourself. Set a limit to the number of drafts you will write before you put your story aside and/or *get an outside reading*.

Which kind of writer are you?

Whether you find it too easy to quit — or too hard — you're going to have to ask yourself a few hard questions.

1. Have I taken this piece of work as far as I can take it?
2. Have I made everything clear or am I leaving too much to my reader's imagination?
3. How does it stack up against other stories of its kind?

Now, how are you going to know the answers? It's time to distance yourself. You can do this in several ways.

SEEING YOUR STORY AS A WHOLE

There are three ways in which writers learn what stories are shaped like, and find out how to tell whether a particular story is in working order. You will learn:

1. By writing so many stories that you as writer know *from*

the inside what stories are shaped like and how they work. If you write enough stories over enough years, you'll see this for yourself. If you're willing to be flexible about when to revise — and when to quit. If you keep at it long enough, you will eventually develop the professional's *sense of rightness*. This is the click — as if of a camera's shutter — that lets you know the picture is complete. Part of the business of this book is to help you to write, and write enough so that you can find out what stories feel like *from the inside*. It's one of the best ways to find out whether they're in working condition.

2. Through reading.

3. Through distancing.

4. With the help of outside readers.

BACKGROUND IN READING

Writers probably ought to spend as much time reading fiction as they do on their own writing.

To answer questions about your own work honestly and accurately, you need some basis for comparison — a sense of what the competition is like, and what the winners are doing. I'm assuming that if you want to write fiction and care about what you're doing, you already do a lot of reading.

You need to read as widely as you can, to have such a broad background in fiction that you escape the danger of focusing on one writer or one particular style of writing and getting trapped writing second-rate imitation. If you read hundreds of stories, dozens of novels, you'll develop a built-in sense of form — what good fiction looks like to the reader. If you know what *hundreds* of short stories look like, then you begin to develop a sense of what makes a good short story. You're not doing this in order to imitate. Instead you're finding out what fiction is about by reading as much as you can make time for.

The same is true of longer fiction.

If you know what kind of a writer you are — mainstream or science fiction or romance or mystery, it makes sense to read a lot of the specific *kind* of thing you think you are writing, everything from acknowledged classics to what's being published this year. Reading work by new writers, you're going to come up against their successes and failures. Judging their work, you'll know better how to judge your own.

In a way, it's like judging show dogs. You have to know what the *best* Scottie looks like before you can tell whether or not you have a good one. Yours may be adorable, but unless he measures up, he's not going to qualify for the show.

As a writer and not a Scottie trainer, you have a major advantage: *You can be as original as you like as long as your fiction succeeds in its own terms.*

Reading widely and writing extensively, you will begin to develop a sense of whether or not a story is working. Notice what characterizes traditional stories, with beginnings, middles, ends—and how far experimental writers go in nontraditional stories. The sky's the limit AS LONG AS THE STORY IS WORKING. If you write enough stories, you will develop the *insider's sense of rightness.* Judging the work of professionals, from the authors of acknowledged masterpieces to contemporary fiction, you'll begin to see when stories work for you, and when they don't. This helps you set standards for your own fiction. You'll know when your own stories are working. As you gain confidence, you can begin to explore and experiment. Remember, you can do anything you want in a story as long as it works.

DISTANCING

If you've done everything you can with a story—taken it through several drafts—and you're doubtful about whether this piece is a success or not, and how you feel about it, you're still too close. You may need help moving out of the story or novel you've built so you can see it from the outside.

You're going to want to find out:

1. Whether it's really finished.
2. Whether it works.
3. Whether after your revisions, it still needs revision.
4. Which parts need work.

5. What to do.
6. How to go about it.

You're going to get specific suggestions for revising in chapters to come, but right now we're talking about how you, as writer, can find out what about your work may need revising.

It's time to distance yourself so you can make some harsh judgments.

First we'll talk about informal distancing. There are a couple of ways to do this. For many of us, the first is the hardest.

1. *Put it away for a while.* My resident critic calls this letting the lasagna set before you serve it. A few days, or weeks, or months of distance from the actual writing of your story give your pulse and heartbeat time to return to normal. If it was love at first sight, a second look may change your mind.

By the time you return to the piece of work you were so proud of, the first fine flush of romance will have given way to the clearer light of reality.

Faults are going to be easier to spot. Gaps and missing links will be more apparent. Things you as writer knew but failed to tell the reader are going to show up because in time, you'll finally be able to forget what you knew as writer and start to function as reader. The flush of inspiration gives way to the harsh light of a critical reading. You may even find yourself saying, "I can't believe I did that."

Unfortunately, most of us hate to *lose the time*. We have a hard time putting away work we think is finished. We're pleased to be finished and a little proud. There's no fun in having a new toy if we can't show it to the other kids. More important, we're anxious to find out whether others like it as much as we do.

2. If you can't stand to put it away, then *read it aloud*.
   a. To yourself. Reading aloud gives you another kind of distance from what you've written. Those words are no longer private things, secrets kept between you and the page. Instead they're rolling around in the room. Klunky prose and untrue dialogue become particularly apparent in this kind of reading.
   b. To somebody else. This kind of reading aloud is excruciating for most of us and extremely productive. In addi-

tion to hearing that klunky prose and untrue dialogue *along with* the listener, you're going to become painfully aware of boring stretches—things that go on too long for what they do, dramatic moments that don't come off, missing links or gaps in the narrative. If you've done your work well, there's also the possibility for instant gratification—the gasp at what horrifies, laughter at what's funny.

OUTSIDE READERS

Let's say you've done some or all these things. If you've read this piece of work aloud to a patient listener, you've already moved into phase two: audience. Let's say you're sensitive; if anybody says a harsh word, you're going to die. One of the first things you're going to need to learn as writer is how to *not die.* This means learning how to subject your work to scrutiny and take criticism as calmly as possible. Nobody is going to like your work as well as you do, but your work doesn't have much of a life for itself until somebody else reads it.

Remember, unless you're a closet writer, writing for yourself with no intention of letting anybody else see what you've done, eventually you're going to run up against the outside reader. You can call the shots, however, by deciding whether to try your work out on a trusted friend or a teacher or, at the formal level, by submitting it to an editor or magazine. Although there are dozens of possible ways to get readings, there are three routes to an audience:

1. Informal readings.
2. Workshop or classroom setting.
3. Hitting the front line—aiming for publication.

One-on-One Readings

If you opt for individual, or one-on-one readings, there may be questions you can ask your readers—trusted friends, mates, relatives. Since informal situations are sensitive at best and depend heavily on your relationship with the person you've asked to read, you'll have to feel your way to some extent, tailoring questions according to the story in question. Because no two stories—or readers—are alike, there are no hard-and-fast rules on this one. Some of these attitudes, however, can also help you in workshop or classroom. When getting one-on-one readings, remember:

1. You may be feeling fragile, but this is a sensitive situation for your reader, too. If a negative response is going to ruin your friendship, find a reader who has less at stake.
2. Try to leave your reader alone with your work. If you're rattling around the room or hanging over your reader's shoulder, you're not going to get as close a reading as you'd like.
3. Don't prejudice your reader. Hold comments and questions until the end.
4. Don't go fishing for praise. Be direct: "What do you think?"
5. After you get the reader's general impression, ask for details.

Let's assume your reader did not respond with a standing ovation. There are things you want to know. Base specific questions on:

a. What your reader just said. If there are things your reader likes, you'll want to know what they are. If your reader thinks there are problems, keep talking until you have the details—what the reader thinks are problems, why and where.

b. Your own questions about the manuscript. Now is the time to raise any doubts you may have about whether your story's all there, whether your reader sees what you were trying to say, whether individual scenes are working, whether you've done what you set out to do—write something funny or dramatic or suspenseful or frightening. Now's the time to ask, "Did you get so-and-so?" "Is it too. . ."

Be a Good Listener

Perhaps the most important thing you need to know in putting your work before an audience—even your mom—is that you're going to get a response, and the response is not always going to be positive. With this in mind, there are several important things to know about getting a reading, beginning with how to listen to criticism. The attitudes toward criticism you form in one-on-one readings will help you in group situations.

1. Keep an open mind. You asked for this reading. Unless you listen to the response, the effort is wasted.

2. Don't expect applause. If you get it, naturally you're going to be delighted, but if you expect to use this reader more than once, you're going to have to ask for complete honesty and be grateful, not angry, when you get it.

3. Don't expect specific suggestions for rewriting. Remember, readings are for diagnostic purposes. Expect your reader to point out problems, not to solve them. It's enough for your reader to say something makes sense or doesn't, or works or doesn't. It's up to you to figure out what to do about it.

4. If you get specific suggestions, remember: readers aren't always right. Take what advice you can use and reserve judgment on the rest. Sort out what you can use from what you can't use. No reader is likely to be right on target about *every single thing*. Complaints or suggestions are useful at pinpointing *symptoms*. Don't count on your reader to supply the cure.

5. Don't argue. It makes more sense to stand back and reconsider than to use up good time defending what you've written. Even when you think your reader is wrong about something, you're not going to gain anything by arguing. Argument wastes time and alienates your reader. If you fight to the mat with a reader over comments on something you've done, trying to force a change of mind, you're going to lose your reader.

6. Be constructive, not defensive. Look at this in a workmanlike way: If these are my reader's objections, what can I do to my story to make it readerproof?

7. Don't act hurt, either. If you think you're going to be a professional, you're going to have to learn how to be professional in your responses. You asked for an honest opinion, and whether or not you like what you got, you're going to have to act grateful for the time the reader spent on you.

8. Keep the lines of communication open. If you get a negative response, ASK QUESTIONS. Remember, you're pinpointing symptoms. Questions can often help you locate the source of a reader's objections. When this happens, discussion can help you figure out what's *really* wrong, and how to fix it.

9. If you're doubtful about recommendations you get from your first reader, get a second opinion. You'd do this if you were going in for surgery. In a way, this is the same thing. You're trying to find out whether there's anything the matter with the patient, so you can decide what to do for it. If you think you may have to perform surgery on what you've written, it's logical to get a second opinion.

With these general rules in mind, it's time to look for your audience. Here are some ways to go about it, beginning with the one-on-one readings that will help you learn to live with criticism.

1. *Getting informal readings.* Give the work you think is finished to a trusted reader. Most of us are lucky enough to have somebody to try our work out on—the dress rehearsal for friends before the show goes on before a more critical audience. This trusted reader may be a teacher you had in high school or college who is still interested in your work and willing to read it, a fellow writer or a member of the family. Some people like to give work to three or more readers, sending out several copies of a book or story at a time to compare responses so they can triangulate. Because this reader is somebody you know personally, pay special attention to the rules for being a good listener. Friendships or relationships are at stake here. If you can't get along with your first reader, find another one.

2. *Workshop or classroom setup.* Not everybody has a friend, relative, colleague or present or former teacher with solid literary judgment. For people in most cities, towns and communities, there are other ways to get your work read and discussed on a relatively informal basis. There are people out there who are interested in the same things you are.

In ascending order of focus, demand for commitment and effectiveness, these include:

a. The informal writing group. Some people like to find others interested in writing, who meet to share work and exchange opinions. These groups are usually made up of beginning writers, which means they may not be as far along in what they're doing as you are. As most writers, particularly beginning writers, usually criticize fiction in terms of what they themselves like to write, they're likely to think you should solve your problems the way they solve their problems. The difficulty, then, is taking the criticism for what it's worth, considering the source in each case.

Like all groups, however, the informal writing group fulfills a key function. If you show your piece to eight people in a group and seven out of eight don't get it, chances are you have a problem.

b. The writing workshop. In these days of proliferating undergraduate and graduate writing programs in American colleges and universities, there are plenty of writing classes available. Many colleges and universities open some classes to people who aren't regular students. Others have special extension programs, offering classes at night or on weekends. Community colleges offer classes. Often they are taught by people who are writers themselves, and they offer the opportunity for active and detailed group discussion at an essentially professional level.

c. The graduate writing program. This involves a big investment of time and money, and all-out commitment. You're going to give up a year or two of your life in exchange for classroom experience, advice from professionals and the benefit of workshop discussion of your fiction.

Another option is the summer writers' conference. With the exception of the workshop at Bennington and the Clarion Writers Conference, most of those available offer courses for no more than two weeks at most, which means they are not as useful as long-term arrangements in helping you locate regular readers.

In all these situations, you make friends outside group meetings, including, perhaps, the one who becomes your trusted first reader. Most people in discussion groups and workshops exchange work on an informal basis outside group meetings, with writers zeroing in on the others in the group who are most in tune with what they are doing.

3. *Hit the Front Line*. You have to be feeling fairly strong to do this, because we're talking about sending your manuscript to somebody who's going to judge it as fit or unfit for publication. Your story or novel has to be in good enough shape to withstand professional scrutiny, and you personally have to be feeling strong enough to live with rejection.

There is, however, an interim position. You may want to get your feet wet by sending a covering letter and a brief sample of your work to a literary agent in hopes that you'll find somebody willing to represent you. Naturally, your letter should be as compelling as possible, and you're going to stand a better chance if you've managed to garner a couple of publications.

Assuming you're at Square One, that brings you to the bottom line, which is also the front line. You're going to have to try to get published.

This means mailing your manuscript to an editor or publisher who you think may like it. The risks are clear:

a. The rejection slip. Once it comes, at least you know not everybody loves your manuscript. By now you've achieved some distance from your story — the weeks or months it takes the professional reader to make a decision. If your story comes back, don't send it right back out automatically. Sit down and reread it. If it still looks as good to you as it did the first time you mailed it, then by all means try two or three more submissions. If the rejection has identified story problems for you, *go back to the drawing board*.

b. The qualified rejection. This is the letter or rejection slip that says no, and then explains why. In spite of what you might think, most writers take the qualified rejection as a good sign. It means the editor or publisher was interested enough in the manuscript to take the time to dignify it — and the writer — with a personal comment. Editors don't write these notes just to be nice. They write them because they've seen something in your work that interests them. If they respond with details about what you might do to make this story better, you have your blueprint for revision. Rewrite and resubmit. You just may be in business.

Clearly, there are many ways of testing your work. If you've put a story or a novel through one or more of them and you still get negative signals, then it's time to reconsider. It still needs work.

WHAT'S NEXT?

Let's say you've taken one or more or all of these steps, and although people may like certain things about what you've written, they don't like the work as a whole. It becomes clear that there's still a gap between what you thought you were doing and what you've actually accomplished.

This means in spite of what you told yourself when you wrote "the end" at the bottom of your piece and said, "there" and handed it to other readers or mailed it, *you're not finished*. Your piece isn't doing what you wanted it to.

Ask yourself:

1. Are these readers right?
2. If so, do I know what the problem really is?
3. Do I know what to do about it?

If the answers to all three of these questions are yes, then you're ready to go ahead with your revision.

If the answers are no, particularly if you're a beginning writer, you've reached a delicate point in which you have to decide whether to push forward with this piece or whether it's time to cut your losses.

Triage

Hard-pressed medics in the old days went among the wounded on the battlefield, practicing something called *triage*. This meant looking into the faces of each of the wounded and deciding which ones were going to profit most from medical attention. Since the medics were short-staffed, they couldn't waste time working on patients who were going to die anyway.

1. If consistent negative readings and a number of rejections have shaken your faith in a piece of work, then it's probably time to cut your losses. This doesn't mean throwing it out. It means putting it away. In the time you spend working on something new, work that's put aside will either get stronger in your imagination or it will die quietly. Either way, you win. You've achieved the necessary distance and you've done something even more important; by refusing to waste time mourning, you've feathered your nest with a new piece of fiction.

2. If consistent negative readings and rejections give you a clear set of signals that point the way to a successful revision, you've gained ground. It's time to take in the wounded piece of fiction and get your priorities in order.

There's more work to be done.

But let's backtrack. The question posed by this chapter was how to find out whether you're finished when you think you're finished. You let your work fly and saw it shot down like a wild duck on its way to a happier place.

Naturally you don't want that to happen to this story again, or to the next one or the next one. As you revise this time, as you begin the next story or the next, *protect yourself*.

When you send this piece out again, you want it to be as strong as you can make it. This means asking yourself a series of hard questions about style, character and truth of dialogue, story and setting. It means standing back from the whole and considering a structural revision.

I've suggested that wide reading is going to give you a good basis for comparison, a sense of form and a more highly developed power of judgment. It's also going to help point the way to more effective writing.

Add to this background of reading a list of questions you should ask yourself, *as you're writing* and *as you're revising*.

Part of the business of this book is to provide some of these questions. I want to help you shortstop criticism and arm yourself against rejection by making a habit of asking yourself all the hard questions I'm going to pose in coming chapters.

These hard questions are designed to engage you in the process of total revision. Forewarned is forearmed. Once you make them part of your working equipment, you'll be able to make revision a way of life.

Because your house of words is precisely that—something you are making out of words—you'll want to work with the best available materials.

Because this means making the words march *in the right direction so your story will move in the right direction*, we'll begin by talking about style.

From the first page you write, you're making countless narrative decisions—from establishing point of view to naming and placement of characters in time and physical location to the nature of characters' relationships. Because what you as storyteller say is, essentially, *inseparable from the way in which you say it*, we're going to start by discussing style and numbering the kinds of questions you ought to be asking yourself as you write.

CHAPTER 5

BUILDING YOUR STORY

STORIES ARE MADE OUT OF WORDS.

The idea for a story may come before the words do, but if you want to get your idea across to readers, you have to use words to do it. If you're going to be a storyteller and not a filmmaker or a draftsman or a master painter, then words are your materials. You'll want to work with the best ones.

When you're making a house of words, you have to pay particular attention to your opening. *From the beginning* the way you write is important, because the words you choose to open your story are going to invite the reader to pick your story up — or put it down. What's more, the opening paragraphs set the tone and make the rules for that particular story. As author, you're beginning to make choices. With every sentence you write, you're making narrative decisions. Making choices, you're establishing your style.

Now let's look at some of the things style does for you.

YOUR STYLE SETS UP YOUR STORY

The way you write helps define and determine what you're writing. Choosing words to begin a story, you're establishing the ground rules — how you're going to deal with your material.

Say you begin by describing a night. It is an August night in Washington, D.C.: hot, close, noisy, empty of people and crowded with memories. The waters of three A.M. are closing over your character's head: the dark night of the soul from which there is no emerging.

Notice that although we have only four lines here, and this is only a summary, *something is happening*. Each adjective defines and qualifies. Every choice creates something: time, place, mood, situation. Now let's pretend I've decided to make something of these elements.

> Martin had spent too many Augusts in Washington; the streets were filled with wraiths of former selves—happy people who could not hear his warnings. Even though it was so hot that nobody was out and nothing moved, he could almost see the two of them drifting down Independence Avenue—Martin and beautiful, lost Carla walking through shimmering heat mirages. He wanted to reach out and touch the lovers, to beg them to stop and reconsider, but in the next second they were gone and he was adrift again, cut loose in the miasma of three o'clock in the morning.

Enough. In a few lines we know who and where Martin is, that he's trying to outrun an unhappy love story, and that the general tone is going to be both romantic and elegiac. The rhythm sets the mood. Although the time is the present, it's clear that Martin is going to have to come to terms with his past in order to resolve the story. It would appear that the romance was doomed because they made a choice that Martin regrets.

Since this is an example and not the beginning of a story, it has no life beyond this page, but if you or I decided to rewrite it and make a few more decisions, it could turn into something.

This as much as anything explains why I put style and openings together. By choosing words, you are making story. Your prose rhythms become the rhythms of the story. Your word choices become narrative decisions. The words begin working for you. The way you put them together creates your style which in turn defines and distinguishes your story.

Whether you're writing a romance or a mystery or deep psychological fiction, the opening of your story is going to:

1. Identify characters.
2. Determine time and place.
3. Establish point of view.
4. Signal readers as to what kind of story they're reading.

STYLE KEEPS YOUR STORY ON THE TRACK

Good choices put your story on the right track. The English language is one of the richest and most complicated forms of human expression and the possibilities for inventiveness and power are unlimited. So is the margin for error.

Does a character scurry or scuttle or scramble or slouch? Are the speeches abrupt or flowery? Are the prose rhythms jerky or rambling or smooth? Are your adjectives arcane or colorful or of the garden variety, and while we're at it, are they sparse or plentiful? *Each choice you make is going to make a difference.*

Because it's much easier to do things right the first time than to spend hours undoing wrong choices, do your best to *be precise and be specific*. If you try your best to make the right choices for a particular story from the beginning, it will save you work later. You want to choose the words that will tell your reader *exactly what you mean*. Finding the right words, you'll make sound narrative choices.

Making Your Story Different from All Other Stories

Someone once said there were only seven stories in the world. Whether there are only seven basic stories or seven hundred thousand makes no difference.

What's important is that there are as many different ways of telling stories as there are people to tell them. When you're working hard and working well, you'll discover that the particular cadences and vocabulary you bring to a story make it yours and no one else's. You want to be able to tell yourself, This story is different from all other stories *because I wrote it*.

When everything in a story or a novel is working right, style and substance are essentially one thing. Readers may be able to identify the style, but they aren't going to be able to separate it from what's going on. Once you've written enough fiction, you'll begin to feel this for yourself and you can see it working in your own stories.

STYLE TELLS THE READER WHAT TO THINK

A writer friend was watching TV with us. I switched to a channel that gave me a movie sequence of a country cabin, a door opening, a teenager heading up the stairs to spooky music copied from the score Bernard Herrmann wrote for *Psycho*: violin scrape-scrape-scrape/screech-screech-screech. I said, "Oh, horror movie." We watched for a while and it turned out to be *Friday the Thirteenth: Part III*. After a pause, my friend asked, "How did you know it was going to be a horror movie?" How could I NOT know?

Style told me what to expect.

In the same way, prose style can tell your reader what to expect from a story. Prose style gives signals in some of the same ways a movie presents itself. It simultaneously makes the thing what it is and prepares the reader for what's coming.

One kind of prose suggests romance, another suggests the hard-boiled detective story, another the nostalgic first-person narration that signals a story of remembered childhood, or coming of age. The words you choose and the way you put them together let your readers know what kind of story they're reading, whether it's going to be a mystery or a psychological exploration or speculative fiction or gritty, hard-edged urban realism.

It can set and maintain mood, whether it's comic or romantic or taut with suspense or fraught with terror.

When you get really good at what you're doing, you're going to be able to use words to make readers feel what you want them to feel and think what you want them to think. You can use crisp prose to make them race along to find out what's going to happen next or you can slow them down with complex sentences rich with detail.

WHERE STYLE COMES FROM

I think style is not so much developed as discovered. We all have our own thought patterns and when we talk, our own ways of expressing ourselves. But something happens when we start putting things down on paper: fits of self-consciousness and imitation. It takes a while for most of us to work through all the stages of learning to develop a style of our own.

You can learn about style *from the outside* by reading. You can learn about style *from the inside* by writing. You have to write and write and do more writing in order to find out the best way *for you* to say what you think you want to say.

1. Reading helps you develop an idea of what's good because reading shows you how established writers do things. You find out what succeeds and what doesn't, what you like and what you don't like. Try to figure out how writers you admire use words—whether in excessive sweeps of rhetoric or in tight, simple sentences. You won't want to imitate them, but you will want to know how they manage to do what they're doing.

2. If you read enough different kinds of writers, you begin to get an idea of what style is. You'll discover that there are as many possibilities as there are writers, from the terse prose of Ernest Hemingway to the spare present tense of Jay McInerney and Bret Easton Ellis to F. Scott Fitzgerald's almost romantic treatment of the language to William Faulkner's long, complicated, powerful sentences. You need to read so many different writers that *you don't imitate any of them*.

3. You can learn through listening. When you begin concentrating on dialogue, you'll want to listen to the way other people talk. Right now, try listening to yourself. When you're writing or thinking about writing, or simply thinking about something that's just happened, what are your rhythms? What does your prose sound like? Chances are it doesn't sound the same way it does when you've just finished reading somebody

else's work. You're likely to walk away from a novel by Henry James or Raymond Chandler or Samuel R. Delany framing sentences like James or Chandler or Delany, but if you're patient, the symptoms will pass. You're listening for your own prose rhythms. Eventually you're going to find them.

4. Try to get it down on paper—the way *you personally* describe things. You're going to find your style through writing, writing and more writing. This is where the real work comes in. Sitting down to write the first time, or even at the end of the first year or the second one, you're not alone. You're probably hearing echoes of the last thing you read. In the old days beginning writers sounded like Faulkner or Hemingway; now they're likely to sound more like Bret Easton Ellis, a beginning writer himself. You have to work past this stage, and the best way is by reading widely as you write more and more. If you read enough, you'll read so much that you won't be able to remember it all. If you keep writing, sooner or later you're going to break through all the borrowed styles and hit your stride. It's not easy, but it pays off.

5. You can learn through revision. Revising a first, second or fifth draft, you'll sharpen and determine *what you are doing* by paying attention to *the way you're doing it*. This will help you:

1. See the work as a whole.
2. Complete your thinking.
3. Bring your story to satisfactory completion.

In the next chapter, we'll move on into specific questions you can ask yourself about the opening of your story—and the way you tell it.

CHAPTER 6

THINKING LIKE A WRITER

How DO YOU MOVE from a first draft to a finished story?

Try to stop being a writer for the moment, and become a reader. Sit down and read your story. Now ask yourself:

1. Is my story doing what I want it to do?
2. If not, why not?
3. Have I said *exactly what I mean*?
4. What can I do to make my story do what I want it to?

You are already thinking about revision.

Now it's time to reread that story. This time, you're going to think like a writer.

Remember, revision should be part of the process of composition. If you learn to revise willingly, you're going to become so familiar with the process that in time you will start making some of these decisions *as you compose*.

The questions you ask yourself after reading a first draft or a tenth one are the same questions you ought to be asking yourself from the minute you sit down to write. Ask them AS YOU GO. The better you answer them, the surer your touch is going to be as your story unfolds.

Once you get in the habit, revision is going to become part of your working equipment.

WHERE TO BEGIN

Even as there's no right or wrong way to compose, there's no single right way to go about revision. There's no right or wrong

order in which to ask yourself specific questions about revision.
In an ideal world, you'd be able to think about all questions *all
at once* — as you write and as you revise.

Because most of us find it difficult to do this, we need to
sort out the elements of fiction so we can stand off and take a
good look at our work. The detailed series of checklists that
follow will give you an opportunity to take apart and analyze
the different elements of fiction and will provide you with a
series of questions to ask about your work.

Writers may differ on where to begin but everybody agrees
that you've got to start somewhere. Although some writers prefer to try to separate style and substance, saying that they're
reading first for story or shape or organization or whatever, and
will fix up the prose later, it's clear that at some level they, too,
are reading to find out how well the words they've chosen do
the job.

Since I believe strongly in the organizational power of
words, I'm going to make the checklist on style the first of our
series of checklists designed to help you read for revision.

Since word choices create beginnings and establish narrative ground rules, you'll find it useful to read for revision to find
out *how well the words are telling the story.* As you're using words
to tell the reader what to think, you'll want to be sure they're
working for you.

Remember, *by getting the words in order, you're getting your
thoughts in order.*

I'm not talking about proofreading. Making the right words
march in the right direction, you are controlling and shaping
your story. Style isn't cosmetic. It's not like paint, that you put
on a house after it's finished so it will look nice. It is the fabric.

Reading with attention to the way the words are telling the
story, you're also:

1. Getting a sense of organization — whether events are in
the right order.

2. Getting a sense of shape — whether your story is all there
or whether there's something missing.

3. Completing your thinking. If passages are unclear to you, they're going to be unclear to your reader. *You are figuring out what you have to say as you work on the way you're saying it.*

4. Reading for consistency of style and tone and character and story.

Judging how well your writing does the job, you can ask yourself several questions. Answering them, you're on your way to sounding like yourself and nobody else.

CHECKLIST I: QUESTIONS ABOUT STYLE

1. *Am I saying what I mean?* If math is one of the two major systems of logic, language is the other. Put your prose in good working order and you'll get your thoughts in order.

When you sat down to write you may have been fired by inspiration, but every one of your sentences had better parse — subject, predicate, clauses all in order and all in the right place. This is easy to do with simple, unadorned prose. If you're just beginning it might be wise to keep it simple until you've learned control. Once you have control of your prose, you can do anything you want with it. You can build elaborate constructions. You can grab a sentence by the tail and swing it around your head.

If you don't have a grammar manual, get one. The old classics are Fowler's *Modern English Usage* and *The Elements of Style* by Strunk and White, but most publishers now offer up-to-date and easy-to-read references. You should have one at hand when you're composing and again when you're rewriting. The rule? *When in doubt, look it up.*

Bad grammar can further confuse your thinking and shoot down your story before it ever gets off the ground.

2. *Are my word choices working for or against me?*
    a. Can I find a fresher way to say what I want to say? If you can't think of a new way to say what you have to say, you may not have anything new to tell the reader. Working hard to avoid cliché, you are going to sharpen your thinking. Wide reading is going to enrich your vocabulary and a little

thought will help you choose words that say precisely what you mean.

b. Am I overloading my text with too many adjectives, distracting readers with bizarre word choices or trying to force words into new meanings?

c. Am I using this word right? If you're working with an unfamiliar word—OK, let's say, something as exotic as *etiolated*, or *querulous*—you'd better be sure you're using it right. Again,
When in doubt, look it up.

d. Do I have the right word in the first place? This is the question you need to ask yourself now, as you begin revising, and at every stage of composition. Part of the process of finding out what you have to say is choosing the right words to express it. Is it spelled right? At best, misspellings alienate editors and make you look like an amateur. At worst, misspellings change meanings—guerilla/gorilla, complaisant/complacent—and things as simple as hear/here and their/there are examples that come immediately to mind. They get between you and what you have to say.

Another rule: *Precision creates and emphasizes meaning*.

e. Can I be more specific? If you have a character getting into her car, is she getting into a '79 Datsun or an '89 Mercedes or what? Is it hers or is it stolen? Specifics advance your story. If somebody is being assailed by an armed mugger, what is he carrying—a knife, a gun or a banana wrapped in a handkerchief? It's going to determine how both characters behave.

3. *What about sentence variety*? There's no immediate rule of thumb here, but if you have a story in which every sentence starts with *he*, you may need to wake up your reader.

4. *Are my sentences run-on*? Teachers fight like tigers to get students to break up overloaded sentences because they know that they can obscure meaning and exhaust the reader. Some writers think fiction lowers all the barriers and that rambling can create velocity. Think again. Go back and make certain that, long or short, all those sentences are perfectly clear.

5. *Do I need to break up paragraphs*? If a paragraph runs for more than half a page, you're going to need to subject it to close

scrutiny. Ideas get lost in overblown paragraphs. So do readers.

6. *What about mannerisms?* Omitting articles isn't style. Neither is putting a period between each word of a sentence and neither is coining words the way some poets do (made up words like wave-shifting and feather-troubled are not effective adjectives). Strange typographical setup isn't style and neither are sentence fragments.

7. *Do I sound like me, or like the last writer I read?* If there's something *faintly familiar* about the way your story tells itself, try to step back and see whose work it looks like. Whether consciously or unconsciously, most beginning writers imitate. If you've written a William Faulkner story—or even one by the new literary brat pack—you're going to want to try to find a more individual way of expressing yourself.

8. *Do I need to make word or phrase cuts to make my prose more effective?* Look at these two versions of one sentence:

After he got up and got dressed that morning sleepy Harry went slowly down to the corner store, where he walked inside and found Mr. Bissell being held up by an armed robber.

Set this against the more specific:

Sleepy Harry shambled into the corner store, where he found Mr. Bissell being held at gunpoint by an armed robber.

BEGINNINGS

This last example brings us neatly to the next matter. It's clear that by making cuts in the Harry sentence in the last of the style questions, I was doing two things:

1. I was sharpening a sentence to make it more effective.

In the process, I was taking the most direct route to the action.

2. Reaching for more expressive words, I was writing an opening.

When you've read widely enough you'll be able to see for yourself that when fiction is working, style and content become the same thing. Refining word choices and forging the logic of the sentences, you're completing your thinking and developing your story. Even the rough example above shows how this works. Refining those few words, I was making several narrative decisions.

It's clear in one sentence that the Harry/armed robber story is being told in the third person, but from Harry's point of view. That means Harry is the camera. It also begins more or less in the middle of the action, with a Harry/armed robber confrontation. Moving through a few more sentences with Harry, I'd know better who he was by how he *reacted* to this situation — familiar store-owner (remember, Harry knows his name) at gunpoint, and so early in the morning!

Because I am a confessed block constructer — rewriting sentence by sentence before I move on — I believe that the opening casts the style at the same time the style casts the opening. As I suggested in Chapter Five, it's these opening sentences that invite or discourage readers. You want to give them your best. As you do, important things are happening to your story.

Let's look at the openings of three novels, beginning with F. Scott Fitzgerald's *The Great Gatsby*:

> In my younger and more vulnerable years my father gave me some advice that I've been turning over in my mind ever since.
> "Whenever you feel like criticizing anyone," he told me, "just remember that all the people in this world haven't had the advantages that you've had."

In these two short paragraphs we're introduced to the narrator, who clearly is a member of what used to be called the upper classes. He's going to tell us this story, and although we don't yet know what the story's going to be, we know him pretty well through his speech rhythms. The author has, furthermore, established that this is going to be a first-person story and because the narrator is talking about judging people, and his tone is just a little distant, it's fairly clear that although he's involved in what's going on, he's not at the center of the action. What's more, he's talking about the past.

Fitzgerald has grabbed you by the lapels and told you how to listen to what his narrator has to say—reserving judgment. He's also setting the tone for what is to follow.

Now listen to this first-person narrator.

> If you really want to hear about it, the first thing you'll probably want to know is where I was born, and what my lousy childhood was like, and how my parents were occupied and all before they had me, and all that David Copperfield kind of crap, but I don't feel like going into it, if you want to know the truth. In the first place, that stuff bores me, and in the second place, my parents would have about two hemorrhages apiece if I told anything pretty personal about them . . .

That's J. D. Salinger's Holden Caulfield; again, the narrator has gotten your attention and he's pulling you into *Catcher in the Rye*. These much-imitated rhythms let us know the narrator is a rebel, and he's young.

In both cases, the authors have used first-person narrators to gain our confidence and involve us in what's going on.

Using the third person present tense, Bobbie Ann Mason begins *In Country* this way:

> "I have to stop again, hon," Sam's grandmother says, tapping her on the shoulder. Sam Hughes is driving, with her uncle, Emmett Smith, half asleep beside her.
> "Where are we?" grunts Emmett.
> "Still on I-64. Mawmaw has to go to the restroom."
> "I forgot to take my pill when we stopped last," Mawmaw says.

In a few short lines of dialogue, Mason has pulled us right into the middle of a scene and introduced her principal characters. She has set the narrative tone and established the style.

In these three cases I think manner and matter are inseparable, as they are in all successful fiction.

This means the careful writer is going to give extra time and thought to the opening pages of any short story or novel, revising sentence by sentence, draft by draft, going back after the last draft to read once more for style and appropriateness of the opening.

One good way to develop an ear for good openings is to go back and read the first paragraphs of every story in an anthology, or to pick up a bunch of novels at random and look at the first few lines. You're going to know soon enough which ones take hold of your imagination on first sight and pull you in.

I've already listed a number of questions you can ask yourself about style. As you look at your story, add to them these questions about your opening.

CHECKLIST II: QUESTIONS ABOUT YOUR OPENING

1. *Does my story really begin here?* Too many beginning writers have to talk their way into a story, describing settings and characters to themselves at great length before they can get them moving. Now it's time to go back and *get rid of everything you wrote in order to find out what you were writing*.

2. *Is my opening too long for what it does?* There are many areas of risk here:

 a. The lengthy description narrowing in on a house, a room, a person—the fictional equivalent of the movies' slow zoom in. It works better in pictures.

 b. Several minutes of people talking in which nothing happens.

 c. Several minutes of your character getting up in the morning.

Check your openings on a case-by-case basis. You're going

to need the whole story in front of you before you can be really sure.

3. *Is my opening too long in proportion to the rest of the story?* Because the first scene is usually on paper before anything else, some writers may be inclined to keep reworking until it's over-developed—an overelaborate setup for something that should be neat and swift.

4. *Is my opening interesting?* Is there a narrative hook—some incident, some question posed here that will catch the reader's interest? Is anybody else going to like this as well as I do or is an outsider going to think it's boring? Keeping this question in mind, ask yourself the next one.

5. *What about action?* Is there something going on? Are my characters immediately engaged in a clash of wills or brought face to face with an impending problem or surprise or confrontation? Openings should imply coming action and interaction.

6. *Is my opening clear?* Is my reader going to know who these people are, who's talking, what's happening? Can my reader tell what's going on? A touch of mystery never hurt anything, but the reader who is left at sea in the middle of unexplained happenings may not stay around long enough to have them explained.

7. *Have I chosen a flashy opening at the expense of continuity?* Often beginning writers will start with the right instincts—finding themselves engaged with character in mid-scene, only to have to go back to explain everything in an attack of what I call the *had-hads*: "It *had* been ten years since Mary and Todd *had* gotten divorced and Todd's new wife Reba *had* ..." You can avoid this by starting at the beginning—or assuming your story starts here and filling in background by implication (phrases like "since the divorce" or: "in this postwar society" give the reader the idea and you, as writer, *take the past for granted* instead of feeling compelled to explain) or by well-handled flashbacks, if they don't get in the way.

Other beginning writers start with a bang and then find that they've left themselves with *too much to explain*. Trying to cover their tracks by accounting for everything, they're likely to slow down action and distract the reader with a muddy time scheme — too many flashbacks and, worse yet, flashbacks within flashbacks. A good exercise for a story that has developed time problems is to identify and number events *chronologically* and then do your best to reduce the number of time shifts.

Still others begin with a prologue set in the deep past and then leap forward to time present without ever intending to return to the past. Since readers remember best *the first thing you tell them*, be sure you want this moment from the past to be central to the story. See if you can make it work without the initial flashback.

8. *Now that I know how my story comes out, is this the right opening?* Sometimes, this is a matter of tone. You thought this was going to be a serious story but early on it became a funny one. Now go back and rewrite so the parts of your story match.

At other times, rereading a finished draft with the benefit of hindsight, writers discover that there are things they know now that they didn't know when they began. There may be details they can add to the opening they have, or they may find out the story doesn't begin quite where they thought it did. This may mean adding a new scene — or getting rid of one.

9. *If I've written a wonderful opening, does the rest of my story measure up to it?* This means making sure you've maintained the level of energy and excitement you started with. It may mean rewriting the rest until it is as good as your opening.

10. *Are all the shotguns I planted in the first scene fired by the end of the story?* Sometimes we throw in details in the heat of invention — a long-lost sister or an undiscovered secret or a family battle going on somewhere offstage — and then lose track of them. *Everything in a story has to function in terms of the story*. If that long-lost sister or undiscovered secret or family battle doesn't turn out to be relevant to your finished story, *take it out*.

REVISION AS ORGANIC WHOLE

Notice that although I chose to begin the checklists with considerations of style and opening, these are really questions about the work as a whole, as are all considerations of revision.

By the time you've asked yourself question five — Is there something going on? — you've moved past reading for style and effectiveness of opening, and into looking at your story as a whole.

Everything you do to a story affects the story as a whole. This is because living, breathing stories are not assembled out of spare parts stuck on like the moustache on Mr. Potato Head.

Stories are whole.

Moving on from reading for possible revision of style and opening, we can identify the rest of the areas we need to look at to see whether we need to do revising. They are:

- Character
- Dialogue
- Point of view
- Showing versus telling
- Story and structure.

We can even look at them one by one, *as long as we understand that they too are part of a whole*. Revision is an organic process, and although we can look at areas that need revision and talk about ways of revising, we need to understand this. Choosing, cutting, reorganizing — however we revise, we're engaged in a single process.

There's more.

These various ways of looking at and carrying out revision are part and parcel of writing. These questions need to be considered every time you sit down to write. It should be clear as well that although for your convenience I've divided the possibilities for revision under separate headings according to aspects of fiction writing, and am providing separate checklists, every question you ask yourself about revision and every individual step is part of this organic process. At every step along the way, you are:

WRITING FICTION.

CHAPTER 7

READING FOR REVISION: CHARACTER, DETAIL

LIKE EVERYTHING YOU WRITE, characters are made out of words. The words you choose create and breathe life into fictional people.

The writer working with character has to create an entire person different from all other people — somebody readers are going to like or dislike according to the writer's intentions, somebody readers can believe in and care about.

Judging our fictional characters, we're going to start with the checklist.

CHECKLIST III: QUESTIONS ABOUT CHARACTER

1. *Is my character complete?* Although I don't have to put his entire life history down on the page and I don't want to bore readers with explanatory accounts of his emotional state, do I have enough detail here to make a whole person?

2. *Is my character believable?* We can believe in the hopes and fears of college students and early cliff-dwellers and extraterrestrials with neon spines *as long as the psychology is working*. This means examining your character's motives and actions. You may not need to explain why your characters behave in a certain way, but if you want readers to believe in them, you have to understand and believe in the state of mind that brought these people to this moment.

3. *Is my character consistent?* Would this character, as drawn, do what I asked him or her to do? Again, even a loving mother can become a hatchet murderer *if the psychology is working.*

4. *Is my character distinctive?* Another way to ask this question is, are there ways in which this character is different from all other characters? Unless you're writing experimental fiction, it's more or less understood that the people you introduce to your readers should have something that distinguishes them — something they do or say or wear or care about that gives the reader a reason to follow their adventures.

5. *Does this character function in this story?* Even the tightest short stories may have a cast of more than a dozen. All of us, however, get caught up in the idea of the occasional colorful character — somebody our protagonist runs into on the way to the real action of the story. If these colorful characters are going to be anything more than extra faces in a crowd, they need to justify their existence.

For example, if your hero has a conversation with a bum on the sidewalk and then goes on to the store and we never hear anything more about the bum and nothing the bum says has anything to do with the story or the outcome, you'd better move that bum out of the story. If on the other hand your hero has a conversation with a bum on the sidewalk and it changes his mood or his mind or his course of action or his way of looking at things, that's another matter.

In short, your secondary characters have to justify the space they take up in your story.

6. *Is this character a stereotype?* Another way to ask this question is, does my character look more like a comic-strip character than a living person?

Some of the broader stereotypes include the prostitute with the heart of gold, the possessive mother, the weedy-looking guy with outrageous daydreams, the misunderstood teenager. This is a list to which you can add some of the stronger characters in the fiction you read. Because we get committed to our characters, this is a hard question to answer honestly. Try.

If your character seems stereotypical or two-dimensional,

ask yourself: Is there some way in which this prostitute/day-dreamer/possessive mother is different from all others? If there is, go back to your story and be sure your reader sees what you see — the quirks and yearnings that make this an individual.

GETTING INTO CHARACTER

I start with character because I believe characters move together to make story. As there are hundreds of thousands of individual human characteristics, there are hundreds of thousands of indicators of character. They are too many and varied to list, but you can work your way through to an understanding of character by looking at what you've written in the light of your answers to Checklist III.

Talking about what characters *aren't* is sometimes the most direct route into finding out what characters *are*.

If you've reread your story and answered no to most of the questions about your central character, it's time to rethink.

Remember, *character is built from the inside*. Like a method actor, you need to be able to get inside your character's head. For the purposes of the story, you need to be able to see the world as your character sees it and talk and act as your character would.

Let's look at your story again.

COMPLETENESS

We're going to begin with problems of completeness. If your character is more than a one-dimensional comic-strip stereotype, you're also working with problems of believability, consistency and originality from the moment you start this person moving on the page. Notice I say person.

You're not building an artificial person out of spare parts, which means all the considerations raised in the checklist should be dealt with more or less at the same time.

Because I don't have your story in front of me, I'm going

to run through the checklist with an example of my own. Let's say it begins this way:

The girl hated her mother.

For our purposes, we'll say I have a fairly sensitive story about a young woman who is having a terrible time with her mother. Let's also say I don't have a very good grasp on who this person is *until I begin to complete her*.

You don't need to write an entire fictional autobiography or even a one-page monologue to turn your character into a whole person. You can understand your character better and make the person complete and believable by:

1. Naming. Names are people. Your Alistair and your Aloysius are not the same as Bob or Barry or Zorg, for that matter; your Celeste and Tiffany are not the same as Jane or Mary or Martha or Sylvia, and they aren't going to behave the same way in a story. Add the last name and you get national and ethnic overtones as soon as you move away from the nonspecific Evans or Jones to O'Malley or Chiappa or Wu or Cohen or Washington or Stuchinksi.

While you were out, I named my character Marilyn Zorn. I named her Marilyn because I realize now she's not a girl at all, she's an older woman—thirty-seven, and as I write I understand that the reason she still acts and thinks like a girl is because she is under her mother's thumb. This mother named her Marilyn expecting this would make her beautiful. Our Marilyn isn't. The last name? It expresses the way she feels about things—forlorn.

2. Listen. Characters reveal themselves through dialogue—and thought patterns. The character who says, "Ain't no use even thinking about it" is a different sort of person from the one who says, "Me? Think about that? Are you kidding?" Every time a character speaks or thinks he or she is helping you make narrative decisions.

"Mama, if you would leave me alone for a minute, I'd be able to figure this out—what to do about it." That's Marilyn, and I understand that she's a simple working girl who hates the fact that she's thirty-seven years old and still living with her mother.

3. Put your character into action. What would my imaginary person do when confronted with that robber Harry ran

into in the last chapter? If she picks up a window pole and knocks him out, you have one kind of person. If she goes home and goes to bed and considers the fragility of human arrangements and the relative lack of safety in the urban world, you have another.

But Marilyn isn't even thinking of going to the store. She has other things on her mind. Fixing her mother's pillows, setting up her lunch tray and aiming her at the TV, she is preparing to escape to the office. The "it" she's worrying about in her speech above turns out to be the fact that a man from the office wants to come home to her apartment for dinner. The mother appears to have been badgering Marilyn to invite him and now she's full of suggestions about what Marilyn should wear and what she might do to herself to make herself better-looking.

a. The jerky, agitated pace at which Marilyn does these chores will indicate her state of mind.

b. As her mother begins giving beauty tips, Marilyn becomes brisker. There is something final about the way she goes about these tasks she performs every morning that indicates she's at the end of her rope.

4. Ask yourself: What does this character want? What is this character afraid of?

What Marilyn wants is to be left alone in a world without her mother. She would, in fact, like to be left alone with this man who's coming to dinner. Marilyn would like her mother to shut up and disappear for the evening because *this is what Marilyn is afraid of*: she is afraid that her mother, a chronic invalid who may or may not be really sick, will use her fragile good looks and womanly wiles to steal the potential boyfriend away from her.

5. Put this character into confrontation. Back to the robber—or to the mate who wants a divorce, or the mother who accuses our character of never phoning and never coming to visit. How does this person behave?

In this case, Marilyn has put the room in order and set up the trays, and is preparing to make her escape when she says, "I'm not bringing him home, Mama. I've put some extra graham crackers and some Cheez Whiz on the tray because I'm getting Bradley to take me out to dinner."

To which her mother says, "Argh," clutches her throat and falls over in a real or perhaps a pretend seizure.

Which is it? What will Marilyn do?

Stay tuned. We aren't talking about story here, we're talking about character.

But you will notice that poor Marilyn, who didn't exist fifteen minutes ago, has begun moving around in her story. We will leave her at her moment of confrontation and hope I've made you care a little bit about the outcome.

BELIEVABILITY, DISTINCTIVENESS

Let's move on to more detailed ways to address the questions of believability and distinctiveness. If you believe, your readers are going to believe. You are going to believe in your characters *because you're going to become them.*

Begin by hypothesis. Ask yourself, what would I do if I were in this situation I've created for this character? Think it through. Are there differences between you and the character? Say you're a woman writer writing a grandfather. If I were a grandfather I might be more philosophical about what's happening, or angrier; I'm sure my judgment would be affected by rich and complicated memories. About Marilyn. If I were Marilyn I'd prop Mama up in bed, split and call the paramedics from the office, but she's probably a nicer person than I am, and she really cares about this mother in spite of everything. But I'm moving into what comes next.

Continue with imagination. Instead of seeing this character from the outside, try to see the world through his eyes. Start with physical details — his health, how well he's getting around, his eyesight. What about his mood? Is it pessimistic or cheery or what, and do you know why?

Marilyn, as it turns out, is feeling particularly fragile today because she hasn't had a boyfriend in years, she's terrified of being left alone and there are new wrinkles and new sections of dry skin sagging at her throat every time she looks in the mirror. For this woman who still thinks of herself as a girl, every negotiation is hard, every big decision even harder. Shall she leave her mother and go out with Bradley? What will she do if Mama is really sick this time, and may just die on her?

Move into the character so you can move with the character. For the purposes of this revision, you are this character. Later you will become every character you write, seeing all the faces, doing all the voices.

Marilyn flutters between the door and the telephone. She tiptoes back to the bedroom door and sees her mother still lying in that unnatural position, with her beautiful head tossed back and a thin thread of saliva staining the pillow.

Next, move outside so you can see your character. Notice I have left this for last, because I believe that if you're able to *become* your character, you may not need to know what this person looks like because you feel it. But now it's time to see how she looks to you — stature, coloring, clothes, way of moving. As you might guess, our Marilyn is underweight, pale and timid. Unlike her vivid mother, who has just thrown this real or imaginary seizure, she moves slowly and cautiously, as if afraid of disturbing the air in the room around her.

Now ask yourself how she looks to the other characters — attractive or not, bizarre or off-putting or lovable or dangerous. You will see this by moving them into scenes together. Becoming both Marilyn and her mother/Bradley/other people at the office, you'll discover *how she acts when she's with other people*. There is always a gap between self-image and the way others see us. Until they meet other people, our characters often think like — well, *ourselves*. Encounters make fictional characters three-dimensional.

Although Marilyn sees herself the way I do, she is attractive to Bradley, at the office, because she has good features and the delicately drawn romantic look of some tuberculosis victims. To her mother, who I know now is only pretending to be unconscious, she looks awkward and funny and juvenile and stupid.

This moment of crisis is going to prove to Marilyn — and us — *who she really is.*

Now that you've seen your character from the outside, notice how the other characters treat him or her and how this character responds to others in the story. By this time, you've moved far beyond consideration of character into matters of story — but you probably also understand that you moved into story the minute you got inside this character.

I know I did. If I stick with Marilyn for a few more minutes I'm going to have to put this chapter aside and write her story.

By the time you've done all these things for your imaginary person, your character has become real to you — speech patterns established, everything from costume and likes and dislikes to loves and hates seems to follow naturally. You already know what this person is going to do in a given situation. But you need to know how to make the reader see and hear what you see and hear, to set this character apart.

Distinctiveness

You can use physical detail to make your character's differences apparent. If a character is wearing trousers, are they jeans or baggies or gray flannels or tennis whites or what? If they are jeans and the character is a woman, are they Levis or Gloria Vanderbilts? It makes a difference. If your woman character is a compulsive reader it's going to make some difference to let us know whether she's hooked on SF or Barbara Cartland or running around with a copy of Kirkegaard.

You can tell us more about this person by describing the room or house or the apartment — whether it's furnished in high tech or threadbare stuff from a second-hand store or ancestral bits and pieces or outmoded Danish modern and you can tell us even more by letting us know what objects this person cherishes — the string bracelet given by an old friend or the religious medal from a teacher or the Mexican sculpture, or . . .

The possibilities are endless.

Let's say that for her day's adventure, which I think now is going to end not at the office but in the Emergency Room (while we weren't looking Marilyn has phoned the paramedics), Marilyn has selected a pretty three-piece knit in a soft beige, something that would look appropriate on a much younger person. Because she has something of the madcap about her, she has added to the rosy pearls with matching clip-on earrings a little girl's barrette, the pink plastic kind in the shape of a bow ribbon. She has it flattening a curl she particularly wants to have look nice when she gets to the office, but I already know she's going to forget to remove it when the time comes for the big confrontation with Bradley.

She and Mama live in a one-bedroom apartment. Marilyn sleeps on a daybed in the living room, and on the walls you will find a tiered shelf with Marilyn's collection of angels, including the Hummel angel that sits on the edge of the shelf and blows a trumpet. Although she doesn't go to church, Marilyn seems to be a somewhat religious person. Let's say she's afraid there is a God with a hell He can send people to, which may be why she called the paramedics.

Deciding on such things, I am dealing with detail. So will you, in making your characters more specific. Each detail shows the reader something specific to that particular character and helps make your character distinctive.

CONSISTENCY

Because you're working with your character *from the inside*, you've automatically done away with problems of consistency. If you are consistently this character, then this character is going to behave consistently. If your loving mom does indeed do a remarkable about-face and turns into a hatchet murderer, she's going to be a believable hatchet murderer *because the psychology is right*.

By the time you know your character this well, you're going to know what this person is doing in this story and you won't even need to ask yourself how this character responds to other people. Characters imagined *from the inside* justify their presence in the story.

Did you have any doubt Marilyn would call the ambulance and take her mother to the Emergency Room? I didn't.

But the laugh is on Mama. There's nothing the matter with her, but they're going to keep her overnight for tests and further observation. In a truly just world, the doctor would come back to Marilyn and tell her the mother has been fooling her all these years, and for both of their good they should have separate apartments. But because doctors are conservative in their judgments (as are Mama and Marilyn) and are unlikely to suggest radical changes, he'll probably send Mama home with a tranquilizer the very next morning.

But meanwhile Marilyn is going to have one evening of bliss with Bradley, and we can hope this means the beginning of good things for her. Released by her mother's doctor, who has told her to leave this in his hands and get about her business, Marilyn has gone back to the office. Bradley greets her, smiling.

"What about my dinner invitation?"

"Tonight," she says.

He'd always thought she was attractive. What he can't figure out now is why she's smiling quite so broadly.

TWO KEY QUESTIONS

Now you have to ask yourself whether a given character belongs in a story. The rule of thumb, I think, is that if the character functions in some way—acting and reacting with the central character—if the presence of a given character *affects the outcome*, then that character has justified his or her presence.

The hardest question any of us can put to ourselves about our characters is whether they are stereotypes. Notice how fond I have become of Marilyn in a few short pages. Unfortunately she—and Mama—probably are stereotypes, because I am not delving very deeply into imagination and I'm not drawing on memory at all to make this story.

If they are at all distinctive, it's because I've identified them with specific details—Marilyn's collection of angels, the ailing mother's fading beauty.

I think that if you are working with people you know from the inside and you care enough about them, you can—and should—avoid stereotype. Precision and detail can turn even minor characters into living, breathing people. In spite of the fact that she's a stereotype, the prostitute with the heart of gold turns up again and again in fiction—which succeeds only to the degree that the writer has cared enough about her and her story to turn her into a real person.

The adolescent who is coming of age is another staple character in fiction, but usually the authors avoid stereotype through use of *specific detail*. Because coming-of-age novels are usually semi-autobiographical, authors automatically avoid stereotype because they're using specific, intensely personal details from their own lives. The trick, then, is to bring this kind of specificity to all your characters as you bring them to life.

DETAIL

You'll do this the same way I brought Marilyn and her mother to the page: through use of detail. Think about the physical details—what your characters look like, what they wear, use, buy, eat; what kinds of rooms they live in; what the streets they walk through look like and what the weather's like.

Then, looking at what you've already written, ask yourself:

1. Have I used enough detail? You want to give readers enough information so they can see what you see—where your character is, and what's happening. Details bring people and scenes to life. Although there's no absolute rule for giving enough detail, you can proceed from the assumption that sentences like: "She had a lot of things in her apartment" and "He put on a hat" sound a little vague. Read authors like John Cheever and John Updike to see what you can make detail do for you.

2. Have I used too much detail? If the detail doesn't enhance the story or advance the action, cut it out. There are no hard and fast rules but I can give some indication of what I'm talking about by saying that if any of your sentences look like this next one, you may be in trouble.

She was wearing her purple silk dress with the brown peplum with the little tucks in it and the matching shoes with
the purple silk stockings that she had bought with Harold
on the first day of their honeymoon which was in Cape Cod
instead of Bermuda because even at the beginning Harold
didn't have any money.

I'd probably get rid of the peplum and the tucks and the first
reference to Harold and come up with something like this:

She was wearing her purple silk with the matching
stockings that she'd bought at the Cape, where they'd hon-
eymooned because even at the beginning Harold didn't
have any money.

This brings us to questions of cutting, which I'll discuss at length
in later chapters.

3. Can I be more specific? If you've sent your character out
to a restaurant, you're going to tell your readers more about the
character and the situation if you identify it as a fern bar, greasy
spoon, three-star restaurant, chili dog stand or Chinese take-out
place. If your character has bought her lover a watch as a present, we're going to get a clearer idea of what's going on if we
know whether it's a Swatch or a Cartier tank watch.
    The idea is not to fill space with further details, but to select
carefully and make the details you do use go to work for you.

4. Do the details I've chosen enhance meaning? This is a
clever question, and one you want to ask only after you've chosen details to set the scene and make your characters specific
and distinctive.

You may be surprised and delighted to discover that some of
your choices have extra significance. If your thwarted lover
sends roses and they arrive dead, you're saying more than something about the roses. You're sending signals that the romance
is in trouble.
    If your out-of-work watchsmith picks up a hammer and
starts smashing clocks and watches, he's doing more than indi-

cating rage. He's destroying all those emblems of time passing and at the same time trashing his way of life.

Enough. I think you should choose details because they are the right ones to make the reader see what you see and believe what you believe. Be precise and careful and every detail you choose will add meaning to your work.

Now ask yourself:

1. Are my characters complete and believable?
2. Are they consistent?
3. What makes them different from all other characters?
4. Have I used the right details to bring them to life on the page?
5. Do they sound like real people?

This brings us logically to the next section.

What's Next

You've probably already noticed that it's impossible for me to talk about any one part of a story without talking about all the other parts. This means that my suggestions for revision to further develop and strengthen character are really ways to make story. As I move on to discuss reading for revision of dialogue, this same thing is going to be true.

I'm talking about dialogue next because dialogue informs character in two ways.

1. Speech patterns determine and define character.
2. We know character through action, and *dialogue is action*.

CHAPTER 8

READING FOR REVISION: DIALOGUE IS ACTION

BEFORE YOU CAN ASK YOURSELF whether your dialogue passages are working as well as they should, you need to know what makes good fictional dialogue.

You're going find out where dialogue comes from and develop a sense of what makes good fictional dialogue by paying more careful attention to a couple of things you're already doing.

You need to learn to listen more closely. Most fiction writers walk around with their heads full of voices. These include things heard, remembered and imagined — the raw material for fictional dialogue. These voices come from a number of places — the present, the past and, perhaps more important, from your own imagination.

Unless you are a hermit without TV, telephone or even radio, you hear voices all day every day — voices of friends and family, what comes in over the airwaves, overheard conversation.

Add to the voices you hear coming in every day, the hundreds of recent and past conversations replaying in your memory. As you remember them, you're already editing, cutting and ordering these conversations, omitting nonessential speeches and digressions. You remember not complete conversations, but the *sense* of these conversations.

Now for imagination. If you've begun writing fiction, you probably spend time thinking about your stories even when you aren't actually writing. Most fiction writers hear voices all the time — their characters telling, complaining, remarking. Listen carefully and your characters will tell you who they are, what they want and what they care about. They can even let you know what's going to happen next in your story.

You can learn technique through reading. Reading annual "best" anthologies, contemporary magazines, acknowledged masterpieces and new fiction, you can learn *how other writers create good dialogue*.

A look at a dialogue passage in any story by John O'Hara or Ernest Hemingway, for instance, can teach you a lot about technique. Both of these rather spare writers catch the sound of human speech—notice, I don't say they catch *human speech*. Instead they go through a process of editing and refining that catches the *sound*. They skip the uhms and ahs and repetitions and awkward pauses of actual-time-elapsed conversation between two people to give readers tight duets and trios. These two literary tough guys have much to show us because they strip the process of writing dialogue to the bare bones.

Because Southern writers are particularly attuned to cadences—the "tune" people keep when they say what they have to say—Southern writers like Flannery O'Connor and Eudora Welty have a lot to teach you about natural speech rhythms.

Reading widely, start looking critically at dialogue passages by writers you admire. Ask yourself:

- Is this scene effective and is everything clear? An effective scene moves the characters from point A to point B—from accord to conflict, for instance, or from ignorance to discovery. Successful scenes demonstrate a change in the relationship between the speakers. This is another way of saying that in successful scenes, something *happens*. Try drawing a line through the scene—seeing what the dramatic movement is, who the speakers are, what's at stake. How did the writer manage this?
- Is this dialogue realistic? If so, why? Is this ordinary speech, or is it really ordinary speech that's been edited and intensified for effect?
- If not, why not? Writers like William Faulkner and Joyce Carol Oates are given to writing occasional long, complicated speeches that don't sound like the usual exchanges between ordinary people. What gives these

speeches their power?
- What did this writer put in and leave out to make this scene dramatic? Swift?

ELEMENTS OF GOOD DIALOGUE

Working on your ear for dialogue—the way you *listen* to voices, and looking at the way other people write good fictional dialogue, you're getting ready to start asking similar questions about your own work. It may help to add a few simple rules.

Rule One: Dialogue Is Action

Except in extreme circumstances, most late 20th-century people don't hit and yell very often. They are, however, capable of acts of enormous power and violence which they carry out through speech.

Every time one of your characters says something to another of your characters and the other says something back, they are *acting* and *reacting*.

This means that every scene you write where people meet and talk should have some movement through it. Dialogue passages should move characters from point A to point B. Your characters can meet and do something as big as falling in love or having a fight or as subtle as shifting from a position of initial wariness to one of trust. They can demonstrate like or dislike, dominance and submission, or deception or betrayal. Anything can happen *as long as something happens* in every dialogue passage you write.

Read for this as you listen to your characters talk. If there is no interaction and no movement, then you need to go back and rewrite.

Rule Two: The Most Direct Route to Good Dialogue Is Cutting

The writer climbs into the head of two or more characters and *listens* to what they have to say to each other, recording everything more or less verbatim. There are certain things we all have to write to find out what we're going to write.

When they get going, fictional characters, like ordinary people, are likely to be long-winded. Even more than people do, fictional characters need to talk and talk in order to find out what they really have to say.

This means the writer has to read and reread dialogue while composing and again while revising, eliminating speeches in which *nothing is happening*. This means getting rid of everything these people said on their way to saying what's important.

Because dialogue is a strangely personal thing, specific to each writer in relationship to each individual piece of fiction, there's no real way to make one or two writers' work stand for all fiction. Although it would be interesting to apply these rules to the work of Faulkner and company, what you really need to know is how they're going to affect what you're doing.

With this in mind, I've constructed a simple example to show you how to make them work. We'll call the following exchange between Harry and Joe our *working example*.

> *Harry:*   Hi Joe.
> *Joe:*   Hi, Harry. What's new?
> *Harry:*   Nothing much.
> *Joe:*   Nice morning.
> *Harry:*   If you say so.
> *Joe:*   Well, it *is* a nice morning, isn't it?
> *Harry:*   How am I supposed to know if it's a nice morning?
> *Joe:*   I just thought I would ask. How are you?
> *Harry:*   Don't ask. How are you?
> *Joe:*   I'm fine, how are you?
> *Harry:*   I'm OK, except for the roof.
> *Joe:*   What's the matter with the roof?
> *Harry:*   It fell on the dog.
> *Joe:*   It *fell on the dog*?
> *Harry:*   After the hurricane.
> *Joe:*   What hurricane?
> *Harry:*   I can't help it if you don't tune in the Weather Watch.

Now this made-up dialogue is mildly amusing, but it can be tightened considerably, as follows:

Harry:	Hi Joe.
Joe:	Hi, Harry. Nice morning.
Harry:	If you say so.
Joe:	Well, it *is* a nice morning, isn't it? How are you?
Harry:	I'm OK, except for the roof.
Joe:	What's the matter with the roof?
Harry:	It fell on the dog in the hurricane.
Joe:	It *fell on the dog in the hurricane*? What hurricane?
Harry:	The one that leveled your house. I can't help it if you don't tune in the Weather Watch.

As you'll notice, while I was tightening our *working example*, something new developed that gave it a dramatic point. In the course of cutting out some of what these two said on their way to saying something important, I discovered what that something important was.

I can't say it often enough: *Revising the way we say things, we find out what we have to say.*

Rule Three: Dialogue Should Be Dramatic, Not Expository

The best way to demonstrate this is to go back to Joe and Harry and show you what dialogue should *not* do. Let's say that Joe and Harry are back at that first exchange in which Joe says, "Hi, nice morning." Let's say I want my reader to know a number of things I haven't managed to get in until now and I think I can do it by shoveling everything into my dialogue. The scene begins:

Harry:	Hi Joe. Even though we have been working side by side in this office for the last twenty years and you are the success and I am the failure and I'm worried about you getting the Finkle account and causing me to lose my job, I still have to say hello to you.
Joe:	Hello, Harry. Even though I spent last night running specs on the Finkle job which I think

I'm going to lose, I manage to stay cheerful so
I'm going to say, Nice morning.

Although that particular rendition has a kind of antic charm, it's off the point of the scene. If we need to know these things about these characters, and although I just made them up it's clear we probably do, there are better ways to render them.

When Harry came into the office, Joe was already at his desk, looking as if he'd been there all night, probably nailing the Finkle account. He had never liked Joe, in spite of which he had to say, "Hi Joe."

"Hello, Harry." Although he was the office star, Joe envied Harry his good looks, which meant he had to smile particularly brightly, saying, "Nice morning," although as far as he was concerned, it wasn't.

But you will notice that as I cleaned up the speeches, returning them to their simpler form, I discovered yet another new development. Although Joe is the success, he resents Harry because Harry is good looking and Joe isn't.

Rule Four: Attributions — Keep It Simple

Naturally as your characters play their scenes, you want readers to know who's talking. Some beginning writers do this in spades, tagging every speech with some variation of he-said-she-said. Because they're beginners, they're likely to go overboard in finding original and inventive ways to say this: for instance, he or she expostulated/ averred/ added/ explained/ questioned/ remarked/ added.. .etc., etc. You name it. Too many beginning writers have characters *doing* speeches: "Come in," she beamed, or "That's very nice," he smiled, when in fact *beaming* or *smiling* or *laughing* words is a physical impossibility.

Remember:

1. There is absolutely nothing the matter with saying, *she said*.

2. If only two people are talking, you don't need to make

attributions more than once every five or six lines. We can keep track of at least that much in our heads.

3. You can also make attributions by giving stage directions, supplying hand gestures or expressions. Let's look at our *working example*.

> When Harry came into the office, Joe was already at his desk, looking as if he'd been there all night, probably nailing the Finkle account. He had never liked Joe, in spite of which he had to say, "Hi Joe."
>
> "Hello, Harry." Although he was the office star, Joe envied Harry his good looks, which meant he had to smile particularly brightly, saying, "Nice morning," although as far as he was concerned, it wasn't.
>
> Harry smirked. "If you say so."
>
> "Well, it *is* a nice morning, isn't it?" Because he had never liked Harry and couldn't afford to show it, Joe had to smile through gritted teeth and add, "How are you?"
>
> "I'm OK, except for the roof."
>
> "What's the matter with the roof?"
>
> Harry could not stop smiling. "It fell on the dog in the hurricane."

Notice that you and I are altogether clear about who's talking at all times, and that nowhere in this example did I find it necessary to use any of the usual attributions—not even the simple and honorable "he said."

Rule Five: If in Doubt, Read It Aloud

Most writers working on dialogue can be caught muttering under their breaths or replaying speeches in their heads. Some will even get up from the desk or shift in the chair as they do all the voices and act out all the parts. This is because these are people they are dealing with, and not chairs or tables or ideas. Perhaps the best way to find out whether your characters are talking like real people is to take a deep breath and read each dialogue scene aloud.

More than one actor or actress has reduced a playwright to

tears by refusing to make a speech that is humanly impossible —
because the playwright has written a flowery or complex speech
that is quite simply unsayable. Reading aloud demonstrates to
you whether the words you have put in the mouths of your
characters sound like the things people actually say.

Rule Six: Characters Should Sound Like Individuals

To be be specific, your characters should sound like themselves
and not like each other. Again, reading aloud is going to help
you identify this problem.

Once you've identified it, there are a couple of things you
need to do.

First get firmly back into character and *listen hard*. Your old
lady isn't going to sound like your college student, and your
southern farmhand isn't going to sound like a businessman from
the North. Listen carefully and you will probably hear them. If
you don't, then look at what you have on the page and weigh
their word choices carefully. Your old lady is likely to deal in
euphemisms and not use contractions very often. She's likely
to say she "perspires" instead of sweats; she thinks people are
"disagreeable," a dated word that nails her age group on the
spot. College vocabularies change from year to year but we all
know what the speech rhythms are and some things have more
or less passed into the language. The southern farmhand is going to say, "Hey," instead of "Hi," will probably use ain't, and
the northern businessman? If you don't know any, you'll probably find the diction of any newscaster is going to be close to the
mark.

Now, test your characters' speech patterns against the
rhythms and word choices of people you know. If your characters sound like people you know, you can't go far wrong.

Rule Seven: Good Dialogue Is Transactional

The transaction completed can be as simple as Joe and Harry
recognizing and re-affirming the fact that they really don't like

each other or as complicated as a pair of lovers deciding to break up. Essentially this rule sums up what good dialogue is: it is *action*, dramatic and not expository. Yes, a straight line exists. You can trace it and pull it tight, as characters move from point A to point B.

Think of a dialogue exchange as one in which *something happens*. It takes two people to make a dialogue, and the interplay between characters gives it direction and shape — it is a *transaction*. You are marking the path of the transaction — with each party stating terms.

In some cases, the transaction is completed. Whether or not the transaction is completed is very much up to you as author and your individual characters *as long as the possibility for the transaction exists*.

You have set up the possibility, and part of the tension in any scene is going to be discovering whether things work out the way your characters hope they will. It helps to know that most characters want different things, which means that even in our *working example* between the mythical Harry and Joe you have the added drama of people at cross purposes. If the emotional deal doesn't come off, you have frustration, which has a dramatic power of its own.

Enough. With these simple rules, it's possible for you to go back to a piece of fiction you've written or are writing and apply the following checklist.

CHECKLIST IV. QUESTIONS ABOUT DIALOGUE

1. Is something happening in this scene?
2. Will what's happening be clear to readers through what my characters say?
3. Can I draw a dramatic line through a scene, demonstrating that they've moved emotionally from point A to point B?
4. Is this dialogue going to benefit from judicious cutting?
5. Do these speeches make it clear what's going on in the scene or do I need to clarify or further develop by adding

    a few lines?

6. Have I overloaded my speeches by trying to sneak in expository details?
7. Is it clear who's speaking in each case?
8. Are my attributions klunky and unnatural or are they unobtrusive?
9. Can I better use my external attributions to advance the action or demonstrate my speakers' states of mind?
10. When I read aloud, do these people sound like real people?
11. Do they sound like each other or do they sound like individuals?
12. Can I intensify or sharpen what they're saying to each other by making a stronger or more individual choice of words?
13. Have I set down the terms of a transaction in this scene:
   a. By letting my characters set down their own terms?
   b. By showing where they diverge?

If you've gotten into your characters' heads and listened to the way they talk, chances are your dialogue will stand up well to this kind of close scrutiny even in a first draft. The wonderful thing about dialogue is that writing it does come more or less naturally to most writers. It's — yes, as natural as speech — which means that any refining or improving done in the course of revision is fine-tuning of the kind that sharpens scenes and makes them exciting, effective and true.

    If your characters are in trouble, then it's time to stop and revise.

HOW TO PROCEED

First you're going to see whether your dramatic line is clear: what you need to put in or take out to define the movement between point A and point B. If it's not, there are steps you can take.

    1. *Tighten.* You'll begin by cutting, going through and get-

ting rid of excess — places where speakers repeat themselves, or where two lines will do the work of four. Learn to take shortcuts between strong, functioning lines, like A: I love you. B: Get out. If the characters have said too much between speech A and speech B, cut or compress.

Cutting is simple. Compression means making one speech do the work of two. For instance, if one character says, "I love you," the second says, "Really?" and the first says, "Really. Ever since the first day I saw you," it's easy to shorten the sequence by having the first speaker say: "I've loved you since the first day I saw you." You've made one line out of three.

Get rid of any extra phrases or word choices that ruin the rhythm or get between your character and the point. Get rid of any unnecessary attributions. If we already know who's talking, we don't need to be told again and again.

2. *Sharpen.* Then you'll go back, line by line, to be certain your characters are saying exactly what you want them to say. They may not be saying what they *mean*, but the intentions behind each speech should be clear to you.

3. *Intensify.* Fill in the gaps. If you've cut away everything that does not apply, you're going to have extra space to move around in. Be certain that your characters are saying *enough* to each other. This doesn't mean spelling things out. It means giving the reader enough information to carry the dramatic business of the scene.

4. *Fine tune.* This means more reading aloud, or replaying the speeches in your head to make certain the word choices and rhythms are exactly as you want them.

As you test and revise your dialogue passages, *making each scene as good as you can make it,* you'll find that major story decisions have taken care of themselves.

CHAPTER 9

FOCUS AND BALANCE: POINT OF VIEW, SHOWING VS. TELLING

AS YOU GET MORE AND MORE COMFORTABLE with the elements of fiction — the tools you use to build a story — you'll discover you're ready to move on to more complex considerations.

The first is *focus*. Do all the signposts in your story point in the right direction? That is, does the *way* in which you've written your story tell the reader:

1. What the story is about?
2. Which is the big moment?
3. How to feel about it?

The second is *balance*. Have you *gotten rid of everything that does not function in your story* in order to highlight what's important?

Your selection of point of view and decisions about where to use description and where to demonstrate in scenes both sharpen focus and create a good balance.

POINT OF VIEW

As you sit down to write, and as you sit down to revise, you need to ask yourself: Do I as writer of this story or novel know where to stand? This means establishing a consistent point of view. To maintain focus and narrative control, you as author need to write from one particular vantage point.

Unless you're an omniscient narrator, detailing everything each of your characters thinks and feels and, perhaps, pulling the whole thing together with authorial commentary, you're going to need to ask yourself some hard questions about point of view.

If you're writing a first-person narration, this is relatively simple. Your character says, I did this/did that/am doing this/will do that. Because you're speaking in your character's voice, you know what that person sees and hears and you tell it *as that person would tell it*. All you need to do is keep it consistent.

The third person offers a number of options:

1. You can use your viewpoint character like a camera, observing only what that character can see and hear or think or remember.

2. You can be a fly on the wall, observing everything everybody does and says but, like that fly, you're going to know what these people *think* only through their actions and what they have to say to each other.

3. You can be omniscient, knowing all and telling all, but remember, the risks are enormous:

    a. Loss of control. Trying to tell *all*, you may lose track of your central story.

    b. Loss of focus. It's a little like trying to keep the audience's eye on one particular performer in a three-ring circus.

4. You can employ multiple viewpoints. Some very good stories intercut first- and third-person narration, giving an overview in third person and then bringing various characters front and center for monologues. Again, the potential for loss of control and focus grows as your story spreads.

Although many novels and some successful stories employ multiple points of view, it's wise for beginning writers to keep it simple. You need to know whether you can control a simple story before you try juggling several points of view in a more ambitious one.

If you're just beginning to write fiction, it's a good idea to choose one method—first- or third-person narration, and if you're writing third-person narration, choose one character as your point-of-view character or "camera."

Picking up one of those collections of "Best" short stories, analyze several for point of view. Reading, ask yourself:

1. What is the point of view here? Is it written in the:
   a. First person.
   b. Second person ("you" do this and that in a story—a risky mode that's becoming more common).
   c. Third person with point-of-view or "camera" character.
   d. Third person "fly-on-the-wall."
   e. Third person omniscient.
   f. Or does it contain multiple points of view? If so, see who the viewpoint characters are, and how many. Try to figure out how the author made the decision. Notice how the author makes the shifts from one viewpoint to another. Does multiple viewpoint enhance or damage the story?
2. Does the point of view pull me, as reader, into the story?
3. If I were retelling this story, what viewpoint would I choose?
4. Which of these viewpoints am I most comfortable with?

Having studied established writers' use of point of view, you're ready to examine your own stories. Reading for revision, ask:

1. Is my narrative told from a definite point of view? As author, where do I stand? Am I omniscient, or have I taken the point of view of a first-person narrator? A third-person character who becomes the point-of-view character?

2. Am I consistent? Do I stay with my point-of-view character or have I jumped into some other character's head? If so, how can I give the reader the same information about that second character without leaving the head of my viewpoint character?

3. Am I playing according to the rules? If you're telling your story in first person, or with a third-person point-of-view character, you're entitled to know *only as much as that character*

knows. Any excursions into the heads of secondary characters disrupt the narrative and diffuse focus.

4. If I am telling this story in alternating first- and third-person prose, or using several first-person narrators, is this piece of fiction *long* enough to support more than one narrative point of view? Some writers like to tell stories through more than one narrator, or to intercut first-person narration with third-person accounts. Everything is technically possible, but you as writer need to think carefully about what you have on the page and to be willing to change tactics if multiple viewpoints are going to distract your reader or pull your story apart.

Multiple viewpoints are difficult to bring off in any case, but it's particularly hard to use multiple viewpoints and still maintain focus in a short piece. If your multiple-viewpoint story seems to fly apart under close scrutiny, it's probably a good idea to try to retell it through one of the characters — or to pull back and become the omniscient narrator, taking the reader by the hand through the thicket of your story.

5. Is this piece of fiction *strong* enough to support more than one narrative point of view? This is a question you may have to put to your first reader. If the story carries in spite of the diffuse narrative method, i.e., if it's strong and clear in spite of shifting points of view, then your first reader is going to "get it" and tell you so. If not, it's time to pull back and think about another narrative strategy.

6. If I do decide to alternate viewpoints — first- and third-person narration, for instance, or cuts between two or more first-person narrators — *am I signaling the reader where the narrative is located after each shift?*

There are several ways to do this: through space breaks or sections named for characters, places or times, or through something in the text that makes it clear who's talking, some internal reference that identifies the new viewpoint character in each section — as that character takes over the narrative.

SHOWING VS. TELLING

Having sharpened focus by establishing a consistent point of view, you can make your story even more effective by considering the relationship in the story between showing and telling.

Most fiction is made up of scenes and description. Authors *describe* or *tell*:

1. What people or places look and sound and feel like.
2. What's going on inside characters' heads.
3. What's happening along the way from the last scene to the next scene.

Through the use of scenes—units in which characters say or do something, acting and interacting, authors *demonstrate* or *show*.

The temptation, particularly for beginning writers, is to tell too much. Because dramatic scenes are often emotionally complicated and tricky to write, they're inclined to chicken out on the big moments, giving the reader "Harry and Martha had a fight," instead of showing the two characters in violent confrontation.

Showing too much can be just as bad for your story. If the characters bound and rebound from one fight to another to a third, every fight begins to sound like every other fight and the drama is diffused before the reader ever gets to the big one.

Good writers use both showing and telling, and work hard to strike a balance. A safe rule of thumb for beginners is to cut back on telling and *show* more than you *tell*, but eventually, you're going to want to use both.

Showing—demonstrating through action and dialogue passages, you keep the thread of the story tight.

Effective *telling* can enhance drama and prepare the reader for the story's big moments. Although the effectiveness of telling depends in part on how good a writer you are, too much telling can distract your reader, who may lose track out of confusion or, worse, boredom and indifference.

As you revise, ask yourself:

1. Am I describing too much of the action instead of letting it happen in fully rendered scenes?

2. If I'm telling too much, can I let some of it emerge in dialogue exchanges between characters, or by putting my characters in action in some other way?

3. If I'm telling more than is necessary, do I need to cut back? The answer is built into the question. You do.

Be prepared to get rid of passages that come *between* scenes — the kind of detail in which your character gets up and dresses and drives to the office, where the scene you're heading toward is actually going to take place.

Take a clue from the movies. You don't have to show us a character arriving, or tell us what that character does in his spare time between the last major scene and the next. Just cut from one day to the next.

Never tell when you can show. If you have a lethargic character, instead of describing this person at length, give us this character rolling out of the rumpled bed and tripping over the half-empty candy box, demonstrating the effort it takes for this person to move through stages of sleep back to life — or work. If two characters hate each other, don't tell us; let us see them fight.

When in doubt, cut. Even if you as writer are heavily committed to a long descriptive passage that doesn't advance your story, let it go. Chances are your readers won't miss it.

Looking at your story one more time, ask yourself these questions about focus:

1. Is the viewpoint consistent?
2. Am I telling too much?
3. If so, do I need to demonstrate with fresh scenes, cut description, or both?

Once you've been writing for a while, you'll be thinking about all these elements — and all the other elements, which are essentially inseparable, and all part of the same process — more or less at the same time, *from the moment you sit down to write.*

Even when you've gained control of your work, however, you're going to find there's still work to do. This will be true for you this year and every year for as long as you keep on writing; it will be true whether you're a draft writer who's taken a story through several drafts or a sentence-by-sentence writer who's taken weeks or months or even years to arrive at what looks like a final version.

It's the moment at which writer as insider has to move outside the work for one more sharply critical examination.

The time has come to read one more time, making one more revision to judge the success of your work in terms of story and structure.

CHAPTER 10

READING FOR STORY AND STRUCTURE

No matter how you work, you won't know for sure whether your work of fiction is doing what you want it to until you think it's finished. You have to believe it's finished before you can really step outside and try to see it the way others do.

Now that you think it's finished, it's time for another look. You need to reread and if necessary revise to make certain the story you carried in your head for so long has made it to the page all in one piece. You want to make it as strong as you can make it before you send it out.

You're ready to move on to the third major kind of revision, which I described in Chapter Three—revising to strengthen story and perfect structure. I've saved details for now because this crucial kind of revision has to wait for until you have the entire story or novel essentially complete.

Now that you have the whole thing, you're ready to consider it as a whole. This makes it possible for you to see more clearly whether you are indeed telling a story and whether or not the story comes off. Is there something at stake here? Does the tension build and is it satisfactorily resolved? Does it hit the mark or fall short? Why? *Have I done it right*?

These are questions you should be asking as you write. You may even be the kind of writer who proceeds best from a detailed outline of events, working with a roadmap designed to take you from point A to point B. If you're a draft writer you'll be able to ask yourself questions about story and structure after each draft, but you'll still have to ask them *one more time*.

By this time you've worked your way through all the other checklists and, armed with a sense of what's right developed through reading and revision, you're ready for the hardest question of all.

Is it all there?

There are many things to consider. Story and structural concerns are so tightly interwoven that I'm going to present them within a single extensive checklist with several sections.

CHECKLIST V: QUESTIONS ABOUT STORY AND STRUCTURE

Part 1: Action

1. *Is this a story?* By now you've read enough stories to know whether or not you're telling a real story. If you're rereading a novel, the questions become more complex. You may need to read chapter for chapter to see whether individual chapters have *dramatic unity*, that is, to find out whether *something is happening* in each chapter. Then you're going to have to reread the whole and ask yourself whether there is a central story question pulling your reader through the novel as a whole. You're reading for *narrative tug* — the kind of suspense that gives the reader some stake in the outcome. Remember, you're trying to hold reader attention for what may turn out to be hundreds of pages.

If you can't answer this tough question with an immediate *yes*, then ask yourself:

a. Is there something going on here, or is this simply a static description of a situation? Novelists in particular may lose track of this. You may be satisfied with the dramatic shape of individual chapters. Now it's time to read again to be certain there is a unifying concern that makes this a novel and not a series of short stories or, worse, stories and sketches trying to pass themselves off as a novel.

b. If there's supposed to be something going on, have I dramatized this for the reader in scenes or have I only summarized?

c. Is it clear what's at stake here? There should be suspense created, some question raised and answered. Novelist Jessamyn West called this "will-he-won't-he."

d. Have I made clear what my characters care about — what each of them *wants* and how far they're willing to go to get it? Everybody wants something. It's up to you to find out what your characters want and make your readers want it for them.

e. Does my reader have a stake in the outcome? Remember as writer that you can't expect your readers to care about something you don't care about yourself.

2. *Does my setup lead to a payoff?* Some people write beautiful setups — openings lush with description, living, breathing characters — only to shortcut by sketching the end in a few lines, or skipping it altogether, leaving the outcome to the reader's imagination. This may seem subtle, but it's not. Instead it's a symptom of authorial laziness. Be certain to deliver the payoff. This means letting the reader know what you have in mind — completing your own story with the collision of wills or the realization or reconciliation that you had in mind all the time. You may want to end with a BIG MOMENT. If so, be sure it's completely developed so your readers recognize it. *Remember, readers know only what you tell them.*

3. *Have I given enough information so my reader can see what I see?* You don't need to be obvious, but you do need to complete your thinking. You need to supply enough detail to let the attentive reader know what you're getting at, providing insight into characters' motives and background for their dreams. You knew what effect you were trying to create — what you thought you were doing when you wrote this story. Now you're trying to decide whether you've brought it off. This means asking yourself whether the reader is going to be able to make out your intentions. Ask:

a. Is my reader, who is essentially a stranger to this story, going to be able to tell what's going on between these characters I know so well?

b. Have I introduced story strands that I haven't tied up? If so, you may need to rework the section in question or the whole story, making sure that the shotgun you brought onstage in the first scene is fired in the last, and if it isn't, that there's a foolproof explanation of the reasons why.

   c. Have I drawn and dramatized all the major events or do some of my biggest moments happen offstage? If so, can I develop further to make my work stronger?

Part 2: Consistency

Making certain this story or novel you've written is all of a piece, that it does what it sets out to do, you're going to need to ask yourself certain technical questions.

1. Have I been faithful to point of view?
2. What about the time scheme?
   a. Does my story begin at the beginning? As I've suggested in the chapter on dialogue, sometimes we write a lot on the way to finding out what we have to write. Now is the time to take out the excess. If your first scene begins with a lengthy description of setting *that does nothing to advance the story*, chances are it needs to be cut or tightened. Ask: Does my story really begin here? If you can free yourself of commitment to what you've already written, you may be able to *cut to the chase*. If starting here necessitates a lot of explanation or klunky flashbacks, keep asking: Does my story begin here or earlier or later? Where?
   b. Does a complex time scheme help or hurt here? If you're using flashbacks to avoid the had-hads, judge yourself harshly. Ask yourself: how much of this information is important to the story? How much can I suggest or imply in other ways, and how much can I do without?
   c. Can I cut down on the number of shifts? Sometimes telescoping flashbacks—joining two segments of time past to cut down on trips back and forth to the present—can strengthen the time present story line and make it more effective.
   d. Am I shifting in time at the right point? If you're alternating between past and present, is there a logic to the shifts—when you go from present into the past, and when you shift back?
   Is the past line chronological, and if not, why not? Can you justify the chronology? Is there a valid reason for

the story to shuttle back and forth between points in the past?

    e. Am I making it clear on the page when time shifts occur? There are many ways of signaling this, from the use of space breaks and section labels to tag lines that pull the reader into a section. As you're asking for close attention, you'd better be sure you've given adequate direction markers.

    f. Is the chronology clear? Even patient readers need something to go on—the sense that if they follow you faithfully, they're going to find out not only where they are, but *when* they are.

3. What about the tone? It's possible to intercut comic and tragic sections in a novel and have the thing work as a whole, but it's harder to do in a short story. No matter how complex the time scheme or use of tense or point of view, you want your story or novel to look as if it is all written by the same person.

Part 3: Completeness

This is hard for most of us to see without outside help, because the work we've just finished is always the one closest to our hearts. We know it so well that we can't see why everybody else won't too. We've lived with our characters so long that we assume our readers have too.

Now it's time to try to see them through the eyes of a reader who's never met them. We have to be alert to gaps so we can supply what's missing—what we see that the reader can't. An outside reader unfamiliar with the piece can be particularly helpful here.

1. Is my story all there? I know what I'm trying to do, but is everybody else going to?

2. Have I skimped on exposition, assuming my reader's going to know what I know?

3. Have I left too much to my reader's imagination? Even the best readers need a few signposts—descriptive details to set the scene, indications through dialogue, characters' aspect (that

is, carriage or expression) or action to let them know what characters have on their minds.

4. Have I skipped key scenes? Some writers lose their big moments by lapsing into summary—others just leave them out. "You mean you didn't *know* he was in love with his sister?" Instead of berating the reader who doesn't "get it," reread to see what you've left out.

Part 4: Pacing

This is a big consideration, and your answers are going to be determined in large part by how attentive you've been to all the matters of action, consistency and completeness. Whether you've just finished a short story or a novel, you're going to need to ask yourself some of the same questions.

- Does my story take too long to get started?
- Are the individual scenes dramatic?
- Is the whole dramatic?
- Is there a big enough payoff at the ending to justify what precedes it?
- What about the balance between showing and telling? Have I demonstrated all my big moments with scenes or have I only summarized?
- Do I need to cut description or summary to heighten the effect of my scenes?
- Is my reader going to be satisfied that *something important has happened here*?
- Does it end in the right place or did I keep on writing after I should have written "the end?"

Because a novel is a long and complicated work, you'll want to go through, chapter for chapter, asking yourself these questions about each unit. Then you're going to have to try and stand back from the work as a whole so you can see whether the entire piece is in balance—whether your long narrative, made up of individual dramatic units, starts in the right place, moves fast and pulls the reader along to the ultimate big moment.

As you begin a novel, all through the long job and now at this last reading, try to keep in mind what's at stake in the novel as a whole. You can't tell readers everything right away but you do want them to stay with you through however many individual episodes there are, for however many pages it takes you to let them know the outcome. Two things are particularly useful here:

1. *The chapter hook*: the immediate question raised to draw the reader from one chapter to the next. What's going to happen next?
2. *The larger narrative question*: What's going to happen at the end of this whole book?

You want your readers to wonder — and care.

Part 5: Length

It's important to tighten so your readers can keep track of the questions you've raised. You may already have that uncomfortable suspicion that your work is too long, and you may know which section needs cutting or compressing, in which case it's time to sit down with the pencil or marker and get to work.

If you're still not sure, ask yourself: is my story too long for what it does?

Your sense of this is going to depend largely on your ability to step back from what you've done and judge it according to the same high standards you apply to fiction you've read. Try to be objective when you answer the next questions.

1. Is it boring? I know this is a hard question, and if you try and try and still can't answer it honestly for yourself, ask a reader you trust.

2. Does too much detail in one section ruin the proportion? An example: You've spent the first three pages of a ten-page story describing the farmhouse where the action takes place. Chances are, your story is out of proportion and you need to cut.

3. Does this section function in the story? To know this, you'll need to be able to see what you've written as a whole, and you're also going to have to be objective and cold-blooded about it. If you're in doubt, remove the pages in question, set them

aside and try reading the piece without them. Then give it to someone else to read. It's going to be clear whether you need the section in question or not.

Part 6: Organization

Intelligent cutting enhances organization. It's like pruning a tree to make it take its proper shape. Unlike trees, fiction can also be rearranged.

You're showing readers what you think is most important by deciding what to put first.

The longer the work, the more complicated questions of organization are going to be, quite simply because it's harder to stand off from it and get a good look. A short story can go as badly wrong as a novel, but because it's short, its problems are easier to identify and correct.

Even though novels are more complex, you'll discover that in most cases organizational revision does not involve an enormous amount of new writing, or rewriting. Instead it is a matter of being able to divide the work into units and step back and try to see whether in this draft, the units fall in the right place.

You can judge your narrative for organization:

1. According to standards you've developed through reading.
2. With the help of a reader.
3. By applying a simple test.

The technique I suggest applies to both short and long fiction. This simple method can help you locate and identify problems of organization. It offers a low-fault method of trying out different solutions.

This technique can also be applied on the job, as you approach the end of a piece the first time through. Student writers I know have used it successfully to find out how to finish long pieces, making tactical decisions about the end of a story or a novel on a trial-and-error basis *by moving items on a list*. It will not tell you what kinds of things to put in or leave out but it will help you develop a surer sense of where they belong. This is how it works.

1. Break down your piece by making a list. List the major events or units—not in detail, but in two or three words. I'm not talking here about naming chapters, but rather, events, or sequences.

If you'd written *The Great Gatsby*, for instance, the first few items on the list might look like this:

Nick meets Gatsby

Nick's feelings for Daisy

first party

Each item stands for something complicated and each falls into the narrative in a certain order. You should be able to find appropriate labels for major events in anything you've written, no matter how ambitious.

2. Now look at the order.

3. Rearrange the items on your list. Remember, this is a very small investment of time compared to what you've already spent. It's also a low-risk way of trying out alternative solutions. Remember, this is only a list. So far, your story or novel is intact; you haven't changed a word.

4. Keep rearranging items until you're satisfied that the order is right. If it's what you started out with, this is nature's way of telling you that structurally, your piece is as well put-together as you can make it.

5. If you find the list of elements has settled in a different order from the one you started out with, go back to your story or novel and reorganize and revise accordingly.

6. If you do your job carefully and are willing to be flexible about approaching reorganization; if you're willing to spend some time considering and weighing each piece *and* its place, the natural order should assert itself.

7. If you put everything in its right place and find you have some units or items left over because they don't belong in the

new order, take a deep breath and put them aside.

8. Now it's time to go back and read for consistency, especially if your revision has altered the time scheme. If this means making phrase changes or writing connective paragraphs, be prepared to do them.

Once you've responded to all the questions on this last, major checklist for yourself, you've done the hardest part — reading to find out where and how your story and structure need revision.

SUMMARY CHECKLIST

1. Is it a story?
2. Have I made it accessible to my reader?
3. Am I consistent in my use of point of view, time scheme and tone?
4. Is my story complete or do I need to develop it further?
5. What about the pace? Does it move swiftly or have I slowed it down by too much telling and not enough showing?
6. Does it need cutting?
7. What about the organization? Is it unfolding in the right order?

Making decisions about what's working and what's not working and what to do about it is the hard part.

The easy part is carrying them out.

We'll talk about nuts and bolts — the physical ways to deal with and complete revision — in the next chapter.

CHAPTER 11

HOW TO PROCEED

BY THIS TIME YOU PROBABLY have plenty of ideas about what you intend to do to a story or novel that needs revision.

There is one last item we need to talk about before we move on into ways to make words and phrases and entire scenes end up where you want them to. This consideration demonstrates as well as any the link between thought and the physical business of carrying out revision. It is cutting.

CUTTING VS. COMPRESSION

We all develop a sense of which passages in our stories or novels are too long for what they do. If we don't know this instinctively, there's usually a reader or an editor who will point it out to us.

In some cases, it's simply a matter of removing a scene or a paragraph of description or an entire section that doesn't work and isn't necessary. In other cases, what we're doing is OK, it's simply too long for what it does. We are going to have to make it shorter.

There are two ways to approach this:

1. *Cutting*. We either draw a line through or erase parts of the passage, eliminating words to make it shorter.

2. *Compression*. We rewrite or retype the passage to make it shorter. We're not so much cutting as changing the prose in the passage to boil it down—we're trying to say exactly the same

things in the same way, but in a way that makes the passage shorter and tighter.

I'll invent a verbose passage and then show you two ways of making it shorter.

> In the autumn of the first year after she was married to Jerome in a summer ceremony with only Jerome's mother and sister in attendance, Marguerite had a very bad time getting along with her husband Jerome's family. It wasn't that she didn't like her husband's mother Mary and his sister Eleanor, who had a wen on her nose and always walked around in work boots and support stockings, it was simply that the two women got on Marguerite's nerves because they wandered around the house—Marguerite's house!—in their country clothes with their faces fixed in faintly negative expressions that to Marguerite, at least, suggested they were feeling disapproval.

First let me edit with a pencil, showing you how this would look if I simply cut out some words and phrases to make it shorter.

> In the autumn of the ~~first~~ year after she ~~was~~ married ~~to~~ Jerome, ~~in a summer ceremony with only Jerome's mother and sister in attendance~~, Marguerite had a ~~very~~ bad time getting along with ~~her husband Jerome's~~ *his* family. It wasn't that she didn't like ~~her husband's~~ *his* mother Mary and his sister Eleanor, who had a wen on her nose and ~~always~~ walked around in work boots and support stockings~~, it was simply that~~ The two women got on Marguerite's nerves because they wandered around *her* ~~the~~ house ~~—Marguerite's house!~~—in their country clothes with their faces fixed in ~~faintly negative~~ expressions that ~~to Marguerite, at least,~~ suggested ~~they were feeling~~ disapproval.

It's clear that I can get rid of a lot of verbiage that way, but as a writer more accustomed to compression, I seem to need to *re-write*, not so much cutting as compressing.

> In the autumn after she married Jerome with only his

mother and sister present, Marguerite had trouble getting along with them. It wasn't that she disliked Mother Mary or Eleanor, who clomped around in work boots and support stockings, it was just that she found them unnerving, wandering around the house—Marguerite's house!—in their country clothes with fixed expressions of faint disapproval.

Remember, this is only an example constructed to demonstrate method. None of these versions is going to win any prizes, but versions two and three are definitely shorter than the first, and I would submit that the third is smoother than the other two.

Cutting your own work, you may settle on a combination of cutting and compression, crossing out words and then rewriting to make a smoother, shorter version.

Now you're ready for the final consideration—which tools and which methods you're going to use to make your revision.

Looking at your work, judging it according to standards you've developed through reading and asking yourself some of the questions on the appropriate checklists, you've made certain decisions about what needs cutting or compressing, what needs changing, what organizational changes need to be made. Once you've made the artistic decisions, only mechanical choices remain.

Now it's time to get down to nuts-and-bolts considerations—how to make the best use of your tools of the trade. By this time you probably know whether you're most at home writing by hand or on a typewriter or a computer, or using some combination of the three. Even with the major decisions already made, you may find the idea of getting all the right words in the right place somewhat daunting.

This is a good time to let method take over. If you know *where* you're going to do a revision and *what* you need to do, it helps to develop a few working habits. Knowing *how* you're going to do something makes it easier to get started. There are no shortcuts, but there are some mechanical techniques that make the physical business of revision easier.

THE NOTEBOOK

If you compose with pen or pencil, you've already developed a couple of systems—crossing out or replacing words, X-ing out sections and marking sections you want to move from one place to another. You also know that at a certain point you need to copy the whole thing over so you can read what you've written and that either you or a professional typist is going to have to make a typescript.

Once you have a typescript you're likely to want to make more pen changes and have a corrected typescript made. Before you submit your manuscript to an editor, you'll need to have a clean copy of the entire work, typed or printed double-spaced with pages accurately numbered and your name and address on the title page.

There are several tricks you can play on yourself to make composing easier and help yourself get started on revisions.

1. Even when writing by hand, double or triple space. Leave margins where you can. This gives you more room for the notes, expansions, word changes and additions of phrases you're going to make as your story develops.

2. A loose-leaf notebook will make organization easier. You can move entire sections and add, expand or remove scenes without having to recopy the entire story or chapter each time you want to change something.

3. Using a loose-leaf notebook, you can add pages of notes or outline pages as you make them, and move them as necessary without disrupting your text.

4. In some cases you may be able to cut and paste, taping four or five replacement lines over the original text, or cutting the page in two so you can insert a new scene. This makes it possible to make changes as you go without having to recopy. If you use both sides of the page, cut up a photocopy.

5. When your text gets too messy to be legible, it's nature's way of telling you it's time to copy the whole thing over. You'll find developmental changes and ideas for expansion occur as you go.

6. There is a point when you need to move into typescript. Before you can consider yourself finished, you're going to have to see what you've written in cold, uncompromising type. Because hand-writing is intensely personal, some writers get so committed to the way the page looks in an abstract way—all those loopy Ls and Ys—that they have a hard time seeing what they've written in a cold light. If you can type, move to the type-writer or the computer. If not, pay to have a draft typed with the idea that you're probably going to need to keep revising.

7. If in doubt, copy it over. If you have the vague sense that a scene or an entire piece isn't working right and you don't know what to do about it, recopying is the best way to solve the problem. You'll discover that faulty sentences straighten themselves out and the logic of what you're doing asserts itself as you reproduce it on a fresh page. Dialogues seem to develop and grow. Often the donkey work of copying frees the mind to solve narrative problems.

8. Copy over yesterday's work if you're having a hard time getting started. This is also an excellent way to avoid the mythical writer's block. If you're copying, at least you're *working*, and at some point you'll gather momentum, writing on to discover what's on the next page.

9. Duplicate your manuscript and put the photocopy in a safe place. Notebook writers are inclined to carry their work with them—on buses, planes, taxis, to the beach. Because they're portable and easily damaged by water, manuscripts in note-books are particularly accident-prone. You're going to want to take this simple step to insure yourself against loss.

THE TYPEWRITER

I began my career as a writer on a Royal Standard office model—manual. Naturally I became heavily committed to typing as a way of composing—and as a way of life. Composing on the typewriter seemed easier than writing by hand—or making handwritten changes or corrections—because I could always re-type to make the page look the way it ought to. As I typed, I discovered the words kept rearranging themselves until they said the right thing.

Along the way, I developed a few techniques for revision that may be useful to anybody who works on a typewriter.

1. Always double or triple space to leave room for changes, expansion or notes. Wide margins are a help for the same reason. Double space your final draft.

2. When in doubt, retype. You are integrating composition and revision. This simple procedure works on sentence drafts, page drafts, completed first drafts. There is a connection between head and hands that allows the brain to keep working and developing your thoughts even as you type. This is one of the best and most significant things about working on a typewriter.

3. Begin the day by retyping the last two or three pages you finished the day before. This gives you continuity. The pages you retype will get better in the process and you'll have a running head start on the new day's work.

4. At the end of each day, sit down with a pen or pencil and look over what you've done. You'll catch typographical errors immediately but, more important, you'll begin to see how your work may change and grow when you get back to it the next morning.

5. If you need to make word changes on what is essentially a finished typescript, you can do it easily, either by retyping (see above) or with the help of White-Out or correction tape.

6. If you need to reorganize:

a. Number the sections that need moving. Put corresponding numbers in the text in the pages where you're going to insert these sections.

b. Cut apart the page in the place where you're going to make the insertions.

c. Use glue or tape to make the reorganization.

d. Retype the affected pages. If you're making large changes in a short story, it makes sense to spend the extra time and retype it from the beginning. You'll need to make your own decisions about longer pieces of fiction. Suffice it to say that almost every work of fiction benefits from being typed over by the author, from the top, and that potential publishers may be unnecessarily prejudiced by numbering changes on a manuscript that looks as if it's been taken apart and put together again.

7. If you need to cut:

a. Cross out the sections you're doing away with or earmark them for compression.

b. Cut the page to remove the section in question.

c. If you're compressing, you can either retype the page including the compressed paragraph, or cut and paste or tape in the new section to see what it looks like before you retype the page.

8. If you need to make insertions, you can follow the steps listed above. If you're inserting several pages but not retyping the entire manuscript, be sure to renumber all the pages or add A, B, C, etc. to the new pages, as: 28A, 28B, 28C, etc.

9. Most editors don't like corrasable bond because it smudges, but it's the easiest way to make corrections and last-minute word changes and still have a presentable typescript for submission. Corrasable will give you the flexibility to make changes at the last minute. A good, clear photocopy will bypass the editor's prejudice. Most editors will accept *a clear photocopy* so long as you let them know this is not a multiple submission. If this is a big project and you're in any doubt, inquire before you submit.

10. Every time you accumulate a significant number of pages—pages you don't want to have to try to reproduce from memory—have them duplicated. You're not as likely to lose a manuscript as a writer who carries handwritten work around from place to place, but these things do happen. A photocopy also gives you a record of what you had on the page before you began revising. Naturally you'll keep a copy of every finished manuscript you send out for possible publication.

THE COMPUTER

Notice that I call the instrument in question a computer, not a word processor. Machines don't process words. They don't even work with them. People do. The computer with the so-called word processing program makes the physical process — all those deletions, all that reorganization, all that cutting and pasting — considerably easier. Remember, I say it makes the *physical process* easier. Decisions are just as hard, as is the demanding business of thinking through what you're doing.

Critics like to say that computers lend themselves to automatic writing: all those words, and on a screen, too, and so fast! It's not writing, they say, it's more like TV! Only amateurs think so. Although there's a certain glamour to technology, it's only technology. Think of the computer as a super typewriter, with built-in functions that make it possible for the demanding writer to go back to the text again and again in the attempt to make it *right* — functions that encourage the writer who'd like to think of the work as finished to push each revision even farther.

Everybody knows computers make typing (notice I say typing, and not *writing*) quicker and easier. In spite of the speed of the machine, *it takes me exactly as long to compose on the computer as it did on the typewriter*.

If it takes me just as long to write a story or finish a novel as it ever did, where does the time go? I'd like to think that it goes into development through revision. Instead of typing and re-typing up to seventeen versions of a first sentence to arrive at something that satisfies me, I have the liberty to push to twenty, twenty-five, twenty-eight. Instead of having to spend quite so much time on donkey work, typing and retyping, I have more freedom to think about what I'm doing.

I will never know whether I was at some level calling my typescripts finished before they were really finished because I was physically exhausted from all that retyping, but I do know that it's easier for me to keep grappling with something when the medium is as flexible as the computer. For me, it seems as swift and mobile as thought. I'm thinking and rethinking, organizing and reorganizing on the screen.

Demonstrating my new toy to the poet Richard Wilbur, I showed him how quickly, almost magically I could consider some eight options in the choice of a particular verb. We both agreed this was no way to write poetry, but the mobility — the potential for thinking through, unencumbered by ink and paper — amazed him.

The computer makes me reread everything I do from the top every morning. As an inveterate typist, I used to retype instead of reread. Because typing is long and life is short, I'd redo only the last scene I'd done the day before. Now I begin at the top of the file and page through the story or chapter from the beginning, screen by screen, correcting typos and making small changes and large ones, before I pick up where I left off the day before.

I am fairly certain that the computer has made me more open to possibilities for revision. I can look at a novel I think is finished and see it in terms of what needs to be done without facing the grisly prospect of retyping some 300-plus pages in order to make a presentable-looking manuscript.

In the course of working with beginning student writers, I've made an interesting discovery that suggests that in spite of the fears of its critics, the computer can make us better writers.

The student faced with the prospect of revising a typescript will go to any lengths to defend those perfectly typed pages — *anything to keep from having to retype*.

The student who works on the computer listens carefully to group discussion of a faulty story, says, "Oh, OK," and goes away to see how the story in question ought to be reworked.

I can report firsthand that the computer makes it easier to get started. When I moved from the Royal Standard office model manual, I threw out my scissors and glue and my corrasible and my White-Out. I still go through all the same processes. I work just as hard. Freed from the messy, mechanical business of incorporating changes, I may work even harder.

If you're already composing on a computer, I don't need to describe the advantages of computer over typewriter or my computer over yours, and there's no point in discussing the relative merits of so-called word processing programs. Most of us are committed to our own hardware and software because it was quite simply a case of love at first sight.

If you don't compose on a computer and have managed to avoid the usual prejudices, I suggest that you beg, borrow or rent a session on one with a helping hand from a friend who can show you just exactly how it works. You'll come to your own conclusions and make your own decisions. If you decide to buy one, you'll get plenty of advice about which is a good computer and what is the best program for the kind of work you do from colleagues with computers.

I might even suggest that even though you think you hate and fear computers, you ought to consider making your final typescript on one, for all the above reasons. Even when you think you're finished you may need to revise one more time at the request of an editor. With your work recorded on a disk, you can still take advantage of some of the following tricks for revision.

Computer Revision

1. Naturally you will begin by storing what you write frequently, and backing up every file with a copy. You may also want to print at the end of every working day. If you work on floppies, copy onto a backup. If you're working on a hard disk, back up with a floppy. Be certain to store and copy all changes at the end of every working session.

2. When you begin revising, you may want to keep at least one copy on disk of every version you write of a story or novel, in addition to a printout. This gives you a permanent record of your progress through various drafts, and enables you to retrieve things you've cut but may decide later that you want to restore.

3. If you're having trouble with a particular passage, copy it into a separate file so you can go back to it and work on it without distractions. You may want to put it through several versions before you replace your original version.

4. If you've learned how to use your word processing program, you already know how to make word changes and how to reorder sentences within paragraphs. You'll use block marking and moving procedures to reorganize the order of paragraphs.

5. You may want to print out at the end of every day's work and revise on hard copy. Moving away from the screen helps distance you from your text in the same way that revising on a typescript helps somebody who writes by hand. It will help you see your piece as a whole. It makes sense to read every finished story or chapter over in hard copy with an eye toward possible revision.

6. When you go to work, page through yesterday's file from the beginning, reading for typographical errors and making necessary word changes as you go.

7. Before you move on, enter the changes you made on hard copy. Using hard copy as a reference, run your FIND function, using a distinctive word or string to take you to each spot where you're making changes.

9. You can use your FIND and REPLACE function to change character or place names throughout. You can also use it to locate distinctive words and phrases — the kind that are too big or unusual to be used more than once, even in a novel. It will also help you eliminate repetitious phrasing. The computer is going to be quick to let you know whether you've already used a word like "bizarre" or whether a phrase like "as she liked to remember" turns up·one time too many. Once you've located repetitions, it's easy to make substitutions. Knowing is half the battle.

10. If you're cutting a section or a scene, move it to a specially named file until you're certain you really want to get rid of it. If you know where it is, you can always get it back in case you decide you want to replace it.

11. If you're reorganizing, sometimes it helps to set up a separate file for the passage in question instead of moving it from one place to another only to have to move it again. Once you have it in a file of its own, it's out of the way but you know where to go if you decide you need it.

12. Reading for story and structure, make your list of elements *on the screen*. This gives you flexibility in ordering and reordering until you're certain that your organization is the right one.

13. If you think you need to expand a scene, you may want

to copy it onto a separate file and do your revision there, before reading it back into your story or chapter.

14. You can move entire sections or chapters, trying things out first here and then there in order to find out where they sit comfortably. It's wise to keep an unchanged backup.

15. Unless you're a meticulous speller with an infallible eye for typographical errors, wait until you're truly finished and then run your spelling check before you print.

16. Many editors refuse to read products from dot matrix printers. If you don't have a letter quality printer you may want to find one you can use to make your final copy. If none is available, put your dot matrix printer on double strike and photocopy the product. In many cases, editors won't be able to tell the difference, and if they do, they can't really complain because you've done your best to make it immediately legible.

17. Even though you think you've proofread on the screen, proofread on hard copy. For whatever reasons, typographical errors are more obvious once they're on paper.

WHAT'S NEXT

Once you've read and reread and rewritten your manuscript, asking most of the questions I've suggested in earlier chapters, and taking some of the steps, you've gone as far as you can go without some concrete news from the outside world.

It's time to start sending out your manuscript. You can do this yourself, trying to target your market by learning as much as possible, as I suggested in Chapter Four, or you can look for an agent to offer your work, using tactics I described in Chapter Four.

You will see to it that your manuscript is cleanly typed, double spaced, with the pages numbered, and that your name and address are on the title page. Mail it flat, not folded, and enclose a self-addressed envelope with return postage. Keep a record of where you're sending it, and when, and as a healthy next step, list one or two other places where you might like to send it if this editor rejects it.

And then?

The best thing to do while you're waiting for a response from the outside world—in short, while you're waiting to find out whether or not this bird is going to fly—is to start something new.

You've already done the best job you could on the manuscript you began with. Now you're going to discover an unexpected payoff. An agent I once had put it this way: "Nothing you write is wasted."

Every time you revise, you learn something about writing.

This means that you're likely to find that the work goes better on the new story because you've confronted certain artistic problems and found new ways of solving them. This is true after one year of writing, or ten, or a long lifetime. The better you get at writing, at judging what you've written and rewriting, the surer your touch is going to be.

As a result, you're going to develop a stake in the new piece you're writing—and you're likely to turn to it with increased confidence.

Whatever you do, keep working. It's the best way to keep from dying if the response from the outside world this time turns out to be no.

And if your work comes back, not once but several times? You'll look at it one more time, trying to decide whether you can put it over on the next submission—as soon as you rewrite.

Good luck.

CHAPTER 12

KNOWING WHEN TO QUIT

BUT YOU'RE STILL HERE. You think your manuscript is ready to go but you want to pass your hands over it one more time before you send it off.

It's time for a quick once-over.

Before you do anything else, ask yourself: Is this a story? Does something *happen* here? Is there the kind of development that makes it clear this is not a sketch or an essay but a story? If you're finishing a novel, ask yourself: Is my central story thread pulled tight enough to hold my reader's attention throughout?

If you're confident that the answer is YES, it's time to move on to the final checklist.

1. Does this begin at the beginning?

2. Is the beginning effective? Will the reader know and care about what's going on here?

3. Have I used enough detail to set the scene and give the reader a sense of what's going on? Have I used the right details? Can I be more specific?

4. Are my characters believable? Would they behave the way they do in this story?

5. Is the dialogue dramatic? Convincing? Characteristic? Do my people sound like real people? Does the dialogue need cutting? Or do I need to develop scenes further?

6. Am I faithful to the point of view I've chosen? If there are multiple points of view, are the shifts clear to the reader?

7. Does the story unfold logically? Is the chronology clear? If there is a complicated time scheme is it justified, and have I made the time shifts clear to the reader?

8. What about focus? Are all the signs pointing in the right direction? Do all the scenes and descriptive passages lead up to and away from the key scene, or big moment?

9. What about organization? Is everything in the right place?

10. Is my story too long for what it does in any section? Do I need to make cuts, or to keep the passages in question but compress for dramatic effect?

11. What about the balance between showing and telling? Am I giving my readers enough scenes or am I describing too much?

12. Am I taking too much for granted? Is the reader going to get the point or do I need to expand?

13. What about narrative tone? Whether it's comic, tragic, a mystery or historical, *does it sound like what it's supposed to be?*

14. Have I proofread?

If you've answered all these questions to your satisfaction, you're ready to mail. Most of you are already reaching for the 8 × 11 envelope.

What about the rest?

At this stage some of you are still holding on to your manuscripts, whether through feelings of anxiety or inferiority or simply because you feel safer fussing endlessly over the same old familiar thing than putting your work out where it will be judged — or starting something new.

For the moment, you may need to cut loose and send out your work before you think you're ready. If you're still doubtful, instead of mailing to an agent or editor, or asking for an outside reading, put it away and *start something new*. Getting into a new piece of work is going to put things into perspective for you. It may even give you the courage to put that much-revised piece before an audience — a key step if you're going to grow as a writer.

Everybody's got to find out the truth sometime. You may be delighted to discover that somebody out there likes your work. What if they don't? There are three things you need to remember:

1. This isn't the only thing you're ever going to write.
2. You won't die if this particular work is a flop.
3. An individual failure is easier to take *if you don't stake everything on one work*. Starting something new is the best insurance I know.

As you write more, you're going to develop the *insider's sense of rightness*. With practice, you're going to be able to keep most of the major artistic questions in your head all at the same time instead of thinking of them as separable elements. The better you get at what you're doing, the more quickly you're going to know whether something's working or not working so you can make sound decisions as you go.

This growing sense of rightness is the ultimate payoff to the time and effort you've spent on writing and revision. It will tell you when to persist and when to quit. It's going to make you feel good about your work.

Appendix

It's clear that one of the best ways to show you how to revise is to let you see how professionals do it. Beginning this book, I asked two writers for manuscript samples of early drafts—and copies of the work as it finally appeared in print.

Lois Gould has published six novels, including *Such Good Friends*, *A Sea-Change* and *La Presidenta*. Manuscript page and page proofs from her newest novel, *Subject to Change*, appear in Chapter Two. Gould has also written nonfiction and originated the *Hers* column for the *New York Times*. Explaining why she composes and revises in longhand, she says, "I always felt punished, chaining myself to a machine with a plug and having it hum reproachfully at me." Her interest in this project prompted The Writers Room exhibit on revision and through her kindness and the cooperation of Renata Rizzo-Harvi, executive director of The Writers Room, we reproduce a portion of it here.

Also reproduced here is the manuscript extract by Thomas M. Disch, discussed in the second chapter. Drama critic for *The Nation*, Disch has published everything from SF and an interactive novel for the computer to poetry. His novels include *Camp Concentration*, the pseudonymous *Clara Reeve* and *The Businessman, a Tale of Terror*.

He is currently working on an adaptation of *Ben Hur* for an off-Broadway company. He says, "I write in longhand in a spiral notebook only when I'm out of the house away from a typewriter."

His extract from a short story titled "Hard Work" is included in the Appendix. It appeared in the British magazine *Interzone*.

The rest of the manuscript samples come from The Writers Room exhibit, which garnered national attention and prompted a series of public readings by the authors included. At Lois Gould's suggestion, the exhibition was organized by executive director Renata Rizzo-Harvi, who has provided the accompanying text.

Although the exhibition included manuscripts by poets and writers of nonfiction as well, the Appendix focuses on manuscript pages of works of fiction and writing for the stage.

Founded in 1978, The Writers Room was designed as an alternative for New York-based writers who had been working in the Frederick Lewis Allen Room at the New York Public Library. The object was to provide office space at low rates on a twenty-four-hour basis.

Any writer with a serious writing project may be considered for admission. Admission is for three months and may be extended. There is a $50 initiation fee due upon acceptance and quarterly fees for writers are $150. The Room, located at 153 Waverly Place in Greenwich Village, welcomes writers from all over the country who are visiting New York and is supported by contributions which are tax deductible.

Here are illustrations of manuscript pages and page proofs indicating first and final drafts by these writers. They are number keyed to details about the authors and discussion of their work habits. The illustrations follow.

Note that no two writers go about revising the same way.

— Kit Reed

Figures 1 and 1*a*. From *August*, a novel written in The Writers Room by Judith Rossner. Rossner is the author of more than seven novels, including *Attachments*, *Emmeline* and *Looking for Mr. Goodbar*. This is the third draft of the first page of the novel that was to become *August*, part of 100-odd pages that were ultimately "thrown away," the author says, "or at least consigned to a file someplace."

In a departure from her usual method of starting novels on

lined pads, Rossner began her current novel in progress on a computer. After writing 400 pages, however, she discovered that the book's plots were proliferating wildly. "The story was branching out instead of turning into an overwhelming stream," says Rossner. So she closed down her computer and went back to her typewriter to complete the novel. "Using a computer offers you so many possibilities," Rossner says, "and it never forces you to choose between them."

Figures 2 and 2*a*. From a screenplay in progress by James Lapine. Lapine co-authored *Sunday in the Park with George*, and is the writer and director of the Broadway musical *Into the Woods*, for which he recently won a Tony award for Best Book.

Figures 3 and 3*a*. From *Shuffle, Shuffle, Jive, Shuffle*, a play in progress by Ted Bent. Bent has written extensively for magazines, film, television and radio.

Bent generally starts writing on large lined pads, then goes back and forth between longhand and computer. He revises both on the monitor and by printing out copy and making changes in longhand. For a given project, he may write four drafts, with "endless" revisions within each draft. "I find writing on a computer is like writing on water," Bent says. "It's wonderful because it allows endless flexibility in experimenting with changes."

Figures 4 and 4*a*. From a work in progress, *Identity Papers*, by Signe Hammer. Hammer is the author of *Passionate Attachments: Fathers and Daughters in America Today* and *Daughters and Mothers, Mothers and Daughters*.

Hammer begins writing on a computer, and also revises on a computer until she senses that her work is ready to print out. She then makes revisions on hard copy, often seeing things that she didn't catch on the computer screen. These changes are ultimately entered into the computer, and the cycle begins again. "This process can be done several times for one piece of work until I think it's finally finished," Hammer says. "But it never really is."

Figures 5 and 5a. From a novel in progress by James Whitfield Ellison. Ellison is the author of seven novels, including *Master Prim*, *Proud Rachel* and *Buddies*.

Ellison begins writing by making longhand notes, which he eventually transfers to a computer. He edits both on the monitor and on hard copy, but feels that final editing is best done on hard copy where he can see the text as it might appear in published form.

Figures 6, 6a and 6b. From *The Deal*, a play by Matthew Witten, which has been produced in Boston and Philadelphia and which will appear in *Best Plays of 1987-88*. Witten has had eleven plays and musicals produced, and was the First Prize Winner of the 1987 Clauder Competition for Playwrights.

Figures 7 and 7a. From "Beholding," a short story by Sheri Stein, who is currently working on a collection of short stories and a novella.

Figures 8 and 8a. From *Orchard Song*, a new novel by Lucinda Franks, which is being published by Random House in 1989. Franks, a Pulitzer Prize winner for National Reporting, is the author of *Waiting Out a War*. She is a member of the board of directors of The Writers Room.

Franks wrote *Orchard Song* on a typewriter, making continual revisions on pages. "My revised pages often look like a ten-car pileup with all the carats and cross-outs and inserted words," she says. She is thinking about working on a computer in the future, but has reservations. "I think a lot of novelists who use conputers have found that they lose control of their prose," Franks says. "One argument is that computers are counterproductive to the creative process because writers become so infatuated with the toy that their intense concentration on their work becomes diluted."

Figures 9, 9a and 9b. From *This Is Your Life*, by Meg Wolitzer. Wolitzer is the author of the works *Hidden Pictures* and *Sleepwalk-*

ing. Much of *This Is Your Life* was written in The Writers Room. Wolitzer bought novelist David Leavitt's computer from him after the typewriter she received for high school graduation fell apart, and has since learned to work comfortably on it. Wolitzer prints out "as soon as I've done anything that I can stand to look at," and revises on hard copy. "I usually work only on the computer," she says, "but if I'm away from it I will do whatever I can to write, which has involved various hotel and motel stationeries."

Figures 10, 10*a* and 10*b*. From *Natalya, God's Messenger*, by Magda Bogin. Bogin is the author of *The Women Troubadours*, numerous translations (including Isabel Allende's *House of the Spirits*) and has worked as a journalist.

The only longhand writing that Bogin does is in her journal. She started her first novel, *Natalya, God's Messenger*, on a typewriter and then moved on to a portable computer. She prints out rarely—every six months—but revises every day on the screen. "The attachment to a series of versions is rooted in typing," Bogin says. "I suspect that we're in a new technology where the gain of being able to work on the screen—and of always having an apparently seamless text—implies the loss of past layers of work. But," she adds, "I can't get too caught up in mourning that."

Figures 11 and 11*a*. From "Cajun Country," a short story by Frances Whyatt. Whyatt, a novelist and poet, is the author of *American Gypsy* and *American Made*. One of the short stories for her current collection in progress has won the PEN Syndicated Fiction award.

Whyatt does all her writing exclusively on a typewriter, penciling in revisions on typed pages and then retyping until the work is finished. "I'm dyslexic, and wrote everything backwards until I was seven years old," Whyatt says, "so writing much in longhand is not an option for me."

Figures 12 and 12*a*.From *Appomatox*, a play-in-progress by Evan Gubernick. Gubernick is a published short story writer and playwright.

Gubernick begins by writing longhand in notebooks "any place but at a desk." After several drafts in longhand, he begins typing and continues to make revisions on typed pages. After producing what feels like a final draft — written in longhand, incorporating all prior revisions — Gubernick lets it "sit for a couple of days. Then I retype for [he hopes] the last time."

Figures 13 and 13*a*. From *Lamplighter*, a novel by John Simmons. Simmons is the author of *A Teacher's Guide to American Jewish History*, as well as several novels, including *Cried the Piper* and *The Sharing*. He is currently at work on another novel, *Monsieur le Six*.

Simmons sketches plots in longhand, and then moves to his computer, printing out every day, and making revisions on hard copy. "Starting in longhand is important to me," Simmons says. "I feel like emotion and feeling are left out if I don't get to see my work in all its stages."

Figures 14 and 14*a*. From "Objet d'Amour," a short story by James Boyd Miller. Miller is the author of short stories and a contributing writer to *Millimeter* magazine.

Until recently, Miller would begin his work with longhand sketches, often writing first drafts entirely in longhand. Now he works primarily on a computer, sometimes sketching plots in longhand, revising on the monitor and on printed pages. "The computer has made me much more productive," Miller says. "Writing longhand can put me into a trancelike state where I get lost in the story. With the computer, the lines of communication are more open. I see everything immediately on the screen, as if it's talking back to me as I'm writing."

Figures 15 and 15*a*. From "Hard Work," by Thomas M. Disch.

MANHATTAN TRANSFERENCE *or DARK IN AUGUST*

Judith Rossner

[This is the third draft of the first page of the novel eventually named <u>August</u>,
part of 100-odd pages that were ultimately, according to the author, "thrown
away, or at least consigned to a file someplace."]

Suicide, as Freud was the first to point out, is an act of vengeance

and murder, and it is not my intention here to pay homage to the man who

intended to ~~destroy~~ *ruin* my life by ending his own. Having once been the

indirect object of a suicide -- my mother's -- and having come as close

to being ~~ruined~~ *destroyed* as I shall ever come without falling mortally ill, I had

developed, long before Vincent mounted his assault on my life, a full

arsenal of analytic rhetoric, philosophical positions, songs, jokes and

tap dances to deal with matters pertaining to self-termination. I don't

talk to people who talk about it, except in my work, and even there I

try to avoid anyone who's more than a casual browser among the possibilities

of controling ones own death. People who consult me to talk about suicide

I send to those ~~whom~~ *my friend* Bonnie calls the Death Watch Beatles, those serious

and eager doctors who are never entirely comfortable until death and

disaster enter the room. People who talk about suicide tend to sound

very much the same. Of course, not all suicides talk.

Figure 1

1

D<small>R.</small> L<small>ULU</small> S<small>HINEFELD</small> opened the door to her waiting room
and said hello to the girl who was scheduled for a consultation. The
girl, whose name was Dawn Henley, nodded coolly.

"Would you like to come into the office?" Dr. Shinefeld asked.

Dawn Henley stood. She was tall, even taller than Dr. Shinefeld,
and quite beautiful, with dark brown, almond-shaped eyes, a startling, almost olive complexion, and honey blond hair cropped to
shoulder length along a straight and severe line. It was July. Dawn
wore white cotton pants, a white T-shirt, and sandals, but she might
have had on a ball gown for the grace with which she preceded the
doctor into the office, sank into the chair facing the doctor's, and
inspected her surroundings.

The waiting room was nondescript, but the furnishings in the office were attractive, if spare. The walls were white; the couch,
brown; the two chairs were covered in a splendid cherry red wool. A
kilim rug with predominating colors of brown, teal blue, and red
covered a portion of the wood floor. Aside from the rug, the artwork
in the room consisted of a semi-abstract painting, in which shapes
suggestive of humans seemed to be posing for what could have been
an old-fashioned family photograph, and a small sculpture resting
on the table at the foot of the couch that was reminiscent of one of
Henry Moore's primordial shapes, an egg embraced by some deli-
cious, unidentifiable object. On the doctor's desk stood a slender
blue vase that held three purple irises. Through an open door near

                    JANE
                (poking him)
        A water bed! When have you ever slept
        on a water bed?

                    KEVIN
        I read that Hugh Heffner has one.
        There supposed to be great for sex.

She laughs. He kisses her. They kiss harder. He slips his hand on
her breast. She lets out a little moan, then pulls away.

                    JANE
        You better keep driving. ~~or we're going~~
        ~~to get picked up for loitering.~~

EXT. CHEVY/OVERLOOK DRIVE - DUSK - ANGLE ON KEVIN AND JANE

                    JANE
        You'll probably meet some snooty girl.

                    KEVIN
        It's an ~~all~~ *college* men's ~~school~~...

                    JANE
        You'll have parties with those snooty *all*
        girl's ~~colleges~~ *schools.*

                    KEVIN
                (innocent) *you'll be around guys all the time.*
        You're the one g~~oing to a co-ed school.~~

          STET   JANE
        Yeah. ~~Maybe I'll meet a future teacher~~ *I'm gonna meet a lot*
        of exciting guys at the state branch
                    There maybe interesting guys at KEVIN
        ~~It's not just teachers at~~ Kutztown!
        ~~(moment of silence)~~
        ~~Well, that's it for Overlook Drive.~~

EXT. END OF OVERLOOK DRIVE - EARLY NIGHT - CHEVY

pulls off of the road into a wooded area.

                    JANE
        Kevin! *Come on!*

Headlights off. Car engine off.

INT. CHEVY - KEVIN AND JANE

kissing. More heated. She pulls away.

                    JANE
        Not here, Kev. Not for the first

                         2

Figure 2

                          JANE
                        (poking him)
                A water bed! When have you ever slept
                on a water bed?

                          KEVIN
                I read that Hugh Heffner has one.
                They're supposed to be great for sex.

SHE laughs. HE kisses her. THEY kiss harder. HE slips his hand on
her breast. SHE lets out a little MOAN, then pulls away.

                          JANE
                Keep driving!

EXT. CHEVY/OVERLOOK DRIVE - DUSK - ANGLE ON KEVIN AND JANE

                          JANE
                You'll probably meet some stuck-up girl.

                          KEVIN
                It's a men's college ...

                          JANE
                They'll have mixers with girl's schools.

                          KEVIN
                        (innocent)
                You're the one who'll be around guys all
                the time.

                          JANE
                Yeah. Maybe I'll meet a future teacher.

                          KEVIN
                It's not all teachers at Kutztown!

EXT. END OF OVERLOOK DRIVE - EARLY NIGHT - CHEVY

pulls off of the road into a wooded area.

                          JANE (O.S.)
                Kevin! Come on!

Headlights off. Car engine off.

END TITLES

INT. CHEVY - KEVIN AND JANE

kissing. More heated. SHE pulls away.

                          JANE
                Not here, Kev. Not for the first
                time.

                            3

Figure 2a

A turn-of-the-century wood frame house in ~~chronic~~ disrepair.
Renovation has stripped paint ~~from the woodwork~~ and ~~exten-
sively~~ bared lathing ~~through~~ cracked plaster--but no refirbishing has occurred. Nonetheless, the rooms ~~fulfill~~ their
designated purposes.

LIVING ROOM is furnished with overstuffed couches and chairs
~~with worn slipcovers.~~ There is a stereo system, records,
posters on the walls, reproductions of familiar art, magazines and newspapers strewn about, ~~and~~ other accumulations of
a bachelor. ~~Door to exterior, and~~ door to adjacent

KITCHEN has a serviceable eating table with four chairs,
sink, overloaded dish-drying rack, old appliances, and a
~~wheezing~~ refrigerator covered with notes and reminders. A
door to exterior.

BEDROOM has an unmade double-bed box-spring-and-mattress on
the floor, ~~bedside~~ lamps and alarm clock also on the floor,
overloaded book cases, a desk buried under papers, a chair, a
bureau with clothes hanging from the drawers and a closet
bursting with gear. A door ~~leads off-stage~~ to bathroom;
another door to kitchen/living room areas.

SCENE 1:   LIVING ROOM, Wednesday evening:

            (BOB WALKER, 40, enters, ~~KITCHEN from outdoors,~~
            carrying briefcase and sack of groceries. He is a
            heavy-set, clean-shaven and ~~handsomely~~ disheveled,
            ~~not quite~~ wears an old down parka over khakis, a
            faded workshirt and tie, and a tweed sports jacket.
            He holds the door open)

BOB: (urgently) Com'on, com'on in! I don't want to
            lose the heat.

            (LARRY KENNEDY, 30, a lean, trim black man with a
            wispy beard, and wearing pressed jeans and a thin
            cotton warm-up jacket over a clean white t-shirt
            ~~enters~~ carrying a small nylon duffel bag and shakes
            ~~way~~ off the cold) ~~He~~ looks around skeptically as
            ~~BOB leads him into LIVING ROOM~~

            Make yourself at home.

LARRY: You live here?

BOB: Yeah, ~~and now Siobhan too~~. But there's an extra
            bedroom. (calling out) Siobhan!

LARRY: Siobhan? What kind of name is that?

Figure 3

A turn-of-the-century wood frame house in dramatic disrepair.
Renovation efforts have stripped paint and bared lathing
beneath cracked plaster, but no compensating refirbishing has
occurred. The rooms, meanwhile, are lived in.

LIVING ROOM is furnished with slipcovered, overstuffed chairs
and a couch. There is a stereo system, records, tapes, out-
dated posters on the walls, cheap reproductions of familiar
art, and magazines and newspapers strew about. Door to
exterior, and another door to adjacent:

KITCHEN, which has a serviceable table with chairs, sink,
overloaded dish-drying rack, old appliances, and a refrigerator covered with notes and reminders. A door to exterior.

BEDROOM has an unmade box-spring-and-mattress double bed on
the floor flanked by lamps and an alarm clock also on the
floor, overloaded book cases, a desk buried under papers, a
chair, a bureau with clothes hanging from the drawers and a
closet bursting with gear. A door to bathroom; another door
leading to KITCHEN/LIVING ROOM areas.

SCENE 1: LIVING ROOM, Wednesday evening:

>   (ZACHARY WALKER, 40, enters carrying briefcase and
>   sack of groceries. He is a heavy-set, clean-shaven
>   and comfortably disheveled man who wears a stained
>   down parka over khakis, a faded workshirt and tie,
>   and a tweed sports jacket. He holds the door open)

ZACH: (urgently) Com'on, com'on! I don't want to lose
            the heat.

>   (LARRY KENNEDY, 30, enters. He's a wispy-bearded,
>   lean black man who wears pressed jeans and a satin
>   warm-up jacket over a clean white t-shirt and
>   carries a small nylon duffel bag. He shakes off
>   the cold as ZACH closes door behind him)

            Make yourself at home.

LARRY: (looking around skeptically) You live here?

ZACH: (with pride) Eight years. (calling out) Siobhan?
            Siobhan? (to himself) I guess she's not home.

LARRY: What kind of name is that?

ZACH: Irish.

LARRY: For a dog?

ZACH: It's a woman.

Figure 3a

First draft

Yet he was an extremely sensual man. He loved to eat.
He loved to pick a cigar from his humidor and roll it between his fingers next to his ear to test its freshness,
then pass it under his nostrils for a deep whiff. He would
clip the tapered end, roll it once between his lips to wet
it, light up with a series of short, quick puffs, then lean
back in his arm chair and take a deep, slow drag.

He'd pour his liqueur slowly into its tiny glass and
hold the filled glass up, turning it to take the light, then
lower it and inhale deeply, savoring the sweet fumes. He
rolled the first sip around on his tongue to release its
full flavor, then swallowed slowly, to feel it trickle down
his throat. The fumes and flavors of liqueur, black coffee,
and tobacco mingled and infused his mouth, sent his whole
body into a sweet state of wellbeing. These were gentlemen's
pleasures; they gave away nothing of himself to a women.

Figure 4

SIGNE HAMMER
WORK IN PROGRESS

Fifth draft

Not that he wasn't sensual; the men in my mother's life were all sensualists. My father was a man of many appetites, and he liked to convert the little ceremonies of daily life into occasions for their satisfaction. He was master of the rituals that surrounded dinner in those days: fixing the drinks, pouring the wine, carving the roast. Presiding. Smoking his after-dinner cigar. He would pluck it from its humidor and listen to the crinkly music it made when he rolled it between his fingers. (He was tone deaf, but his fingers could feel the sound of good tobacco.)

He drank his liqueur from a small, narrow glass whose thick base was veiled in smoky tones. When he held it up, the liquid amber light shone through the drifting smoke like fire. He held the first sip in his mouth, rolling it slowly over his tongue until it trickled gently down his throat. Mingled fumes of B & B, black coffee, and tobacco infused his mouth, sent his whole body into a sweet state of well-being. These were gentlemen's pleasures; they gave away nothing of himself to a women.

Figure 4a

the answer to life's pains, perplexities and early morning
unanswerables. I would grab Gordon Ames' manuscript and a blue
pencil from the attache case in the hall, bury myself in the
~~nauseating~~ commercially hopeless midlist (there I go, using that
word) jumble of Ames' new and not particularly anticipated novel
and forge out of the tiny smithy of our combined souls a fiction
that, at best, might sell three thousand copies. A fiction that,
with the greatest good fortune, might garner twenty reviews, all
of them ~~out of New York~~ *from the hinterlands (meaning not manhattan)* and ranging in temperature from ~~lukewarm~~ *cool*
to downright polar.

Gordon Ames' seventh novel was another installment, with
assumed names and so on, in the life, times, temptations and
travails of -- can you guess it? -- Gordon Ames.   He figures that
Himself is the most important subject he can put pen to -- one
that will reveal the reader to himself -- and ~~to Himself indeed~~ *over numerous beers*
(maybe he has often argued that position.)
~~it seems to be. But as it happens~~ *of course) II* there is no esthetic choice
involved in the matter: the sad and pathetic truth is that the
poor bastard has nothing else to write about. Critics are
forever carping that writers don't write about ~~work~~. *what their characters do for a* But how can ~~living~~ *o*
they? *be expected to?* Most writers (Ames is by no means alone *in this,* or even the worst
offender) shy away from ~~close-up considerations~~ *precise descriptions* of where the cash
comes from, and that's because the only job most of them know
anything about -- if you call holing up in a room by yourself and
stringing sentences together a job -- is writing. Fictioneers of
my acquaintance think about themselves constantly and are eager
to rush into print with the latest bulletins on their sexual and

Figure 5

the answer to life's pains, perplexities and early morning unanswerables. I would grab Gordon Ames' manuscript and a blue pencil from the attache case in the hall, bury myself in the commercially hopeless midlist (there I go, using that <u>word</u>) jumble of Ames' new and not particularly anticipated novel and forge out of the tiny smithy of our combined souls a fiction that, at best, might sell three thousand copies. A fiction that, with the greatest good fortune, might garner twenty reviews, all of them from the hinterlands (meaning not Manhattan) and ranging in temperature from lukecool to downright polar.

Gordon Ames' seventh novel was another installment, with assumed names and so on, in the life, times, temptations and trials of -- can you guess it? -- Gordon Ames. He figures that Himself is the most important subject he can put pen to -- one that will reveal the reader to himself -- and over numerous free lunches he has often argued that position. Of course there is no esthetic choice involved in the matter: the sad and pathetic truth is that the poor bastard has nothing else to write about. Critics are forever carping that writers don't write about what their characters do for a living. But how can they be expected to? Most writers (Ames is by no means alone in this, or even the worst offender) why away from precise descriptions of where the cash comes from, and that's because the only job most of them know anything about -- if you call holing up in a room by yourself and stringing sentences together a job -- is writing. Fictioneers

Figure 5a

THE DEAL - by Matthew Witten - 1st draft

Scene ~~Two~~ One ~~later that day~~

> Lights up, centerstage. A table in a
> restaurant. Bottle of wine and two
> glasses. PETER and JIMMY.

PETER
That's what I'm talking about.

JIMMY
This is what I'm saying.

PETER
That's--

JIMMY
This is what I'm saying.

PETER
Okay.

JIMMY
Where are these guys coming from?

PETER
Okay.

JIMMY
They come in here, think they can do whatever the hell they want.

PETER
No way, hunh?

JIMMY
You got to deal with the people.

PETER
Sure.

JIMMY
The people in the community.

PETER
Of course. The local people.

JIMMY
The local people.

PETER
Right.

~~2~~ 1

Figure 6

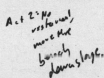

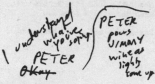

Act 2: No restaurant, move the bench downstage.

Downstage Re-ight Right: PETER's office. [3rd draft
Upstage right: ALEX's office.
Upstage left: JIMMY's office.
THE DEAL Downstage left: ALEX's office.

Downstage center restaurant table.
Upstage center; park bench.

Act One

Scene One

Lights up on JIMMY and PETER, sitting
at a restaurant table centerstage.
On the table, a bottle of wine and
two glasses.

ALEX is in the FBI office, with the
lights down low.

PETER pours JIMMY wine as lights come up

I understand what you're saying

PETER
Okay

I mean JIMMY
The bullshit that's going on...

PETER
Okay.

JIMMY
Fucking bullshit!

PETER
I understand.

JIMMY
Your company comes in here, and they think they can do whatever the
hell they want!   .... yet

PETER
No way, hunh?

JIMMY
You got to talk to the people.

PETER
Sure.

JIMMY
People in the community.

PETER
Of course. Local people.

JIMMY
Right.

PETER
Guys like yourself. Jimmy, this is why I'm here. The boys with the
bucks heard there was problems in this town. People who aren't

1

Figure 6a

THE DEAL

Act One

Scene One

> Lights up on the restaurant table.
> PETER is pouring wine for JIMMY.
>
> Meanwhile ALEX sits in his office,
> with the lights down low.
>
> Restaurant noises in background.

PETER
I understand what you're saying.

JIMMY
I mean the bullshit that's going on...

PETER
I understand.

JIMMY
Your company comes in here, and they think they can do whatever the hell
they want.

PETER
No way, hunh?

JIMMY
You got to talk to the people.

PETER
Sure. Guys like yourself.

JIMMY
Right.

PETER
That's why I'm here. To make sure you guys get what you want. (points
to JIMMY's menu) So what would you like?

JIMMY
Expensive place.

PETER
What's your pleasure, Jimmy? The sky's the limit.

JIMMY
I guess I'll have that filet mignon.

PETER

1

Figure 6b

Here we are in the backyard, the whole family, except my brother. This is
the house he rents in Texas. It's flat as far as you can see in every
direction, giving wide berth to the sky. That's mostly what you wind up looking
at. Garden over there on the left, already half-planted. Even though it's only
March, "the year's more fruitful in the south," as Alan, my brother, says. That
woman poking at the trees is my mother. Short dyed blonde hair, tallish,
robust, black slacks and flowered blouse. She's got that flat-footed step,
always feeling her way on the ground. The girl with her is my oldest niece,
Allison. Something about her begs to be fat and jolly, the way eyebrows and
puffy cheeks crowd her eyes. She hangs up the wash while they chat. Pretty soon
she's got to go inside and prepare dinner. Chicken enchiladas, she said.

Haggai is the one wheeling the stroller with the can of mud on the seat.
That's a spray bottle of cologne in her hand. She stops and sprays herself with
the atomizer. She's five. And the little one who follows her, Deborah, is
three. They periodically convene at the mud puddle to pour out mud from the can
and then scoop some back up. Mud stains cover their dresses. Over there,
playing that paddle ball game imported from east coast beaches, is Saul, the
only boy, and with him, my husband, Jeff. Naomi, sitting here at the edge of my
chaise lounge, has got the baby on her lap. Naomi has stayed this close to me
since about an hour after we arrived.

My sister-in-law, Martha, brings out the sheets for Allison to hang up.
Martha's thin, but has that belly that protrudes as if she were permanently
five-months pregnant. It's hard to remember her now in the John Lennon cap with
inch-long hair barely sticking through, driving fast on the FDR, singing "I Am
Woman" at the top of her lungs. She and my brother used to be leftists, back
when I was a kid. For my thirteenth birthday, Alan gave me a copy of The
Communist Manifesto wrapped with Christmas paper. I tagged along with them to
anti-war demonstrations.

Figure 7

"Smell this sweet Texas earth, Ma," my brother says. "Can you believe it's only March?" As Alan cups a handful of dirt beneath Sylvia's nose, I can almost believe he's my same older brother: tall, straggly hair, easy laughter. His manner, witty but humble, as if he can't help his jokes, still attracts me. Becoming a Christian hasn't affected his style. Now he leads my mother to the other side of the garden, out of earshot. Dressed in slacks and a flowered shirt, Sylvia grasps Alan's arm, her flat-footed step feeling its way between rows of seeds. To me she seems robust, though she thinks of herself as overweight.

Alan stops suddenly and faces Sylvia again. His shoulders hunch to ease the distance between them. Fanlike, his long fingers brush her arm, then wave toward himself. He seems to be saying you, me, you, me. Sunlight dabs Sylvia's bleached hair. She laughs and nods, her smile stretching till her back teeth show. For the moment she devotes herself absolutely to Alan's words. They shake their heads in a mirroring of disbelief. Without hearing them, I can guess that someone did something outrageous, unaccountable, because it has always been those stories that united us as a family--the ones that led to a superior amazement.

Beyond Alan's backyard the land running flat in every direction gives wide berth to the sky. As I sun on a chaise lounge, Alan's five children, all somewhere near, make me feel lazy and sweet. The baby warms my lap, pulling the hair on my neck. At my feet, Naomi, with thick braids straining to her waist, sighs, "Aunt Carol, I wish you had long hair. Then you would look like me." Naomi has stayed close enough to stroke my hand since yesterday, when I arrived from New York with Sylvia and my husband, Jeff. He's gone for a walk to the nearest store, a mile away, to shake off some family dust.

Figure 7a

Christine fingered a little ~~imany~~ portrait /of on ivory.

~~Eliza~~ Chiswell, How... stuck in the back of the drawer with her snug black silk bodice and a string

of pearls around her neck. The centerpiece of ~~his whkxf~~ her great great grandfathrs

fortune was the homestead which ~~ak~~ he built amid twenty-five

acres of apple orchards outside of the villa~~ge~~ in ~~1858~~ and 1868

he seemed ~~xxxxxfxxxxx~~ to have built it, ~~xx~~ in part, as a kind

of shrine in ~~whe~~ which to ensconse ~~kk~~ his wife. ~~Eliza~~, according

to his diaries, was a pale-skinned prima donna and the ~~only~~ one

thing in his life that threatened to slip ~~through his fingers~~

like ~~~~ a honey-dipped a pea. dipped in syrup.

~~pear~~. She had a ~~xxkxxxx~~ xxxx sweet sweet voice and such unique beauty that the

very sight of her stopped the rocking of men's chairs in front

of the post office. Cornelius wanted her tucked away out of town, safe

and sound. Luckily, ~~Eliza~~, who carried herself like a swan

and had that bird's same ~~vxxxx~~ voraciousness, · and was fully as voracious was more than

content to ~~kkxkxx~~ tinker and toy in lonliness with the earthly

pleasures her husband could give her. There was, so it is said,

~~no end to tardenand for her~~

Christine fingered a little portrait on ivory of Hopestill Chiswell stuck in the back of the drawer with her snug black silk bodice and a string of pearls around her neck. Hopestill had been the youngest of five daughters whose parents still hoped for a boy after she was born and that was how they had come up with her name. So eccentrically devoted to her family was she that she wore a wedding gown of silvery gray to symbolize her sadness at leaving her father's home.

The centerpiece of her great great grandfather's fortune was the homestead which he built amid twenty-five acres of apple orchards outside of the village in 1868 and he seemed to have built it, in part, as a kind of shrine in which to ensconce his wife. Hopestill was a pale-skinned prima donna and the one thing in his life that threatened to slip out of his hands. She had a sweet voice, like pear syrup, and such unique beauty that the very sight of her stopped the rocking of the men's chairs in front of the post office. Cornelius wanted her tucked away out of town, safe and sound. Luckily, Hopestill, who carried herself like a swan and had that bird's same voraciousness, was more than content to tinker and toy in lonliness with the earthly pleasures her husband could give her. There was, so it is said, no end to her demand of them.

Figure 8a

~~All day she had traveled through the dark caves and tunnels of the World's Fair, and now, finally out in the wide reaches of ~~day~~ sunlight, she could no longer see at all. That was when her father took the picture: a squinty girl in culottes, standing with her hands out at her sides enduring the embarrassment. All around her cameras snapped. Similar children were posed in front of domes and arches.~~

All day she had traveled through the dark ~~caves~~ chutes and tunnels of the World's Fair, and now, finally out in the wide reaches of sunlight, she could no longer see at all. She couldn't see, and she could barely hear, either; the same song was still weaving through her: a chorus of cricket-children singing It's a small world, after all, and then singing it in other languages, each ~~one~~ less ~~recognizable~~ identifiable than the last — until finally the children seemed to be ~~saying~~ chattering Gikadrutzax faxmazlab. as her car floated ahead through darkness. ~~Where on the globe~~ What language was this? she wondered, Slavic, African? She didn't know, but now it was all over and she had been shunted out into daylight. That was when her father took the picture, the one that proved so important years later. She stood, humiliated in culottes, thongs. ~~as he adjusted the lens.~~ All around her, ~~similar~~ other children were posed similarly before domes & arches. ~~[Father adjusted lenses. Children sighed heavily, flung their arms out, wincing the shot.]~~ "Hurry up already," she said, in exasperation, ~~hearing~~ recognizing already the edge to her own voice. There was no love lost between Grace and her father; That was what he himself had said. Her father was remote. He chronicled everything, he was the family archivist. Silent, nervous and cold in his short-sleeved shirts with pens

Figure 9

clipped to pockets, he took pictures of his
daughters and, occasionally, his wife. ~~The~~ The pic
were always individual portraits, never group shots. ~~I~~
~~they might have all~~ There was nothing to convince any
that these people ~~comprised~~ made up a family. None of then
looked alike, really. Each was imperfect ~~and~~ ~~but~~ in a
different way. Only Nora, the ~~youngest~~ youngest, was animated,
~~enough to make~~ at ~~age~~ eight, she was all knobbed knee
and elbows and nervous jerky motions. She had
not slowed down, like her older sisters.

He took a picture of Grace, and
it was indistinguishable, like the rest of his pictures
~~Still~~ he placed it in the photo album, sealed it behind plastic.
Years later, when she was ~~twenty~~
and everything had fallen apart, she wanted to look at tha
time, to preserve it in some ~~sort of~~ ~~amber~~ way, and s
she brought back the photo album from home. She took it
to Cambridge on the train, and that night she and
Jeff Staples, the boy she ~~was~~ was just beginning to love,
sat and looked through her childhood.

"I want you to see," she said, opening the
big ~~plastic~~ book ~~like a blanket~~ across her lap, First there were the
baby shots, and then some backyard barbecues. Final
they were there at the World's Fair in 196
Everyone had gone; everyone had distinct memories of it.

Figure 9a

through a shaft, and showed you the inner workings of the human brain. God, it was great." He paused. "What I remember most," he said, "is how hot it was. I always had to go to the bathroom."

Opal turned the page. There at the top, among the World's Fair series, was a picture she distinctly recalled posing for. She remembered the day well, and how she had traveled for hours through a series of dark chutes and tunnels, and how at the end of the afternoon, finally out in the wide reaches of sunlight, she could no longer see. She couldn't see, and she could barely hear, either. The same song was weaving through her: a chorus of cricket-children singing, "It's a small world, after all," and then singing it in other languages, each version less identifiable than the last, until finally the children seemed to be chattering, "Gluka brznik faxmilgriv." What language _was_ this? she wondered: Russian? Greek? She didn't know, but she couldn't focus on it any longer because her father was making her pose for a picture. She stood, impatient for him to finish, while all around her, other children posed similarly before domes and arches. Fathers adjusted the lenses on their bulky new cameras, and children sighed and swung their arms out, ruining the shot. Opal could not bear the protracted moment between the focus and the click, but her father had a bad temper, so she didn't dare complain. Instead she stood in the invisible frame he had squared off around her, jerking and rolling her eyes.

After the shot her father faithfully rubbed the print with a sponge soaked in some chemical that smelled like toxic salad dressing, and later, after the afternoon was over, he sat in the family room in Jericho, and pressed it into an album, sealing the image of his younger daughter behind plastic.

Figure 9*b*

Natalya, God's messenger, is my aunt. It was her lucky break right
~~for The Friday~~ a ~~rainy~~ Friday
after the war. ~~Tuesdays~~ after V-E day, ~~sixteen hundred thousand~~
~~Friday~~ after paychecks had been handed out, ~~she lost her job as a lathe~~
~~turret operator at the~~ ~~~~ Factory at the corner of West
4th Street and Sixth Avenue she ~~was~~ got the news: ~~things are going~~
~~to be winding down here, you girls better look for something else.~~ She
~~said goodbye to her job as a lathe turret operator at the~~
~~factory and~~ stopped at the newstand in front of Emiolio's pizzeria.

There it was: "Natalya, God's messenger, retiring. Established palm-
reading practice for sale. No experience necessary." She ~~jumped on the~~
~~cross-town bus and~~ Second Avenue. It was an impulse, but what the
hell. She ran up to 8th Street and caught the cross-town bus. Ten minuts
later she was standing at the corner of 7th Street and Second Avenue ~~and~~
wondering what strange tricks fate had up its sleeve. ~~from where~~ she
could see the ~~seemly sad~~ sign that told her ~~she had come to the~~ Sure
enough, the original Natalya, a Ukranian reader advisor, was packing up
her tarot cards and heading south after a lifetime of reading the upturned
palms of weary immigrants and ~~famous actors~~ and ~~singars~~ who came to see
her from uptown. "You'll make a lot of money and meet many interesting
people," she told my aunt, ~~who paid her $100~~ , her entire savings, and ~~in those~~
~~a considerable sum~~ ~~furnit~~, for a sequined turban, a ~~special~~ ruby with
adhesive backing for the middle of her forehead, a crystal ball, ~~four~~
framed pictures of the Bay of Naples, a box of sandalwood incense, a
folding table and a ~~filing index~~ cards with the names and phone numbers
of all the regular customers.

While Natalya was sweeping up, ~~following her broom around~~ the tiny
store like a cat meticulously licking itself clean, she ~~didn't stop talking~~.
My Aunt Rita didn't know a life line from a crack in the sidewalk or the

Magda Bogin

NATALYA, GOD'S MESSENGER

1.

Natalya, God's Messenger, is my aunt. It was her lucky
break right after the war. One Friday afternoon the summer
of V-E Day rumors began to fly, and no sooner had paychecks
been handed out at the Universal Tool & Die Co. at the
corner of West 4th Street and Sixth Avenue, than she and the
other girls who worked as turret lathe machinists got the
news: the boys are coming home and veterans are going to
have priority; you girls better look for something else. It
was the end of June and the war in the Pacific was still on,
but the first soldiers from the European theater had already
been sent home. For women like my aunt, the handwriting was
on the wall.

On her way to the subway my aunt stopped to buy a copy
of the <u>Daily Mirror</u>. She flipped to the help wanteds, but
before she could focus on the listings for machinists her
eye stopped short: "Natalya, God's Messenger, retiring.
Established palm-reading practice for sale. Two-hundred
dollars. No experience necessary." Destiny's own
determined arms, as she would later put it, propelled her
across town, and ten minutes later she was standing at the
corner of East 7th Street and Second Avenue from where,
looking east on 7th, she could see the palm-shaped sign
halfway down the block.

Figure 10*a*

"I saw your ad," she said when the door to the tiny store was opened by a stooped, beturbaned woman with the bluest eyes my aunt had ever seen; and sure enough the original Natalya, a Ukrainian reader advisor, was packing up her tarot cards and heading south after a lifetime of reading the outstretched palms of weary immigrants and of the rich matrons who came to see her from uptown. "You'll make a lot of money and meet many interesting people," she told my aunt who, after a brief negotiation, wrote out a check in the amount of $140, her entire savings, for a sequined turban, a fake ruby with adhesive backing for the middle of her forehead, a crystal ball, two framed pictures of the Bay of Naples, a fringed red lamp, a folding table with four matching chairs, and a blue damask tablecloth.

"Sit down, darling. I'll tell you everything you need to know."

While Natalya was sweeping up, pressing her broom around the tiny store like a cat meticulously licking itself clean, she distilled her vast chiromantic knowledge into a fifteen-minute course for her successor. My Aunt Rita didn't know a life line from a crack in the sidewalk or the Plains of Mars from the Steppes of Central Asia, but by the time Natalya had finished sweeping, she knew that the left hand was the slate you had been born with and the right what life had written on it. She knew that a thumb could tell you more about a person than a little finger, and that the

Figure 10*b*

He had come in on a motorcycle sometime after midnight and they'd given him the slot
next to hers. It had stopped raining, though the ground was soaked and half the
slots were under a foot of water, so most the campers, those that weren't in vans or
RVs, were still up and talking in those low tones heard in church or when others are
sleeping.

He was young, nice looking in an intelligent way but not meant to be intellectual. And
although the windshield of the big harley was full of bugs and his leather jacket
smelled of damp and was cracked and the fake fur collar tacky with sweat and rain
and his face streaked with road soot and damp, he had the look of a clean person
by nature.

The first thing he did was introduce himself to her, but not in an aggressive way.
He just went over and offered to help her with the tent which she'd been re-tieing
after an earlier wind had loosened the spokes.

"Been like this long."

"Just since this morning. Yesterday was beautiful."

"Never been in the South before."

"Oh?"

"Yah. Drove straight down from Michigan."

"You're kidding. How far is it to Louisiana."

"To where." To here?.

"Layfayette."

"Thousand miles."

"That far and you did it straight."

"Well. Stopped for gas and stuff."

"How long it take you."

"Twenty hours."

"Twenty! Don't your legs feel funny."

"Yah. I'm still vibrating, like when you get off a sailboat."

"You sail?"

Figure 11

CAJUN COUNTRY

He had come in on a motorcycle sometime after midnight and they'd given him
the slot next to hers. It had stopped raining, though the ground was soaked
and half the slots were under a foot of water, so most the campers--those
that weren't in vans or RVs--were still up and talking.

He was young, nice looking in an intelligent way but not meant to be intellectual. And although the windshield of the big Harley was full of bugs,
and he wore one of those cracked leather field jackets with the fake fur
collars which smelled of damp and sweat, and his face had long streaks of
soot running down from it--she saw the care with which he'd stacked and
corded in his gear, and had the sense of him as being an otherwise clean
and orderly person.

The first thing he did was introduce himself to her, but not aggressively.
He just went over, said his name was Ned, and offered to help her with the
tent which she'd been re-tieing after an earlier wind had loosened the spokes.

"Been like this long?"

"On and off. Yesterday was beautiful."

"Never been South before. This is my first trip."

"Oh yah?"

"Yah. Drove straight through from Michigan."

"You're kidding. How far is that?"

Figure 11*a*

APPOMATTOX

LIGHTS UP. FRONT OF TWO STORY BUILDING. WINDOWS GROUND FLOOR AND SECOND.
BETWEEN A SIGN READING "JUANITA'S RECEPTION HOUSE". DOOR CENTER. WESTY
STANDING, KICKS AND BEATS DELEVAN WHO IS DYING ON GROUND BENEATH WINDOW
OF BUILDING UNCONSCIOUS

WESTY:
You see what I mean? Do you see what I mean? Well, fuck, you can't possibly
see what I mean if you don't look. Motherfucker, look at that window.
Those curtains. Geez, look at those curtains. Don't tell me they don't
stir something in your balls. Don't tell me that. I thought there was
a law. Some kind of law. A local law. That's how these things are settled
locally, because people, folks in different places think differently
about things, all kinds of things. Folks in one place say well it's alright
so long as it's kept quiet while folks, other folks somewhere's else
would say we're going to search every stack in this county and maybe
the next one too and root out all that we here in this committee room
see as being an outgrowth of our most evil and vile instincts.

WESTY STOPS BEATING AND WALKS SLOWLY OFF STAGE LEFT. DELEVAN WAKES SLOWLY
AFTER WESTY IS OFF.

DELEVAN:
Ah cut all that poetic crap and say what ya' mean, say what's really
on your mind, go on spit it out, cause Sophie I gotta tell ya' my patience
is wearing thin, thin as the skin on your old dried up face. So you can
just stop pulling your punches don't worry 'bout me, no ma'am. I can
take it. I can take anything you can throw at me, you old lizard you.
You old gila monster. You old prune.

DELEVAN FALLS UNCONSCIOUS AS BEFORE. WESTY THEN REENTERS FROM STAGE LEFT,
CARRYING A TWO BY FOUR.

WESTY:
Crude, but a weapon. What a man cannot do alone, he can with ease and
grace accomplish with a weapon in hand. What sets us apart and above
your everyday ape. God gave us a thumb, so we could grip a stick. Ask
any of our five star boys. Agreed on that, ay Delevan?

WESTY GOES TO STRIKE DELEVAN, BUT JUST BEFORE HE HITS, DELEVAN SUDDENLY
COMES TO.

DELEVAN:
Oh Sophie, you're killing me! You're chompin' away at my insides!

WESTY:
That's it boy, some fire! Let's see some fire!

DELEVAN:
Everyday you're eatin' out another chunk! Oh Sophie!

WESTY:
Okay boy, on your feet. Come on.

Figure 12

APPOMATTOX I

SPOT ON WESTY, WHO DRAGS A BODY TIED BY THE FEET FROM OFFSTAGE LEFT.

WESTY:
You're an idiot, you know that? If I thought I could do it alone, I'd
be doin it alone. See how that works melonhead? No, no I bet you don't.
HE STOPS AND UNTIES THE BODY. HE BEATS AND KICKS THE BODY. LIGHTS UP.
FRONT OF TWO STORY BUILDING. WINDOWS GROUND FLOOR AND SECOND. BETWEEN,
A SIGN READING "JUANITA'S RECEPTION HOUSE." DOOR CENTER.

WESTY:
You see what I mean? Do you see what I mean? Well, fuck, you can't possibly
see what I mean if you don't look. Motherfucker, look at that window.
Those curtains. Geez, look at those curtains. Don't tell me they don't
stir somethin in you. Somethin in your lower half. Don't tell me that.
Christ, I thought there was a law. Some kind of law. A local law. That's
how they settle these things, isn't it? Isn't that how they do it? Locally,
right?, because people, folks in different places, well, they think differe
about things, all kinds of things. Folks in one place say well it's alright
so long as it's kept quiet about, while folks, other folks somewhere's
else say we're gonna search every crack in this county and maybe the next
one too and root out all what we here in this committee room see as being
an outgrowth of our most evil and yes vile instincts. Vile instincts.
WESTY STOPS BEATING AND WALKS OFF STAGE LEFT. DELEVAN WAKES UP.

DELEVAN:
Ah cut all that poetic crap and say what ya' mean. Say what's really on
your mind, go on spit it out. Cause Sophie I gotta tell ya', my patience
is wearing thin, thin as the skin on your old dried up face. So you can
just stop pulling your punches. Don't worry 'bout me, no ma'am. (STANDS
SLOWLY) I can take it. I can take anything you can throw at me, you old
lizard you. You old gila monster. You old prune. (SITS SLOWLY) You old
prune.
DELEVAN FALLS UNCONSCIOUS AS BEFORE. WESTY REENTERS FROM STAGE LEFT, CARRYI
A TWO BY FOUR, PRACTICING HIS SWING.

WESTY:
Big fella gave us four fingers and a thumb but for two reasons, so we
could grab hold of a fork, and so we could grab hold of a stick. What
sets us apart and above your everyday ape. We agreed on that boy?
WESTY GOES TO STRIKE DELEVAN, BUT JUST BEFORE HE HITS, DELEVAN SUDDENLY
COMES TO.

DELEVAN:
Oh Sophie, you're killing me! You're chompin away at my insides!
WESTY PULLS BACK FROM STRIKING.

WESTY:
That's it boy, some fire! Let's see some fire!
DELEVAN:
Everyday you're eatin out another chunk! Oh Sophie!
WESTY:
Okay boy, on your feet. Come on. Up!

Figure 12a

Soon she was extradited to Arkansaa. She was indicted
for assault with a deadly weapon (pistol whipping) and
(a shot was fired)
attempted homicide during the robbery of a Piggly-Wiggly
actual
store in Little Rock. The murder charge, which had
been made in order to involve the FBI, was reduced. But
Jackie was wanted on other charges as well. She had a
long criminal record despite her youth.

At her trial Jackie pleaded not guilty. She had
and
a poor defense, no alibi, and was convicted. The state's
attorney labelled her a "vicious, unrepentant criminal
woman" and compared her to Bonnie Parker, John Dillinger,
Kinnie Wagner, and Lizzie Borden. These likenings were
convicted
not so much hyperbole as/premature. Jackie was sentenced
to ten to twenty years in the State Penitentiary.

Although Jim Starkwell went to Little Rock that summer
she   not
to try and stand by his bride, no one would let him.
Although
He appeared unconcerned about the hatchet, But Jackie
much less talk to him
would not even see him. In the newspapers it was
reported that she hated him. Jim Starkwell sat in the
courtroom every day until the trial was over, but Jackie
never even looked at him. "A cruel hoax," observed the
Little Rock Gazette, "does not deserve such loyalty."
After the jury returned with the verdict, Jim went home.

Figure 13

on the roof and were about to board the elevator, were ruffled and started in a line for the Third Avenue exit. The porter had a time with them. The police took Jackie and threw her into a car and sped away.

Soon Jackie Farrell was extradited to Arkansas. She was indicted for assault with a deadly weapon (pistol-whipping) and attempted homicide (a shot was fired) during the robbery of a Piggly-Wiggly store in Little Rock. There were a half-dozen armed-robbery charges in all. Although the actual murder charge, which had been made in order to involve the FBI, could not be proved, the state tossed everything at Jackie but the kitchen sink. It turned out that Jackie Farrell had an almost lifelong involvement with crime. Her father was the late Bud Farrell, who had robbed the Lilborne National Bank in 1948, capping a long felonious career.

At her trial Jackie pleaded not guilty. She had a poor defense and no alibi. The state's attorney labeled her a "vicious, unrepentant criminal woman" and compared her with Bonnie Parker, John Dillinger, Kinnie Wagner, and Lizzie Borden. These likenings were not so much hyperbole as premature. Jackie was convicted and sentenced to ten to twenty years in the state penitentiary.

Jim Starkwell went to Little Rock that summer to try and stand by his bride. She would not let him. Although he appeared unconcerned about the hatchet, Jackie would not even see him, much less talk to him. In the newspapers it was reported that she hated him. Jim Starkwell sat in the courtroom every day until the trial was over, but Jackie never even once looked his way. "A cruel hoax," observed the *Arkansas Gazette*, "does not deserve such loyalty."

After the jury returned with the verdict, Jim went home.

6

Figure 13a

perfectly sculpted. It gave him an air of authority. His skin was translucent like bisque. His hair a fine weave of white, balded in the middle, with long wisps combed over the bare skin from left to right. He reminded Candace of photographs she had seen of the Swiss psychologist, Carl Jung. This comparison helped to relax her as he intently peered into her eyes and then began palpating her body, squeezing folds of tissue and pressing into her abdominal cavity. As bizarre as everything happening to her felt good to have someone touching her, especially someone who had the fatherly, reassuring look of Carl Jung.

As Dr. Macro explored her body, Dr. Nuance retrieved a reporter's notebook from his shirt pocket, hidden behind the white lapel of his frock, and began taking notes.

Candace was making a mental note or two of her own, the most salient of which was that neither doctor had so much as said, "Hello" to her since walking into the room. She was an object lesson, invisible, suitable for framing, like one of these poor cadaverous souls in a Thomas Eakins painting.

Moving silently, not even speaking to each other, the doctors communicated through gestures, eye movements and head nods. It was a sinister choreography the two doctors moved around the bed, while moving around each other. The younger doctor intermittently showing his senior the scribbles he had made in his reporter's notebook. It all had a fluency about it, practiced and nimble, they moved through their routine like tribesmen through a ritual.

Candace was now fully awake. How could she not be, with all this poking and prodding going on. The young doctor, who Candace thought was kind of cute, had begun kneading her calf muscle and was working his way up to her thigh. Maybe she could convince him to peel her a grape.

All this touching was making her extremely hungry, and between the two appetites competing for her attention, her empty stomach was the stronger of the two. In fact,

-2-

⟨17⟩ So much myth and lore to be passed along, doctor to doctor, Macro to Nuance...

Figure 14

scratch. So, much myth and lore to be passed along, doctor to doctor, Macro to Nuance. The requisite routines and techniques of planned deprivation, medieval torture, and wholistic alchemy. This was an intricate and complex process, and not to be taken lightly. The two doctors were all business, speaking in sober, dispassionate tones, the sub rosa dissonance of medical jargon being exchanged, giving rise to the feeling that an opinion was forming in thin air, in that unoccupied space between the movement of their lips. Candace hated them for their rectitude and (professional) abstraction.

Dr. Macro's eyes were a pale blue, almost a grey blue, and watery as if they h been kept in an aqueous solution too long. His lips were thin, too, like Nurse Padgett's. His nose was narrow, patrician-like, perfectly sculpted. The clean, precise facial planes lent Dr. Macro an air of authority. His skin was translucent as bisque. His hair a fine weave of white, balded in the middle, with long wisps combed over the bare skin from left to right. He reminded Candace of photographs had seen of the Swiss psychologist, Carl Jung. She liked Jung.

He began palpating her body, squeezing folds of tissue and pressing into her abdominal cavity. It felt good to have someone touching her. Bizarre, alien, yet familiar, Dr. Macro's probing fingers, were warm to the touch, giving off a heat t radiated deep inside the tundra.

Dr. Nuance retrieved a reporter's notebook from his shirt pocket, and began taking notes, jotting down Macro's cryptic asides as he examined her.

Neither doctor had said a word to her since walking into the room. The two doctors seemed to Candace like tribal priests hovering over a virgin, abstracted b ritual, they were stoic, enigmatic, the threat of death hanging between them.

Moving silently, the doctors communicated through gestures, eye movements and head nods. It was a sinister choreography as they articulated the space around th bed in a series of overlapping patterns, moving in and out of one another's way, precise, never touching; the younger doctor intermittently showing his senior the scribbles he had made in the reporter's notebook. It all had a fluency about it, practiced and nimble, like ice skaters.

Figure 14a

"Now here's the scenario for the foofist ~~my plan for Rambo~~," Sal said, summoning a ~~screen~~ from the ceiling of the room. "Not Rimbaud Chocolates, ~~spelled~~ spelled flitz flat, but _Rombo_ Chocolates, ~~spelled~~ spelled like it sounds, with a slogon that's got some punch, and no more of these ads in ~~French~~. But a picture's worth a ~~thousand~~ words." He clicked the first slide into place, and the screen burst into giant ~~of~~ fuzzy red white and blue letters that promised.

RAMBO!

Strait on, gay, he'll blow you away."

~~On~~ Slide 2 followed:

RAMBO!

Attack your problems]with a the man's chocolate!

Slide 3:

B.I.FF! POW! ~~SOCKO!~~ BLAM!
RAMBO GIVES A GOOD GOD-DAMN

Slide 4:

RAMBO!
The Chocolate that Led to Victory in Viet Nam!
~~Could~~ Lead ~~you~~ to Victory Now.

Figure 15

"I think you'll all also agree that the Rimbaud team hasn't been performing up to capacity for a long time. Look at that sales graph! Read the report of the market research team. Three out of four gay consumers in Cheyenne, when asked to name and grade seven male chocolates in order of preference ranked Rimbaud Chocolates last on their list. As to the advertising . . ." Here Sal practised the sneer that his namesake had used to such effect in the unjustly neglected *Dino* (1957, script by Reginald Rose). "Aside from the fact one, that the ads nowhere refer to the product and two, that their scripts are written in a dead language, and three that half the ad budget has been in *The New Yorker* and other scholarly quarterlies that have a combined estimated readership of 4,000, aside from all that they're probably great ads. Not speaking French myself, I wouldn't know."

Burgess-King withdrew a silk handkerchief from his breast pocket and honked into it with discrete defiance.

"It's clear as the nose on the face of the Statue of Liberty that the product needs a face-lift, and here's the scenario I've proposed." Sal summoned a screen from the ceiling of the room and dimmed the lights. "Not Rimbaud Chocolates spelled the French way, but spelled like it sounds – Rambo! And a slogan that promises action, adventure, excitement, aggression – the things that a *man* is looking for in a man's chocolate. Here, I'll show you." He clicked the first slide into place, and the screen burst into giant fizzing red white and blue letters:

RAMBO CHOCOLATES
Straight or gay, they'll blow you away!
Slide 2 followed:
Attack Your Problems
with the Fighting Man's Chocolate
RAMBO!
Slide 3:
BIFF! POW! SOCKO! BLAM!
RAMBO GIVES A GOOD GOD-DAMN
Slide 4:
RAMBO!
The Chocolate that Led to Victory in Viet Nam
Can Lead YOU to Meaningful Success!

"Of course, slogans and promises are just the wax on the paint job. To achieve real success a product has got to penetrate more than a consumer's consciousness. It's got to change his life. When he looks at his face in the bathroom mirror, or better yet in the bedroom mirror, he shouldn't see himself there – he should see the product. 'Mythologize,' as all the marketing textbooks tell us, 'eroticize, and taunt.' Consider the Harley-Davidson motorcycle, one of the greatest products in American history. In its heyday there were seven magazines devoted to the proposition that riding a Harley and wearing its livery were a guarantee of sexual potency and homicidal prowess. For its consumers it provided quite literally a meaning for their lives, as can be seen from its most famous slogan, Live to Ride, Ride to Live. Consider, as well, another classic male-oriented product, Jack Daniel's Bourbon. At the turn of the century, many men in the Sun Belt states developed such obsessive product loyalty that they spent from 20% to 50% of their discretionary incomes on not simply the product but on dressing themselves and furnishing their homes with

with advertisements for the product. Truly, a marketer's dream come true. The only problem in both these cases was the higher mortality rates associated with frequency of product use. However, Rambo needn't face that dilemma. There is no inherent danger in eating a pound or two of non-nutritive candy. Only if it engendered dangerous levels of aggression among those aspiring to fulfil its image and become, themselves, Rambo chocolate soldiers, only then would there be a risk of the market self-destructing. So let's have a look at the Rambo man."

Sal zapped a message to his assistant's auricular splice. "Rod, would you step in now and model that uniform?"

On this cue the doors to the Conference Room parted with a trumpet voluntary, and Rod Steiger, in his new position as Sal's executive secretary, entered in the product livery that would one day earn its own proud niche in the Marketing Hall of Fame in beautiful Tuxedo Park in the state of New York. There Rod stood before the astonished manager, the first recruit to the Legion of the Chocolate Soldiers.

Sal went up to him and plucked a bullet from his bandolier, stripped off the foil, and tossed it to Eddie Albee, the Assistant Marketing Director, who was sitting beside old Walt Whitman. "Eat lead, sweetheart!"

Albee nibbled nervously at the tip of the milk-chocolate bullet, and Rod, blushing with shame but proud to serve General Edibles in any way he could, went round the table dispensing a bullet from his bandolier to each of the managers. As he did so, Sal pointed out, and the managers noted, the other features of Rod's uniform: the I LOVE RAMBO jumpsuit; the chocolate-capped toe of his high-lacing boots (which Burgess-King was encouraged to lick); the Rambo C-Rations backpack with its fifty-pounds of assorted candles that the more gung-ho chocolate soldiers would be able to sell to their buddies in the time-honoured sales-pyramid fashion of Amway and Herbal Life; the Rambo Chocolate Milk canteen prettily embossed with the nude body of the immortal Italian Stallion as movie-goers first got to see him in his earlier porno films, and other chocolate accessories for belt and bandolier too numerous to mention. Sal then ran through the figures R & D had developed concerning possible profit margins on each item of the Rambo uniform.

At the end of the presentation, Burgess-King stood up and, after wiping away the last traces of Rod's toe-caps from his lips with his handkerchief, said: "Sal, I think I speak for all of us here when I say this is a truly interesting and bizarre marketing concept. If consumers can be made to buy one-half the product you're proposing, Rambo could assume a role of leadership throughout the male chocolate industry, and not just in the gay segment. Indeed, it could represent a revolution in the whole field of Recreational Foods. The only problem, as I see it. . ." Here Burgess-King allowed a tinge of sarcasm to colour the polished neutrality of his BBC baritone. ". . how are consumers to be persuaded to cultivate such an intensity of brand loyalty? Short of their being abducted, tortured and brainwashed, which I gather the FDA will not yet allow."

There was a rustling sound round the Conference

32

Figure 15a

INDEX

SETTING

JACK M. BICKHAM

*With special thanks to editors Jack Heffron and Robin Gee,
and to William Brohaugh . . . the man who started a lot of this
over a lunch table in Norman, Oklahoma, a few years ago.*

ABOUT THE AUTHOR

Jack M. Bickham taught professional writing at the University of Oklahoma for twenty-two years before retiring in 1991 to write full time. He is the author of more than seventy-five published novels, including *Twister*, *The Winemakers* and five novels published so far in a suspense series for Tor Books. He has written extensively for *Writer's Digest* magazine and his titles for Writer's Digest Books include *The 38 Most Common Fiction Writing Mistakes (and how to avoid them)* and *Scene and Structure*. He and his wife Louanna live in Norman, Oklahoma, where he is at work on three more novels.

CONTENTS

CHAPTER 1

WHY SETTING IS IMPORTANT

SETTING IS A TOPIC seldom discussed at length in writers' workshops or addressed in any detail in texts for creators of fiction. Like the weather, it's mentioned in conversations, but considered entirely out of our control. Yet setting is a vital component of any story, and it does involve a body of technique which you can learn and use to improve your creative work.

Story setting is even defined too narrowly in those few texts which do consider it. It is not merely the physical backdrop of the tale. It may also include the historical background and cultural attitudes of a given place and time, the mood of a time, and how the story people talk. Also tied closely to setting may be such details as the author's style, a period's traditions, and the kind of story the writer wishes to relate.

All of these factors must dovetail properly with the story's plot, its characters, the theme and the desired general emotional tone of the piece if the finished fiction is to "work" for the reader.

Many classic tales are classics precisely because all these factors fit together perfectly. Most can scarcely be imagined in a different setting. Consider, for example, how profoundly different DeFoe's *Robinson Crusoe* would be if the author had chosen to have his hero shipwrecked on a barren arctic rock, rather than upon a tropical island. Could the story have been told at all in such a different setting? Would Dickens's *A Christmas Carol* have the same kind of impact if set in the English countryside? Or would the movie classic *High Noon* work emotionally for an

1

audience if it were set in an early-day English colony—or in a big city in the year 1993?

These are perhaps extreme examples, but you will discover, as you think about it, that setting does more than provide a framework within which the story is told. It makes some things possible, other things quite impossible. In a traditional Old West setting—to use another extreme example—one cannot have the hero leap onto a jetliner. By the same token, a detective in a gritty contemporary urban scene can hardly track his suspect the way Natty Bumppo might have done in one of the *Leatherstocking Tales*. Even character language can be a part of setting, or be tied to it. The kind of character talk that might be appropriate in an urban police mystery could destroy the credibility of a traditional historical romance because people in different places and times speak so diversely.

The moral: When you choose setting, you had better choose it wisely and well, because the very choice defines—and circumscribes—your story's possibilities.

In addition to its importance in terms of credibility, setting also contributes enormously to the general feeling or tone of a story. It creates a mixture of story mood, character feeling, and general ambience which eventually (in stories that work) become as much a part of the appeal and sense of "rightness" as the plot, characterization, or any other factor. Hemingway's *A Farewell to Arms* simply would not work if set in the Vietnam era, for example, because the emotions—so right in a novel of World War I—aren't at all appropriate for a story set a generation or two later. And of course the historical and cultural context of many recent suspense novels could only be believed if clearly dated in the period prior to the demise of the Soviet Union. If set "today," they simply wouldn't work because recent history has changed the feeling of the era.

The setting of a story can affect the author's wording—the writing style, too. Compare, for example, the opening of a novel like Daphne du Maurier's *Rebecca*, a gothic-baroque romance, with that of a contemporary thriller like *Darker Than Amber*, one of the Travis McGee novels by John D. MacDonald.

Rebecca begins:

Last night I dreamt I went to Manderley again. It seemed to me I stood by the iron gate leading to the drive, and for a while I could not enter, for the way was barred to me. . . .

While the Travis McGee book opens this way:

We were about to give up and call it a night when somebody dropped the girl off the bridge.

The romantic backdrop of *Rebecca* fits perfectly with the dreamy, cadenced quality of its prose—a style which would not fit at all in a John D. MacDonald novel. And the opposite, of course, is also true. In both cases, the setting dictated style as well as many other story factors.

Given the importance of a story's setting, it is surprising how often it is selected with little thought—just popping into the writer's head as part of the original idea, and never seriously examined thereafter. Even more amazing is how casually many writers treat setting in all its aspects.

This book is an attempt to change all that.

THE CONTRIBUTIONS OF SETTING

Writers generally recognize that good handling of a proper setting can "decorate" a story, thus enhancing its color and general appeal as well as making it more convincing. Less often realized, however, are the following additional contributions setting can make:

- intensification of reader involvement
- enhancement of story unity
- tightening of plot structure and/or intensification of suspense
- motivation or explanation of character
- clarification of theme
- excitement of the writer's own imagination

While we will look more deeply at most of these aspects, it may be well to consider each of them briefly at this early stage, to provide you with an overview of what is to follow.

Reader involvement may be intensified by proper handling of setting because physical, sensory descriptions of the story world allow the reader to experience those surroundings through his own imagination—as if he were "really there," seeing, hearing, breathing, tasting and feeling the world of the tale. Vivid, evocative physical description of setting can transport the reader into the story's universe. The reader may also derive an additional sense of involvement and satisfaction if he is given, as part of the setting, factual data which fascinates him and makes him feel he is learning something.

This kind of involvement and possible satisfaction not only predisposes the reader to be friendly to the writer, and generally relaxed, it also makes him more likely to believe the story's plot and characters because he is already having a pleasurable experience from the setting, and believes in the story world.

These are not minor advantages for the writer. She should always be alert for ways to soothe, please and enchant the reader, because a friendly reader is more apt to accept uncritically other aspects of the story.

Unity is another element upon which setting can have an obvious favorable impact. A story line may involve complex developments affecting a wide variety of characters; the issues may become very complex; there may even be multiple viewpoints and story lines taking place in different levels of the society. Yet a consistent setting can provide an unchanging backdrop against which even otherwise unrelated story developments or characters will be seen as related simply because they are taking place on the same stage.

Thus the physical setting can provide a unifying background scenery. The consistent tone of language and general story atmosphere which grow out of the physical setting also provide a sense of unity. For example, once an atmosphere of gothic horror has been established, even the innocent play of children in the "great, gloomy house" may become frightening for the already-enchanted reader, who would not otherwise see the children as in any way scary or threatened.

Plot or suspense can be advanced and complicated by setting. As one example, suppose your tale is about a wagon master who is leading a train of Conestogas across the prairie toward distant mountains. Your descriptions of the subtly changing scenery as the mountains become nearer act as a physical "scorecard" showing how the story is advancing toward its ultimate conclusion. If the reader knows that hostile Indians await in the mountain pass ahead, your repetitive mention of the mountains will become a drumbeat of suspense.

Similarly, the emotional atmosphere in an example cited earlier, the movie *High Noon*, was a vital component of the story's effectiveness. Some might quarrel with my definition of atmosphere as part of setting, and argue that the atmosphere *grew out of* the setting. I would reply that in a vivid setting, atmosphere can become so palpable that it seems to assume an identity of its own. Whichever side you might come down on concerning this distinction, I think you can readily see that atmosphere can hardly be considered without relating it to setting, however you choose to describe setting. In *High Noon*, the town's fear and the citizens' cowardly indifference served to isolate the hero more and more as time passed and the moment of crisis loomed; they became as real as the heat and the endless horizon. Without the atmosphere of fear, suspicion and cowardice, the repetitious plot—the hero repeatedly seeking help and being turned down—could have been meaningless and insipid.

Character is significantly linked to setting. The seafaring, whaling world of *Moby Dick*, for example, is crucial to an understanding of Captain Ahab and his mad quest for the white whale. Outside of the specialized setting Melville defines, Ahab's obsession makes no sense at all. And consider poor Amos Herzog in Saul Bellow's classic *Herzog*. The title character could hardly be believed outside the gritty, decaying, smog-plagued urban landscape in which he is depicted. He is a product of that environment, and his motives and thought processes are inextricably driven by it.

One of my own novels, *Twister*, concerns an outbreak of tornadoes across the eastern two-thirds of the United States similar to the actual outbreak of April 3, 1974, when dozens of storms wreaked hundreds of millions of dollars in damages and injured or killed scores of Americans. In this book, the setting of the storm system was the novel's very reason for being, and a cold front spawning many tornadoes actually became the central character in a good portion of the book. Setting seldom becomes this central in a novel, but the fact that it can happen is another illustration of how directly setting can impinge upon characterization.

Theme can also be directly affected by setting. The setting can become a central symbol or metaphor, not only unifying other aspects of the story but illuminating its central idea. Mark Twain's *Huckleberry Finn* is one obvious example that comes to mind. When Huck and Tom step onto their raft and set out down the Mississippi, their voyage becomes a story of life in microcosm. The river setting, so rich in religious and American symbolism, becomes more than a river, Huck's journey finally becoming a voyage into manhood—and life.

The writer's imagination can benefit from setting research. Very often, researching factual information for a story, or visiting an actual site to experience it physically, will fire her imagination in unexpected ways.

Perhaps you'll forgive another autobiographical illustration. When I visited California's Napa Valley several years ago, researching information about winemaking for use in the setting of my novel *The Winemakers*, I was quite concerned about how to open the novel in a way that would establish the setting and a sense of impending trouble at the same time. As I was walking through a winery with its owner one day, he cautioned me not to stumble over a number of heavy electrical cables on the concrete floor.

"Those control the temperature of the fermentation tanks," he explained. "If you pulled the plug, we could lose five hundred gallons of wine."

In that instant, my research into setting had set off my imagination and solved my problem with the opening of the book. If you read it today, you will find that it begins with a young winemaker arriving at her winery—and finding that someone has intentionally "pulled the plug."

TAKE YOUR TIME

Here we've looked at setting in a variety of ways, but in a cursory fashion. I hope I have managed to convince you that your handling of setting may be far more vital to your fiction project than you had previously suspected. In the chapters ahead we'll take a closer look at these and other aspects of setting, and how to maximize their potential in your story.

Let me urge you to work through the chapters slowly, seeking out ways you can reconsider your own work in light of the matters being discussed. It may help you to have copies of some of your own completed stories at hand as you study. As a point is made here, you may benefit by pausing to absorb the idea, and then carefully looking at some of your own copy to see if you have considered the idea in your past work. If not, you should ask yourself why not; if so, you should ask yourself if your new understanding might improve what you did earlier, perhaps without knowing why. If you choose to rewrite portions of your earlier material before moving on through this book, so much the better.

There's no tremendous hurry, you see, and hasty reading without action on your part might let important technical information go in one ear and right out the other. I encourage you to take your time and apply each chapter to your own work before moving on to the next.

After all, you remember the cliché—"Rome wasn't built in a day." *Your* story's Rome, if it's to be convincing, can't be built overnight either.

CHAPTER 2

PRESENTING SENSE IMPRESSIONS

WHEN MOST WRITERS THINK of the word "setting," they think of the physical impressions of the story world: the look, sound and smell of the place or places where the story takes place.

As we move along through this book, we'll also consider many other aspects of fiction which can rightfully be considered part of setting, but first let's consider the sense impressions of the story world.

Your use of description is vital in putting the reader into the story world. Use of vivid descriptions places him imaginatively inside the setting, transporting him to your story world through an appeal to his senses.

Sense impressions, therefore, are tremendously important in presenting your setting and keeping your reader intensely, physically aware of it. An in-depth examination of descriptive methodology is beyond the scope of this book, but we'll take a cursory look at some techniques in chapter fourteen. For now, a brief overview might help.

A truth every writer should keep in mind is that when she stops to describe something in fiction, the progress of the story usually stops while she does so. Fiction readers seek movement in their fiction, and so every "pause to describe" can be a dangerous one, threatening to weaken or even kill the reader's interest.

What is one to do, then, given the equally compelling truth that description of the story setting is vital to reader belief and physical involvement?

The answer is that descriptions generally should be kept to

a few words or a few lines at any given spot. Sensory descriptions should be sprinkled throughout the story, rather than "dumped" in great gobs. Handled this way, descriptive passages won't slow the story for long, and the reader will be reminded again and again — in short passages — how the story setting feels.

THE FIVE SENSES

Psychologists have repeatedly shown that sight is the dominant sense for most normal people. Therefore, it stands to reason that your sense descriptions most often will be dominated by how things appear. Hearing impressions usually rank second, but one can easily imagine circumstances in which tactile impressions might rank higher in story importance. So let's look briefly at each of the five senses you'll hope to touch in most of your stories.

Sight impressions may be of various kinds. There is a common misconception that one has covered the waterfront if she tells what colors can be seen in a given setting. Color is important, but — again according to psychological research findings — we know that a person's sight impressions of a given setting come into consciousness in a specific order.

Spatial dimension is often noted first. How large is the area? How open or closed? How high is the ceiling, if there is one? How far away is the sight-horizon if we're outdoors? How big or small does this space that we're describing feel to the onlooker?

The source of light is usually noted next or may be noticed simultaneously with dimension. Where does the light come from? How bright is it? Is it white light, or a mixture of subtle hues? (If we are "walking the reader" into a room, for example, is there a wall of high windows, or a single slit in a solid gray wall? And if a wall of windows, is the light that streams through sunny or cloudy gray?)

The dominant color of a setting may be striking and important. In describing a desert, for example, you may stress — after the vastness of the scene, and perhaps the glare — the monotonous tan of the terrain under a harsh, copper-colored sky.

Texture may also play a role in sight impression. The play of shadows over a weather-shattered cliff face may be a crucial sight impression; so might be the perfectly flat and placid surface of a small mountain lake on a windless day.

Contrasting shades of color are sometimes a dominant aspect of sight. The leaves of a tree might be green in actuality, for example, but in the context of your story they might look like sharply defined black shapes against the brilliance of the blue sky. That yellow fire truck might be more vibrant if it's seen parked in front of a red brick wall. Contrast often enlivens sight impression.

Hearing impressions are also crucial. The loudness of sound in a given setting is, of course, important, but also consider what is the tonality of the sound. Is it harsh or melodious? Why?

Is the sound a simple, single-source one, or a complex of many sounds? Should you transport your reader by concentrating on the single high wail of an ambulance siren, or would your setting be made more vivid if you depicted the siren sound almost lost in the groan of a garbage truck nearby, the honking of taxi horns, the roar of a diesel engine and the rumble of a subway beneath the pavement?

The identity and direction of a source of sound may be important. Is the sound coming from a distance, or close? Is it in the room or beyond the walls? Is it the muffled echo of a gunshot or the whimper of a child?

Assuming you are telling your story from the viewpoint of a character inside the action, that character's interpretation of the sound or sounds may also be highly significant in your description of it. For example, your character in the woods hears a low, guttural animal sound. Does she interpret it in terms of remembering how her pet dog used to grumble at squirrels, or does the image of a hungry grizzly instantly leap into her mind?

The sense of smell often ranks third in the hierarchy of sense impressions in a setting, usually far below sight and hearing because it is a more primitive sense, one we often tend to overlook or discount in real life. We often notice only strong odors, whether pleasant or unpleasant, and seldom form a strong judgment about a setting on the basis of them alone. Also, for most writers, describing odors is difficult and seldom seems highly relevant.

Yet, a woodland setting might come to life most vividly for the reader through a brief, cogent mention of the scent of pine and fallen leaves. The terror of a fire might come partly from the stinging cloud of smoke that threatens to choke bystanders. In such cases, an appeal to the sense of smell might be called for, or even demanded.

Tactile sensations — feeling with the fingertips or the surface of the skin — are more individualistic than most of the other senses mentioned thus far. Here we are dealing with physical feeling — roughness or smoothness, heat and cold, and the like. While there are imaginable circumstances in which the description of the setting through tactile sensations might be in order — in a story of someone threatened by freezing after being lost in a blizzard, for one obvious example — such sensations usually form a small part of the setting of a story.

Taste impressions, as part of setting, will be highly individualized. This sense is seldom used to a marked degree. But in those rare instances where a description of a taste — sweetness or bitterness, saltiness, acidity — may be called for, they too form a part of the physical setting of the tale.

As a fiction writer, you'll come upon occasions when you want to appeal to most of the senses in an attempt to make your story setting vivid and appealing. However, just as you must be accurate in factual background, you can't allow yourself to be "carried away" by some poetic flight of fancy in describing. Bluebirds *are* blue, and readers aren't going to like it if you change the color to orange because you think it might be more vivid.

HOW TO DELIVER SENSE IMPRESSIONS WITH PRECISION

It is not enough, though, to stick to known and verifiable impressions, and to sprinkle them in with care. Readers yearn for the most vivid and striking physical presentations of setting that you are capable of giving. Here, then, are some additional points that you should keep in mind.

If you know your story setting well, your notebook and imagination will be teeming with sense impressions you want to convey to the reader in order to make the story world vivid. But there is a danger that you might overdo it. The key here is to avoid generalizations or vagueness, and stick to specific, concrete detail.

Suppose, for example, you are trying to describe a fine country morning, and you bog down in generalizations and vague, catchall phrases (the words italicized in the following). You might come up with something like this:

> The *beautiful* day began with a *bright* sun in a *clear* sky and a *gentle* breeze moving through the *handsome* trees behind the *big* house. Beyond the *wide* river, through a *slight* veil of mist, the *buildings* of the *town* could be seen. . . .

Clearly, one might go on for pages with this kind of vague and generalized description, and never really get anywhere. If you search for a few words that are as specific and concrete as possible, however, you may achieve your story goals and get on with things in a hurry, as follows:

> Shading her eyes against the brilliant sun, Cassie squinted into the chilly breeze, trying to penetrate the smokelike haze over the river. Beyond it, the town's buildings jutted up like a child's blocks tumbled onto the ground.

We'll look more deeply at such questions of precision in wording in chapter fourteen. The point here is simply to start you thinking about the relationship between specificity of information and style. If you are specific enough, and strive to write with sharp impact, this in itself will tend to prevent your writing descriptive passages that are too long.

One further thought about "overkill" detail: Repetition of exactly the same sense impressions makes a story dull and predictable. Similarly, repetition of the same background facts can be deadly dull. If you need to repeatedly mention the frigid weather, for example, find a different way to refer to it each time. You can't simply keep saying it's cold outside. Instead, consider dropping in brief mentions of details like the following:

- the shrill wind against the roof shingles
- thick ice encrusting the inside of the windows
- a character's breath issuing from her lungs in steamy clouds
- brittle snowflakes swirling in the misty night
- a character shivering and wishing for a heavier coat
- a stray dog shaking miserably from the cold
- tingling pain in ears and fingers
- eyes watering from the chill wind
- smoke billowing densely from every chimney in sight
- the crunch of hard-frozen snow under a man's boots
- cold-reddened faces and hands
- low, thick snow clouds overhead

All of these small details will say "It's cold!" without ever saying it directly or in a repetitious manner.

In like fashion, suppose you need to say that the town which is your setting has a hostile feel about it — that the people distrust strangers. The reader is likely to get infuriated if you say this straight out more than once or twice. But, again, you can create any number of small details to show this trait of the setting in different words. (As a small exercise, you might wish to pause here and compose a list of possible setting details that would continually emphasize the town's hostile nature without boring repetition of the same words.)

With the selection of small but accurate details like these you can provide continual emphasis on setting without becoming repetitious. Use of this technique, along with cognizance of plot pressure to keep things moving along at a good pace, will put setting in its place as a critical but never obtrusive aspect of your storytelling.

THE VIEWPOINT

In order to be precise and convincing, you must be aware of another angle in your presentation of setting, and that's the viewpoint from which the sensory information is seen.

Beginning writers sometimes thoughtlessly assume an omniscient viewpoint—the see-everything and know-everything viewpoint of a godlike creator standing over the entire setting. Sometimes such a viewpoint is economical and the simplest way of putting down relatively large quantities of data in the smallest possible space.

Virtually all fiction, however, is told from a viewpoint, from the head and heart of a character inside the story action. Therefore, very often your job as a writer depicting some aspect of setting is to determine what the viewpoint character can realistically know or experience at any given moment—then to limit your presentation to that.

How can you know when to deliver information "from on high," and when from a character's viewpoint? The simplest answer might be found by following this three-point procedure:

1. Determine which impressions must be given "from on high" because (a) no character can see or experience them all, or (b) they can be given much more simply and vividly from outside a limited viewpoint.

2. Present descriptions "from on high" only at the beginning of story chapters or sections, when there has been a break in the time or action and you have not yet reestablished a character viewpoint since the break.

3. After establishing a viewpoint in any given section, present all further descriptions from inside that viewpoint, only as that viewpoint person could experience them.

Looking at each of these points in more detail:

As stated in No. 1, above, some sensory information cannot realistically be seen or known by any character inside the story. Suppose you wish to set up in the reader's mind the threat of a dam breaking and possibly flooding a town. If any character inside the story knew about this threat, he would surely sound an alarm. Therefore, in order to show the reader the cracks in the dam and the rising water pressure behind it, you have no choice but to get out of that limiting character viewpoint at the beginning of a chapter, say, and to present your description of the situation from an anonymous, godlike viewpoint. Then, having established knowledge of the setting threat in your reader's mind, you can enter the viewpoint of an innocent character inside the town.

Or, you might wish to portray a gathering storm. A story character *might* see this coming. But in order to alert the reader through a character viewpoint, you would have to drop in some references to clouds on the horizon, a freshening wind, the sound of distant thunder, or a drop in temperature to make the character aware of the storm so that the reader could become aware through that character's observations. Sometimes you might go through all this; other times it might be far more economical to adopt a godlike viewpoint and simply describe the gathering clouds and rising winds on a broader scale than anyone in the story could sense them.

Moving to No. 2, when you do choose to describe from an omniscient viewpoint, you should do so only at the beginning of story segments where no viewpoint for that segment has yet been established.

Why? Because readers like to get into a viewpoint, and once they do, they imaginatively experience everything in the story world from inside the character's head and heart. If you are in a chapter, say, and in character Joe's viewpoint, it's extremely jarring to the reader if you suddenly drop out of viewpoint and start describing things on a broader scale than Joe could possibly know.

Between sections or chapters, the reader tends to relax his viewpoint focus. After a break in the time or action, he'll more readily accept an omniscient passage. So this is the spot where you can most gently drop out of character viewpoint in order to present setting description from a broader perspective.

Note, however, the advice given in No. 3: Once you've established a character viewpoint in a given section, it's important to present all information from inside that viewpoint.

Perhaps two additional illustrations will further clarify these points. Both are from my novel, *Twister*, and in both cases my objective was to describe a part of the setting that was at the heart of the story: a storm spawning multiple tornadoes across more than half the United States. I wanted to describe what such a storm would be like to an individual trapped in it. But I also wanted to show "the big picture" that no single individual could experience. Therefore, I had to assume different vantage points.

One of the limited vantage points I chose was that of a farm woman named Milly, and my primary intention was to show how a tornado might be experienced by someone like her, in the storm's path. Therefore, the segment began in Milly's viewpoint as the tornado approached — this part of the dynamically changing setting being described as she would experience it, in viewpoint. I have italicized the words which establish or reinforce her restricted viewpoint:

> Out in front, not far across the road, a perfectly vertical column of blackness spun wildly. Its hollow interior was lighted by the strange bluish-white light that bathed everything else. The column seemed to be composed of rings of spinning clouds, one on top of the other like a stack of pale tires, and *as Milly watched, she saw* one ring near the bottom work its way upward, seeming to slip over others above it until it was out of view. Boards and small trees and other unrecognizable objects hurled around and around in the rotating column. *She saw* a small tree fly out of the column and flop to the ground like a killed fish. The sound was either *too great for Milly's ears*, or they had been broken by *the intense pain she felt in them.* . . .

There is nothing here that Milly cannot logically and credibly experience. (You may also notice that shape, light and movement are described first, with hearing noted at the end.) This passage achieved the goal set out for it, describing a single person's experience of this part of the setting.

A chapter or two later, however, my intention was to show

a broader view of a storm approaching a town. In this case, no single individual could possibly know everything I wanted to tell, nor could any single character see the panorama I wished the reader to experience. Therefore, the following passage opened a segment after a time-and-space transition clearly marked by extra white spaces in the text:

> The Thatcher tornado, one of three suspended under a single enormous thundercloud cell some nine miles in diameter and towering more than seventy thousand feet in altitude, was at its peak of life as it reached the southwest edge of Southtown, on a northeasterly path that would take it through the heart of the city. It was one mile wide at its mouth, with winds of two hundred miles per hour crushing, smashing and destroying everything in its range, and could not be seen as a classic twister, but rather as a gigantic ebony obscuration from ground to sky, swirling, shrieking with a sound like none other in the world. . . .

Thus you make your viewpoint decisions based on your intent at the moment in the story, and you place them in the most advantageous structural locations. There will be more about these decisions in later chapters, as the need to discuss them arises.

A FINAL WORD ON THE SENSES

Before closing this look at sensory description, one point should be emphasized yet again, and that has simply to do with accuracy. However hard you strive to be vivid, or whatever device you may choose to put the reader into your physical story setting, please remember that you must never deviate from verifiable facts. A single slip—describing a certain known flower by the wrong color, for example—might so offend your reader that many of your subsequent descriptions might be met with skepticism, or worse. *Never* deviate from the factual in your physical descriptions.

Accuracy! It's so important.

In the next chapter we'll look at another aspect of setting where accuracy is also supremely important, one closely related to what we have been discussing here. That involves setting information based less on physical senses and more on hard, cold fact.

Which doesn't have to be cold at all, as we shall see.

CHAPTER 3

PRESENTING FACTUAL MATERIAL

FACTUAL BACKGROUND IS OFTEN AS ESSENTIAL to a story as its physical look and feeling. Thus one of your major jobs as a writer is to know how to handle the presentation of facts in your fiction.

Some aspects of factual background may be simple, such as knowing what kind of weather to portray in west Texas in August. Others may become more esoteric, such as knowing how many strands of barbed wire a rancher would realistically string in your western novel set in the year 1875. And still others might be more demanding yet, such as the need to portray with great accuracy the facts of a surgical procedure being done in your medical novel. Whatever factual material you choose to present as part of your story fabric, it must first of all be right.

ACCURACY

It's disturbing to me how often fiction writers say that they don't have to worry much about factual information in their setting because "I made the town up," or "I never specify exactly where or when it is." Such ideas don't hold water. Factual data about the setting must always be as accurate as practicality allows.

For example, even if you're presenting a fictional town in an unnamed region, there must be an internal factual consistency about the setting. The town should at least be identifiable as being in the South, let's say, or in the Rocky Mountains. Within this general frame of reference, you must be factually accurate.

By way of illustration: In the southern setting you might show crape myrtles in bloom, but you'd better know they bloom late in the summer, and usually have pink or orchid-colored flowers, or they might also be white. In the high mountains, crape myrtles winter-kill; there you may have lilacs—but in the spring. Similarly, it might be possible for your imaginary town to have a snowstorm in June if it were set in northern Montana, but if your general reference area were in the South, such a snow would require a lot more explaining!

Thus even a very vague story setting requires general factual accuracy. And most story settings are much more specific and require far greater attention to factual detail. You as a fiction writer must always remember this principle: even a single factual error in your setting may destroy all credibility for your story . . . all reader belief.

One example: Several years ago, there was a novel (whose title and author have long since escaped me) with a plot about the abduction of the president of the United States in his Air Force One. Much was made in promotion copy and advertising about the research the novelist had done to make the aircraft setting accurate. This might have been quite true. But in reading the novel, I noticed a careless and fundamental error: The author had thoughtlessly guessed about the transmitting range of a communications device on the plane, and he worked out a key aspect of his plot by making a tiny radio transmit farther than it ever really could have done. This error, small as it was in terms of the total factual background in the novel, was so crucial that it destroyed all my faith in the accuracy of the rest of the background—and I was not the only reader who noticed; reviewers did, too, and the novel was not successful partly because this single bad mistake had wrecked its air of verisimilitude.

I once encountered a more serious factual error in setting when a young woman brought me a novel set in Saudi Arabia. She had carefully researched that Arab nation, and her story brimmed with fascinating facts about the country as well as vivid descriptions of exotic sights. Unfortunately, she had overlooked one crippling fundamental error. The whole plot of her book was based on the idea of a young woman visiting Saudi Arabia as a tourist. The author had not uncovered the fact that Saudi Arabia does not allow tourists to enter the country. Thus the novel was factually impossible.

Never assume you know something if you haven't checked it out. I used to test writing students by giving them a number of statements to complete which in reality could have only one outcome. One such statement said the character "shoved the throttle of the plane fully forward." More than half my students, year after year, wrote for a result that "the engine died" or "the motor slowed" or some such, thoughtlessly assuming that the throttle of an airplane must work the same way as a throttle on an old car or a tractor, where pushing the knob forward decreases power. Unfortunately for all those who guessed on the basis of such an analogy, an aircraft throttle works the opposite; you push forward for more power, not less. The correct factual response had to be that the engine roared, the plane's altitude or speed changed, or something close to that.

Once more: Never assume you know a fact about setting if you haven't checked it out. All stated facts about the setting must be accurate if the story is to be believed.

The weather in a given place at a given time of year should, as already mentioned, be in line with actuality. Further, if you happen to be writing about a specific place and a specific actual date, I would advise you to go so far as to check old newspapers or almanacs to find out what the weather really was at that time, in that place. (I thoughtlessly assumed once that a quite ordinary day in June of a certain year was warm and windy in Montana. I received two letters from outraged readers pointing out that I had failed to take note that *that* June period saw the biggest early-summer snowstorm in state history. I have decided you can't be too careful about anything.)

Many readers won't know if you guess, but a surprising number will check up on you . . . and immediately lose all belief in the rest of your story after they find one verifiable error. More dangerous to you as a writer is the fact that if you guess about one seemingly minor thing, you may fall into the habit of guessing about things that many readers may notice, to your everlasting discredit and unpopularity.

Know the kinds of trees and shrubs and animals that should be shown in the area you depict. Know the feel of the place, whether the typical day is sun-washed and brilliant or gray and grungy. Know the ethnic composition of the neighborhood, and how the people talk. Know clothing styles, characteristic shelter and transportation. Know what things cost. Know the local slang and what people are most concerned about.

Did you know, for example (as I learned in my student's doomed novel about Saudi Arabia), that Saudi citizens' idea of an entertaining time is to go out into the scrubland and build a big fire and roast meat on a spit? This current setting fact goes back to the history of the setting, that of a nomadic culture. Or did you know that a Saudi man is allowed four wives—but is obliged to treat all equally, so that if one wife gets a house, all wives must have an equal house, and so on? Again, this cultural/religious rule goes back to the region's history and long-standing traditions, which are a vital part of the general setting. And you have to get them right.

WHEN IS TOO MUCH "TOO MUCH"?

Readers today are better informed than any in history. They receive more information from more sources than readers did even a decade ago, and they tend to want more information in their fiction. In the current information revolution, some of them actually seem to feel guilty about reading fiction unless they can convince themselves that they are also learning something. Therefore, recognizing this trend in readership generally, novelists tend to pack much more hard information into their story settings. If you look for solid data in most novels today—even "frothy" ones—you may be surprised to see how much hard research went into them.

But does this mean there is no practical limit to how much hard fact you should provide? By no means. You must not simply pile page after page of fact onto your setting scaffold. Rather, you should have a rich lode of factual information on hand before you begin to write, and should know how to sprinkle in those facts a few at a time in places where they will best fit into the flow of your narrative. Note that both parts of the equation are necessary in providing readers with sufficient factual data about your setting: having plenty of accurate information, and knowing how to sprinkle it in, a bit at a time, at the right times.

A point is made of this duality of purpose because there are writers who err by ignoring one part or the other. Some research heavily and gather fascinating details, then succumb to the temptation to dump it all, in long, boring imbedded essays which stop the story, shift the focus from characters to encyclopedia-type data, irritate the reader, and finally put him to sleep. Other writers, knowing they can't shovel in loads of facts, respond by not gathering many facts to begin with — or by carelessly guessing at a few. Either course is disastrous.

You can never have too much factual information on hand about your setting. You will often be amazed by how much you manage to work in, a dribble at a time. But even if some of it never gets into your story, your knowledge of this information will enrich your storytelling because you the author will know the story world in all its details as well as, or better than, any character.

How do you know how much setting information to insert into your narrative at any given time? Unfortunately, this is largely a matter of "feel," and you can never be entirely sure. But one aspect of fiction that will help you decide when "enough is enough" is plot pressure. If your story's plot is "working," your characters should be under some pressure — both in terms of story time and emotion — virtually throughout. If you have your plot working in this way, you simply may not have time to dump in too many facts, nor will your characters have time to notice or discuss too many facts at any given moment.

What am I implying here? Simply this: If you find yourself stopping the story action again and again to drop in lengthy information about the setting, this may be a clue to you that your plot is not "tight" enough — is not putting enough immediate pressure on the characters. Often you can answer the question of how much setting information to put in at any given point by looking at the pressure on the characters—and increasing that immediate pressure if you find that you have nothing going on which would realistically preclude someone thinking quietly about their hometown's demographics for half a chapter, or reciting other facts to some other story person.

So if you suspect that you're putting in undesirable gobs of uninterrupted factual information (or excessive sensory description, for that matter), look at your plot. Try to devise ways to make things tougher on your story people so that there simply will not be time for overindulgence in setting details.

PROBLEM SITUATIONS

But what about the times when you may have detailed factual data or story information that you want your viewpoint character to learn in the course of the story? In such cases, clearly, you need to have the information given to the character in his viewpoint. So what do you do? Have someone walk up to the character in the story and start pointing things out to him, and telling him facts?

I hope not. When you want your viewpoint character to observe certain things or learn certain facts, you must not have some other character simply dump the information on his head. What you need to do, rather, is to create inside your viewpoint character a need and desire to notice something or learn certain things. Then you can have him set out to reconnoiter a mountainside, for example, or interrogate some other character.

Having set up a felt need for certain setting information inside your viewpoint character, you can realistically have him go off in search of it. In this way, you set up a little sub-quest in the plot—the character seeking information about the setting and situation.

Following are two examples of such a situation where the author has decided that a character needs certain information. The first is a clumsy and horrid example of how *not* to do it.

Ralph walked into the bar. He did not know it, but it was the same bar where his brother Jake had been seen two weeks earlier.

The bartender came over and squinted at Ralph. "You look familiar," he said.

"I do?" Ralph said.

"You look a lot like a man who was in here two weeks ago. He said his name was Jake. He looked tired that evening . . . said he was going to register at the Zuider Zee Motel down the street. That's the one the police raided the other night, you know. The police chief—his name is Sam Spade—believed there was gambling going on there. But back to this man Jake. I asked him where he came from, and. . . ."

This is pretty bad. The "He did not know it" line at the top is a clear violation of viewpoint, the author clumsily stepping in to say something the character does *not* know, then using another character to dump information on Ralph (and the reader) in a totally unbelievable way.

How much better it works if we have set up Ralph's need to learn information in the bar, perhaps as follows.

Ralph found the bar where his brother had been seen two weeks earlier. Somehow, he thought, he had to learn why Jake had come here, from where, and—most important—where he had planned to go next.

The bartender seemed surly. Ralph ordered a beer, and then tried to collect information.

"Are you the regular man on duty at this time?" he asked.

"That's me," the bartender said. "Why?"

"Would you have been working two weeks ago tonight?"

"Say, fella, what is this? Twenty questions?"

"I'm trying to locate my brother. His name is Jake Wheelan. He was in this bar two weeks ago tonight. I thought you might have seen him. He and I look a lot alike."

The bartender frowned and leaned closer. "I might

have seen him, at that. What is it exactly you want to know?"
"Well, first. . . ."

As this example makes clear, sometimes you can get important information into your story without having to retreat to an "on-high" vantage point. Your viewpoint character can ask questions, and you can get the information into the story that way—both for the reader's use and as motivation of your character.

On the other hand, there will be cases when you must have the wisdom to take a broader view. Suppose you are writing a historical novel which looks at a small section of the country and how it is about to be engulfed in a freshet of immigration. From an omniscient, "on-high" point of view, you can tell the reader about national business setbacks, the influx of immigrants from Europe to the East Coast, even the lingering aftereffects of a recent war. You can paint a much broader canvas than any character inside the story could possibly portray for you.

At this point we need only remember that there are such viewpoint choices—and they are yours to make wisely, with thought. There are a number of other things to consider in choosing and showing viewpoint, but it's necessary to look at some other matters before we go deeper into that. We'll return to the subject in chapter ten, with other aspects considered in the chapter following that.

START THINKING "RESEARCH"

In the meantime, work on your own habits as they relate to accuracy in the presentation of facts in your setting. This will mean research. (One can't always write about the hometown neighborhood she already knows intimately.) Appendix 1, starting on page 155, looks at research methods and procedures, and you should begin dipping into it as soon and as often as necessary.

Start getting more familiar with your local library and bookstores. By all means, browse them! Allot an hour or two, or more, on a regular basis. Stroll past the shelves. Acquaint yourself with the kinds of factual information available. Notice, for example, that travel books deal mostly with physical matters, and can be invaluable to you in learning how to describe a setting, but you may unearth equally crucial information about history or custom or regional attitudes in books to be found in the history section, or in an area devoted to social sciences. The more you browse, the more resources you'll uncover.

Before you go on, however, perhaps this chapter has suggested something you need to look at again in some of your own copy? Is there a fact to recheck . . . or a better way to present your factual material?

Take your time.

CHAPTER 4

FUDGING FACTS: WHEN IT'S OKAY TO STRAY FROM TRUTH

HAVING WORKED HARD TO CONVINCE you of the need for absolute accuracy in setting, I am now forced to confront you with a paradoxical statement:

There are occasions in fiction when *inaccuracy* may be beneficial—when a writer can score considerable gains for herself by deviating from actuality either by bending the facts or making some up.

A number of reasons exist for this.

As we shall explore in chapter five, readers of certain fiction genres expect and virtually demand qualities of setting which may be more mythological than real. Woe be to the unwary writer who deviates from such genre-reader expectations, regardless of actuality!

We'll discuss the matter further in that later chapter, but one example might be mentioned here for clarification. Readers of traditional western adventure stories generally expect the tale to take place in "the warm West," which means that most westerns take place in the heat of summer, and usually in semiarid areas such as west Kansas or Texas. Horsemanship is almost always some part of the setting, and so are firearms and gunplay. The setting almost always includes philosophical ideals of manly courage, independence and quick justice, and the cowboy and land baron, rough as they might be, were building an empire, please remember, not raping an environment!

All such reader expectations about a story's setting may require you to deviate considerably from the actual truth.

ARTISTIC LICENSE

Are there other instances when you can safely deviate from the facts about setting? Yes. Here are some examples of what you can do.

Invent a town or area, within reason. Your story situation may make it necessary to invent a town or area rather than placing your story precisely in an actual one. Most of the reasons you would do this are mundanely practical. You don't have access to every small physical detail of the real town in Bavaria you want to portray, for example, but you have general memories of the area, and access to guidebooks which show pictures of several towns similar to the one you vaguely remember. In such a case, making up your own town might keep you true to the spirit and feeling of a real place, but free you from worry that you might get a street name wrong or a bit of history garbled. Or you might be basing your story loosely on actual events — a murder, say, or grand theft that really took place. Placing your story in the actual town where the crime was committed would lead every person in the real town to look for themselves in your story, and thus naming the actual town might open you up to misidentifications (or real ones!) — and lawsuits. Far better in such circumstances to make up your own town, similar to the real one.

Invention of a town or area as setting may free you creatively and legally, too. But a proviso must be added, and that is this: The invented place must be true to the general area and time in which you invent it. It simply won't work to set a story in 1976 and have your railroad line using mostly steam locomotives; these were generally phased out of use in favor of diesel power in the 1950s. Similarly, just because you happen to make up your particular small town in upper New York state, you can't have everybody speaking in an accent or with slang totally out of keeping with that general geographical area — then plead that you can do whatever you want because the town is imaginary. The rules of credibility apply even in a wholly fictional setting, and most writers who make up a town pattern it closely after a real, known one — or well-researched one — in order to avoid gaffes like having considerable oil drilling taking place in modern-day Oklahoma, where the oil business has declined radically in recent years, or putting a mountain anywhere near Oklahoma City.

Put actual historical (or contemporary) personages in your fiction. Writers often worry greatly about when they can and cannot put real people in their story settings and plots. A rule that perhaps errs on the side of safety is that you can put actual people in cameo roles. It's a fairly popular device, one I've used myself in a series of novels about an international tennis player I call Brad Smith. There is no Brad Smith, and he is made out of whole cloth. But as part of the story setting, any number of actual tennis stars, from Bjorn Borg to Chrissie Evert, show up in cameo speaking roles.

Such a setting device tends to add verisimilitude to the yarn and to make the reader believe in the wholly fictional characters. Generally there is nothing wrong with this, even though making up dialogue for real people, and even minor actions in the plot, is clearly a departure from reality. Again, however, you shouldn't stray too far from the truth: If you put Jimmy Connors on the tennis court in your story, you can't make him right-handed; readers will notice that and chalk it up to your ignorance, thus diminishing your credibility as a storyteller.

The legal ramifications of using real people in your fiction are not complicated. The basics have not changed in over a half-century. In both civil and criminal libel, three elements must be present to establish libel has taken place. The words used must be defamatory; they must be published; and the person libeled must be identified. (Fredrick Siebert, J.D.: *The Rights and Privileges of the Press*; Appleton-Century Co., 1934.)

Beyond this, courts have generally held that the alleged libel must have been written and published "willfully." That is to say, the offended party must prove that the accused writer meant to do harm. This is a very difficult allegation to prove, as many failed libel suits have proven. However, all writers should remember that there have been rare cases where a judge ruled that the writer printed a damaging falsehood, and should have been more careful. In such cases, a "reckless disregard for the truth" — the terminology often used in journalism school lecture halls — may be interpreted as proof of an indifference to fact so sloppy and brazen that the resulting falsehood can be considered "willful."

Also remember that truth is its own defense. If you are sued for libel and can absolutely prove the veracity of what you wrote, you cannot be found guilty of libel. (Of course you might go through a great deal of emotional torment and expense before you are vindicated in a court of law.)

Public figures such as elected officials are almost impossible to libel when the writer is writing about official duties. All such comment, including newspaper editorials, is considered "fair comment."

The published material must bring the subject person into disrepute and actually damage his or her reputation, and you can't libel the dead.

Beyond these basic points lies a swamp of legal nit-picking. Great, fat books have been written on libel. Occasionally a court renders a libel ruling which subtly alters the body of "case law," creating some new precedent every subsequent judge may have to consider in rendering a verdict, but all of these fine points take us far beyond the scope of this chapter.

In addition to libel laws, the writer must be concerned about laws protecting citizens' right to privacy. These are far broader and less specific. If you put a real person in your story, and if he or she doesn't happen to like your portrayal, you might find yourself sued for invasion of that person's privacy.

Such cases might be filed virtually by anyone on any pretext, and there are a lot of people out there eagerly looking for a chance to sue somebody and make some easy money. A writing friend of mine was once sued for millions by the family of a dead official with a shady past. The story mentioned some of the dead man's alleged shady dealings. The family sued for invasion of their privacy by the writer's mentioning the dead man's chicanery, and while they ended up losing their case, my friend spent more than two years in agony as the case dragged on, to his considerable expense in legal fees.

The moral here is that you should be extremely careful in

matters involving real people, living or dead. That rule—and the always-present need for the greatest possible verisimilitude in your stories—guides all the observations that follow here.

My own rule is to use real people only in harmless cameo roles, and to reduce even the use of actual historical personages to a safe minimum. I generally make up my specific locales—at least the restricted area of a known city or state my story may play in—and use real people supersafely.

An actual example might further illustrate the last two points about making up a town and putting real people in cameo roles. In his novel *The Night Hunters*, mystery writer John Miles opens with a prologue that begins as follows.

> In the summer of 1962, the President of the United States flew 2,000 miles in order to cut a ribbon and open twelve miles of two-lane asphalt highway. The new road followed the ridged crest of a wooded hill system—steps to the Ozarks—in the most desolate and beautiful section of southeastern Oklahoma.
>
> The President's aides spoke of his abiding interest in projects designed to preserve natural beauty and stimulate pride in the nation, and the President himself, standing tall and young with the brisk Oklahoma wind in his sandy hair, spoke movingly of our heritage. . . .
>
> It was by all odds the biggest day in the history of the town of Noble in Archer County, Oklahoma. . . .

This segment combines historical and geographical fact with invention. It is a fact that John Kennedy went to Oklahoma in 1962 to dedicate a short stretch of scenic highway. But the town most directly affected was not Noble, but Big Cedar. Newspaper accounts do not reflect remarks by the president that day about "our heritage," but about development of natural resources. Further, there is no "Archer County" in Oklahoma, and although there is a real town of Noble, it is located in Cleveland County, faraway from the story locale, in the middle of the state.

Miles's deviations from actuality were not the type that readers would "jump on" as inaccurate. Clearly, he was taking liberties with actuality in order to lay out the background setting for a story to be played out in and around a fictional town in a fictional county—much like a real town in a real county.

The plot of Miles's novel has to do with a hidden story involving a plot against the president's life on that visit long ago, and the long-hidden aftereffects of that murderous scheme. Far better to make up a town and some character dialogue so that the main plot might be believed, than to try to put the story in the actual town of Big Cedar, Oklahoma, where many readers would know that such a series of events never, ever, took place.

Invent dialogue for real people, even historical personages. What you can't do is try to prettify your setting by having actual persons, contemporary or historical, saying things clearly contrary to everything actually known about them. This is not a legal question but one of simple accuracy and verisimilitude. In a historical novel about Lewis and Clark, for example, you might reasonably show the two explorers discussing the wildlife and day's activities; you could extrapolate conversations like this from expedition journals, and possibly even allude to real past events. On the other hand, it might be going a bit too far to have Lewis telling Clark how frightened he is out here in the wilderness without his night light.

Change the location or timing of real events. You can also mildly alter other established facts, if the changes are not glaringly wrong. In one of my Brad Smith novels, for example, I changed the venue of events leading up to the Wimbledon tournament, making up a couple of warm-up tourneys that don't actually exist, and changing the dates for some others. Why? The different timing and placement of these parts of my fictional setting made my plot work better and more smoothly. In addition, had I used real locations in all cases, I would have had to spend another $10,000 visiting all such locales and tournaments in Great Britain in order to make sure I had every detail about the actual place perfectly accurate. In another Brad Smith book, set around Lake City, Colorado, I sent a car chase south of town and onto a creek-canyon road that does not really exist. Two other creek-canyon roads do exist south of town, but neither exactly fit my needs for the chase.

I don't think anyone objects very strenuously to changes

like these. In both cases, the deviations from actuality remained true to the kind and spirit of the real setting. Only details were altered for convenience.

Invent period jargon or slang. You can even write in such a way as to "fake" the sound of a period. This is especially true in historical fiction. It may be quite impossible to know exactly how the common person spoke in the England of 1700, for example. But writers depict the period setting's language peculiarities and cadences all the time. Sometimes, as more than one novelist has admitted, certain slang expressions were simply made up because they "sounded right," true to the cadence and feel of journals and other written documents of the time. Similarly, writers of science fiction often invent pseudotechnical doublespeak for characters to spout as part of the general technological setting of the story. But again, common sense must prevail. You simply can't have an Elizabethan character saying words like "groovy" or "okay," or starting sentences with the contemporary misusage, "Hopefully. . . ."

Imagine the clearly impossible. The setting of Michael Crichton's *Jurassic Park* is a theme park where prehistoric animals have been returned to life. My own novel *Ariel* was set in a computer lab featuring a large mainframe computer which began making its own telephone calls, and then "came to life." The key to making all such improbable or impossible settings work for the reader lies in making the impossible imaginable and acceptable—making the setting enough *like* something that *does* exist so that the reader can "buy it." The copious use of actual facts in presenting the setting is mandatory to get the reader to suspend disbelief. Crichton, for example, provides heavy detail on real scentific developments in biological engineering—cloning, and the like. I heavily researched work in artificial intelligence, computer design and childhood-learning theory before writing *Ariel*, and put heavy doses of facts about such real aspects of science in the novel as part of its setting.

The moral of this, perhaps, is that even when you make something up out of whole cloth—or perhaps especially when you do so—it's even more crucial that you know what the real facts are and present many of them to make your departure from actuality more credible. There seems to be no escaping the need for careful attention to detail—and research.

In all the cases mentioned in this chapter, the use of a vivid bit of setting that never really existed might be better than use of the real thing, even if scrupulously researched. But in every case we have seen the need for factual information lying behind the make-believe, as a point from which it can take off and still be believed. There are advantages, sometimes, in making up part of your setting, but that doesn't relieve you of the need to be accurate and true.

The trick, it seems to me, lies in seeing what might ring false to your reader—and never taking a chance in such a case. If you can construct part of your setting from memory of a real place, or from your imagination, it can be perfectly all right as long as you don't stray too far from what the reader knows is real. You can set your story in the fictional town of Bickham, nineteen miles outside of Houston, for example, and if you do so, you can make up street names and everything else since the town does not really exist. But you can't have a blizzard in August in that general locale, and if you have a character drive to Houston to shop, you'll have to have the street names and all other details of the real city accurate in every detail.

So, you can see that accuracy is a prime requisite even in an imagined setting. Imagined setting must be just as consistent and detailed as one built on an actual place or time. It cannot deviate from realities about the region or era. You may, for reasons of convenience or legality, obscure the actual identity of a place, or you may play loose with certain aspects of an actual place's history. You can make up a setting from memory or imagination. But your job always is to convince the reader. Specific detail is convincing, and generality is not. That's why made-up details of a setting are so often extrapolations, not wild invention, and why writers so often research heavily into a real setting before making up a similar one of their own; they want to have a lot of detail, and they want to be very close to what's really "out there" someplace.

A "DEPARTURE CHECKLIST"

Assuming you are considering making up part of your setting or deviating from actuality in some ways as you depict an actual setting, here are a few questions you might want to bear in mind — a sort of safety checklist for your departure from reality.

1. "Do I have good reason not to use the actual place or time?" If the only reason you're making up a setting is to make it easier on yourself, you may be making a mistake. You'll probably end up researching a real place, and then basing your imagined setting on hard facts, anyway.

2. "Am I sure that my imagined setting will be more vivid and believable than the actual place might be?" As useful as imagined settings may be, credibility is gained by placing your story in an actual, recognizable place and time. Don't carelessly assume that a made-up town, for example, would necessarily be more interesting than a real one you know well.

3. "Is my imagined setting close enough to a real one to be believed?" In other words, is your imagined setting credible? Are the details close enough to an actual place to be accepted without question by the reader?

4. "Do any of my imagined details fly in the face of reality?" Are you sure the weather is right for your region, for example, and if you are using real people in cameo roles, are you absolutely certain you have basic details about the real people perfectly correct?

5. "Do I have enough detail to be convincing?" Have you thought deeply enough about every aspect of your setting? Do you know everything you possibly could about it? Do you have mental or, preferably, actual drawn maps, for example, as well as biographies, dates and descriptions of places in your imagined history? Are there vague spots in your planning which must still be filled?

THE VALUE OF BUILDING FILES

Clearly, even if you don't fear the harrassment of lawsuits, you will want to make your story settings and people as credible as possible. To that end, for professional pride, if nothing else, you should start setting up some files, whether you intend to work primarily with actual settings or imagined ones. In either case you'll need background facts.

These files may be very general, with headings such as "Science," "Homes," "Rivers and Lakes," "Historic Romances," or whatever. As you read newspapers and magazines, be alert for material that might go into one of these files, or into a new one. I don't want you to become a file clerk, but a growing store of factual data for possible use in future story settings can become a priceless resource.

Even if you deviate far from actual places, persons and times, you need the background actuality as a support for your imaginings. As you move along in your fiction-writing career, you will find that you are building more and more of these files. This is all to the good because it will make your future work on settings easier. Most of us who have been in the business for a while have file drawers full of all manner of factual information that might be useful in a setting someday. Some of the clippings in my files go back many years and have never proven useful as yet, but I keep them because one never knows what strange byway his imagination may take.

CHAPTER 5

SETTING IN SPECIALIZED STORIES

As MENTIONED IN THE LAST CHAPTER, readers come to certain genres — types of stories — expecting certain kinds of settings, certain details, certain intensities and lengths of description. In the example used earlier, it was noted that readers of traditional westerns expect — and even demand — that the setting have certain prototypical aspects.

This was brought out to me most forcefully early in my writing career when I myself was writing westerns. I wrote a novel set in a Colorado town in the middle of a severe winter when an avalanche cut the area off from all outside assistance. Although seemingly acceptable in every other regard, the manuscript was rejected several times on the basis, as one editor put it, that the story setting "lacks the traditional feeling of the warm West."

Since that time, the importance of meeting reader expectations about setting in certain genres has been brought home to me again and again. It's an aspect of setting seldom addressed by the experts, but it's very real. You, as a writer interested in improving your handling of setting, should be aware of how various genres bring with them built-in expectations about the setting that should be used.

The late Clifton Adams, one of the best western writers who ever lived, told me that the advantage of the traditional western setting lay in the fact that "The police won't come in and break up your fight just when you've got it going full-blast." That's one of the hard-core, practical reasons why most westerns take place in isolated settings — no one will break up the fight or jail the bad guys or rescue the hero from his plight.

Another reason for the isolation so typical of the western novel setting, however, is simply this matter of reader expectation. From the time of James Fenimore Cooper's tales of the early frontier, readers of western adventure have expected an isolated setting. Such readers aren't aware of the practical plotting advantages such a setting provides for the action writer; it's simply what these readers are used to, and it's what they want to find again in every new novel of the type that they read.

There are other aspects of setting that fit the western genre, too. Some were mentioned in chapter four. But there is also the matter of expansiveness . . . grand vistas . . . vast, open country. This sort of physical setting and open *feeling* is characteristic of nearly all such books.

The kind of people found as part of the setting in westerns is usually predictable, too. Sympathetic female characters, until the most recent time, were quiet, loyal, long-suffering and hardworking characters whose main function was to serve as romantic interest for the more-important males in the story, or to act as mirrors whose adoration made the men look more heroic. That's changed a bit in recent years, and today you can occasionally find a female in a western who is her own person and has some spunk. But the background cast of most westerns is male to this day, the masculine ethic forming part of the story's setting.

The males tend to form a story backdrop based on traditional values, including the work ethic, belief that right makes might (and not the opposite), and the heroic ideal of a lone man against heavy odds for the sake of justice. While the real West might have had a great number of strong and admirable black men, they seldom appear as part of the setting in a traditional western. And while in truth more men might have been shot in the back with a shotgun than killed in street duels, the setting of a western still often depends in part on the unexamined assumption that Marshal Dillon really did stride out into the middle of the street and outdraw a bad guy every once in a while. In the real West, six-guns misfired with dismaying regularity; in the traditional western, six-guns are as reliable as the finest modern weapon. In the real West, the women who made it as far as the frontier towns tended to be a bit on the tough, gnarled side. In the traditional western setting, they're more likely to resemble Michelle Pfeiffer. And so it goes.

The point here is not to disparage the western or any of the other genres we're going to examine. The point is that you as a writer should be aware of what your genre reader expects, and then remember that it is incumbent upon you to deliver the goods expected, whether they're in line with actual fact or not. Thus, in writing genre fiction, you have to be accurate in terms of the reader's expectation or the myth of the genre, rather than the actual truth.

Knowing your genres, then, will tell you where "accuracy" is located.

So let's briefly consider a few others.

ROMANCE

Readers of romance often turn to this genre for escape from the humdrum, relief from grim reality, and reassurance that life can be both beautiful and romantic — that dreams do indeed come true. What do these expectations say about romance settings?

Perhaps above all else, the romance depends on a philo-sophical setting — a group of beliefs assumed as true by the peo-ple in the story — based on the ideal of romantic love. The hero-ine may indeed be a young career woman quite capable of taking care of herself, and may even speak against "silly romantic love." But she is proven quite capable of being "swept off her feet." A belief in love-at-first-sight, so celebrated in popular songs, is essential to such a story; it is the bedrock belief-setting on which everything else is built.

Further — and bearing in mind that there are exceptions to every generalization — most romances play out in a physical setting which is in some way exotic or faraway or sharply differ-ent from the assumed reader's everyday world. Warm, flower-filled Caribbean islands were once the most popular setting, with small European kingdoms (peopled by princes and wealthy heirs) a close second. When these settings were used in too many novels, Central and South America came in for considerable play. There was a brief vogue for the hot Southwest, and Hawaii, and some romances continue to take place in mountain settings, including ski resorts. An occasional useful setting is the large city, but when such a setting is used, the author usually tries to make it out of the ordinary and exciting by stressing fabulous restaurants and clubs, great mansions of the rich and powerful, or the inner workings of some presumably intriguing business firm, a law office, perhaps, or bank.

What all these settings have in common is concrete detail in abundance showing a lifestyle environment far from that known in the everyday life of the average romance reader. Thus the physical setting provides a voyage of escape into an imagined world rich in wish fulfillment.

Because these escape settings form such an important part of the appeal of such stories, they are often written with a loose plot structure that puts relatively slight immediate time pressure on the characters, which in turn allows the author to dwell lovingly and at length on her descriptions of the setting or settings. Because the characters are not pressed to take immediate action in the plot, they have time to notice details of the setting, and the author can credibly devote lengthy passages to description while the characters presumably are doing little if anything.

This softness of plot tension in romances and its resulting opportunity for lengthy descriptions of the setting tend, in turn, to encourage a writing style which is comparatively loose, discursive, heavily ornamented and sensuous. When setting details are described from inside a viewpoint, such descriptions are often tied directly to strong emotional response in the character, so that further coloration of the prose results.

The total effect: Stories in which physical detail is heavily, even sumptuously described, and in which plot tension is usually slight in order to allow for such handling of setting. Thus, if you intend to write romance, you must not only observe acutely for colorful, exotic setting detail, you must also cultivate a full and rich prose style, and you should be careful not to create plot situations which put too much immediate pressure on the characters. For these elements—setting, style and plot—as different as they might appear on the surface, are inextricably tied together in the romance.

SUSPENSE

Readers of suspense fiction bring quite different expectations to this genre. Here the basic appeal is usually either intellectual puzzle (the mystery) or dire physical threat (the classic tale of espionage). While such stories may be very specialized, demanding a deeply researched and meticulously presented setting involving technology or the expertise of a specialized field, the background is not the primary reason why people read them. Here the plot and perhaps the characters are the thing.

What does this imply for you if you want to handle setting properly in such a genre? Three things:

1. The physical detail you present should be described briefly.
2. Your style should be crisp and understated.
3. The emotional background of the story — the tone of the piece — should be as chill as the romance is warm.

Physical detail should be shown briefly for two reasons: The reader of this genre is more interested in plot, and the plot usually will be so pressure-packed and suspenseful that neither character nor author can be involved for long periods of time (or long paragraphs on the page) in setting descriptions. This generalization is violated in novels such as "techno-thrillers," where heavily researched, in-depth factual or physical detail are a considerable part of the writer's appeal. But unless you are writing such a tome crammed with often-esoteric "inside information," the rule of brevity applies.

The style should be crisp and understated because, again, a flowing and discursive style is not what the reader of this genre likes, and is not really fitting in a story of high tension and rapid movement.

The emotional background in suspense stories should be

chill because such a feeling-state in the major characters is the only believable one for story people in such grim situations.

The result of these reader expectations in suspense fiction generally is a tighter, colder writing style.

Here, for example, is the total description of a new bit of setting used in a novel of mine called *The Regensburg Legacy*:

> The next morning, Friday, Dugger drove out of Stuttgart to the suburbs to the south. The sky was blue porcelain, relief after all the foul weather. A brisk breeze blew. Following small road signs with an American flag and the words KELLY BARRACKS on them, he turned off a routine German street and found himself approaching a gate to the military installation like any of a thousand others in the world. There was a high chain-link fence, a black-on-white sign, broad paving, and a guardhouse manned by smartly uniformed MPs.

There is no more description of the new setting. The plot continues immediately with Dugger's attempt to gain admittance to the installation.

While this limited amount of attention to setting, and this sort of unornamented prose, are perfectly fitting in suspense, let me ask you to pause for a moment here and give some thought to how much differently this setting segment might have been written for a romance novel. How much longer might it have been? How much looser and more flowery might the language have been? How much more emotional content—the feelings of the viewpoint character—might there have been?

I think it would have been three to five times as long, and perhaps longer. There would have been much heavier specific description of all kinds—details about the buildings and pavements, the colors of the flower boxes, the sounds of traffic, the sight of birds overhead, the smell of diesel fumes. The writing would have been looser and more ornate, and *everything* in the setting would have been related somehow to the viewpoint character's interior life, her emotional reactions to the environment.

Such differences in handling of setting are often overlooked by the unwary writer, so that even promising stories fail because their emphases and modes of delivery don't fit the genre.

HISTORICALS

Readers of historicals bring still different expectations to that genre, making different demands on the writer. In this kind of story—almost always a long, thick novel—breadth of focus, width of historical sweep, and richness of factual information are expected, even required. If you wish to write such a book, be sure to provide for:

1. Vast background content.
2. Heavy doses of minute period detail.
3. A variety of vantage points.
4. A plot deeply intertwined in the setting.

In terms of content, the setting should contain both vast historic and regional background. At the same time it is offering broad scope and panorama, it should give the reader heavy doses of setting minutiae, little tidbits about the cost of snuff in the colonies, for example, or how milady powdered her hair in those days.

Since both of these focal lengths—very long-distance and extremely close-up—are required in the historical, the writer will be forced to use both the wide-screen omniscient view "from on high" and the tightly restricted, intimate experience of the viewpoint character dealing with fine details. This will probably make the writing style itself fall somewhere between the lushness of the romance and the chill brevity of suspense.

Whatever is presented in the plot, the setting will remain very much in evidence, with the plot intertwined with it, and it will have considerable wordage devoted to it, because it is in the setting that the historic facts and ambience will be transmitted to the reader—who chooses this sort of novel largely to get such input.

The plot may be considerably tighter than in the romance,

for example, but probably will not be as rigid as in the suspense story; a strong plot will be needed to keep the long, broad-canvas story moving, but it will not be such a tightly pressing plot that characters don't have adequate time to experience (and notice) the setting details which form such an important part of the appeal for the average reader of historicals.

SCIENCE FICTION

Readers of science fiction are a bit different from those of any of the genres mentioned so far, and their expectations may give the writer more latitude than in any other genre in terms of what kind of setting and how much setting should be emphasized in the telling of the story. This is so because science fiction may have a primarily suspenseful slant or can, on occasion, be quite romantic. These varying tendencies within the broad genre can result in stories which handle setting in vastly different ways.

Virtually all science fiction, however, has the following characteristics:

1. A background of solid scientific data.
2. Extrapolation from known current facts.
3. A plot which grows out of the setting in some way.

One almost universal truth that can be seen concerning science fiction is that all the genre, from "space opera" to the weightiest technological tome, emphasizes data. In other words, in almost all science fiction the emphasis is on the factual background in the setting and the ideas tested in the plot, rather than on, say, romantic character interaction or straight physical suspense.

What does this mean to you as a potential writer of science fiction? First of all, it means you're going to have to know some cutting-edge science; you may start your research by reading a short, speculative piece in a magazine like *Omni*, but chances are that you'll soon find yourself delving into heavier publications such as *Scientific American*, which can be very heavy going indeed.

In addition, you will use your research findings to invest your setting with some technological trappings, and more often than not you will extrapolate this setting into the future from present-day science, while making sure that your plot problem grows out of the technological setting, rather than just being in the same story with it.

The point made in the last part of the preceding sentence was a whopper, so let's consider it further. What do I mean when I say the plot problem should grow out of the setting, rather than merely be in the same story with it? Simply this: It's a mistake to think that the science or technology setting for such a story is merely a backdrop; the setting should make the story go — should include the basis for the problem or quest itself.

This obviously requires that you do more than make up a glittering scientific setting and then arbitrarily stick any old story into it. The setting has to *cause* the story, almost; it has to contain the germ of the basic plot problem.

Earlier I mentioned *Ariel*, one of my novels that I liked the best when I wrote it. Although the novel sold as a "mainstream" book, it's basically science fiction put into a setting of research on artificial intelligence in computers. The story provides an example of how setting becomes the core of the plot problem, and how the two are completely tied together. The setting is a research lab in which there is a mainframe computer being modified and programmed for artificial intelligence; once this setting changes dynamically, however — and the computer asks *"Who am I?"* — the plot can never be the same again. A change in the setting has changed everything, forever.

Good science fiction almost always works like this.

Another aspect of science fiction setting, briefly alluded to previously, is the fact that the "science," wild as it might be, is rooted in real, contemporary science. That is to say, the story might turn out to be about strange clone-characters trying to take over the world; but this yarn would include in it as setting and background some information about actual chromosomal engineering and gene-changing being done in the world's labs today. The use of real, present-day research as a springboard into the extrapolated story setting is very common, and that's because the existence of some actual research now makes it easier for the reader to accept the story premise, even though it might be a wild departure from today.

STUDYING MARKETS

Often writers are encouraged to "study the markets" and "see what's selling." One of the bases for such advice lies in the genre expectations of readers such as those discussed in this chapter. It's fatal to try to handle a setting for a suspense story in the same way you would handle one for a romance, or even a science fiction story. Therefore you must know what the generalities of each genre are if you are to handle your settings in an acceptable manner.

Remember, however, that such genre expectations are somewhat general. A common mistake is to look too specifically at "what's selling," and then to slavishly copy the detail rather than the generality. For example, one might notice a colorful Caribbean setting, then write his own story against an identical colorful Caribbean setting, when what he should have done was notice the broader principle of exotic locale behind the specific Caribbean setting, then search for a *different* exotic setting that would also fit the pattern.

Most studies of genre expectations and requirements fall into this mistake of being too specific and failing to see the general principle at work. In handling setting for genre, nothing can be worse; by the time you've finished your book, the specific acceptable locale may have changed again and only the general requirement for the exotic, lushly described setting will remain.

Study the genre you want to "hit." Then search for the general rules about its setting. One flies in the face of such generalities at grave risk. But by all means also recognize the freedom of choice this study still leaves to you!

CHAPTER 6

HOW SETTING ACTS AS YOUR STORY BACKBONE

A COMMON PROBLEM IN WRITING a long story, especially something as lengthy as a novel, has to do with story *unity* or cohesion. "I have six subplots going, and how do I keep a sense of unity in my story with so many?" a writer may ask. Or: "I simply must change viewpoint several times, but what can I do to maintain a sense of coherent, cohesive story line?" Or (scariest of all!): "My story seems to be flying all to pieces, and I don't know how to hold all the diverse elements together."

Expert use of setting can often provide an answer to such questions.

Setting—especially the concrete, physical setting experienced through the senses of the characters or described in occasional panorama by the author—can provide a constant, stable, reassuringly familiar backdrop against which all manner of diverse plot developments can be played out.

In this sense, story setting functions very much like the setting of a stage play. The backdrop may be the brick walls of office buildings, with perhaps a streetlight and a mailbox as the only other features; two characters may move out in front of this setting and talk about plans to rob a bank, then exit stage left; next may come a young couple talking about his new job, and how excited they are about it. Superficially there may be no clear connection between the two bits of action that have taken place, but because they both have played against the same backdrop, the audience will be quite sure that *there is a unity here*—that the two bits of action definitely are linked in some way—

even though no overt connection has been demonstrated. The setting has done the job.

Multiplot, multiple-viewpoint novels often achieve a similar feeling of unity almost entirely by reliance on common setting as the binding factor. The suspense novels of writers like Tom Clancy and Clive Cussler rely heavily on same-setting unification. A few years before these writers attained their present popularity, Arthur Hailey made unifying setting the bedrock foundation of his novels like *Hotel* and *Airport*. In the novels of Phyllis A. Whitney, setting is always an important unifying factor as a bewildering variety of characters assail and confuse the first-person narrator; further, in the Whitney novels, the setting very often includes hidden history — past events concealed by some of the characters — whose eventual revelation is central to working out of the plot and the main character's personal problems.

Consider, for example, Cussler's breakthrough novel, *Raise The Titanic*, in which the long-sunken wrecked ship is constantly at the center of discussions, maneuvers, plans and counterattacks. If the Titanic were not at the heart of the setting as both focus and target of everyone's quest, the dozens of viewpoint changes would be hopelessly confusing.

Or consider *Hotel*, in which the very purpose of the novel is to place a wildly mixed batch of characters and plot problems within a single setting and show how the problems all work out within that unifying setting.

In the case of Whitney, try to imagine how a novel such as *The Trembling Hills* could work at all if the setting were not San Francisco at the time of the great earthquake there. Without the unification of constant references to that colorful historic setting, the multiple story lines would seem to "fly all to pieces" in apparent lack of relevance to one another.

Let me encourage you to study a number of recent novels of your own selection; look at the setting and examine the different viewpoints and plot lines. Ask yourself how many of the varying elements tie directly to one another in ways other than through reference to the setting. I think you will be surprised to see how often divergent aspects of plot and character would not be seen as related at all if they did not play against identical setting back-drops.

Further, you might want to consider how the *tone, mood* and *atmosphere* of setting will unify a story. From Edgar Allan Poe to Stephen King, horror writers have known this to be so. The consistent emphasis on darkness, dankness, isolation, eccentricity and occult intervention gives King's novels, for example, a unifyingly frightening feel that no single plot element or character can provide. To put this another way, in the novels of King and other horror writers, sometimes the consistent feeling of dread and fright comes not so much from what happens as it does from where it happens, and how that place feels.

Thus you can not only make your story more believable and convincing through sound use of setting, you can also unify it both in terms of making disparate plots and characters seem related and in terms of building up a story atmosphere which will cloak all characters and events within a single feeling matrix.

This is another reason why setting is so important, you see. You get not only obvious credibility advantages from proper handling of setting, but also unification of other story elements.

UNIFYING TECHNIQUES

A variety of techniques are available that will help you use your setting as a unifying "binder." We will look at six of these techniques, those used most often by writers to create a strong sense of cohesion in their stories. Study each technique, and use them to unify your own stories.

Consistent and repeated reference to a single aspect of your setting will keep that aspect uppermost in your reader's mind. Then, as you show different characters noticing this single aspect, or as you play out different scenes near it, or include a reference to it, you consistently remind the reader that, "Hey, we're in the same place, see? The same story, see?"

One example might be use of a clock tower on the main street of your story's small town. To transform the clock and its tower into a potential unifying device, you would first give it some considerable notice and description, perhaps something like this:

> Middletown's Main Street was dominated by the First National Bank's old brick clock tower, built in 1889 and a landmark to the present day. No other structure on the street stood more than two stories tall, but the clock tower extended a full three stories taller. Its dark red bricks were stained by generations of soot and rain, its conical copper roof was green from decades of corrosion. It had a clock face on all four of its sides, each face almost six feet in diameter, with ornate Roman numerals and hands festooned with spidery black curlicues. It struck every fifteen minutes and tolled out each hour, its vast and metallic voice an echo from times gone by. At night, four small spotlights shone on it, illuminating it like the rampart of a mighty old castle. Whenever anyone looked for a symbol of Middletown, they almost always came back to the clock tower, for it dominated the town; it always had, and it always would. Some said it *was* Middletown.

Such a lengthy description, as useful as it might be in building up story mood, could hardly be allowed, even in a novel, unless the tower was also being set up as a constant unifying aspect of the setting. You can be sure that the reader would "latch onto" such an elaborate description, and remember it. (Remember that lengthy descriptions ordinarily are to be avoided. When you insert one such as this for a very special reason, the reader notices immediately.)

Having thus gotten the reader's attention, you could use the clock tower again and again as a unifying reminder:

- Characters could agree to "meet under the old clock."
- Someone could hear the old clock striking the hour.
- The author could comment that the tower looked especially dark today against the rainy sky.
- Traffic might be described at some point as being backed up from First Street all the way down to the clock tower corner.

- An elderly character might comment that he feels "as old as that clock downtown on the bank corner."

I leave it to you to imagine many other ways the clock and its tower could be mentioned repeatedly in a story as a unifying factor.

Repeated reference to certain aspects of the setting by one or more characters is closely related to the technique just discussed, but a bit different. In this case, the author does not focus on a single item in the story environment such as the clock tower, but on some angle about the setting which is dominant. This might be how isolated a setting is, for example, or how grungy, or how it might be sandwiched in between a steep hillside and a fast-moving river. In such a situation, the author (through her direct description) and the characters (through taking notice in viewpoint, or in making dialogue comments) repeatedly refer to the general angle that is set up early in the story as particularly noteworthy.

Here's an example of how a general setting angle might be set up at the outset (here focusing on a town's isolation):

Middletown stood on the prairie halfway between Junction City to the north and Emersonville to the south, eighty miles to Junction City, ninety to Emersonville. To the east and west, the next hint of "civilization" was much farther away. On a clear summer day, someone once said, you could look in any direction, for as long as you could bear it, and never see anything at all but sagebrush, rolling sand dunes, and an occasional dust devil.

Having once set up this aspect of the setting in the reader's consciousness, the author might salt into the story dozens of references like the following:

- The brilliant sunlight made her shrink from the vast distances.
- "You can't get anywhere from here in less than two hours," he said.

- She drove to the edge of town and looked out toward — nothing.
- Sleep would not come. She felt like she had been dropped into the middle of the Sahara desert. . . .
- An old pickup truck, coated with the red dust of a million desolate miles, rolled in from the empty prairie to the north.
- The town felt like a place on a distant planet, so isolated was it.

Again, you may come up with small references that would do a better job than any of these in referring back to isolation as a general, unifying aspect of the setting.

Continual, subtle expansion on a detail or aspect of the setting will also serve to keep it in focus as a unifying element. How would such a process work? Rather than beginning with a large description, as in the case of the clock tower mentioned above, you would start small, and build. As the story went along, the element of the setting chosen for such treatment would grow larger and larger in the reader's awareness.

As an example, in one of my earlier novels titled *Katie, Kelly and Heck*, I had five distinct plot lines and some dozen viewpoints working from quite early in the book. Although all the events took place in the same small town — one unifying factor — I worried that something further was needed to assure an additional sense of unity. The setting device I discovered, and built more importantly as the story progressed, was a back-alley whisky still which no single character considered centrally important.

I first showed the still, freshly loaded and beginning to cook a new batch of sour-mash whisky. It was simply mentioned as being located in the alley.

A chapter later, I showed a secondary character examining the still in more detail. This time I revealed the ownership of the apparatus and its importance to him. Two more sentences of description were added to what had been provided in the earlier segment, this time telling the capacity of the still, its temperature, and its internal pressure. I also described a pressure gauge on the equipment.

Fifteen pages later, I showed the still being sabotaged — the pressure valves being closed, the heat starting to increase, and the aforementioned pressure gauge beginning to rise.

From that point, with metronomic regularity, I returned in brief segments to the still, unattended in the alley; each time, a bit more description was added, and each time it was noted that the temperature was still higher, the internal pressure continuing to rise toward the red line on the gauge. While all the characters in the story went about their own business, and the physical setting changed from place to place around the town, the repeating, expanding progress reports on the still, described objectively from a viewpoint "on high," maintained a central setting detail focus point for the book until very late in the story when — you guessed it — the still exploded, bringing everyone's attention back to it.

In your story the central aspect of setting might be a house, a room in that house, a street, a gathering storm. Whatever it might be, if you first merely mention it but then continually return to it with greater and greater attention to descriptive detail, you may be sure your reader will focus on it and cling to it as a unifying factor in your yarn.

Ongoing references to different aspects of the setting which have something in common is slightly different again. Here, rather than seeking different ways to refer to generally the same phenomenon, as in our examples above about isolation, you provide the reader with different looks at various parts of the setting, building a complete and detailed picture, finally, by a process of accretion.

For example, you might show a factory worker in a small town paying his home rent to an office operated by the same company that pays his wages. A bit later, you might show the same worker shopping and getting additional credit at the company store. Still later, you might have him taking his sick child to the clinic (the only one in town) operated by the company. And later yet you might describe how the local newspaper is run by an editor who happens to be the brother-in-law of the owner of the local company. As you added references to other aspects of the setting, a composite picture would emerge which would give the reader a convincing picture of a "company town" where anyone trying to be independent would face grave odds indeed.

Such a technique is very convincing to readers, incidentally, because it allows them to experience and draw conclusions about a story setting in the same way they operate with real-world environments: by collecting small bits of data and finally drawing conclusions from them. In addition, of course, the quiet drumbeat-like presentation of different aspects, all pointing to the same generality about the setting, give the story a wonderful cohesiveness.

Careful comparison-reference back to what the setting was before it changed can allow setting to remain a unifying factor even when the actual setting changes. Suppose, for example, a basis of your plot lies partly in the stress caused to the characters because they are forced to move from the city to an unfamiliar rural area (change in setting causing the plot). In such a circumstance, you would be required to describe the city setting in order later to show how different it is from the new rural one. All well and good, but the sudden change from urban to rural in the middle of the story might create a sharp feeling of discontinuity—loss of unity—for your reader.

In such a situation, the unity of the plot problem would be emphasized by your references to the conflicted feelings in the characters as caused by the move; by comparing new setting versus the old in an author-objective passage or two; by having characters talk about the new setting and how it differs from the previous one; or by having characters homesick for the old setting, talking about how good it was, how unfamiliar they are with the new. In this way, the change in setting would itself become a constant setting reference point!

In my novel *Katie, Kelly and Heck*, mentioned earlier, Katie Blanscombe is dislocated from Cleveland, Ohio, to a sorry, isolated little outpost in Arizona, where she gets into all kinds of trouble because she simply does not understand the new territory. In the course of the novel, I found it useful to have Katie fall prey to homesickness again and again, and to criticize her new hometown as being barbaric when compared with Cleveland. Thus, even as Katie moved from a boardinghouse to a hotel, and from poverty to ownership of a restaurant, and from nervous self-restraint to a scene in which she danced and kicked up her heels on a cafe stage, her basic personality was kept unified and consistent — and her essential personal problem kept in focus — by the fact that she kept being homesick and kept moaning about "this dreadful little town," comparing the setting to the one she had left in Cleveland.

You may think of other examples in which the very emphasis on change in setting becomes a unifying factor of its own. The story of a wagon train going west, for example, might pass through a number of contrasting macrosettings — grasslands, prairie, deserts, rivers, mountains — and might in part be held together because the microsetting, the wagon train itself, remained much the same. Additional unity might be given such a story also, by having the characters notice and comment on the changing backdrop during the journey, saying things like, "I thought the rainy weather on the prairie was bad until we reached this Godforsaken desert, where it never seems to get below a hundred degrees."

Showing that the setting is contributing to the course of events can add unity to a story. Here the trick often is to have characters in the story point this out, saying things like the following:

- "This couldn't happen except in Middletown."
- "A company town always enforces its rules on troublemakers."
- "If that wall of snow and ice starts to move, we're trapped."
- "A mother-lode discovery like this one always brings in the lawless element, and we should have expected it."
- "When the store was robbed last Tuesday, it changed our lives forever."

There are occasions when it may seem like overkill to have characters comment on the impact of setting on plot — when it's so obvious that mention of it may sound silly. But real people tend to belabor the obvious when they're under stress, and realistic story people will, too. So as you build credibility sometimes by allowing characters to worry aloud about obvious problems, you may also improve the sense of story unity by pointing out to the reader that the setting is holding things together by contributing to story happenings.

A SETTING EMPHASIS TO AVOID

If you believe from this discussion that I consider setting a primary unifying factor in many novels, you are absolutely correct. As long as each mention of setting is done briefly—ordinarily a few lines at a time, at most—I believe constant reference to setting will have multiple salutary effects on your copy.

However, there are times in your story when you must be careful *not* to dwell on setting, especially avoiding mention of any new aspects of it. This is when you are just opening a new story segment which involves transition in viewpoint or immediate locale.

Suppose, for example, that you are writing a novel in multiple viewpoint, with multiple plot lines and numerous settings. Suppose further that you have been away from character Martha's viewpoint and plot for a number of pages, and now wish to return to her.

Making such a transition in story focus and interest is difficult for your reader. It is incumbent upon you to make the change as painless and unconfusing as possible. The last thing you want to do is confuse him. If you open up your new segment returning to Martha's viewpoint and emphasizing the new setting she is in, the new and unfamiliar detail makes the reader's reorientation more difficult and potentially confusing.

To put this another way, you're asking the reader to make a hard enough jump in going from, say, character Sam's viewpoint and locale back to Martha's. You want to make it as easy as possible. How would you do this?

1. Avoid introducing new setting detail at the outset. This

in itself will eliminate one possibly disorienting element in your
transition.

   2. Remind the reader how your character was feeling when
last seen. Given any clue at all, your reader will recall how your
viewpoint character was feeling when the story was last in her
viewpoint. By mentioning this same feeling again when you return to her viewpoint, you give the reader a vital "connection
point" for a successful transition.

   3. Refer to a unifying aspect of setting already established.
This will give the reader a familiar landmark as a point of reorientation. Only well after you have eased the reader into the
changed viewpoint—and reminded him of the setting in terms
already familiar to him—can you risk the potentially disorienting tactic of adding new details about the setting.

Let's look at an example to clarify number three. Suppose you
were returning to Martha's viewpoint downtown after you had
devoted a few chapters to other viewpoints elsewhere, perhaps
on the far outskirts of your town. You might ease the initial
transition something like this (italics added for emphasis):

> *Still angry and worried* as a result of her argument with
> Bill, Martha parked her car on Main Street a block from
> the center of town. As she got out of the car, *the familiar
> sound of the old clock on the bank corner* reached her ears.
> It was tolling noon. *Fighting tears of frustration*, she walked
> toward the *tall, sooty brick tower where the clock had tolled for
> a century.* . . .

The first italicized words avoid any new detail and reestablish
Martha's point of view by harking back to the last time she was
seen in the story, reminding the reader of the exact same emotion Martha was experiencing then. This returns the reader to
Martha's viewpoint in the least difficult way possible. (This matter of identifying a character's feelings—her *emotional focus*—is
a subject we will consider in greater detail in chapter eleven.)

   The second group of italicized words further eases the transition by mentioning something in the physical environment
that is already familiar to the reader from earlier parts of the
story: the clock.

The third and fourth brief segments elaborate briefly on the first two.

This works. But imagine how confused the reader might be at such a time of transition if the author had begun the new segment by describing previously unmentioned aspects of the setting, such as, say, false storefronts along Main Street, advertising signs, small shrubs dying from a drouth, or a beggar often seen on the curb. Introduction of such new setting detail would only disorient the reader. When making a transition, the familiar must be emphasized first!

Later in your story section, of course, you might well add a few new details about the setting, but only after you had written a reorientation paragraph (or two) would it be safe to do so.

But how would such tactics work if Martha had really traveled far from her small town while we were away from her viewpoint for a chapter or two? What if she had gone all the way to London, for example?

The same basic procedure would work. Here's how that kind of transitional opening might be worded:

> *Still angry and worried* a full week after her argument with Bill, Martha felt very much alone as she walked along the Thames. She looked across the river toward Big Ben in its ancient tower that so symbolized London. The great old clock began to toll the hour. It sounded so *familiar, so much like the old clock on the bank corner back home*, that her eyes filled with tears. . . .

Later, of course, new details about the London setting would be added a few at a time, as necessary. But reader reorientation takes precedence over any such additional detail.

SUGGESTED EXERCISE

An exercise might help you firm up your understanding of the techniques outlined in this chapter. While no single bit of homework is guaranteed to touch all the bases, the following exercise is one that has helped a great many writing students. Perhaps you would like to try it:

1. Carefully write an author-objective description of a major, noteworthy aspect of a setting, something like the clock tower used in illustrations in this chapter. Make this description, up to three hundred words, as vivid and detailed as you can, appealing to as many of the reader's senses as possible, and try to tie the physical description to some feeling or mood you want to set up in a story.

2. Add two or three brief, cogent paragraphs to this description from the viewpoint of a character, adding a bit about how the setting looks to the character, or how it makes her feel, or what it makes her think about. (Not more than a hundred additional words for this.)

3. Simply list five additional and related aspects of setting you might use in the same story if you were pursuing it through several additional chapters.

4. Imagine that you have been away from your chosen viewpoint character's head and heart for twenty-five pages, and now wish to return to her, in viewpoint, near the place where your major, noteworthy aspect of setting is located. Write the first four sentences of a segment that would return the reader to this viewpoint and locale.

Having done these things, put the pages aside temporarily and reread this chapter on setting. Then go back to each of your assignment pages with a critical eye and ask yourself these questions:

1. Is the noteworthy aspect of setting which I selected a good and central one for the story I want to tell? Is it interesting? Unusual? Sure to stand out?

2. Have I described it vividly, in as few pointed words as possible?

3. Is my list of additional features (to be added later) the best I can come up with? Taken altogether, do they tend to complete a coherent, evocative picture of this place and/or time?

4. In my "returning episode," have I carefully noted my imagined character's emotion? Have I carefully mentioned only

that part of the setting which forms my central, noteworthy aspect?

If your answer to any of these questions is "no," then rewrite! It's important to have the material in this chapter clearly in your mind before moving on to other dynamic ways you can use setting to improve your story.

CHAPTER 7

HOW TO USE SETTING TO ADVANCE PLOT

IT'S FAR TOO EASY TO FALL INTO THE TRAP of thinking of setting as a fixed and static aspect of your story. As implied in some of our earlier discussion, setting is not necessarily static at all: The weather may change, a storm may develop or collapse or move on; the background attitudes of characters may be radically altered by plot events; virtually anything may happen to alter the environment in which the story is playing out. Just as a story's plot must move forward and its characters must experience things, and change, so too the setting can seldom be allowed to stand in the background as a totally predictable, immutable element. When writers get bogged down in a story, sometimes it's because they have forgotten all this.

ADVANCEMENT OF PLOT

Setting can be used in several ways to help you advance your plot.

First, you can emphasize setting in a new way, bringing out a previously unseen problem. Imagine that you have built a story setting involving a small business depicted as thrifty, energetic and competitive against larger firms. Now think about how you might complicate and advance the plot by putting much greater emphasis on the company's competitive situation and the size of its rival firms. Suddenly your reader (and perhaps some of your characters) might begin seeing the company setting as precarious rather than comfortable, as too small to compete successfully rather than as a cozy Ma-and-Pa operation, as a place to escape from rather than a place to settle in. Once you have begun emphasizing these ways of looking at your setting, imagine how your plot might be advanced in terms of character problem (and reader interest).

It might come in a passage like this:

> The constant jangling of telephones suddenly struck Calvin as discordant, harshly demanding. He saw the driven expressions on some of his coworkers' faces, understanding for the first time how desperately all of them were working to stay ahead of the Acme Company down the street. He smelled frightened sweat—his own—and felt his stomach tighten as Meg hurried in from the front office, carrying a stack of change-orders. He had seen change-orders a thousand times, but suddenly they looked different to him. Now, instead of a challenge, they represented a threat. What if that stack of papers represented cancellations that could sink the Blodgett Company ... and threaten his future?

Now the office setting is no longer comfortable. Now today's business is not merely important, but a matter of life and death. Now the meeting this afternoon must perhaps deal with a crucial marketing decision, rather than with routine business. By emphasizing the setting in a new way, you may dictate inescapable results in the immediate plot. To put this another way, by emphasizing the setting in a new way, you make something happen in your plot.

Or as another example, suppose you're writing a story about a small mining town in the Old West, bound inside a tight river canyon by high mountains on both east and west. You might first describe this town setting as secure, walled in from intruders, protected from the winter weather and cool and shady in the summer. But you could easily use the same setting to advance your plot simply by choosing to emphasize other aspects of it: The great gray massiveness of the surrounding mountains, their enormous bulk seeming to hang poised over

the town, ready to wipe it out with a landslide at any moment;
the way the tight river canyon walls in the town and makes it
impossible for anyone inside the town to see approaching attack-
ers; how the encapsulation of the town in its stone cocoon has
made its people closed-minded and suspicious.

Even more dramatic in terms of advancing the plot is the
introduction of new aspects of the setting not previously seen,
so that your reader worries more and your major characters are
forced to take some unexpected action.

Suppose again that your setting is the mountain town described above, with only its friendlier aspects identified. Suppose
that Ted, your viewpoint character, learns something previously
unknown about the setting, as in the following example:

> "I love the mountain behind the town," Ted told Max-
> well. "It gives a feeling of solidity — strength. You just know
> this town is as solid as that granite."
>
> Maxwell's face twisted with pain. "Solid as that granite,
> eh? That's all *you* know, my friend."
>
> "What do you mean?" Ted shot back.
>
> Maxwell squinted upward at the rock face overhanging
> the buildings, and pointed. "You've seen those deep fis-
> sures, the shadowy cracks in the face?"
>
> "Of course. What . . ."
>
> "Those cracks go deep, Ted. It isn't generally known,
> but the entire face of that mountain is crumbling. That
> granite is rotten. Give us the slightest earth tremor, or even
> a heavy and prolonged rainstorm, and the face of that
> seemingly solid mountain could fall right onto this town —
> wipe it out in an instant."

This new aspect of the setting changes everything. It has to jolt
your character into a reassessment of everything, and possibly
change the course of the story from that moment forward.

Often most dramatic of all is the basic, abrupt change in the
setting itself. Such a change upsets all expectations and must
result in new plot developments.

When I mention change in the setting, I am not talking
about actually moving the locale of the story, although you

might elect to do that sometimes, too. Here I refer to having something change drastically in the essential makeup of the existing story backdrop. For example, rather than having Jennifer move from Peoria to San Francisco, we would stay in Peoria, but have three closely timed murders create an atmosphere of terror and suspicion inside the same general physical environment. Or, rather than leaving our car race at the Indianapolis 500 and changing the setting to Dayton, Ohio, we would stay at Indianapolis but show the sky clouding over, threatening a dangerous downpour on the track.

Or perhaps the setting could change in a way similar to the following example:

> The Sparger family had been near the heart of power in Middletown for more than fifty years. Ted's father and his father before him had been leaders of the local Democratic Party's machinery, and had always had a voice in political decisions. It was this political power that had made Jim so confident he could get the block of Main Street rezoned to allow him to tear down the old bank building and sell the property for a new apartment complex.
>
> By midnight, however, as the election returns kept coming in, he saw that everything in this comfortable world of his had suddenly changed.
>
> "We've lost," the Democratic chairman told him bitterly around 1 A.M. "This is no longer our town. We have no control now. Nothing is ever going to be the same again."

Thus the physical setting is the same, but the cultural-political setting has become vastly different, and for people like Jim it is really no longer the same setting at all.

Changes inside the setting are almost always threatening to story characters in some way, and because they are threatened, those characters do something about it. And when characters do something about it, your plot is jostled off dead center.

A change in the setting can also be used much more dramatically, of course, to make the plot action change as well, and instantly. If your quiet suburban hospital suddenly catches fire, this change in the setting has instantaneous results in the plot as people run for safety and/or try to put the fire out.

What's the moral here? Simply this: Any time you feel a need to move your plot along, look at the possibility of introducing a real or just perceived change in the setting you've been using, or changing the way you've been describing the setting. A dark cloud scuds across the sun, plunging the street into darkness; a character learns that someone died in this rented house last year; suddenly the town no longer feels friendly; a rock tumbles and a landslide begins to gain momentum. In each case a different reader perception of the setting has started us toward movement in the plot.

ENHANCEMENT OF TENSION

In virtually all such situations the change does more than motivate characters to do something, thus advancing the plot; it also increases dramatic tension in both the characters and your reader. You can capitalize on this fact by consciously tailoring your setting change to increase tension in any of the following ways (or with a combination of them):

1. by darkening the mood of the story
2. by introducing new threatening element(s)
3. by creating mystery
4. by overturning previous character expectations
5. by demanding immediate action.

In an earlier chapter, a suspense novel by John Miles, *The Night Hunters*, was mentioned in an illustration. The same novel might be used as a source of illustrations of all the points just listed.

Two paragraphs in chapter two of the novel begin to darken the mood as follows:

> She wished . . . that she hadn't found that Bartelson had died by his own hand. There was something still depressing about the picture that the scant facts portrayed: a man coming west, as they said, to make good, and doing

all the "right" things—serving in the army, opening his own business, serving the community. But for Bartelson it had all gone sour. Ruth tried to imagine how it must have been, staking one's life in this remote place, walking every day under these brooding old trees, feeling the heat of late summer suck the energy out of every pore, watching the forces that no one could understand take everything that had been worked for, saved, built against the future.

She shivered again, for no reason, and hugged her arms about herself. . . .

The first paragraph breaks almost perfectly in half, first recapping new and worrisome information just learned about the setting; then, with the "Ruth tried to imagine" sentence, moving into the viewpoint character's feelings and using emotionally charged words like "remote" and "brooding" to darken the mood.

Such work on the mood of the setting is especially important in a novel such as *The Night Hunters*, set in a small southeastern Oklahoma town which ordinarily would not be thought of as threatening. Many short passages clearly designed to darken the mood are found throughout the novel.

The book is, however, not merely a mood piece but a suspense novel. Only a few pages after the segment quoted above, another character close to Ruth is seen driving home late at night. Here there is another touch of the darkness of the first paragraph, and then the introduction of a new threatening element:

Preoccupied with her and his own feelings, Doug drove the few blocks to the little house he had rented. He did not think deeply into the questions she had raised about the missing records or seeming lies, because he well enough understood the clannish, suspicious nature of the people of Noble. It was simply one more manifestation of their kind of hate, he told himself. It meant nothing more. . . .

Because of his preoccupation, Doug Bennett did not see the black Ford cruise quietly down the street moments after he had gone inside. The car was parked and the engine shut off. The lone occupant remained behind the wheel, watching. Long after the lights had gone out in Doug's house, the shadowy figure remained in the car, watching, moving now and then as a pint bottle was raised, sipped from and put back on the seat.

Such a passage, of course, creates mystery, too.

Setting or a change in setting can also be used, as previously stated, to *overturn character expectations*. Later in the same novel, the character Ruth Baxter expected to leave the town of Noble on a short trip. But her plan was thwarted just at the end of a previous chapter. Now, having been out of her viewpoint and setting for about a dozen pages, the reader is returned to her at the start of chapter nine like this:

> The impulse was to scream — to scream and keep on screaming, to let the fear burst out. Ruth fought it and held it back by the tiniest margin of control.
> The tunnel was less than ten feet in diameter. The only illumination was an urnlike, battery-operated fishing lantern on the loose gravel-and-earth floor. Its yellowish light shone against chalky stone walls, seeping water here and there, braced in X patterns with heavy, rough-cut timbers gone black from age and rot. . . .
> Ruth, her hands tied in front of her, was made prisoner to one of the huge support beams by another length of rope looped through her arms and tied to the beam. . . .

Here the transition is eased for the reader exclusively through identification of a carry-over emotion from when Ruth was last seen. But the setting is new and totally unfamiliar, a tactical fiction situation we earlier warned against because it creates confusion. But here the gambit is acceptable and even desirable because clearly one of the author's goals is to make the reader experience just a little of the fright and disorientation that Ruth herself is feeling. In effect, the near-vertigo experienced by the reader in being plunged headlong into a new and alien setting works here, because confusion is exactly a part of the effect being sought. In such a drastic change, the character Ruth obviously is not—and will never be—the same; all her expectations and assumptions have been altered forever by finding herself suddenly in this new setting.

Finally, and perhaps the easiest method of all to understand, you can increase story tension with a change in your setting that *demands immediate action*. Such action-demanding setting changes are often dynamic and highly dramatic, like the following:

- Setting: a quiet town. But then the dam breaks above it.
- Setting: a small hospital. But then a deadly epidemic breaks out.
- Setting: a peaceful street. But then gunshots are heard.
- Setting: a nice old house. But then the eviction notice is served.

I leave it to you to conjure up any number of other static settings in which a change dramatically increases tension.

THE POWER OF REPETITION

Although the emphasis in this chapter has been primarily on dynamic setting—setting in change or with changing perception—it is also possible to increase story tension simply by drumming away at a static setting that is threatening or scary to begin with, such as in the novels of Stephen King. Often there is no really new development in the setting at the times when the story intensifies. What we get instead is further moody description of the same setting, which has a cumulative emotional effect. To reduce the process to absurdity: One cobweb across the face means nothing, but a dozen may mean a haunted house; one momentarily glimpsed light in the old mansion may be a trick of moonlight, but several such sightings almost surely mean something dire is afoot.

By all means, then, you should realize that handling of setting can be an invaluable tool for you in increasing plot tension and making things happen. It's axiomatic in fiction that characters make things happen in the plot. But it's equally true that setting can motivate characters. So you needn't always look inside your character's mind for motive; sometimes it might be simpler to examine your story environment, and do something with it that *forces* mood to darken, action to take place, or character to get moving.

All of which brings us to a closer look at the way setting forms and motivates character. That's the business of chapter eight.

CHAPTER 8

HOW SETTING AFFECTS CHARACTER

IT MAY SEEM A BIT STRANGE to you that a separate chapter should be devoted to setting and its impact on character when it's been clear from the outset of this book that setting obviously has such impact. We have already seen how setting affects story characters in a variety of ways, potentially playing a part in their background, expectations, beliefs, hopes, ideals, problems and goals. Here, however, we want to take a deeper and more precise look at setting's impact on your story people and to point out how you should work to make setting and character harmonious.

The use of certain settings often tends to foreordain certain kinds of characters. This is because of reader expectations of the type discussed back in chapter five.

While there are exceptions to every rule, one of the most obvious examples of setting predicting a certain kind of character is the traditional western. Today you may find more short, scruffy and even "antiheroic" male leads in the traditional western setting, but the vast majority of male leads in the latest western novels are still close to the stereotype introduced all the way back in Owen Wister's *The Virginian*, the man who told someone to "smile when you say that." This character, predicted by the setting, is close to Gary Cooper in *High Noon*, or Alan Ladd in *Shane*. He is a loner, brave, soft-spoken, slow to anger, self-reliant and incredibly competent in outdoor skills and gunmanship; he is Anglo-Saxon, tall, blond or sandy-haired more often than not, vaguely in his 30s, with a background that has alienated and slightly embittered him, and possibly put him on the wrong side of an unjust legal system. Usually he has no permanent home, and owns little more than his horse and what he can pack into his saddlebags, if that much. He is a fundmamentally decent man who respects women and the underdog. He seldom seeks a fight but backs down for no man.

This prototype of the western hero does not endure simply because it seems to work in terms of reader expectation. It also works because such a character is completely in harmony with the traditional western setting; the mythic "Old West" is the kind of setting that would produce such a man, and such a man is the kind who would best survive in the Old West environment. His ideals—individualism, truthfulness, self-reliance—are the values that fueled the American psyche during the country's great expansion into its western frontier. In short, the traditional western hero is true to his setting.

Thus the setting can be a predictor of character. Publishers of romance fiction, for example, see this clearly. Some romance editors issue detailed "tip sheets" which define not only the kind of setting they want for their stories, but details about desired lead characters. Setting and character have been carefully outlined to "fit" one another.

One such publishing house recently said it wanted its stories to feature an urban or suburban woman, single, age twenty-eight or so, with a dismaying and unhappy love affair or marriage in her background; she is allowed a lively sexual appetite, but shouldn't act upon it except with the man she learns to love in the course of the story. Another publishing house said it wants younger women in college or blue-collar work situations, and expects such heroines to have more vivid sexual exploits. Still another line features older women in highly professional occupational settings, and for such characters problems in their professional lives must somehow dovetail with romantic entanglements—which, given their experiences, they should approach more cautiously than their younger sisters in the genre. And so it goes. The existence of such tip sheets proving that editors realize the intimate relationship between setting and character.

SETTING PREDESTINES CHARACTER

The impact of setting on character goes well beyond tip sheets and genre expectations, however, and you as a writer of fiction should remember that. Setting—in real life as well as in fiction—tends to form character in ways you can analyze and use in your work.

This was brought home to me most forcefully a number of years ago when, as a journalist, I was given the assignment of doing a twenty-county tour of Oklahoma to ask questions of the person on the street for a series of newspaper stories on "the mood of the state."

This was no small task, and I approached it with some trepidation. The reason was not simply the size of the task, but the fact that Oklahoma is a border state, quite different in its farm belt north and tourist campground south, its wooded hill country in the east and dusty open plains in the west. I sensed—but did not fully appreciate at first—the fact that a state with such drastic differences in topography, incomes and occupations might offer a bewildering variety of outlooks and opinions.

I set out to the western sections first, driving across vast, dusty, open prairie where you can see another car on the road five miles ahead, and a distant farm silo may be the only relief from a barren horizon. On my first day I visited three small rural towns, parking near the drugstore or courthouse and buttonholing passersby, ready with my notebook and list of questions.

To my surprise and delight, almost every one of these "plains people" responded with a cautious but open attitude; they were almost uniformly friendly and willing to help by expressing opinions. They seemed generally to trust me at once, and take me at face value.

This assignment was not going to be as hard as I had feared, I thought as I worked through other parts of the prairie country.

About three days later, I worked through the southern part of the state, visiting tourist campgrounds, fishing cabins, and

little towns catering to sportsmen and sightseers. Again I found
that the people were friendly. But then I drove farther east into
the hill country.

I love the hills and mountains, and I grieve to report it, but
the deeper I moved into tightly hill-bound terrain, visiting small
hamlets dense with trees flourishing in the dark shade of over-
hanging cliffs and bluffs, the more chilly my reception became.
Gone was the open, trusting attitude of the plains, and instead
I met narrowed eyes of suspicion, sharply hostile counterques-
tions, and a growing number of outright refusals to so much as
"talk about talking." There were open, friendly people, to be
sure, but suddenly they were in a distinct minority. There were
times when I felt like I had been plunged into a scene from the
movie *Deliverance*.

Later I moved out of the hill country and into the northern
farm belt, where attitudes toward a stranger like me seemed
halfway between those I had met earlier. Only then did something begin to dawn on me with greater impact than ever before.
Roughly, the realization (and I hesitate to admit I had been so
dumb as not to have known it long before) went like this: "Hill
people and plains people are *different*."

Why? Psychologists and social historians probably have a
much better answer than I do. Surely it can't be as simple as the
fact that life on the plains is marked by open horizons, vast
winds, and a sky that comes down to eye level, while life in the
hills is closed-in, almost hermetic at times, more isolated from
the broad view.

Whatever. The basic fact is what's useful to us as writers,
and that is simple enough: *Define the kind of setting a character is
to be found in, and by so doing you go far toward defining the kind of
character it must be*.

It may be such an obvious fact that we sometimes forget it.
In more than two decades of teaching fiction, I shudder to think
of the number of times I have encountered story characters like
the backwoods girl who had never been out of her valley, but
spoke in a brisk, "Britishy" accent; or the college-president character who dressed and acted like a gross and illiterate idiot, or
the working cowboy set in an eastern courtroom and brilliantly

defending a suspect in a complex lawsuit. We forget the strong link between setting and character formation only at grave peril; readers usually are quick to balk at believing story people who appear completely out of tune with their setting.

Does this mean that you should attempt to delineate characters who are perfectly typical of their story setting? By no means. If you try to do so, you risk creating stereotypes rather than vital story people, creating only dull and predictable characters. What you must aim for is the credible, not the stereotypical.

PROTOTYPES AND STEREOTYPES

Ordinarily this means that you should be aware of reader expectations in the traditional genres, and also the kind of people most typical of various real settings. It will help you in making characters and settings harmonious if you do some real-life observing and then draw up a "setting list" for your desired character.

Suppose, for example, you wish to create a character who is a famed brain surgeon. You might immediately draw a character who is a tall, middle-aged man, with gray hair, a distinguished manner, a big country home, and a workplace environment in a huge city hospital. This is all believable enough. It might work. But it is also predictable — and a bit dull.

So let's suppose for a moment that you haven't been paying attention to this chapter, and try to create a more memorable character-and-setting combination without real-world study or the knowledge that character and setting must in some way fit one another. Your new character, in such circumstances, might turn out to be a short, fat, unkempt teenager with a bad case of the shakes who spends most of his time in the pool hall, lives under a railroad bridge, and practices medicine in a clinic serving a rural community of 300 souls.

Of course I grossly exaggerate for the sake of illustration. But stranger setting-character combinations have been known in student manuscripts.

How would you avoid both the character who is credible

but dully predictable and the character who is unbelievable both in terms of his fit to the environment and the credibility of his story setting?

First you would make real-life observations. I suspect you would find things like the following about famed brain surgeons:

- They tend to be mature men. *But there are women in the field.*
- They almost always work in major hospitals in very large urban centers. *But some work in large clinics that happen to be located in smaller communities.*
- They work killingly long hours.
- They are extremely well paid — most are wealthy.
- They tend to live in large suburban homes. *But some live on ranches and some in inner-city apartments.*
- They deal daily with life-and-death situations.
- Most are in private, individual practice. *But some are members of medical firms or clinic teams.*
- Most are dedicated, and love — and live — their work. *But a few are at the burnout stage, longing to escape the pressurized life.*
- They come from well-educated family backgrounds. *But a few represent the first person from their family ever to go beyond high school.*
- They drive Mercedes and Lincoln cars. *But some drive pickup trucks, and some don't own a car at all.*

Having begun to create such a "prototype list" from actual observation, rather than from what you think you already know, you would have the stuff to begin drawing a character in a credible but not stereotypical environment. You might be able to begin creating a character who is a woman, five feet tall, the first of her family ever to attain a college education, who drives her Ford Bronco to the big clinic on the edge of a small rural community every morning. She might live on a ranch, and she might be suffering from premature professional burnout after several years of working seventeen-hour days in the operating room.

Now, having done this, I would suggest that you take further steps. You should make personal contact with a brain surgeon—or some other surgeon with a highly specialized craft—and try to spend some time with him (or her) in order to see and better understand his typical setting. Ideally you would see his home, meet his family if any, ride to work with him one day, ask questions about his background and beliefs, and even seek permission to stand beside the scrub nurse in the surgical arena and witness the environment in which he works. (I did this—with great hesitancy—for a medical novel once, and it was not as scary as I had imagined it would be; I didn't even faint.)

With all this research behind you, I suspect you would create a brain surgeon character who was not only more vivid than you might otherwise have been able to make her, but you would also have a story setting rich in the kind of detail that convinces the reader and enhances the character.

Even if you are not quite willing to go this far in making sure the wedding of setting and character is a good one, go as far as you can! Don't let laziness or shyness hold you back. In the extreme, remember that the New York City corporate executive is *ipso facto* not the same as the college English teacher at a rural Kansas junior college; and remember further that ordinarily you couldn't just switch the two characters, moving the executive to Kansas and the teacher to New York. Look long and hard at your setting, and grow characters out of it. Or look long and hard at your character and provide him with a setting that fits. Just don't ignore their relationship; to do so is to risk having unbelievable characters in a good setting, or good characters in an unbelievable setting.

CASTING AGAINST SETTING

"But"—you may be protesting—"what about that western character I just read about who was a little weasel from Chicago? Or that brain surgeon—for the luvva Mike!—whose story setting was a ranch in Arizona? Or how, Bickham, do you explain the success of the character Dr. Joel Fleischman in the popular TV show *Northern Exposure*, a young Jewish doctor in the godforsa-

ken setting of Cicely, Alaska? Where is the harmony of setting
and character in any of these examples?"

Such notable exceptions don't change the rule. They only
prove that no rule is absolute, and that sometimes, with good
reason, a writer can take a big risk. Such examples as cited above
illustrate the process of *casting against setting* for the sake of surprise and contrast. The technique has notable triumphs, and
you may wish to try it. You should be warned, however, that
you walk the precipice of incredibility every time you do, and
there are many failed experiments of this type for every one
that works.

Parenthetically, I don't know about the weasel western character or the brain surgeon on a ranch. But Dr. Joel, in *Northern
Exposure*, gets his humor and sympathy not just from being out
of harmony with outback Alaska, but because he is so perfectly
a product of his fictional New York City background setting. To
put this another way, Joel doesn't fit his present setting, but
that's a large part of the point—his continuing plot problem.
On the other side of the same dramatic card, his character would
not work in this predicament if he did not act *exactly* as his stated
background setting ("I'm a New York City Jewish boy.") suggests. Joel fits his background, the setting from which he has
been transplanted, very well indeed, and that's why he is effective as a character out of his element.

You can probably think of many other successful fiction
characters who seemed to be cast against their setting. Sometimes they were; other times they are shown out of harmony
only with a particular setting and were perfectly consistent when
considered against the larger setting of their entire life. Wherever the truth lies, however, casting radically against setting remains a dangerous tactic.

USING SETTING TO CHANGE
A CHARACTER

Whether the setting changes during the course of a story or
remains essentially the same, it can cause changes in your char-

acter's perceptions, feelings, thoughts, motivations and actions.

A moment's reflection will show why this is so. We live immersed in the physical world, dozens and perhaps hundreds of impressions entering our consciousness at every instant. Because no single mind could absorb and meaningfully process all these impressions, our conscious mind ignores many of these stimuli, and gives many others only the briefest notice before dismissing them. It is even possible to act upon some aspect of our environment without consciously giving it much thought.

As an example of ignoring stimuli flowing in from our environment or setting, consider the background music piped into many shopping malls and stores. Often, we simply don't even hear it. Or suppose you happen to live on a busy street, with constant traffic sounds; unless there is a siren or a particularly loud sound, you seldom notice the routine noise at all. Similarly, we get so accustomed to seeing some routine things in our daily lives that we seem not to notice them at all: the trees in the park, perhaps, or the familiar old elm in the front yard, or (tragically, perhaps) the habitual look of strain or pain on a loved one's face.

As to the mechanism by which we take only the briefest notice and then jettison thought about a stimulus, I refer you to the television commercial. Have you ever noticed how you sometimes forget to press the mute button on your remote control because your mind has muted the message already?

But how can someone act upon some aspect of her setting without much, if any, conscious thought? Again, your own experience can provide you with examples. Perhaps a prime one might be the way you drive your car on a familiar route. Haven't you ever had the common experience of getting home after such a jaunt and realizing that you have no recollection whatsoever of changing lanes, making turns, dodging other drivers, or even stopping for traffic lights? You noticed, and acted, without really knowing it.

It has even been suggested that post-surgical depression in some cases may be caused by the fact that the unconscious mind remains alert during anesthesia, that it remembers quite vividly the pain of the operation, and takes time to get over that trauma.

If our real-life setting can din into us in all these ways, then isn't it clear that we are never really out of the impact zone of our environment? And isn't it even more obvious that our setting can affect our personality and actions at those times when we are not conscious of it?

The lesson to be learned, then, is that you as a writer of fiction can tailor changes in your story setting to affect your character. You not only can do so, but almost must do so, if your story is to function like real life. So let's look at the most obvious ways you can consciously craft your setting in order to change a character.

Moving your character into a different setting is the most obvious and perhaps simplest device for using setting as an agent of character change. To be sure, thrusting a character into a new and different setting does not guarantee he will change; in adventure fiction, where the action is the thing, a character can be pushed into all kinds of wild setting variations and yet be the same person throughout. (Think of Indiana Jones.) But if you are writing another kind of fiction where character change is desired, you can show the character first noticing the change in setting, then definitely reacting as a result of taking notice.

This means that you must not only delineate the new setting and how it differs from the previous one, but you should show the character taking note of the change. Ordinarily, if you are in the character's viewpoint, this will be no problem. Just make sure that you include clauses like "She noticed how different this new neighborhood was. . . ." (with specific details added) or "He felt tense here, and knew it was because the unfamiliar area was so dark and isolated, with the great bulk of the mountains. . . ."

Having taken this step in viewpoint, don't forget the next: showing the character reaction as a result. This reaction might be shown in considerable detail, as the character slowly or swiftly goes through feelings about the new setting, then comes to thoughtful decisions designed to make everything feel better or safer again; at other times, showing how the character was reacting would be quite quick and simple.

In the above situation, for example, after showing the character's observation of the new setting (the different neighborhood), you might add three sentences like the following showing resultant immediate action and the beginning of a major character change (the immediate action and suggestion of character change italicized for clarity):

> She noticed how different the neighborhood was . . . how empty the streets, how shabby. Every black alleyway seemed like it might hide an attacker. She heard voices somewhere behind her. *She shivered and walked faster. Already she knew she was a different person here. She would never trust anyone again.* . . .

Sometimes, of course, it simply isn't practical for you to move your character to some drastically different physical setting in order to produce a desired character change. In such cases, however, it is often possible to keep the character in essentially the same setting, yet introduce significant alteration in that setting.

Any number of possibilities come to mind, and a few examples will help you see what I mean:

• When Jill opened her curtains onto the dear, familiar street, she immediately saw the big moving van next door, and the strange boxes being unloaded. . . .

• "Bill," the boss said, "we are going to redecorate your office to reflect the new duties I have in mind for you."

• Clouds scudded over the sun, and it began to rain. Marianne's depression began to grow. . . .

• The *Detour* signs went up Monday morning, and Ted's store was shut off from traffic.

The key to success in handling all such instances lies in locating the kind of change within the present setting that is most likely to jar the character and create the possibility and even the need for character change. Obviously, you must mix and match properly.

What do I mean by this? Well, look again at the examples

above. When Jill opens her curtains and sees boxes being unloaded from the van, she would possibly worry about that kind
of change. Storekeeper Ted, however (in the fourth example),
wouldn't worry about boxes being unloaded nearby, but the detour (which might not worry Jill) is a potentially disastrous
change in *his* setting.

So you can change character by moving him to a new setting, or by introducing the right kind of changes in his present
setting. That leaves the third basic way of using setting to change
character, which is, essentially to leave the setting the same, but
have the character notice new things about it.

One of the most obvious examples of this that I've ever seen
involved a friend who had always been physically active and
cheerful. One day he happened to fall and slightly injure his
back. As a result of this minor injury, which at first had seemed
frighteningly serious, he became more cautious and began looking for other possible dangers in his environment. He noticed
floor tiles which might be slippery, pavement that was even
slightly uneven, area rugs that might slip. He began to see every
familiar staircase, escalator and change of floor level in the local
mall as a place where he might fall again. He began to see almost
everything in his familiar setting in a new way, and so he began
acting in a new way, no longer taking walks or going out much
by himself . . . finally becoming almost a recluse.

I'm happy to report that my friend went into therapy and
managed to overcome the irrational fears that had made him
see his setting in a new and dark way, which only fed those fears.
Finally he saw quite clearly how the mechanism in his case had
worked:

1. A sharp experience jolted him out of seeing things as he
always had.

2. A growing alertness to a familiar setting, with his new orientation, caused him to notice things he had never noticed before.

3. Interpretation of the new things he noticed made him
begin to act differently—he "became a different person," as he
later put it.

This is the machinery by which you can get your character to experience his story setting in new ways, and so change as a result. You should first make something happen to get your character looking at his setting freshly, in a new light. You next show him finding "new" things in his setting (new to him, that is). Then you show him changing as a result.

In a few cases you might not even need a dramatic or sharp experience to get the ball rolling. Stories of boredom or desperation are quite common, and in many of them the character finally goes bonkers because *nothing* has changed in the setting, and seemingly never will. Once the character becomes aware of this dreadful unchangableness, then the very lack of change itself becomes a powerful potential instrument of character-change.

You can also use setting to create longer-term and more subtle character growth. Consider the change in the TV series character mentioned earlier, Dr. Joel Fleischman in *Northern Exposure*, over the first two seasons the show was on the air. At first he was in a panic and only wanted out of Cicely, the fictional town. Later, however, as he began to know people in the area and see some of the area's natural beauty, his attitude subtly changed and he became more human and forgiving. (Even his dress changed from modish New York to sloppy Alaskan bush pilot.) He became more calm and the hard edge of sarcasm dulled. Even later in the series, when he learned his forced stay in Alaska was to be longer than he had previously thought, he remained a man changed by his setting even as he bemoaned the fact. The setting's impact on his character, while slow in taking effect, is obvious.

This kind of interaction between character and setting almost always takes place, whether the writer designs it or simply allows it to happen. You should be as aware of it as possible, and use it to your advantage whenever you can.

SUGGESTED EXERCISE

As an exercise at this point, you may wish to write a short story segment in which you quite consciously delineate how a setting changes a character. Place yourself in the character's viewpoint and show him or her observing something about the setting, and reflecting on the observation. Then show, in viewpoint, that the character realizes he is seeing the setting in a different light. Define how his perception has changed, and, if possible, why it has changed. Finally, show the character reflecting on this changed attitude and wondering how the change is going to affect his plot motives and interaction with other characters.

Doing an exercise like this may feel mechanical. No matter. I urge you to do it, writing it step-by-step in the order I've just given you. I think the work will give you a better feel for how setting can have direct impact on character. The better you come to understand this interrelationship, the better you can tailor setting to character, and vice versa.

USE OF SETTING AS A CHARACTER

The tactic of making a setting into a character was mentioned previously in connection with my novel, *Twister*. It seems appropriate to reiterate the point in the context of this discussion. In short, the point is that sometimes a setting (or aspect of a setting) can be so overwhelmingly important in development of the plot (and the characters' lives) that it seems to take on a life of its own. This is a dynamic which cannot be forced; nothing could be cornier than trying to breathe life into a setting not vital and central enough to "take over" a story. But setting can become a character when setting, plot and characters blend perfectly.

In Arthur Hailey's *Hotel*, for example, the setting also becomes something of a character in its own right, practically taking on a life of its own. Similarly, in Hailey's *Airport*, the terminal building and everything it contains seems to become for the reader almost a huge living organism itself. In stories of the sea, the sea often becomes the central antagonist, and seems (even in a classic narrative poem like "The Rime of the Ancient Mariner") to become malevolent.

Clearly, setting and character are inextricably tied in the dynamic of fiction. But setting can affect fiction in other ways, too, as the next chapter describes.

CHAPTER 9

HOW SETTING ADDS TO STORY MEANING AND VITALITY

IN DESIGNING THE SETTING or settings for your story, it's important to remember that the setting, and how you handle it, may go far toward finally defining what your story means. In addition, your work on the setting may stimulate your imagination to explore story angles and ideas that weren't at all in your original concept of the tale.

STORY MEANING

Selection of setting can profoundly affect story meaning because some themes may be difficult or even impossible to examine in a certain kind of setting, while a different setting could make these same themes seem almost inevitable as a concern of the characters in such a place and time. If you begin planning your story to be played out in a rough, isolated wilderness setting, for example, that choice may at the outset be nothing more than a convenience for you, or the first idea that leaped into your mind. But selection of such a setting virtually eliminates some story themes and makes others likely.

For example, if you choose to set your story in a rugged, isolated mining town in the Klondike a century or more ago, it's hard to imagine that your story's meaning could have much to do with any of the following:

- The pressures of high society on a young woman's marriage plans
- The difficulty of choosing a college curriculum
- Country club exclusion due to racism
- The desperation of urban slums
- The choice of an apartment complex roommate
- Finding a date for the prom
- Lost airline tickets
- Harrassment by telephone calls
- Concern about AIDS
- Worry about environmental pollution and endangered wildlife.

The first six themes in this list relate to physical location of the setting. The situations listed would not likely exist in a place like the Klondike. The next three themes on the list relate to the time of the setting. Airlines, telephones and AIDS would not exist in a Klondike setting.

The last theme on the list, environmental pollution, would not be likely because of the attitude existing in such a setting: Until fairly recent times, environmental concerns were not much of a worry, and certainly old-time miners repeatedly raped the environment with no thought whatsoever of the consequences in pollution and destruction of wildlife. As a matter of fact, prevailing frontier attitudes toward wildlife were the opposite of today's; killing off all wolves, coyotes and bears was a positive value in those days.

So choice of a setting limits the themes you can deal with.

Conversely, choice of a setting immediately suggests themes which are possible. Using the same isolated, old-time Klondike setting, some possible ideas and themes come to mind at once:

- Greed for gold
- The threat of starvation in the wild
- The danger of wild animal attack
- The quest for food and shelter
- The value of friendship
- The terror of being lost in the wilderness
- Homesickness for civilization.

Once you realize this interdependence of setting and thematic ideas, you can better tailor your setting to your ideas. That wilderness setting might be chosen and developed consciously in order to state as clearly as possible a realized theme involving courage against great odds, perhaps, or the saving strength of religious faith in a time of isolation and trial. If you also emphasized certain other aspects of the wilderness—the cruel and random death of prey animals, as one illustration, or the seemingly hostile persistence of the killing winter gale—you might more clearly develop a theme about personal courage.

We often see this relationship between setting and meaning most clearly in movies, because so much has to be shown and not explained in words. In the *Treasure of Sierra Madre*, for example, the war between good and evil impulses in the characters is emphasized and made clearer because of the savage and primitive conditions under which the men exist, leaving little or no room for pretense or manners. The recent *Batman* movies derived part of their meaning from the dark, towering, crumbling city infrastructure that formed their setting. Many critics saw serious ideas about the human condition depicted in these films. The setting put the audience in a somber frame of mind, and gave outrageous activities a semblance of verisimilitude. Played in a less menacing and terrible urban setting, the stories might have been seen merely as comic book nonsense.

This relationship between setting and story meaning was brought home to me most vividly when I was writing a novel a few years ago titled *A Boat Named Death*. The story is of an old mountain man, quite mad, who stumbles upon a woman and her small children in a cabin in the wilderness. Through being touched by their total vulnerability and dependence on him to save their lives, he is changed from practically an animal to a love-filled man who faces his own death for the sake of others.

The novel met with some success, but probably could not have done so if the choice of setting had not been right. Most of the story is of the man's attempt to get the little family to medical help by taking them down a wild river in flood in an old rowboat with the word "Death" painted on its side. The trapper's struggle against the river—which seems to him a character bent on their annihilation—becomes a symbol of his entire life struggle, and explains how he became the man he is. But, at the same time, his journey down the river becomes a spiritual one, his heart changing as the river batters and almost destroys him. The setting, the boat in the careening river, makes possible the themes of man against nature, and man against himself. A final change in the setting, to a small and hostile town bent on the trapper's destruction, makes possible an emphasis on the transforming power of love, even on a man whom the wilds had practically turned into a beast.

Every writer comes upon situations like this, where the choice of setting not only defines the kinds of ideas that can be explored, but suggests ways that all or part of that setting can be transformed into a symbol that contributes to story meaning. In an example earlier in this book, we used an old clock tower, visible from all over a small town. One immediately thinks of using the clock tower as a symbol for the passing of time, or for a town's living in the past as if time had stood still, or to illuminate the story's meaning.

In such ways, setting can have a profound impact on your story's meaning. You should be alert to this fact, and remember it in matching plot to character, and both to setting. In a proper blend of the three, a story meaning and depth of ideas will come much more clear. To put this another way, the perfect setting can make all the difference in what your story ultimately means.

You should also remember, however, that conscious manipulation of the setting and other story elements does not mean that you should set out on a mad quest for symbols and metaphors in your setting. Symbolic meaning, when it occurs, is usually an outgrowth of the creative process itself. Such meaning usually develops fully in your mind only as you write the story. It's very dangerous to set out on a piece of fiction with the idea of "making something a symbol." The result too often is artificiality.

What should you do, then? Simply remember that setting can affect meaning in the ways we have mentioned here. Work to make setting harmonious with your other fiction elements. If symbolic or metaphorical meaning comes clear to you as you write the story, consider ways you might point it out more clearly. But never force it; that way lies disaster.

STORY IDEAS

We've seen in earlier chapters how good setting makes the story world vital and vibrant and real to the reader. But there's also a quite different advantage of good setting: The impact it can have on the writer herself as she researches and creates her tale.

Many writers have experienced the "turn-on" that research digging can bring. What happens is that new and previously unsuspected facts turn up during the research, or some new detail or anecdote provides unexpected delight. In either case, the writer gets newly excited, and sometimes gets new story or character ideas from the experience. What can also happen is that the writer imaginatively gets so deeply into her setting as she writes, that she actually sees possibilities in it that were previously not seen.

The late Clifton Adams, one of our most gifted western writers mentioned earlier, told me once with great pleasure how he had stumbled upon a historical record of French foreign legionnaires actually assigned in south Texas during frontier times. This unusual historical sidelight so fascinated Cliff that he did considerably more research about it and found material for use in several later novels. Phyllis A. Whitney has remarked that she researched a setting for an adult suspense novel and found enough material for an additional young adult book. In my own career I have had numerous similar experiences: Medical research done for my novel *Halls of Dishonor* gave me considerable additional information about the medical setting, which was one of the inspirations for a later book called *Miracleworker*, another medical story. The germ of the plot for *Miracleworker*, as a matter of fact, came from an accidental encounter with a medical supply "detail man" (salesman) during a research visit for the other novel.

Careful research is required to make sure your setting is accurate and believable, as discussed back in chapter three. But such research very often pays the considerable dividend of inspiring new ideas for setting, as well as indicating how story people in such a setting might think and act, and how a plot in such a setting might play out.

The moral? Never shirk research. Learn to love it. Even when you think you have done enough research for your story setting, try to dig just a little deeper — conduct that one more interview, visit one more site, write one more letter or read one more book on the subject. Trust the process of research. It will feed your imagination in ways you may never have dreamed of.

You may indeed find that the inspiration continues through the writing process, even after you thought learning about your setting was finished. In a curious way, the process of writing sometimes intensifies a writer's vision. In fact-writing, putting the words on paper sometimes helps clarify the very thought the writer is struggling to record. In fiction, it is even more common for a writer to begin writing a description or factual passage about a setting, and suddenly find herself imaginatively transported into that setting in a more vivid way than was possible before she started writing it down.

So research provides inspiration, and writing down ideas can help the imagination focus and crystalize the very imagining. The ideas form words and then the words, as they are written, clarify the ideas. It's a strange process and I don't begin to understand it. I just know it happens, and very often it happens when the writer is describing a setting, and suddenly finds herself so deeply immersed in that setting, in her imagination, that she is amazed.

Try it. Write a detailed description of a setting you know a lot about. Put down concrete physical details, emotion-packed observations of feelings about the setting. As you write, you will almost certainly find your imagination further stimulated by the process itself.

Many writers, knowing how research and writing can fuel the imagination, take the learning process a step further. They become a fond joke among their friends because they always seem to be making an unnecessary trip or going to a meeting they don't have to attend, or starting with great vim and vigor into some new hobby which their previous life gave no indication about.

Such writers do these things because they want to seek out new experience. They know you can never predict when such an experience might suggest an entirely new backdrop for a story. They also do these things because they have learned to love information for its own sake.

I admit to being one of those who constantly leaps into new hobbies. I have been at one time or another a photographer, a guitar player, a hunter, a fisherman, a private pilot, a camper, a ham radio operator, a golfer, a tennis player, a pigeon-raiser, a carpenter and a model train enthusiast. (And I've probably forgotten some hobbies that should be mentioned, too.) I went into each of these activities with enthusiasm, wanting to learn just as much about it as I could. I've had a great deal of fun. But I've also derived great benefits in terms of story settings because every specialty or hobby exists in its own arcane little world.

I think, for example, of standing in an airport hangar listening to pilots swap flying stories; there is a characteristic preoccupation here, and special lingo based on special shared skills and knowledge. Then I recall the days with amateur radio operators at events like the annual American Radio Relay League "Field Day," when operators set up in the out-of-doors to train for emergency situations; again the interests are unique, the people are unusual, and the lingo specialized. Each hobby's microworld has its own informal oral library of folk tales and jokes, some of which can stimulate your imagination with ideas for plots as well as settings.

Entering such a hobby world can bring all sorts of new information and ideas for story settings. And it can also be a lot of fun; such new experiences and learning keep you young ... keep your brain nimble and eager.

In addition, your enjoyment of learning new things and meeting different kinds of people will help you maintain your enthusiasm, help keep your mind open to new experiences and ideas, and, quite simply, help you maintain a focus broader than your own private world of work and family.

This last point is very important, although it does not relate solely to the setting in your story. Writing is a lonely business, and it is all too easy to become so focused and intense about your work that you start closing doors and windows, turning down chances to meet new people, and begin to resemble a hermit. If your story world is to be vibrant and convincing, you must be out in the world, continually drawing from new and stimulating experiences. Research — and hobbies — make sure you maintain this outer focus.

A word should also be said about "painless research" of a different type: travel. As mentioned before in a different context, we tend to get so used to our everyday environment that we take many things for granted, and practically don't see them anymore. Familiarity breeds a kind of blindness. Traveling to a new locale, where nothing is familiar, awakens all the observational apparatus; we look, *really* look, at a church or store or office building that we might drive right by without seeing if it were in our humdrum, everyday setting. A change of scene sharpens all our observational skills. Even after we return home, we see things with fresh and inquisitive eyes for quite some time.

I'll talk about travel for on-site research of setting in Appendix 1 on research techniques as well as in chapter fifteen.

SUGGESTED SELF-EXAMINATION

Perhaps this chapter has suggested a course of self-examination that might help you analyze your own "research" and setting work in its broadest possible definition. Let me offer a few specific ideas for such a self-exam.

Look at the settings you have used in your last four stories or books. Are they very much the same? Are they small-town settings, for example, or all contemporary, or perhaps all big-city neighborhood or all business? If they are, ask yourself what other different setting you should research for your next creative effort.

Can you see many things that your settings have in common, even if they appear different on the surface? Do your story people always come from similar backgrounds, for example? Do they always have the same values? What different backgrounds or values could you research for your next setting?

Study the way you described physical settings in recent stories. Do you always stress what is seen, at the expense of mentioning other sense impressions? Is it possible you could enrich your descriptions if you took a trip or tried a new hobby which might excite your mind and make your observations—and writing—more acute?

Have you done as much research as you should have for recent stories? If not, why not? List ten sources of setting information you regularly use—or *should* be using. Have you taken an interesting trip, even a short one, in the last six months? Have you looked into or begun taking part in a new hobby in the last year? Think about these things!

Finally, one more exercise. Select a setting for a story which would be quite uncharacteristic for your work: a place and time and set of attitudes you have never used as a story backdrop before. Don't make this selection easy; pick something really "out in left field" in terms of what you usually do.

Now research this setting, and prepare a fact portfolio about it. Make up and fill out a setting research form for it. (You will find one writer's setting research form as an example in Appendix 2.)

This work is guaranteed to open your eyes to some of your tendencies about handling setting. It will also, I feel sure, stimulate you to find new ways to handle your setting problems.

CHAPTER 10

SETTING AND VIEWPOINT: IT'S HOW YOU LOOK AT IT

AT MANY POINTS IN THE TELLING OF A STORY, an author faces the decision of where to put the vantage point—the point from which the setting is to be described or discussed. Fundamentals concerning this decision were discussed in chapter two and mentioned again in chapter three. Let's briefly review those points and then look at other aspects.

Essentially, what you often have to decide, as the author of the piece, is where you stand—where you place the reader's imagination—in experiencing the story setting. In the broadest terms, you have the two choices already mentioned: The omniscient or author-objective panoramic view, told as a god might tell it, seeing everything and knowing virtually everything, or the view as experienced from inside a character, and limited to what that single character can realistically experience and know.

Each approach has its pros and cons. So let's reconsider them as briefly as possible.

THE OMNISCIENT VIEWPOINT

The omniscient approach offers three distinct advantages:

- It offers the broadest possible scope.
- It allows the author to provide information no character knows.
- It is economical—allows summary.

Useful in describing scenery, landscape, and great movements over time, the omniscient viewpoint allows you the author to show anything you wish from as far away, or as close, as you desire. It allows you to provide a long-time sense of history. Such "on high" observations can also include information that no character inside the story could possibly know. Therefore, the omniscient viewpoint has many applications in broad-sweep situations.

Such a viewpoint is not used only in broad-sweep situations, however. It is a very efficient way of showing information about a setting, and allows for summary because you the author are not stuck in the lifelike narrative of a story character, whose experience often must be told moment-by-moment, with no summary, in order to be as realistic as possible. That's why you sometimes find a writer getting out of character viewpoint at the start of a story segment in order to provide a few broad brushstrokes of setting as quickly as possible. In such situations, the omniscient viewpoint is the most effective.

Here, for example, is a brief use of the technique by novelist Jeff Clinton in a recent western titled *Big Sky Revenge*:

> Night came, and with it a clear starry sky and the sliver of a rising moon. The ground quickly gave off its heat and in the dark it was cold, the kind of cold that sinks quickly to the bone.

This is economical writing. A broad and general picture of the setting is provided in fewer words than might have been necessary if the same description were put in the viewpoint of a character, who might have had to walk outside and look around, shiver, etc., in order to experience the same thing. The brief passage also illustrates the ability to summarize. At least an hour passes in two sentences. If told from a character's viewpoint, the passage of so much time could hardly have been summarized so deftly because there is no summary in real life, and little in the lives of fiction characters; rather, the writer would have had to add considerable minute details in order to show time passing, rather than simply summarizing it, as the omniscient approach allows.

Just as the technique has advantages of sweep and compression, however, it has disadvantages which you must weigh before making a decision to use it:

- You may lose your character identification.
- You may get carried away and overdescribe.

Since omniscient writing by definition is told outside a character viewpoint, there is always the danger that the reader may lose contact with the viewpoint character if such passages go on very long. Your shifting to a broad, godlike viewpoint takes your reader to that mountaintop or place out of space and time, too, remember. He may stop thinking about your main story character and her outlook during such on-high journeys. Such a loss of contact with the viewpoint character may mean loss of reader sympathy and identification with that character—and, consequently, loss of interest in the human story.

To put this another way, there is a danger that such a passage, if extended very long, will turn the reader's attention from the story people to the setting exclusively, and all storytelling will be lost as the reader studies a kind of stop-action photograph in words. Make sure the advantages clearly outweigh dangers such as this one if you "go omniscient."

The other disadvantage noted above—that one might get carried away in omniscience—is easier to deal with once you realize the danger exists. Sometimes a writer gets so deeply into the broad-scale imagining that she is carried away and starts putting in great gobs of purple prose. Or she may start lecturing the reader about the facts.

I think most of us have cringed at one time or another when encountering an awful purple patch of overheated description in a story. Perhaps most of us have almost dozed off, too, when confronted by a huge block of solid factual information that stopped the story dead in its tracks. Almost always such errors come when the writer is in an omniscient mode. Always keep in mind the reactions of your readers.

THE RESTRICTED VIEWPOINT

What should we remember about using the restricted viewpoint of a story character as our place for viewing the setting? Again there are advantages and disadvantages you may already be aware of from the earlier discussions in chapters two and three. Here we'll review and then move on. (You may wish to return to the earlier chapters as part of your study here.)

The advantages of viewpoint restriction:

- It's convincing because it gives the reader this information the same way he experiences real life: from the limited view of a lone individual.
- It's simpler because there will always be many aspects of the setting that the single individual cannot sense or know — being on the wrong side of the mountain to see the waiting outlaws, for example, or standing too far from the scene of the crash to hear the clashing of metal.
- It tends to be briefer because a character caught up in the action and problems of your story ordinarily just won't have the time to notice a lot of things.

We've looked in earlier chapters at the major disadvantages of restricted viewpoint, and need only mention them by way of review here:

- There may be times when you want to show a broader picture, and simply can't find a character who could experience all that.
- There may be information you want to provide that no single character could possibly know.

THE URGE TO TELL TOO MUCH

I've known writers who got very uneasy — or downright panicky — because they thought they needed to get certain broad-scale information or sense impressions into their story at a given point, but couldn't find a character to experience all that they desired to convey. If you ever get that feeling, let me suggest that you sit back for a minute and ask yourself if the reader really needs that panoramic view (or additional information). Often you may discover that she doesn't, and that your feeling is an *author* concern, not a *reader* concern. You may be wanting to tell more than necessary just because you happen to know it.

It's hard sometimes to accept that a reader doesn't need to experience or know something. You know everything about the setting, can see it all in your imagination, and your natural impulse is to want to share your vision with your reader—to put in everything for the reader to know, see, hear, smell, taste, feel and believe about the setting at that moment of story time. It's a brave impulse, and one that's very hard to dissuade writers of sometimes, but nearly always it's fallacious.

Your reader seldom needs to know all you do at any point. You might think he would benefit from a vast and panoramic view of that city setting, but he does not experience his real life that way, and he does not want to experience the story setting that way, either. Belief comes from identification with the viewpoint. Identification with the viewpoint comes from a restricted view of the setting. The reader's concern is with what the character knows. Your authorial concern about showing the big picture often has nothing whatsoever to do with telling a good story in the most effective way.

However, if you decide after reflection that broad-scale information is vital to the reader, you obviously may elect to assume the omniscient view for a short time. Or you may elect to keep your viewpoint limited to a single person at a time, but hop around among several characters in order to show what each is experiencing.

Let me offer one example here of how the omniscient viewpoint can provide a sweeping picture. This is from an early segment of the novel by Jeff Clinton mentioned earlier, *Big Sky Revenge*:

It was a magnificent day: brilliant blue sky, a few low clouds forming a silvery haze on the lower slopes, the upper reaches already blinding white under their winter coat.

Crossing a swift stream, its banks encrusted with ice, Ford spooked an elk—a flash of tan and orange—in the long declivity a quarter-mile behind his house, on higher ground. He didn't fire. He saw some deer, a doe and a buck, higher up and at some distance. The light snow under the trees was crisscrossed with the tracks of rabbits, beavers, otters, and skunks. Ford walked steadily, his breath a huge cloud around him, and reached the turning in the creek designated on Craddock's map. He moved on.

A brief analysis of this short passage may be helpful. The passage comes after a transition in time, clearly marked by double white spaces in the text, so the reader presumably begins reading without too strong a thought connection to any viewpoint.

But even if circumstances make it possible for a switch to omniscience here, why does the author choose to use it? I think the answer is clear. Especially in an outdoor story of the Old West like this one, a feeling for the vastness of the country and its visual beauty are vital elements. The reader yearns imaginatively to see the mountains. And, as in virtually any story, he needs a periodic recontact with the physical setting to remind him of his physical orientation. Therefore, in this example, the author meets reader needs by "fleshing out" the setting with a panoramic view, and he takes advantage of a natural transition point to do so.

Notice, however, that the purely omniscient view is not maintained for long. The character Ford's name is mentioned midway in the second sentence. The fact that his name is mentioned does not in itself establish his viewpoint, because the god-like observer can see him just like he sees the mountains and snow. But mention of the character's name begins to set the reader up for insertion into a character viewpoint, and sure enough, two short sentences later, a viewpoint is established with the words *He saw*. Only Ford can know what he saw. Therefore, when these words occur, the reader is again placed in Ford's viewpoint.

You might also notice, however, that considerable material not necessarily in Ford's viewpoint follows this single viewpoint identifier. The light snow, Ford's heavy breathing, and all the rest of it contain no intrinsic evidence that they are from Ford's restricted viewpoint. So additional panoramic material is inserted. But a reader, once put into a viewpoint, will invariably tend to assume that everything which follows is experienced by that viewpoint. So here the additional panoramic material is assumed to be from Ford's viewpoint, and author Clinton is careful to make sure that nothing that comes later in this segment is from a viewpoint that the character Ford could not possibly experience. Clinton seems to know well one of the cardinal rules about handling point of view in setting as noted in chapter two. To state it negatively: Once in a viewpoint in any given segment, don't get back out of it.

A BRIEF RESTATEMENT

A brief restatement of the principles mentioned here and in earlier chapters relating to the subject of viewpoint may be in order.

- Use the "on high" omniscient viewpoint to establish general story setting, tone, the look and feel and possibly background of a place.
- Move inside a viewpoint character to gain reader identification, and to reflect character outlook and mood.
- Move from viewpoint character to "on high," if you must, at the beginning of segments, after a transition of some kind.
- Return to character viewpoint at the earliest opportunity.
- Always think about what the reader needs to know, not what you may know or want to inflict on the poor soul for no good reason.

If you follow these principles, your story setting will be presented fully, vibrantly and convincingly. But your job in handling your viewpoint will not be done. What's left? Pegging your presentation of setting to *feeling* and *mood*. Which is the subject of chapter eleven.

CHAPTER 11

SETTING THE MOOD: HOW SETTING VIEWPOINT CREATES ATMOSPHERE

BACK IN CHAPTER SIX WE BRIEFLY CONSIDERED emotional focus of a character as a unifying factor in storytelling, and promised to get back to the matter at an appropriate time. Having looked at viewpoint in chapter ten, we can now look more carefully at emotional focus and story mood, and how both interact with your story's setting.

It may be that you will choose to open your story, or relate parts of it, from the broad, omniscient viewpoint. In such situations, you still need to be conscious of the general emotional mood you wish your story to evoke in your reader; you will need to select details designed to create or enhance that general mood, be it joyfulness, sadness, fear, dread, anger, or whatever. More often, however, you will probably tell virtually all your story from the viewpoint of a character inside the story action, as discussed in chapter ten. In these cases, it is even more critical that you understand how the viewpoint affects story mood.

Your character's emotional set and the general mood conveyed by a story at any given point are inextricably bound together. Given a central character who is sad and lonely, for example, the depiction of the setting must reflect details generally in keeping with that mood, even if you happen to be writing from an omniscient viewpoint at the moment. When you are in character viewpoint, the need to dovetail character emotion and story mood is much more vital.

If you walk your sad and lonely viewpoint character into a bright and happy setting, the story mood will not be bright and happy despite the objective nature of the setting because your sad and lonely character will not see the setting in terms other than his own internal emotional set. Thus, walking into a joyful wedding, for example, he will see it all as a contrast to his own plight; you the author must show that the happiness around him only reminds him of his own sadness.

Three crucial aspects — *who* the story is about, *what* you show about the setting, and *how* everything feels to the reader — must be consistent in mood and reinforce one another. Your viewpoint character, like people in the real world, will interpret the setting through the lens of his current emotions. If you want to write a story with a sad and lonely mood, you will write about a character whose feelings are sad and lonely. If you write about a character whose feelings are sad and lonely, then your setting will look (or be interpreted as) sad and lonely because your viewpoint is that of a character who cannot interpret things in any other way.

Once you have recognized this dynamic interaction, you can consciously manipulate your story elements to give the story exactly the general mood you desire.

In writing any story, you need to think about the following generalized questions, all of which are closely linked:

- How do you want the reader to feel while experiencing the story?
- What is the general mood you hope to convey from the setting?
- How do your character's emotions color what he sees?
- What setting details impact both the character's feelings and general mood of the story?

Every story, you see, elicits a general feeling matrix in its reader. The poet T.S. Eliot, writing about this subject years ago, talked about what he called "the objective correlative," that precise relationship between what is presented and how it makes the reader feel. No story should leave the reader emotionally unmoved, or thinking, "So what?" Your setting must fit the desired feeling or your story won't work. So consciously analyzing how you want your reader to feel will help you plan and present your setting.

You attain this reader feeling through story mood. If you want your reader to feel sadness, for example, you need to present your story in a setting which includes somber details, unhappy elements, dark shades of gray, items designed to create a mood that will lead to the desired feeling.

And how will your character's emotions color what is shown of the setting? We have already seen how a happy character might "reach out" into his environment and notice happy things, while a sad one is likely to notice the sad, or interpret whatever he sees in a sad way. You can't simply depict a sorrowful setting, for example, without making sure that your character's feelings are such that sad details are what he will see because of the sorrowful tint to the emotional lenses through which he experiences the story world.

And what kind of details do you need in your setting to reinforce the desired mood? If the story is to leave the reader angry and resentful about some wrong in society, and if the mood is to be somber and bitter, and if the character is to be hurt and rejected, what specific details do you have to locate and present in the setting to make sure the character—and through him the reader—gets the desired feeling clearly and forcefully?

Sometimes, of course, a particular setting virtually demands a certain kind of emotional response in the character, a certain story mood, a certain reader feeling. A graveyard, for example, is difficult to imagine as a setting for a lighthearted, humorous story. Yet Peter S. Beagle achieved exactly this effect in his novel, *A Fine and Private Place*, through the viewpoint of an extremely unusual character. But Beagle's story is the exception which tends to prove the rule. More often than not, you should give some serious thought to the kinds of feeling a particular setting can predictably engender, and then make your setting decisions accordingly.

But general thoughtfulness and planning will not necessarily get the whole job done for you in terms of emotion and mood.

Your general questioning invariably must get down to specifics like some of the following:

1. In the opening of your story—What aspect of the setting should be shown at the earliest possible moment in the story to establish an opening mood or tone? What specific details should be included in this opening? From what vantage point should the opening be presented?

2. During the course of your story—What central unifying aspect of the setting should be shown repeatedly? What different views or experiences of this central aspect will be used to avoid obvious repetition? What other aspects of setting will be developed, and in what order?

How many different viewpoints will be employed? If settings change drastically, how will each new setting be established, and with what mood or tone?

If different viewpoint characters are to experience the setting, how specifically does each character's emotional outlook color his or her individual experience of the setting?

How will all differing views and aspects of the setting be unified in a coherent, consistent story mood or tone, and how do you want this general tone or mood to make the reader feel?

3. In the ending of your story, what feeling do you want to leave your reader with? What aspect of setting will you stress as the ending to help evoke this mood? From what viewpoint will this last look at setting be shown? Is there a possibility of developing story theme more clearly through employment of the closing look at setting?

Many of these questions are intimately interrelated, of course, but let's try to separate them and consider them individually insofar as it is possible.

STORY OPENING

In deciding what general aspect of the setting should be shown to establish a story-opening mood or tone, it is important to remember that the opening feeling you engender in your reader sets up his expectations for everything that follows. You need to be quite sure what mood you wish to evoke right from the outset.

Here we are talking about the broadest possible definition of mood, such as sadness, fear, joy, apprehension, isolation or engulfment. Every story *feels* a certain way, and this is what you need to define. Then, having defined it in your own mind as clearly as you can, you need to think about your setting and decide what you should present first to make the story feel that way to your reader right from the outset.

Perhaps you have envisioned a large city with teeming traffic, streets alive with business people during the daytime and crime at night; rivers, trains, air traffic, skyscrapers and large wooded parks; rich neighborhoods and poor ones. If the tone or mood of your story is to relate somehow to the dynamism of all this humming activity and the nervous electricity of a complex city environment, perhaps your opening should stress all of these aspects in a broad-view look written in a staccato style that adds to the electricity and confusion. On the other hand, if your story is really the sad and nostalgic tale of a couple growing old in Brooklyn, perhaps your focus at the outset will be as narrow as the description of a single potted violet on a windowsill behind the dusty front window of an upstairs apartment.

Suppose you opt for this second example. What other details besides the little potted plant will you show? A roach crawling on the glass or a small, silver-framed photo of a young serviceman killed in Vietnam? An old lamp with fringed shade on the marble-top table or the latest issue of *Penthouse*, folded open to the letters section? An unopened letter or an old-style telephone ringing? The distant scent of sachet or the stale odor of marijuana? Harsh street sounds or the soft sound of a recorded string quartet? Obviously, the specific details you choose will immediately serve to begin establishing your desired opening mood.

Also in terms of your opening there is the question of viewpoint. As discussed in chapter ten, description from the omniscient view is best accepted by the reader at times when a character viewpoint is not firmly in the reader's mind. Certainly the prime time when this is true is in the very opening of the story. For that reason, you may well choose to begin with an omniscient viewpoint and only later go into a character viewpoint. It is also true that writers very often wish to establish a broad setting picture at the outset of the story, before narrowing their focus, so this too may dictate an "on high" viewpoint at the start.

Your desire for a particular mood, however, may suggest the immediate presentation of setting from the viewpoint of a character. If, for instance, the emotional mood of the central character is vital to the feeling of the story throughout, you might plunge your reader into that character's viewpoint (which is to color everything) at once.

As an example, compare and contrast the following opening lines of a story about a lonely person living alone in a squalid setting. What is the general story feeling conveyed by this:

> A cold, steady rain pounded the deserted streets of the neighborhood, making the chill night more bleak and lonely. An old man in a dark raincoat hurried along the crumbling sidewalks and vanished into the shabby yellow light of a tavern on the corner. A police car trundled slowly through the dark, its headlights yellow, like the eyes of a great cat. . . .

As opposed to this:

> She bit her lip to keep from screaming. The pounding of the rain on the window of her small room was driving her mad. The night outside mirrored her feelings: blackness . . . desolation. Fighting back tears, she watched an old man in a dark raincoat hurry along the deserted sidewalk and enter the corner bar. Another derelict, she thought in despair, another loser like me, waiting to die. Her head throbbed with pain. She felt nauseated. She looked at the bottle of blue pills on the cheap plastic end table, knowing they offered what she wanted most: oblivion . . . death.

Clearly the mood evoked by these two openings is quite different. One is from the omniscient viewpoint and establishes a dark, lonely, brooding, and perhaps threatening feeling in the setting. The second is *deeply* in a character viewpoint, so that the setting is as much inside her head as anywhere in the outside world. The mood that's established is in contrast with the first example, here being more desperate, anguished, miserable and limited.

What decisions will you make about your opening? Remember that you will be establishing reader expectations that you should be ready to meet with consistency in your handling of setting throughout the rest of the story. What you set up, you must follow through on.

STORY MIDDLE

Which brings us to the main course of your story, and some of the questions you have to consider for its progress.

As noted above, selection of a central unifying aspect of the setting is almost always a "must." Earlier we looked at setting up an old clock tower as such a unifier. What aspect will you select? Will it be a specific thing like the clock tower, or a more general repeated emphasis on setting, such as its isolation, or its place in the mountains or near the ocean shore?

It's important to avoid reader boredom as you return again and again to this central aspect of setting, so it will pay off if you plan carefully all the different ways you might refer to it. Can you describe or present it from differing locations which present different angles of view? From different viewpoints? Different times of day? Different emotional or intellectual perspectives? You will find it useful to plan some of these different approaches, making notes on how and when you might use them, including notations on how they will appear different to the reader, and perhaps the kind of wording that might be used.

Again using the clock tower as a basis for an example, the beginning of your brief and preliminary list of different ways of describing setting might look something like this:

Clock tower —

Seen from street below; from window across street; from edge of town; in noon sunlight; lighted at night; on city stationery masthead; from passing car a block away; possibly from private aircraft?

Vantage points to include omniscient, viewpoint of Stephanie and Roger.

Omniscient vantage-point descriptions objective but evocative of small-town, the great age of the tower, the town's parochialism. Stephanie sees tower as dear, familiar, reassuring, always nostalgic, happy. Roger, however, sees it with anger, resentment, a symbol of how the town holds Stephanie so she won't go away with him.

There will, of course, be many other details and aspects of the setting which will be presented during the course of your story. You need to know what most of these will be, so that setting references come instantly to your mind as you follow your character's journey through the plot. (It can badly slow down your plotting if you have to pause often in the first draft in order to think up what bit of setting detail should be inserted. If you know the details in advance, you will tend to drop them in quickly, without being distracted from your plot and character by the need to dream up something about the setting on the spur of the moment.)

Naturally, if your story is going to move into several settings, you need to do this kind of planning for each of them. As you do, you will find yourself beginning to see each from various viewpoints, and this will improve your imaginative connection with both your characters and your story world.

STORY ENDING

Little needs to be said about questions like those mentioned above, because most of the points involved have already been touched upon in the context of earlier story development. It should be noted, however, that the concluding feeling or mood conveyed by your setting may be almost as important as the opening one because this is the emotional hook on which you hang the entire tale—the feeling you hope to leave with your reader at the story's conclusion. It may or may not be precisely the feeling that you established at the outset. In a story of any length, it will have changed subtly because something has changed in the course of the story—events have taken place, characters' lives have been altered. For this reason, your characters are not likely to see their setting at the end of the story exactly as they saw it at the outset; their feelings have changed and they will see the setting differently, too.

So don't mechanically assume the end mood will be exactly as it was at the outset. It may be close, but some variation, some dramatic progress, nearly always will have taken place.

Finally, consider the possibility that some part of your setting—the clock in the old tower, for example once more—might ultimately be made to mean more than anyone realized it meant earlier in the story. Is it possible that your character, in the ending, suddenly sees the inexorable movement of the giant minute hand as the moments of her life slipping away? Does the tolling of the hour become the tolling of the bell "for thee," as in John Donne's poem which concludes, "Send not to see for whom the bell tolls,/ It tolls for thee." Or can the crumbling bricks of the tower come to be a metaphor for the crumbling dreams of your characters?

ALL SETTING IS EMOTIONAL IN PART

From all this you can draw an obvious conclusion: No mention of setting in fiction can be said to be wholly objective. Selection of viewpoint, as well as selection of the emotional lens through which the described place or event is seen, must be made with constant reference to the desired emotional feel of the story, its present plot situation, and the characters at the time of description.

Obviously, you need to plan carefully in this entire area. It's planning that will pay off in consistency of story mood and maximum impact on your reader.

CHAPTER 12

SHOWING SETTING DURING MOVEMENT AND ACTION

MOST OF THE TIME UP UNTIL NOW, we have been tacitly assuming that your handling of setting was being done in a kind of stop action — that you could present or describe setting details in relatively static terms. In writing fiction, however, you often confront situations where you have to show a character movement into a new setting, or where the action is swift enough that you can't realistically "stop to describe," and must get the job done on the fly, while things are happening. In this chapter we'll consider such common situations.

It's possible that you may be able to stand back in the omniscient mode to reorient the reader to a change in setting, or even rapid character movement through setting details. If you are moving the character into a new setting at a time of transition, as at the opening of a chapter, you of course have the option of doing an "on high" omniscient introduction, then moving into viewpoint. In such situations, principles we've already discussed will see you through the transitions involved. More often than not, however, you may find yourself already in a character viewpoint during such times of change. Then, you have to stay in viewpoint and at the same time show as much broad detail as possible in order to reorient the reader.

STAYING IN VIEWPOINT WHILE MOVING

The thing you have to remember in such cases is that your viewpoint character is probably in movement, and has other things beside the setting on his mind. Therefore, for the sake of realism, you must carefully pick broad-brush details that will stand for the whole setting, evocative brushstrokes that you can paint in a very few words because the character can't stop and "notice things for you" endlessly.

In such cases, ask yourself the following questions:

• What two or three broad details will best suggest the new setting to the reader?
• How can I capsulize these details in a few sharply evocative words?
• What is my character's preoccupation right now — what is he probably concerned with, in terms of the plot, which might color his perception of the new setting?
• What is my character's mood right now, and would this likely color his perception of the new setting?

Here is an example of a chapter opening written with these questions in mind. It's from a recently completed novel of mine, *Double Fault*. (Tor Books, New York, © Jack M. Bickham.)

The cosmic question (Brad Smith Faces Life, Chapter 600) was answered for me when my flight into Los Angeles was delayed several hours and I didn't clear the airport until almost 1 A.M.: I would not call Beth tonight.

In the morning there was nothing much to do around my motel in Burbank, and I could have called her at her office. I didn't, and this time there was no handy excuse. She would ask why I was in LA and I didn't like lying to her but telling her the truth would only restart the disagreement that had already begun to feel old.

There would be time to call her later during my visit, I told myself.

Whether I would do it or not was a question still occupying a part of my mind early that afternoon when I drove toward Whittier and the tennis club where the FBI report said Barbara Green always played tennis on Thursday.

It was a hot day and the air quality wasn't very good. I couldn't see the mountains. The sun looked like a big silver cottonball through the heat-haze. Traffic on the free-

way was dense as always. I watched my mirror, but saw no
signs of being followed. In the traffic, that meant nothing.
This entire mission seemed to me today to be a classic waste
of time. I tried to convince myself that I was just feeling
sorry for myself because of the simmering anger at Beth,
the continuing erosion of hope.

The Redlands Racquet Club turned out to be a medium-sized facility parked behind the palm trees and lush
grass of a municipal golf course. The builders had tried to
make it look like San Simeon, or maybe an old-time movie
theater. I found a parking place among the glittering Toyotas and Volvo station wagons — mommy's day at the club,
children — and went in with my racket bag slung over one
shoulder and my duffel over the other.

I hoped for an observation deck, the better to spot her
and stage our "accidental" encounter, and I was not disappointed. Walking out onto the utility-carpeted upper deck,
I had a nice view of the sixteen courts, cement with green
plastic paint, all in use. For a few seconds, scanning, I didn't
see her.

Then I did: out on Court 8, two women slugging it
back and forth in a singles match far more vigorous than
any of the games on nearby courts; a tall, lithe, leathery
blonde in pink, blasting every ball with a controlled feroc-
ity, and Barbara — a slender, pretty brunette with a red
headband and graceful oncourt movements that made it
appear she never had to hurry to make a return. Thank
you, FBI. You have done good and now my deception can
begin. I looked for the staircase that would take me down
to court level.

The problem I faced in this segment was how best to handle a
transition in both space and time, from the character Brad
Smith's home near Missoula, Montana, to Los Angeles, after a
day's air travel. Needed: the speediest possible setting change
that would reorient the reader, leaving him feeling comfortable
in the changed story environment.

First I selected the two or three broad details about the
southern California setting that I thought would "say Los

Angeles" to the reader in a few words. I picked *hot weather*, *smog* and *heavy freeway traffic*.

In terms of time reorientation, I decided simply to mention the time of day or night without resorting to such tricks as showing clocks or having a character reset his watch.

This still left the question as to what familiar attitudes, feelings, character preoccupations or physical objects I might use to show the reader that some things were the same although the physical setting had changed. In this case I chose the character Brad's habitual glum preoccupation with his friend Beth, and the deterioration of their relationship.

The first paragraph thus mentions Brad's characteristic preoccupation immediately ("The cosmic question," etc.). The remainder of the sentence establishes both place and time in a factual way: "It is now later, dear reader, and we are in Los Angeles."

The second paragraph continues to focus on the preoccupation, moves the setting to a Burbank motel, and changes the time setting to the next day. The third brief paragraph is a bridge designed to move the character — and the reader — off the preoccupation for the moment in order to let the story proceed on another line. The fourth paragraph changes the time setting again, this time to afternoon, and puts Brad in a car moving from the motel setting to a tennis club setting.

Paragraph five, beginning "It was a hot day" is the one designed to put the reader more concretely into the new physical setting. Here the selected broad details — heat, smog and traffic — are inserted. Brad's emotions are shown as another help to the reader, to keep him feeling he is on familiar emotional turf during this setting change.

Then the picture of setting is narrowed from the broad Los Angeles area to the specific tennis club. Again, suggestive details are used rather than a detailed description, and the character is kept on the move.

The following paragraph, beginning "I hoped for an observation deck," again narrows the focus of setting, this time to a specific part of the club, and shows the character's motive for making this move inside the setting. Finally, at the very end, he reaches his new specific place in the setting, and the stage is set for interaction with other characters to resume.

Note the specific wording and phraseology designed to make the new setting as vivid as possible with the fewest suggestive words, and at the same time to keep place movement and time defined. Some of those specifics include the following:

- didn't clear the airport until 1 A.M.
- in the morning
- around my motel in Burbank
- early that afternoon
- drove toward Whittier
- hot day and the air quality wasn't very good
- couldn't see the mountains
- sun looked like a big silver cottonball through the heat haze
- traffic on the freeway was dense
- Redlands Racquet Club
- medium-sized facility
- parked behind the palm trees and lush grass
- San Simeon
- glittering Toyotas and Volvo station wagons
- my racket bag and duffel
- observation deck
- sixteen courts, cement with green plastic paint.

Please understand that I don't offer this excerpt as a particularly wonderful piece of scene-transition work, but as one that might be instructive. As with most of the illustrations in this book, my own work is used as illustration because I can at least tell you what I was thinking when it was written. And here my memory of the transition problem, and how I chose to work it out, is quite fresh.

The brief approach used in the excerpt you've just studied will work equally well from first person or third person perspective, and from a limited or a broad, "on-high" viewpoint. The overriding concern you the writer should have with scene transitions is clarity: The danger of reader confusion is serious at such times, and so is the danger of losing your story movement. Brevity, and new plot development as soon as possible, will help you avoid loss of forward movement. Key broad details, shown vividly, will help provide quick reorientation for the reader. Remembering your character's mood or preoccupation will help the reader stay oriented to the continuing problems which the change in setting do not alter.

With awareness of these principles and a bit of practice, I think you'll find such transitions becoming easier to handle.

DESCRIBING SETTING DURING SWIFT ACTION

A more difficult problem with setting can come when there is rapid character movement inside the general setting, or when the setting itself is changing with great speed (as when a storm is developing, for example). Most such situations occur within the body of a chapter or section, after you have established a character viewpoint. Telling the reader everything he needs to know during such rapid action is a challenge to any writer in terms of clarity and brevity.

To help you handle these situations, remember that your viewpoint character will be preoccupied with the action and therefore able to catch only fleeting, dominant impressions and sense images. Detailed description will be out of the question.

In planning and writing such a sequence you must keep yourself imaginatively wholly within the viewpoint, seeing only what the character sees, hearing only what he hears, and so forth. A danger during very rapid change in setting, or character movement through the setting, is loss of contact with the viewpoint. In other words, the movement may be so swift and exciting that you the writer may slip, in your own excitement, and include setting observations that the viewpoint character could not know. You must work hard to immerse yourself deeply in the viewpoint, and deal only with what he can possibly experience.

You must remember also that the viewpoint character will often experience setting impressions that are fragmentary and confusing; the source of a sound may be unknown, for example, or various impressions may seem to crash in simultaneously and confusingly. Don't worry if fragmentary impressions seem confusing. Your character may be confused, and if so, that's precisely the view of the story environment you want to portray.

Broad, dominant impressions may be all the character can experience at the moment. At time of such rapid movement, your character realistically won't have time to notice a great many fine details. Therefore, you must content yourself with including only the dominant, overwhelming impressions—all the character could realistically be expected to take in.

Strong action verbs will help carry the reader swiftly along with the movement. At all times of rapid movement in the setting, one of your aims as a writer is to convey that movement not only in what you show, but how you show it. Nothing can kill the sense of swift movement more surely than passive verbs or weak, limping sentences. You must strive for the strongest possible action wording.

Any descriptive segment must be extremely brief. There is never time for much description at such times. A pause to describe something can destroy the very sense of speed you must convey.

The character's reaction to the setting stimulus may be more important to the reader than the actual stimulus, but you have to show the setting stimulus or the reaction won't make sense. What happens in the setting at times of high action may not be nearly as important as your character's impressions of it and its impact on him. Is that loud bang a gunshot or a car backfiring, or possibly a firecracker? No matter; if identifying the source ruins the story, then the viewpoint can't know, so you *can't* tell. What's important is that the sound makes the character jump and run to the window to look outside. So you must always focus on the result inside the character.

Here's an example of a rapid-fire action sequence using these principles. It's also from *Double Fault*:

> Running outside to his rented Taurus, he glanced south and saw that the Buick had already vanished around

a slight turn in the highway where it started to ascend into the foothills. He grabbed his door handle and almost broke some fingers, forgetting he had locked up. Getting the key in the lock and jumping inside took another few precious seconds. Backing out seemed to take an eternity.

Floorboarding the Taurus's accelerator, he swung onto the pavement and headed in the direction the Buick had taken. Startled faces looked up from an open-air vegetable stand as he rocketed past them, the Ford's transmission screaming in protest at such violent treatment. *All I need is for the town constable or somebody to arrest my ass for speeding.*

Reaching the curve where the Buick had vanished, he had to ease off a bit and allow the transmission to upshift. Then he poured power to the engine again, and it responded sweetly, the speedometer going up around 70.

Ahead — well ahead, too far ahead — Davis could see the Buick nearing the outskirts of town, brake lights flaring brightly in the evening gloom, then swinging to the right and off the highway. He kept standing on the gas until he was almost on top of the place where the Buick had turned, seeing only at the last second that the intersecting road was gravel. He swayed violently onto the gravel, half-losing it as the back end slewed around, then catching control again and pouring on more power. The guy in the Buick with Brad had turned on his headlights, which made two nice red tail-light signals for Davis to watch for. He kept his lights out to avoid detection if possible.

The gravel road swung through a series of curves and came out in the deep canyon of a shallow river off to Davis's left. He was having a bad time seeing the road in the dimness without headlights. A pale cloud of whitish powder put in the air by the Buick ahead didn't help matters.

Sweat stung Davis's eyes. He was walking a tightrope, and knew it: get too close, and the bald man would realize he was being followed and possibly kill Brad — if he hadn't already done so; fall too far back in an over-abundance of caution, on the other hand, and you could lose him altogether. Davis took several gravel curves in controlled drifts, and was rewarded with a glimpse of the Buick tail-lights well ahead. The bastard was driving like a maniac.

Which he probably was, Davis thought. Davis hadn't had time to see much, but he had seen enough to know that the driver of the car ahead fit the sketchy description he had of the conspirator who was still at large.

What did he want with Brad? Revenge? If so, for what? Far more likely, he had learned somehow that Brad might know where Kevin Green was. But how could abducting Brad help the loony in any way—abduction being far and away the best Davis could assume this was?

Sheer red rock walls closed in tightly on the road, which had begun to get worse, narrower and washboarded by traffic and erosion. Ahead was a tighter curve to the right around an outcropping of the hundred-foot rock face. Davis eased off a little and then swung wide into the turn. At the last possible instant he spotted the yellow glare of headlights just around the bend somewhere. Jamming his weight hard on the brake, he spun the wheel and felt for an instant that he was losing the Taurus altogether.

Dirt flew around the windows as the Ford skidded, swinging over jagged bumps in the dirt. Davis spun the wheel the opposite direction and got a semblance of control just as he went into the deepest part of the curve. A little Jeep, headlights yellow, poked its snout around the turn ahead of him. It immediately veered right as far as it could go without hitting the shoulder dropoff into the streambed. Davis took the Taurus back right, over-correcting as he regained full control and hitting the gravel shoulder nearest the cliff face. The right side of the Taurus brushed the rock wall with an ugly crunching sound, and then Davis was free again and speeding on into the thicker dust-cloud left by the Jeep.

The dirt road narrowed and straightened out for several hundred yards, paralleling the rocky stream on the left. Davis didn't see any sign of the Buick's tail-lights ahead. Gritting his teeth so hard they ached, he floorboarded the accelerator again, making the Ford leap anxiously into passing gear as the tach needle swung into the red.

Another curve—Christ, it was almost impossible to see now!—and a side road right that was little more than a cow path back into what appeared to be a shallow box canyon, part of it fenced, choked with willows or some similar tree. As he roared past, Davis looked for dust in the air down there, but didn't see any. He wondered if it was too dark to see it if it were there. He had no time for speculation. Every ounce of his energy was funneled into the job of driving.

The roadway became narrower still and the canyon walls closed in on both sides, the stream much narrowed, marked by water rushing through a narrow rock ravine with such speed that its whitewater looked silvery even in this terrible light. No turnoffs here, Davis thought. The Buick had to be still ahead.

Up ahead he caught a momentary flash of pinkish red light—the Buick, surely. He could get closer than this. He eased the Taurus a bit faster, feeling the back end slip and slide in minute losses of rear wheel bite. He didn't have time to glance at the instruments again, and maybe now he couldn't have read them in the gloom anyway.

The river canyon suddenly began to widen, and Davis drove out onto a broad meadow area, the stream off to the left somewhere behind a grove of aspen, a fenceline along the right to protect perhaps as much as sixty acres of what looked like cultivated field of some kind. The mountains seemed to have receded all around, were off in the dark where he couldn't pick them up now.

Ahead he saw the lights of the other vehicle flare for braking. He could not allow for much time if the bald man stopped; he might be stopping only to finish Brad off and dump his body in the ditch. Davis maintained speed.

The other car did stop, pulling off to the side of the road. Davis didn't know what the hell to do now, but he knew it wasn't a good time to count eenie meenies. Flicking on his headlights, he tipped the high-beam switch and started braking hard as the lights came fully onto the Buick on the roadside less than a hundred yards ahead.

Only it wasn't the Buick.

It was a dark-colored Japanese 4×4 pickup, and a youthful man and pretty girl with flaxen hair had just clambered out onto the roadway, fishing poles in hand. They looked up and froze with alarm as Davis skidded the Ford to a halt on the shoulder behind their truck, fixing them with his brights.

Rolling his window down, he yelled at them, "Did you see a Buick sedan on this road somewhere?"

"You'd better be careful!" the boy replied hoarsely. "I've got a gun in the truck!"

"Goddam it, did you see a dark-colored Buick back up the road?"

It was the girl who answered. "Yes, but we passed him when he turned off at Box Canyon."

"Shit!" Davis cranked the steering wheel hard left, pulled partway across the narrow roadway, backed around, and spun the wheel left a second time. The racket of his tires in the dirt and gravel was far worse than what the bald man had made back in town. The Taurus held a straight line, however, and pressed Davis lightly back in the seat as it accelerated.

Within ten or fifteen seconds he was going so fast that the car felt decidedly light on its springs, almost a projectile out of control. Davis did not ease off. He had screwed up. Maybe he had lost the trail altogether. Caution was the last thing he could afford now.

The situation portrayed here is roughly as follows: The viewpoint character in the chapter, Collie Davis, a close friend of hero Brad Smith, has just seen an unconscious Brad in a car speeding away from a motel in the small Colorado mountain town of Lake City. Davis recognizes the driver as a man intent on killing Brad, so Davis must pursue and try to prevent it.

The setting problem: Show rapid character movement during a car chase; remain focused on the desperate, high-speed action of the chase; yet keep the reader physically oriented to the movement through the setting, as well as to the car being pursued and the micro-environment inside Davis's vehicle.

Consider some details in the excerpt:

In the first paragraph, words like "running" and "grabbed" establish the high-speed, hectic quality of the action to follow. The direction, south, is established, along with the make of the other car and the existence of foothills in that direction. The last sentence sets Davis's car in motion for pursuit.

In the second paragraph, Davis gets the briefest glance at bystanders, a necessary detail to prevent the setting from being abstract at this point. Then the sound of the transmission is added for realistic impact on another of the reader's senses. (While most of this sequence stresses sight perceptions, you may notice a continuing attempt to mention other senses such as hearing whenever it seems appropriate.)

The fourth paragraph, beginning "Ahead . . . ," establishes spatial dimension, in this case the distance between the cars. The mention of red tail-lights and gravel gives the reader further concrete physical details — to put him into this setting.

The next paragraph, beginning "The gravel road. . . ," compresses a few moments, but gives additional details ("a series of curves" and "deep canyon") to keep the reader oriented. Dimness and the powdery dust thrown by the other car are again very specific physical orientation markers.

The sixth paragraph, beginning "Sweat stung," moves description of the setting almost inside Davis's brain, focusing on minutiae of the setting in such a way that a transition is then possible all the way out of the physical environment for a moment and inside Davis's thoughts. The remainder of this paragraph and the ones immediately following it are for reader contact with character emotion and thought process.

Later, an attempt is made to get the reader back into closer touch with the broader setting. "Sheer red rock walls" and the "hundred-foot rock face" plunge him, we hope, into physical awareness of the deepening canyon and the worsening condition of its "narrow and washboarded" road. In the next paragraph, the near-collision with a Jeep coming from the opposite direction is designed to put the reader more intensely in contact with the speed and dangerous lack of control involved in the setting. When Davis's car brushes the rock wall, we again become aware of sound.

In the paragraph starting with "Another curve," the reader, does not know it at the time because the viewpoint character doesn't know it, but the small canyon is where the pursued car actually turned off. It is important to orient the reader to this bit of the setting so that a return to it later will not come as a total surprise, but at the same time the view must be fleeting. Note that the viewpoint character looks for dust, does not see any, but wonders if it's too dark to see it even if it were there. Also notice a later sentence — "He had no time for speculation." You will find that inserting such statements into fast-moving descriptions of setting will help greatly in keeping the details brief and vivid; if the viewpoint character has no time to notice details, you can't be tempted to put them into your copy, and the reader is more likely to accept the ongoing rush of brief glimpses and impressions.

A few paragraphs later Davis moves out of the tight canyon setting and into different terrain with details such as "broad meadow area," "sixty acres," and "cultivated field." When he sees lights ahead, he reacts in action, rather than with any fine description, his response to the stimulus being the important thing.

The setting detail of the 4×4 vehicle and the two passengers changes the dramatic situation in a startling way. Details are brief, but the "dark-colored" pickup, "youthful man" and "pretty girl with flaxen hair" give enough evocative detail that the reader can imaginatively fill in the picture.

The remainder of the excerpt deals almost exclusively with a plot twist, returning Davis's, and the reader's, mind to the small box canyon mentioned so briefly but importantly at an earlier stage of the action. As Davis gets back into new violent action, the desperation of his inner setting — his mood — is shown by the startling expletive. The "racket of his tires in the dirt" is a concrete appeal to hearing, and is compared with the sound Davis heard earlier (prior to the portion quoted here) when the abductor's departure first alerted him to the situation. Davis's mood of intense worry and haste is emphasized again for several reasons: to motivate continuation of the chase at dangerous high speed (plot); to continue to characterize Davis's internal feelings (characterization), and to keep the reader mentally prepared for brief, fragmentary description as rapid movement through the story environment resumes (setting). This, it seems to me, is an excellent example of how setting can seldom be considered in isolation from other elements of storytelling; it relates to all of them, and they relate to it.

Although it is not readily apparent in this excerpt, the brief descriptions here set up reader orientation for much of what is to follow. The reader knows the next action will probably be in that box canyon glimpsed earlier; he knows the area is remote, that it is mountain country, that there are few people around, and that darkness has fallen. Thus one part of your story's description of setting can set up reader orientation for what is to follow in a subsequent section.

As a suggestion for further detailed study: You may wish to go back through this excerpt and study the language. For example, you might underline the strong action verbs in red and the sharply specific noun phrases (such as "hundred-foot rock face" and "crunching sound") in green. Count the number of words in many sentences and compute an average sentence length for my description of high-speed movement through setting. Can you draw any conclusions which might help you in your own work?

CONCLUSIONS

If you began this study of setting with the idea that it's a static physical backdrop for your story, this chapter more than any other so far should have opened your eyes. Setting is a dynamic aspect of storytelling. Movement can drastically alter your method of dealing with the setting. How you handle the setting can have a direct effect on your reader's story involvement and sense of plot pace. Setting is not a piece of canvas stuck on the back wall of your story; it is a moving, changing, exciting part of your total story fabric.

Most of the time, when you are showing a quick change of setting or rapid movement through a setting, you will be in a character's viewpoint. It may sound paradoxical when I say it, but the quality of your handling of setting at such times may be as dependent upon what you don't tell as on what you do. You must always remember how limited and fragmentary a viewpoint character's awareness may be . . . how overwhelming may be the sense of haste or confusion . . . how strong may be a few broad-brush impressions which can block out character awareness of any fine detail. Your ability to use highly selective detail may "make or break" your story sequences in which movement is part of the experience.

CHAPTER 13

THE STORY BEHIND YOUR SETTING

AT THE OPENING OF CHAPTER ONE, we defined setting as including historical background and cultural attitudes of a given place and time. Implicit in much of the discussion throughout later chapters has been the assumption that setting can indeed affect characters and their behavior. And we have mentioned history briefly, as well as mood and tone. In this chapter, however, we will look more specifically at the history of a setting and how such history might develop certain prevailing attitudes and feelings in its people, aspects you need to understand if your total story setting is to be convincing.

Now, you might assume that if your story setting is a totally imagined town and local area, knowledge of any real history or cultural attitudes is irrelevant. Nothing could be further from the truth. Except in science fiction, where you may be creating a wholly alien setting, your stories will be set in an identifiable region—the South, say, or eastern seaboard metroplex. So even if your particular town doesn't exist, it has to be convincing to the reader. And it can't be convincing if its history and cultural attitudes are totally at odds with what the reader knows and expects about the actual region.

STORY BACKGROUND

In an earlier chapter I told you about a tour of Oklahoma I did once, and the differences I found between people in the hills and on the plains. That's one example of how regional setting affects attitude. Here's another aspect of the same idea: Can you imagine taking the history and resulting cultural attitudes of a small midwestern town in the United States and trying to create a setting in South America based on the same kind of background and value system? The history of a place, and the outlook that history has created, is as vital and unique a part of story setting as any other factor—and it has to be right.

Your story setting in terms of past time—and the likely general attitudes and feelings the past will engender in its people—has to be correct if your story is to convince the reader. Even if you're writing a science fiction tale of an alien universe, you'll have to know the prevailing attitudes there, and you'll have to invent a history that would credibly create those attitudes. More often than not, however, you'll be dealing with an imaginary place in a very real region of the world, and your imagined microcosm has to be in harmony with the realities of that region.

The importance of history and regional attitude was forcibly brought home to me years ago when I moved from my native Ohio to central Oklahoma. I knew little of Oklahoma history, either long- or short-term, and had a devil of a time understanding how most of the people seemed to feel and think about some things. Only when I began to understand the history of the region could I see where some of the puzzling comments and behavior came from.

Here is what I started out knowing, or *thinking* I knew: Oklahoma was a western state, probably with a lot of cowboys in it. There were Indians there, and oil production. I thought it was prosperous and optimistic, with at least traces of a frontier adventuresomeness.

What I found in general was somewhat different. One of the first things that struck me was racism; there were still segregated lunch counters and restricted sections on public buses, and in the county courthouse I was shocked to find a restroom marked "White Men Only." Jokes based on racial stereotyping were all too common. I didn't see many cowboys, and the Indians I saw were generally acculturated into the lower economic strata of white society, and the victims of a racial bias quieter but even more pervasive than that afflicting blacks. The small towns seemed broken-down and poor, and large sections of the larger cities looked bright and shiny, as if they had been built yesterday. Most surprising of all, perhaps, most of the white people I met in all walks of life seemed angrily defensive about being Oklahomans, and went to great lengths to protest that they were *not* "Okies." The state seemed to have a galloping inferiority complex, and an anger to go with it.

As I listened to the people, thought about my experiences and studied the history a bit, many of these surprising attitudes were explained.

Oklahoma only became a state in 1907, less than half a century before I first moved there. It had seen a continual cycle of booms and busts in the oil business, and was at that time in something of a bust. The small towns looked run-down because I was seeing the original housing in many instances, cheap pioneer construction now falling down after a life-span of almost fifty years and not being replaced because times were presently hard. In the more prosperous cities, some of the buildings that looked like they had been built yesterday *had* been built yesterday; the cities were in the process of rejuvenating themselves after the initial cycle of poor construction and subsequent decay.

As to the social attitudes, nothing was forgiven but a great deal was explained when I began to learn that Oklahoma's land runs were made primarily by poor *southern* whites who had failed other places and went to the new territory for one last desperate try. (Similarly, I understood a later-detected narrow definition of moral acceptability—Oklahoma was still a dry state then, for example—when I read of the early influx of conservative fundamentalist religious groups and their stubborn adherence to their traditional strict, unyielding view of what constituted acceptable behavior.)

A certain air of lawlessness puzzled me at first, and then began to make sense in a way when I saw how decades of prohibition had created a society with laws against liquor—and a flourishing bootlegger business which circumvented the law.

The state's seeming inferiority complex was hardest to understand. Despite everything negative I have mentioned, Oklahoma had a dynamism about it, and clean air, and great freedom and opportunity. Why, then, did everyone seem so angrily defensive?

I learned that John Steinbeck's novel *The Grapes of Wrath* had infuriated and insulted Oklahoma people. I had read the novel as a collegian in Ohio, and thought the Okies portrayed were splendid, brave, noble people, the impression I feel sure Steinbeck intended. But in Oklahoma people were already hurt and oversensitive to imagined slights because of insults from Californians who had not welcomed a flood of homeless "Sooners" who went to that state during the Dust Bowl days. The result was that Oklahomans felt Steinbeck's novel made them all look stupid, dirty, poor and worthless, and they bitterly resented it. This was why they were so defensive and argumentative.

Thus a growing understanding of Oklahoma's history — its land runs, the primary regional background of its people, its youth, its oil booms and busts, and its disastrous part in the Dust Bowl and in Steinbeck's novel — helped me understand prevailing attitudes which otherwise made little sense.

I've told this rather extended personal story merely to make a point: A people will be influenced by their past; a people's general attitudes and moods will influence the world of your story — will be a vital aspect of the setting. If you want a totally convincing setting, you must include history and the feelings and attitudes which come from it.

This does not necessarily mean that you will dump huge blocks of history into your story, or inflict on your reader sociological explanations of character attitudes or behavior. It does mean, however, that some brief explanations may be salted into omniscient passages or casual observations by characters. Such brief comments linking history and attitude will add great verisimilitude to the setting.

GETTING INFORMATION

The best way to get the feel and history of a region, of course, is to visit it and stay long enough to get past whatever tourist veneer may disguise the cultural reality. This may mean an extended stay, or several short ones. If you can afford such an expedition or expeditions, you will be richly rewarded with continuing discoveries that will give your resulting story a vitality and depth it otherwise could not have.

But what if you don't have the time or money to spend days or weeks in your desired regional setting? Then you are reduced to studying books, maps, brochures and possibly video or film about the region.

This is not as much fun, but it's a possible alternative.

There are many "remote" sources available for learning about a region's history and attitudes. As you begin your inquiry into an area, you will likely develop specialized sources of information in a short time. Appendix 1 makes a number of suggestions on developing such sources. You might want to read the few general comments that follow here, then turn to that appendix for a fuller discussion.

Here are some of the possible sources you may check for information about your setting:

1. Your public library. A regional or area history will almost surely be available off the shelf or via interlibrary loan. Consult your librarian if a search of the card file or computer database doesn't suggest a few titles. Remember that most states require a grade school or high school course in local history; such textbooks should be available, and often include the kind of general information you seek. Also, social and cultural historians began contributing valuable state studies during the 1930s, when government projects funded them, and such work continues today. Many states also are the subject of a "roadside history" book, designed so motorists can visit historic sites on the highways, and state or local magazines and special periodicals may be a gold mine of information.

2. Your college library. If you can gain access to a college library, further resources are available to you. More specialized histories of towns, religious groups, etc., may be found here. Don't overlook master's degree theses and doctoral dissertations in such areas as history, sociology, economics and social work.

3. Your state or area historical society. Although these spe-

cialize in your own area, you may be surprised to learn what resources are available through interlibrary loan, on microfilm or microfiche, or on computer disk. Genealogical collections often reside in state libraries of this type, too, and could include basic genealogical references for other areas of the country. Such materials may provide valuable insights into long-standing attitudes and values of a region.

4. Government documents. The United States has studied and analyzed virtually every aspect of life in this country, from agricultural history and practices to sexual behavior and consumer spending. Most cities of moderate size or larger have a telephone number listed for assistance to citizens. You can order documents this way, or procure a guide to many documents available by mail order from Washington.

5. Your local bookstore. Most will have a variety of magazines. There probably will also be a "travel" section, and browsing here may uncover a specific guidebook or history you will find relevant. Be sure to consult the bibliographies in the back of such books for leads to other source publications on the subject.

6. Correspondence. Even small towns these days have Chambers of Commerce and/or tourist bureaus. Don't hesitate to write for historical or cultural information. These offices exist to answer such queries, and some material you may receive free of charge. States have tourist bureaus, too, and industrial development offices designed to provide demographic, attitudinal and all sorts of other information for potential tourists, PR firms or businesses considering relocation. This material may answer many questions for you.

7. Computer sources. If you have a CD-ROM drive, you may already have a source of historical information on compact disk. Whole encyclopedias are available, and many regional histories. There are several fine commercial products for sale on floppy disks, including some which show historic trends, industrial production, religious groupings, financial standings, and many other aspects of an area's attitudinal life. To find out where to obtain any of these materials for your computer, browse through any of the top monthly computer magazines for a wealth of ads for them.

8. Interviews. Don't forget to ask about them among your friends and associates. You may often find that a friend has a

friend who was raised in the area you're interested in. If you get lucky this way, by all means seek out an interview. People usually love to talk about places in their past, and you will get not only information but a real insight into the attitudes of the person you are interviewing; such attitudes may be typical of the region.

USING THE INFORMATION

Having consulted some or all of these possible sources, you'll be ready to take the same steps another writer would take after visiting an area to study its history and attitudes. Essentially, you will ask yourself:

- What in the history of this place is uniquely formative of prevailaing attitudes and feelings?
- What are these prevailing attitudes and feelings?
- How can I present the characteristic area attitudes and their background cause in my story?
- What part does this aspect of setting play in the working out of my story?

If you have done your homework and then honestly decide that there's nothing especially significant in the historical background or regional attitudes of the people as far as your particular story is concerned, well and good. Your effort still will not have been wasted because you can proceed confidently, knowing you aren't likely to make any factual errors such as having a Dallas cabdriver view the world the way one in New York might, or having upstanding citizens openly frequent a roadside bar in a small town in the heart of Southern Baptist country. And more likely you won't just prevent such obvious setting errors. You will also get a keener feel for your entire story world because you will know where the story people have come from — what makes them and their peers "tick."

That's why history and attitude are such an important part of your story setting. Getting them right will not only prevent

mistakes damaging to credibility, it will also help you better plan
the events likely to motivate your characters . . . stir them
up . . . make them feel passion. Your story will be made more
believable at the same time it is drawing additional feeling and
even fervor from the historical background and prevailing senti-
ments of the place.

As an exercise, pause here and consider — on paper — your
own area, the place where you live now. Briefly write down what
you believe the general feeling of the place is in terms of how
people feel about themselves, their setting and their lives, and
what they believe in and care about. Then try to find and write
down some of the historical background for the area that tended
to make people the way they are. Can you identify the attitudes?
Can you define any of them as special to your area? Can you
find the historical or perhaps sociological reason for them?

Such practice on an area that you know well should help
you prepare for checking out an area that's relatively unfamiliar
to you.

If you haven't done so earlier, this would be a fine time to
consult Appendices 1 and 2. These go into further detail and
other aspects of researching a setting and may provide you with
additional ideas for investigation of how a place was, and how
the past influences the present.

CHAPTER 14

SETTING AND STYLE

A THOROUGHLY DETAILED STUDY of writing techniques in presentation of story setting is well beyond the scope of this book. But questions often asked — and errors frequently seen in student manuscripts — suggest that a few observations and bits of advice would not be out of order.

Your style as a fiction writer may have already developed over time, or may just be in the process of developing. In either case, it is likely that you will write best if you force yourself never to try to be "fancy" or "inspiring" or anything of that kind in developing your writing style. The best style usually is no visible style at all — prose that is crisp, clean, clear and transparent: a pane of glass through which your reader experiences the story directly, without ever being aware of the words. Far too much "stylish" writing is really affected writing, and while there may be a few readers out there who would appreciate such stuff, the fact is that your story has been lost the first moment a reader starts noticing your style rather than following the story's events.

The bottom line: In handling setting, as in all other parts of your fiction writing, strive for directness and simplicity. Such writing is the most graceful and effective of all.

SOME TRUTHS

It is also a fact that handling setting often involves description of some kind, and it is in description that writers most often fall prey to the temptation to write "pretty" or "poetic" passages. Therefore, it's vital in talking about setting to begin any discussion of verbal technique with truths which have been stated before, and will always be true:

- Write simply and directly, and don't get fancy.
- Never use a big word when a small one will do.
- Write short sentences. Write short paragraphs.
- Never strain for an effect, and never try to be poetic.
- Remember that clarity is your bedrock stylistic goal.

These rules might all be summarized briefly: When in doubt, take it out. If you are not absolutely certain that a turn of phrase is accomplishing the desired effect—and the story can go on without it—then don't put the phrasing in at all, or if it's in your draft, delete it on rewrite. Few things will disgust a busy editor—or more quickly brand you an amateur—than overwriting.

You know what that is: a seemingly endless round-and-round the verbal rosebush, trying to pile more and more adjectives on something in the setting so it will be "clearer." Or tacking a batch of weak adverbs onto a verb that was wobbly to begin with, in an attempt to make the verb more forceful.

Here is an example:

A warmly cheerful and welcoming fire was burning brightly inside the large, dark, sinister cavern, while slow-moving shadows could be discerned on the high, pale walls of rock.

What's wrong with this? Just about everything! Consider: The writer wants to show the setting in a vivid way, but the approach is all wrong. Instead of seeking out strong basic words, the writer stuck on all sorts of qualifying adjectives and adverbs ("warmly cheerful," "welcoming," "large, dark, sinister," etc.) instead of trying to be simple and direct. You may come up with a better rewrite, but here is one possibility:

A campfire blazed inside the great cave. Shadows danced on the high rock walls.

You may quarrel with use of the verb "blazed," and wish to substitute something like "burned brightly." You may argue, too, that "great cave" is not sufficiently evocative. Is "danced" a clichè? Perhaps you can come up with better wording.

Regardless of such quibbles, I think you will agree that the second effort is improved by slashing some of the weak adjectives and adverbs and attempting to find stronger nouns and verbs that don't require such crutches. A good, specific noun will seldom need many adjectives to modify it. A strong action verb will seldom require the help of an adverb. Therefore, it's obvious that you can, as one editor advised me, "look for adjectives and adverbs, and kill them!" or you can possibly avoid the temptation to use them in the first place by seeking out strong specific nouns and strong action verbs.

A further observation about these examples may be in order. You may have noticed that in the original a fire "was burning," while in the suggested revision a "fire blazed." If we had chosen to substitute "burned" for "blazed," the basic meaning would have been the same, but for better style: Always use the simple past tense if you can in describing things. Thus you will not write, "Rain was falling . . . ," but instead will teach yourself to write, "Rain fell. . . . " You will not write, "Evening was nearing . . . ," but instead, "Evening neared. . . . " (or perhaps better: "Darkness neared," darkness being more specific than evening).

Also, avoid the pa.sive voice. You will *not* say things like, "The night was made worse when the rain began . . . ," but instead will say something closer to "The night worsened when the rain began." The use of compound verb forms and weak passives in description is often tempting, but almost always bad. Compound verb forms are not the most direct way to get the job done, and passives are weak; description always walks on the dangerous edge of being too slow and dramatically weak anyway, so don't make the risk greater than it already is.

When this was first pointed out to me years ago, I protested (briefly) that it's not quite the same thing to say "a fire burned" and "a fire was burning." Being a refugee from an English department, I argued that "fire burned" implied that the fire had burned in the past and was now over, while "fire was burning" connoted that it was still burning in the story present. "Pick nits all you want," my writing coach replied. "Try it my way and you'll never go back." He was right. Once I habitually used the simple past tense, all my descriptions of setting seemed magically more vibrant.

Look for weak verb forms, pallid nouns, crutch adjectives and limping adverbs in your own copy. If you find them, fix them!

THE PURPLE PATCH

Another aspect of straightforward descriptive writing style is the ability to avoid poetic flights of fancy and unnecessary big words. You have perhaps encountered such a flight in someone else's copy—surely not your own!—and know why composition teachers call such an effusion a "purple patch."

Here's an example of a purple patch:

> Rising, chanting, ever-changing, in a never-ending cacophony of ululation, the zephyr-breath of the mighty planet's ceaseless, restless celestial motion, driven alike by the massive depth of ocean and rising of a miniscule breeze from the golden, petal-like wings of a gossamer butterfly, pressed insistent lips against the diaphanous opacity of the chill pane.

Wow. Gorgeous, huh?—until you stop and figure out what the writer was trying to say, which was: Cold wind blew against the frosty window.

It's been said before, but the point is worth making again. Such outrages against writing style most often occur when the writer has "stopped to describe." Therefore, one good way to avoid the temptation to write purple patches is to seldom stop your storytelling to describe. If you are intent on keeping your setting descriptions brief and maintaining focus on the characters and the plot inside the setting, then few chances to write a purple patch will arise.

Instead of burying yourself, your story and your reader under a trash-pile of verbiage, look for the *feel* of a place or time, and then seek out concrete details to evoke that feeling. As mentioned in chapter eleven and elsewhere, the feeling might be one of joyfulness or isolation or loneliness. Identify it, then ask yourself what specific concrete details will evoke the feeling in as few words as possible. You can count on your reader to fill in the details if you give him precisely the right clues on which to build.

That's why, for example, I risked using the word "blazed" in an example earlier in this chapter, and why I contented myself with calling the site a "great cave." I am not sure precisely what the word "blazed" will conjure in the reader's mind, but I feel sure it will have something to do with bright, leaping flames, great heat and vigor. Exactly what picture "blazed" will give the reader beyond that, I don't know. But I don't care; his own imagining will be better for him than any further avalanche of details I might try to foist upon him. Similarly, I count on "great cave" evoking in his mind his own mind-picture of the feeling of greatness and cave-ness. Will it be Carlsbad, or an earthen hole he played in as a child? I don't care; I would rather he work from my feeling-evoking words, and draw his own feeling-packed mind-picture, than try to study through some laborious description of mine.

Readers love to draw setting pictures in their own imagination. They will, provided you give them the right feel for the place, and the few precise words designed to evoke that feeling.

How do you find those few precise words? You do so by seeking out specific, concrete details in the setting which will produce the desired evocation. As an example, suppose you first laboriously wrote something unacceptable like the following:

> It was a cold and bitter night. Phillip felt chilled, and when the sleet began, he felt colder. Dark clouds rolled in. The mercury fell. Icy wind began to blow. Walking home alone, Phillip was buffeted by the wind.

This is not too bad. Short words, short sentences, little strained "poetry." But it lacks feeling-focus. What are we trying to evoke here? Cold? Wind? Loneliness? Darkness? A short segment like this can't evoke everything at once, and maybe the story situation dictates brevity, as it often does.

But perhaps we can improve things. Let's decide that what we want to evoke in the reader concerning this bit of setting is a feeling of *chill and loneliness*. Having decided this, we can have a stab at revision something like this:

> Alone, Phillip trudged home. Violent wind battered him, driving pinprick sleet into his face.

Possibly this brief segment will get the job done for us. Suppose, on the other hand, we wish to use the same general setting details to evoke a different mood in the reader, one of *longing for home*. In such a case we might produce a segment like this:

> Hurrying against the strong wind, Phillip squinted through the darkness for the first sight of his cabin window. It would be good to get home to the warmth of his stove and the stout protection of the cabin's log walls.

In both of the above examples, notice that indentification of desired feeling provides the framework inside which a brief and focused description can be written.

ADDING CONTRAST

Another helpful gambit you can use in seeking brevity and evocative accuracy is the use of contrast. On its simplest level, what we are talking about here is how a dark cloud will look darker against an otherwise bright sky, or how much more dreary an old building will look if you stand it beside a fine, fresh new one for the sake of the contrast. It always helps the vividness and evocativeness of your writing if you can pinpoint a sharp contrast: barren black tree branches seen against a snow-colored wintry sky, for example, or a scream piercing the total silence of a summer afternoon in the country, or the glitter of diamonds on a black velvet cloth.

The trick here is to identify the object you wish to emphasize, figure out what specific sensuous characteristic of that object should be stressed, and then find the right object to stand it beside, or background to display it against, for the maximum contrast.

In sight contrasts, look for dark against light, smooth against rough, color against pallor, smallness against vastness, or brightness against dullness. In sound contrasts, look for loudness against silence, pleasing sound against discordance, harshness against smoothness. Ask yourself: "What specific aspect of the setting do I want to make vivid?" Then: "What can I place beside it to make it stand out even more?"

Suppose you want to show how loudly that truck is idling at the corner traffic light? First make sure no other cars are on the street when you show it, and make the scene a lazy afternoon or evening, very, very quiet otherwise. Then the truck's idling will be not only loud, but deafening. Or perhaps you would like to emphasize how small a house is, and how isolated; take it out of that tight little woods and stand it alone on a vast and windy hilltop, surrounded by a thousand acres of empty prairie. (Does this mean, incidentally, that you will sometimes tinker with minor aspects of your setting simply to make things more vivid? Of course.)

LEARNING TO OBSERVE

First-hand observation will help you clarify some of these stylistic techniques for yourself once you are aware of them. I encourage you to look at parts of the real setting-world around you, and think about how you would portray them. Look at the tree in your yard or nearby park — *really* look at it, for a change. How could you place that in your story setting and make it real and vibrant for your reader? Really look at that city bus as it approaches your stop. How could you put that bus into your story and make it practically leap off the page for your reader, so that it becomes a tremendously vital and real part of the setting?

Make notes as you hone your observation-description skills, write practice paragraphs. Make sure they're not long, static paragraphs, but brief, evocative ones, centered on a mood. If you don't like a description you've produced, go back and re-write it using stronger verbs and more specific nouns, or using a different feeling as the focus point, or putting something different into the setting for useful contrast.

Such accurate observation, creative thought and careful verbal revision will soon result in surer and more skillful use of all the other techniques we have covered in this book. In handling setting, the use of precise language is mandatory, because your words are the conveyance of everything you know and your reader needs to know. Nothing else will work unless your verbal arsenal is on target.

So important is verbal technique in setting, as a matter of fact, that we cannot leave the subject with the discussion given in this chapter. In chapter fifteen we will pursue the subject a bit more, with a number of highly specific exercises and work suggestions.

CHAPTER 15

EXERCISES TO SHARPEN YOUR SETTINGS

BE WARNED IN ADVANCE: This chapter is designed to make you practice some of the things you've learned in earlier chapters. None of it will be especially difficult for you now, but doing the suggested exercises correctly will require some investment of time as well as effort—and there's even a requirement for that aspect of fiction-writing which all amateurs dread and all selling professionals do: rewriting.

FACTUAL DATA IN A SETTING

Let's suppose you have the following information in your notebook after visiting a small town and making observations and then doing other factual research at the library.

The name of the town is Elk City, and it's in the western part of Montana. In a valley in the Sapphire Mountains. Population is 3,000. County Seat of Morgan County. Courthouse on town square downtown, old brick building, two stories, with a dome. City hall, a small stucco structure, is nearby on Main Street. The town is quiet, but sometimes trucks going by on the nearby highway make a big racket. A bell in the tower at the First Presbyterian Church tolls the hour. Elk City has a city manager and city commission, five commissioners elected at large. Small police department and fire department, antiquated equipment. Sheriff's department in the basement of the courthouse is old and grungy. Sheriff has four deputies. It's cold in Elk City in the winters, cool in the summers. The surrounding mountains are tall, jagged and beautiful. No other town of any size nearby — people drive ninety miles to Missoula for major shopping expeditions. It's an easygoing place with a population on the elderly side, and hunters and fishermen visit a lot. Nothing much ever seems to happen. Some of the side streets are dirt only, and in the summers they're dusty. An old, open-pit copper quarry nearby, now abandoned, has water in it which sometimes smells bad on the hottest summer days. During the long, snowy winters, of course, this is no problem. It was a pleasant summer day, seventy degrees, when you visited last July 7 and 8.

Elk City was founded by a man named John Jergens in the 1880s. He found a small vein of silver nearby, and for a few years the town boomed with silver mining. When the silver played out in the 1890s, copper was discovered and the big quarry, now an abandoned pit, provided steady work and income for about a hundred families. As copper production decreased, the town declined steadily, and by the 1920s it was about the size it is today. Old-timers still yearn for the good old days. Every year they have a Frontier Days celebration on September 1. Parade, community picnic, band performance in old Jergens City Park. People are proud of sticking it out in Elk City, and think one day the town will come back. They've been saying that for more than fifty years now.

The town's five churches provide the center of social activity. There's also a Moose Lodge. People often gather for coffee at the Chicken Shack Cafe on Main Street or the Big Sky Motel's coffee shop on the edge of town, on Highway 16. The local paper, a weekly, is called *The Bugle*.

Elk City used to be on a railroad passenger line, but that's long since closed. The old rock station is falling down. Once a day, about 4 P.M., a Montana Rail Link freight train pulls through on its way north, not stopping. The diesel engine usually blows its whistle at the Main Street crossing and farther north, at Bryson Road. The train comes back through, headed south, about midnight, and blows its horn again. It's a mournful sound at night.

Movie theater, the Ritz is closed permanently and boarded up. Major street names other than Main, which runs east-west: High Street, Bluff Street, Sapphire Ave., Higgins Street, Selby Ave. The grade and high schools are on Selby. Sometimes in the winter, deer and even elk wander down out of the aspens and lodgepole pines on the mountainsides and walk right down Main Street. There are black bear nearby, too, and sometimes a mountain lion is reported. Area ranchers and sheepmen are bitter about federal and state laws protecting wolves and the occasional mountain lion.

Study the above information, then duplicate Nancy Berland's Setting Research Form (Appendix 2), and fill in a copy of the form from the facts given.

After doing this work, think about the kind of characters and plots that might be used in this general setting. For example, you might write about members of the local political scene, suddenly thrust into a crisis when it is discovered that pollution from the old copper mine has poisoned all local sources of water. Or you might put a romance in this setting, with the conflict stemming from the fact that the heroine is a native who loves the place, and her lover is a visitor intent on buying up property and changing everything by turning it into a gaudy gambling oasis.

Think a bit, too, about some of the stories that might not work well, or at all, in this setting: a grim, police-method murder investigation might never work because the town's law enforcement is small and primitive; a plot involving members of a large juvenile gang would probably be out of the question because the town does not have large numbers of juveniles on the loose, and no stated crime problem. (I suggest that you think of these "impossibles" briefly just to further clarify your understanding of how setting enables — or precludes — certain kinds of stories.)

Having done all this work, take another step. Select the bare bones of a plot and a cast of your own that you believe might work in this setting. Then, on another sheet of paper or two, make a preliminary list of other general aspects of the setting which you believe you would have to learn about if you were actually going to write this imagined book. This list might include "ethnic makeup of population," "voting record in general elections," or even something like "worst drouth in area history." This will be *your* list, growing out of your ideas about what your story plot should be in the given setting.

Having done this, if you can hone your list into one or more specific questions—about anything at all that you think you might need to know—be sure to do so, making them as detailed and lengthy as possible. Then ponder a bit where you might get all this additional information if you were really getting ready to write the book.

Finally, write a 300-word description of the setting as you would use it in terms of mood and viewpoint. If you were planning a romance, for example, your selection of sensory details might be generally sunny, summery, ruggedly inviting. And your selection of factual material would tend to emphasize the positive and upbeat. If you were planning a gothic terror story, on the other hand, you would be shooting for quite a different tone, and your selected details probably would tend more toward the dark, the isolated and the bizarre.

If you worked conscientiously on this assignment, you went through the essential process for checking out, analyzing, and using information in order to present a credible and effective story setting. In addition, although no stress was placed on the fact at the time, you also produced a lengthy piece of writing about setting.

Going through the process in this way is its own reward; nothing teaches better than practice. To assist you further, however, here is a suggested list of questions which might help you analyze how well you did on the job.

- What viewpoint did you select to describe this setting? Why?
- What mood did you select? Does the mood grow directly out of your perception of the given facts about the setting,

from your idea about a plot problem to put in that setting, from your conception of the kind of character you would use as the viewpoint in such a setting, or on some other factor?

- Did you find or imaginatively add some salient setting aspect which might recur in your story as a central point of focus or symbol? What is it? Why did you choose it?
- What single, dominant impression about this setting did you identify as a centralizing point for your treatment of it?
- Did you identify anything in the history of the setting which would contribute to a prevailing cultural attitude which might be useful in your story?
- What kind of central character would work best for you in this setting?
- Did you introduce that character in your 300 words? If not, should you have done so?
- Was your description of setting static, a "stop-action" picture, or was there movement of some kind? Does consideration of this question suggest possible revision to you?
- Could this setting unify an otherwise fragmentary plot? How?
- Could this setting possibly become virtually a character itself?
- What contrasts if any did you use in describing this setting?
- Did you avoid weak passives in your writing?
- Did you use strong action verbs and specific nouns?
- Do you find a lot of adjectives and adverbs that ought to be "killed?"
- Do you habitually do this much work on setting for your stories?

In thinking back over previous chapters, you may come up with other self-check questions you want to ask. My list is, as stated, only suggestive. We learn our writing craft from trial and error, from failure, from praise, from teachers, from studying other writers, and from analyzing our own work in a critical (but not negative) manner. It's not enough to read about technique.

Practice—and thoughtful self-analysis—are mandatory if you are to grow in the craft.

For these reasons, it's never wise to rush through an assignment like the one above. Even if some of the work seems unnecessary, you never know where it might lead you. Work that may seem like drudgery at times may provide an insight that will vastly improve your fiction.

OBSERVATION IN THE FIELD

Find a local site that's outside your usual haunts. This may be a park you've never visited, a courtroom downtown, a cafe down the road somewhere, or a church or school you've noticed but never visited. Taking a notebook (and small recorder, if you have one), go to that unfamiliar place and spend at least an hour. Observe details. Make notes. Record sounds if possible. Try to identify the feel of the place. If there are people there, note how they look, how they dress, how they talk, their ages, their general demeanor, what they talk about, how they seem to feel, and what they are doing. Think about using this place in a setting.

Upon returning home—and within twenty-four hours while your memory is fresh—write a 300-word description of this site as if you planned to use it as the setting for a story.

After completing the setting description, use the questions listed for the first exercise to analyze this story setting.

Additionally, this exercise provides a good self-analysis of your writing style in handling setting material. Consider the following questions, and others like them:

• How many different senses are represented in your writing? (To facilitate analysis, you may wish to go through your copy and underline sight impressions in red, let's say, sounds in blue, odors in green, and so on.) Does one sense predominate? Did you overlook something that you might have usefully said about the setting if you had remembered another sense?

• How many adverbs and adjectives do you find? Can you kill any?

- Look for weak passive constructions. Repair them.
- Can you strengthen any verbs? Make any nouns more specific and concrete?
- Does your writing here evoke a specific feeling or mood in the reader? (Did you think about that while writing?)
- How many words of three or more syllables do you find? There shouldn't be many — big words usually hint at obscurity, and you want clarity.
- Write down what conclusions you can draw about your own writing tendencies at this point. For example, do you tend to use weak passives? Do you tend to adopt an omniscient viewpoint without thinking about it? Do you enrich your copy with multiple sense impressions, or do you tend to concentrate only on sight, for example?

Finally, rewrite the segment you prepared for this exercise. Improve it, knowing what you now see more clearly following your self-analysis.

LEARNING FROM A WRITER YOU LIKE

Seek to become a more consciously aware critic at the same time you read for pleasure or relaxation.

For this assignment, study a few pages of a story by a writer you admire. Find a section in the work which clearly deals with story setting. Mark up this copy — photocopy pages from the magazine or book, and work from the copies, if you can't bear to mark on the original.

Try to note, look for, question, and mark as many aspects as possible of this writer's handling of setting. Marginally annotate mood. Underline strong verbs.

Repeat the process outlined in the first two exercises. Again, try to write down some conclusions, even if the work seems only to verify things you knew before. Noting them again will deepen your understanding and retention of principles.

LEARNING FROM YOUR OWN COPY

Go back into your own story files and pull out a chapter or section dealing with setting. Go through the entire process of analysis outlined on earlier pages of this chapter.

Then, rigorously analyze any mistakes or slips you may have uncovered and ask yourself how you would handle this setting problem differently today. Are there gaps in your factual base? Does the setting lack feeling? Is the prose "purple" at times?

Rewrite the segment if you are now dissatisfied with it — even if it's part of something you previously sold. (The day you can't improve is the day you stop having a future as a writer.)

KNOWING YOUR OWN TENDENCIES

With regard to most of the work done for this chapter, you should seriously consider a fact mentioned fleetingly at an earlier point. That is: In going through the exercises, you may have exhibited previously unexamined creative tendencies of your own in dealing with setting. Having done this work and thought about it, you can perhaps see yourself more clearly. Did you let yourself get impatient? (I always do, and have to struggle against this known tendency in myself.) In the sample of your earlier work that you looked at, did you perhaps discover a previously unnoticed tendency toward purple prose or weak passive constructions in your writing style when describing setting? Did you discover that you always tend to adopt the same kind of story viewpoint in dealing with setting, and had never realized before that you did this?

Some of your ingrained creative tendencies are probably excellent. Others may be counterproductive or even destructive. Study yourself as well as others, and try to see your own work in a clearer, more objective light.

Such self-analysis of your tendencies as a writer not only

makes you more aware of what kind of writer you are at the moment, it may reveal to you new directions . . . new tasks to be undertaken . . . new possibilities for growth. In this way, the truth will truly set you free to become a far better writer than you ever imagined you might be.

CHAPTER 16

A PROGRAM FOR FURTHER STUDY AND GROWTH

IF WE HAVE ACCOMPLISHED anything in this study, I hope it has made you more aware of the importance of your fiction settings, and how setting interacts with so many other story factors. Setting, as you now see clearly, is far more than a painted physical backdrop behind the stage of your story's action; its effects ripple into all other aspects of your storytelling.

The observations and brief assignments included in this book were designed to increase both your awareness and technical agility in working with setting. You may already feel better qualified than ever before to handle setting problems. But work in this area, like most aspects of writing fiction, is never entirely done. All of us must continue to strive to sharpen our perceptions, our skills, and our ability to observe our own work as well as that of others.

Having finished this book, you are now just at the beginning of continuing work. How you proceed from this point will depend on many factors, including available time, the kind of fiction you want to write, and your discovered strengths and weaknesses. However you work to grow from this point forward, there are a few things you can do, and a few questions you can keep in mind, that will provide focus for the days ahead.

KEEPING TRACK

First and foremost, you need to develop a repository for your ongoing study of setting. You may already have one, in the form of a daily journal or one or more notebooks in which you make notations about the writing craft. Or perhaps you have a series of file folders where you collect notes, newspaper and magazine pieces or photos that might be useful one day in depicting a setting. If you have such a system for regularly making notes or keeping research material, I urge you to expand your use of it in ways to be mentioned shortly. If you do not have a journal or any kind of file for observations and general writing data, then consider starting one immediately.

I happen to have three such information repositories. One is a simple spiral-bound notebook of the kind students use. The second is a modest collection of file folders in a metal cabinet. The third is a small bookcase whose shelves are packed with maps, travel brochures, books, photographs and a few travel tapes (both audio and video), most of which I made myself.

In the notebook journal I regularly record information on my sales and royalties, as well as ideas for future projects and personal observations about possible characters, plots and settings. This is the place where I transfer short setting notes that I might have jotted down during a trip somewhere, for example.

I always carry some sort of smaller and easily portable notebook on trips, even short ones to places where I have been before. A company called Stationers, Inc., in Richmond, Virginia, makes a "Reporter's Note Book" that I favor; it's spiral-bound, with vertical flip-over, lined pages, and its dimensions are eight inches tall by four inches wide, a size that I can slip into an inside coat pocket, or a female writer might easily carry inside a normal-size purse. My setting notes might include a page or two of specific description or something as brief as a note made recently which read in full: "Ample late-summer rainfall makes aspens turn more red in the fall?" When I return from a trip somewhere, as already stated, I transfer these notes, often fragmentary, to the pages of the journal and discard the original notebook pages.

The same procedure serves well if you are making a more carefully planned trip to "scope out" an actual setting. In such cases, however, a still camera, a video camera if you have one, and a small cassette recorder will also come in handy. As discussed in Appendix 1, the recorder and camera may be invaluable during interviews. But also, you can sometimes gain great insight into the sounds of a place by simply recording several minutes of general background noise, then replaying it later.

Why is this so? While on the site and engrossed primarily in what you can see, you may overlook normal sounds that are vital to the setting, such things as the sound of traffic, a distant train, foghorns in the night, perhaps the barking of dogs. When you play back such a random audiotape later, you often hear things you missed at the time because you were distracted by something else entirely.

On any field trip, you should look for the local tourist information office or chamber of commerce, and see what brochures and maps may be free for the taking. These can go into one of your file folders or on a bookshelf.

When you know you have repositories for setting information, that very fact can motivate you to be more alert to gathering new data, whether you plan to use it immediately or not. If you are actively researching for a known project, you might use a variation of the Nancy Berland setting form found in Appendix 2. Having worked with a form like this a few times, however, you will find that asking some of its questions becomes second nature to you, but later transfer of data to a file copy of such a form puts information into a more-or-less standard format, making it easier to file, quicker to find later, and simpler to use even long after the observations have been made.

What form your own setting repository will take is up to you. These few observations are meant to stimulate you to come up with your own system. You may elect to use 5×7 file cards, or a directory on your computer's hard disk. Format is not as important as having a place, and feeding it information on a regular, sustained basis. The work will pay dividends for immediate projects and future ones that you haven't even imagined yet. It will also keep you focussed on aspects of setting vital to your stories.

Several chapters in this book have suggested aspects and uses of setting that should alert you to the kinds of information you should record. The Nancy Berland form is another fine guide. If at first you worry that you might forget crucial questions to ask when you are researching a setting, let me provide you with a short list to keep in mind as a starting point:

- What does this place feel like to you?
- What specific aspects of the setting make you feel that way?
- What do you know of the history of the place?
- What do you know about identifiable local attitudes?
- What is the dominant source of light here? How bright is it? What is its color? How does it contribute to the feeling of the place?
- What is the sense of space here? Vast? Cramped? Open? Closed?
- What three characteristic sounds can you identify?
- Is your sense of smell important in this setting?
- Is there a central landmark or possible setting symbol?
- What dramatic plot possiblities do you see here?
- What kind of character would you most likely put in this setting?
- How would you describe this place from an omniscient vantage point? From the viewpoint of a character?

Of course this is only a suggestive list, the kind I happen to carry around in my own mind. Your genre, interests and tendencies may lead to the development of different questions. The point is that any general list of questions helps focus your efforts in gathering new setting information, and having a general focus also helps you organize whatever filing system you choose to set up for such information.

CONCLUSION

Learning the value of setting is just the beginning of your quest for excellence in storytelling. As you hone your skills and develop your setting-presentation techniques, you will build a database and sharpen your powers of research and observation through field trips and careful recording of the things you find.

It's a lifelong process, learning to be more sensitive to the places and people around you, but it's a process that is not only rewarding in terms of your craft, but richly rewarding, too, in the way it expands your personal horizons and makes you ever more keenly aware of this wonderful world we all share.

Good luck to you!

APPENDIX 1

RESEARCH RESOURCES AND TECHNIQUES

Reference is made throughout the text to various research resources and methods for gathering information. As a central reference point, this appendix will recapitulate most of that information as well as offer additional suggestions.

For one setting project, a single source may furnish almost all the information that's needed. For another, you may need to try several research avenues in order to come up with sufficient data to build a credible setting in your story. Here we'll consider each primary research source in its own right, touching upon the special value of each and upon specialized techniques, if any, involved in mining that source.

On-site visits almost always represent the most desirable way to get information about an area to be used as part of a story setting. Nothing quite beats being there and experiencing the place yourself. There is a freshness and immediacy to the experience that no other kind of research can quite duplicate.

The moral: If you can possibly visit an actual site, whether you plan to use the site itself or one similar to it, by all means do so.

You should try to do some homework about such a site before you visit. Studying a map, glancing through a local history, or finding something about the place in a travel guide may give you a fine running start when you get there in person. It helps amazingly to know things like which way Main Street runs or where the local college is, for example. If you know a little about the local history and problems, so much the better. The more you know ahead of time, the less time you are likely to waste getting oriented once you arrive. On most visits, time is of the essence and you simply can't afford to use half of it trying to figure out where you should go or what questions you should ask.

Don't hesitate to write ahead to possible local sources, including the chamber of commerce, the visitors' bureau if there is one, the local newspaper, and even the mayor or city manager. State when you plan to be in town, what your propject is, and the general kind of information you're seeking. Most local sources will be flattered by your interest and eager to help. It may even be possible to start your visit by interviewing one or more local experts. (See below for more on interviewing.)

When you arrive on the scene, you should be prepared with a collection of notebooks and pens or pencils, an audiotape recorder, and a videotape recorder if you have one. Plan to make notes on everything, and record as much as you can.

Finally, try to avoid the natural tendency many of us have to be shy in a new situation and to worry about bothering people, although common courtesy, of course, is always desirable. And while it is possible to make a nuisance of yourself, you will usually find local people more than happy to answer questions and give assistance. It's flattering to be told your visitor is a writer interested in using your town, area, neighborhood or business as a story setting; most people will go out of their way to be helpful in such circumstances.

Interviews are the major sources of information during on-site visits or other data-gathering expeditions. Interviewing is a minor art. I've been interviewed by people who made it a pleasurable and interesting experience, and by others whose awkwardness and lack of preparation made the interview from my standpoint both boring and irritating. You can make your interviews as much fun for your subject as they are informative for you if you will follow three basic principles: prepare ahead of time; have plans for the meeting; be professional.

Preparation for an interview is always possible to some degree, with perhaps the exception of a rare occasion when you happen to run into a source person unexpectedly and conduct an interview on the spot. But such spontaneous interviews are rare. Usually, whether you're on a field trip or meeting a local expert, you know about the interview well ahead of time.

What kind of preparations are required? They vary, but you should at least have some idea about who your source is — her name (and how to spell and pronounce it!), her job title or area of expertise, and other such fundamental biographical information. This information may be sketchy if you have written for an appointment, for example, and were unable to question anyone else about your subject's personal data. But get what you can. (As an interviewee, I have found that there are few things less likely to inspire confidence and a desire to be helpful than having an interviewer say something like, "Good morning, Mr. Brickman!" And yes, it has happened to me.)

In addition to knowing what you can about your interviewee, you should also research whatever is available about the field or area you plan to ask about. If you'll be talking to someone about local history, for example, you should have at least a smattering of information from books or brochures so that you are not totally ignorant about the subject. This not only saves time during the interview, but makes your interviewee feel more relaxed and confident in you because of your obvious preparation. (It also helps your confidence in dealing with a stranger and asking questions which may include some that might sound impertinent.)

If you are seeking other kinds of setting information — if you are planning to ask a business executive about how his company works, as a takeoff point for building a similar story setting, for example — then it helps if you go in with some idea of what the source's area of expertise is. This doesn't mean you have to understand quasar theory to interview an astronomer, but a quick trip to the library or the encyclopedia would give you some idea about quasars before you meet her, and any background is better than none.

In addition to preparation before the interview, you should also have other plans for the meeting. Obviously you should also have a list of factual setting or story-background questions written out in advance to guide you through your talk. You

might also have a list of fundamental biographical facts you want
to verify at some point—job title, background, telephone number where your subject might be reached, etc.

It may be that the interview will go splendidly, and quickly
become a mutually enjoyable chat. That can happen when
you're well prepared. But there will be other times when your
interviewee is tense or impatient—or you are—and things do
not go well. Having the list of prepared questions is helpful as
a "fallback position" in such cases; you always have them to run
through, and won't likely find yourself stuck in an uncomfortable silence while you wonder frantically what you should say.

All this, of course, is part of how you should conduct yourself before and during the interview. You should be professional.

What does that mean? In addition to preparation ahead of
time and having your plans for the interview written down and
in mind, it also means having a specific time and place set for the
interview, being there on time, and looking presentable. Don't
overdress. But don't go looking like you just crawled out of a
mineshaft, either.

Once the interview begins, strive to be cool and confident.
You needn't apologize for being there. Remember that it's your
interview, and you can quietly control the situation.

It may be intimidating to walk into an interview with a revered local historian, for example, or with a famous doctor. The
impulse may be to start apologizing for being so uninformed in
the expert's field. But what you have to remember is that your
subject may be an expert in her field, but you are the expert in
yours. I have often told a subject something like, "I don't know
a lot about quasars, but I'm a professional in my field just as you
are in yours. If we work together, we can make it possible for
laymen to get a much better appreciation for all this."

This is not an egotistical attitude, but simply a realistic one.
You will be far superior to most of your interviewees in communication skills. They respect that, if your attitude and demeanor
demonstrate that you are.

A professional attitude and conduct during an interview,
in other words, means that you will not be apologetic or syco-

phantic. You will be cool and friendly, as relaxed as you can be, properly respectful, and organized. You will ask your questions, get your information, say thank you kindly, and use no more of the subject's valuable time than necessary.

Should you ask to tape an interview? Yes. But some sources will say no, or be so nervous about the machine that they watch it instead of you, and never get into the interview. In such situations, the recorder has to be shut off and put back in your attaché case. In any event, the recorder is no substitute for your notebook; it is at best a fall-back device used to clarify some point in your notes, or double-check the accuracy of a quote you've written down. You can't present a sound recording in your story; you have to transcribe information and recast it for story use. Notes taken at the time will show your instant reading of what's most important about the things being said. They will have none of the "hums" and "hahs" and background noise of the tape recording.

It is not necessary to know shorthand or speed writing to take good interview notes. You will be looking for information and can condense your notes. Often you will quickly jot down fragmentary facts, which are all you need for your setting.

Finally, when the interview is over—when you have the needed information or your allotted time is up—close the session promptly, express gratitude, and be on your way. It always helps to close with the suggestion that a later question might arise, and a request for permission to call or write back if such occurs.

Library sources are not as dynamic as an interview, but often are extremely vital. Some of these are mentioned in various parts of the main text, but the most common ones should be mentioned here.

Whenever you visit the library, it goes without saying that you should be armed with notebooks and a couple of ballpoint pens or pencils. Many materials can't be checked out, and you will have to make notes in the library's reading area.

Much of the following will be old hat to you if you are a regular user of your local public library, but if you haven't visited the library very often, or are possibly intimidated by it, then it's probably time to get reacquainted.

Libraries of medium size or larger have long since been computerized. For a person unfamiliar with such systems, walking into the lobby and being confronted by video display terminals rather than the old, familiar card catalogs, can be off-putting. But cards and computers work similarly, usually being cross-indexed by subject matter, titles and authors' names. A few minutes' work with either system will set you at ease. And librarians usually are most eager to be of assistance.

Travel guides, atlases and local or regional histories can be found in even smaller libraries. These are always worth checking into. You may find specialized materials such as genealogical collections which sometimes contain rare old photographs. (Some libraries have collections of old photos that can give you priceless insights into an area's history.) Encyclopedias may provide good general information and old newspaper files may be most helpful. Larger libraries will contain extensive microfilm collections of many older archives and collections. The Draper collection, for example, is a massive collection of documents and written interviews pertaining to the early history of Ohio, Michigan, Wisconsin and Indiana; filling hundreds of rolls of microfilm, its home is at the University of Wisconsin in Madison, Wisconsin. But copies are available in numerous other libraries. Your librarian may be the easiest source for information about such materials.

Don't overlook the periodicals room in your library; it may contain local or regional magazines with just the information you want. There will also probably be a subject cross-index to more recent magazines if it's a larger library, and this might quickly send you to a magazine article that you did not know about.

When checking any library source, of course, carefully study the footnotes and bibliographies; these can often lead you to the titles of other source materials. And if some of these are not available locally, ask about getting them through an interlibrary loan.

If you check a book or periodical out of the library, remember that it is still incumbent upon you to make notes on information you may wish to use in constructing your story setting. Taking a book to the local copy shop and duplicating many pages is in violation of federal copyright law, and even if you find an unscrupulous copy shop that will do it for you, you should resist the temptation. Writers, of all people, should be keenly aware that unauthorized copying of printed material is not only illegal, but grossly unethical. Information from a publication can be used, but such use without giving credit to the source is unethical. Copying someone's exact literary style violates copyright.

If you are planning a major piece of fiction in a certain setting which requires that considerable research material be used over a considerable period of time, you may not want to be restricted by the library's limited borrowing time. Or you may learn that there is an edition of a book published later than the copy in the library's possession. In such cases you may turn to other sources of information.

Commercial sources is just a fancy phrase meaning your local bookstores. These stores will have sections devoted to broad categories such as history, travel, sociology, etc. By visiting a few of them you will quickly learn which one has the best specialized sections.

You may find books at the store which are not in your library. I will be surprised if you don't, as all libraries seem to be strapped for funds and behind in their acquisitions. If you buy books, be sure to keep your receipt for possible tax-deduction purposes. If you're like me, you'll buy only books that you can see will have long-term research value to you, but that won't keep you from buying quite a few as you begin to build your research library.

Many colleges and universities have presses which specialize in certain areas of information. The University of Oklahoma Press, for example, has for years published many fine histories and biographies involving the western frontier, and not just Oklahoma-related items. Some of the best books currently in print about gold mining and outlawry in Montana have been published by Oklahoma. In like manner, the University of Nebraska Press has published many very fine books about Native

American history and lore. Most bookstores will either stock
some of these specialized university press titles, or have access
to their (as well as commercial publishers') catalogs. They'll also
have a list of books currently in print, probably on microfiche,
and can check specific titles and publishers for you.

Just browsing a good bookstore will sometimes reveal a
magazine or a book you didn't know existed. Don't forget to
browse the travel section, especially. Such books as the Fodors
travel guides or the Michelin guides include detailed maps, brief
histories and descriptions, and wonderful photos that can give
a feel for a place.

Another commercial source, often overlooked, is your local
travel agency. They're in the business of making reservations
and selling tickets, so I wouldn't expect one of their busy (commission) agents to spend much time answering your questions,
but most agencies have racks of tourist-luring brochures and
maps free for the asking. Invariably such materials include an
address where you can write for additional information.

Government sources of information for story settings
range from your local county or state agricultural agent to national and even international organizations. Your city hall or
courthouse might be the place to start. Is there some kind of
agricultural extension service available? You may not want to
know much about farming, but maybe your story setting includes a backyard flower garden; extension service offices often
have tremendous amounts of information available in pamphlet
form for such activities as this, too. Almost surely there is a local
Civil Defense office of some kind. There are dozens and dozens
of CD brochures available on everything from drinking water
to weather forecasting to nuclear radiation. There may be an
extensive library of area legal documents somewhere, and these
could provide setting information in the form of history that
you could get no other way.

In larger cities you can call a United States Government
number to order government pamphlets of all kinds. Some are
free, none are expensive. There is even a document you can buy
which lists all the other documents available. This is a valuable

resource because a myriad of federal agencies are in the publishing business.

The United Nations is a gold mine of printed information on matters of industry, health and science around the world. The organization's materials can be mail-ordered out of New York. If you are looking for factual data to be used as part of the setting in a story set abroad, the UN may be your best source, and again the cost is reasonable.

Most government agencies of the kind we're talking about here have public information as a priority part of their agenda. (If you were head of a federal government agency dependent on taxpayer support for existence, you would want to tell the taxpayers all about your operations and expertise, wouldn't you?) A simple letter to an organization such as NASA (National Aeronautics and Space Administration) or NOAA (National Oceanic and Atmospheric Adminstration, including what we once called the weather bureau) is likely to inundate you with information if you ask for it. The Department of Agriculture is another gold mine.

Computer research is another possible avenue of setting information. A number of standard library-type sources such as encyclopedias are online with major computer database services such as CompuServe or Prodigy. If you are heavily into electronic communications via the computer, there are specialized databases of all kinds. You may also be interested in commercially available computer programs available on floppy disk (or on CD-ROM); these let you "dial up" deeply detailed information on various regions of the world, or even major cities. More of such material is coming onto the market all the time.

Correspondence may go well beyond sending for brochures and pamphlets. If you locate the name of a company or individual that might have information useful for your setting work, it never hurts to write a letter asking specific questions or seeking an interview. I had a cordial response to such a routine letter of inquiry and enjoyed months of letters back and forth as I explored a topic in far greater detail than I ever imagined possible.

In a letter of this type, it's important to say who you are

and how you're qualified (as a writer, not in their field!), generally and briefly what your project is, and to provide a sample specific question or two. Then sit back and see what returns. Sometimes it's a joyous surprise. (Once I got a thirty-pound box of materials from a scientist at NOAA, for example.)

Local experts are another source of setting information not to be overlooked. It may be the old codger sitting on the park bench downtown who knows the town's history better than anyone. Or it might be a woman living nearby who has devoted half her life to learning all she can about a city and a lifestyle halfway around the planet. By all means ask your friends and associates if they know of anyone in the area you're researching. Ask at the library as well, as librarians often know such experts. Such a person will sometimes give you not only good factual information, but a sense of the feeling of a place or time, anecdotes, a loving look at something or someplace otherwise unavailable.

In all cases, whatever kind of research you do, keep good notes. Develop a standardized method of hanging onto them, be it file cards, file folders, computer disk, or whatever. Learn to honor research, and it will be your best companion now and for all your writing career.

NANCY BERLAND'S SETTING RESEARCH FORM

Nancy Berland is an Oklahoma novelist who is active in the Romance Writers of America. This form is one she uses in workshops she gives around the country.

Copyright © 1992, Nancy Berland. Used by permission of Nancy Berland.

Date/time/season of visit ⎯⎯⎯⎯⎯⎯⎯⎯⎯⎯⎯⎯

City/town name ⎯⎯⎯⎯⎯⎯⎯⎯⎯⎯ State ⎯⎯⎯⎯⎯⎯

County/Township/Borough (indicate which) ⎯⎯⎯⎯⎯⎯

County seat? yes ⎯⎯⎯⎯ no ⎯⎯⎯⎯

Area of state (northeast, northwest, panhandle, etc.) ⎯⎯⎯⎯

Community's population ⎯⎯⎯⎯⎯⎯⎯⎯⎯⎯⎯⎯

County population ⎯⎯⎯⎯⎯⎯⎯⎯⎯⎯⎯⎯

Form of government ⎯⎯⎯⎯⎯⎯⎯⎯⎯⎯⎯⎯

Location of city hall or seat of local government ⎯⎯⎯⎯⎯

Impressions

Three adjectives which most closely describe your first impression of community (friendly, fast-paced life, sleepy community, etc.) ⎯⎯⎯

⎯⎯⎯⎯⎯⎯⎯⎯⎯⎯⎯⎯⎯⎯⎯⎯⎯⎯⎯⎯⎯⎯⎯⎯⎯⎯⎯⎯⎯

⎯⎯⎯⎯⎯⎯⎯⎯⎯⎯⎯⎯⎯⎯⎯⎯⎯⎯⎯⎯⎯⎯⎯⎯⎯⎯⎯⎯⎯

General attitude of citizens (friendly, snobbish, etc.) _____

_____

_____

How would you describe town's populace? (Old-timers who sit on
street corners? Yuppies? Blue collar? Well-educated? Minorities?
Mention all groups noticed.) _____

_____

_____

Sensory Impressions

Odors you detected in the air (specify day/time smelled) _____

_____

_____

Sky and air quality (Overcast—is this typical during this season?
Smoggy, foggy, clouds—what kind? Clear?) _____

_____

_____

If weather affected your skin, note how _____

_____

_____

Weather on day you visited (temperature, direction of wind and
velocity—general) _____

_____

_____

This area's unique climate conditions (electrical storms, hurricanes,
ice storms, etc.) _____

_____

_____

Foods unique to the area and your reaction to these _____

_____

_____

Sounds you noticed (testing of jet engines, freight train rumblings, sonic booms, plant whistles, etc.) _____

_____

_____

Other sensory information unique to the area _____

_____

_____

Physical Features

Predominant geographical features (mountains, buttes, mesas, lakes, rivers, canyons, etc., noting specific names if these have been utilized as recreational areas) _____

_____

_____

Layout of community (town square, streets intersecting at right angles mainly, streets radiating like spokes from central point, as in Washington, D.C.) _____

_____

_____

Street surfaces (note differences and where) _____

_____

_____

Predominant architectural forms (Victorian, A-frames, adobe huts, high-rise apartments. Note types for different socioeconomic groups)

_____

_____

Predominant landmarks/statues, noting materials of man-made structures _____

_____

_____

Shopping centers _____

_____

_____

Local amusements (parks, tourist attractions, noting locations) ___

_____

_____

Nearby communities _____

_____

_____

Public transportation & name/locations of terminals/airports, etc. ___

_____

_____

Flora, Fauna and Such Stuff

Soil type/texture/color _____

_____

_____

Types of trees (note if in bloom) _____

_____

_____

Flowers (same info, note colors) _____

_____

_____

Observations about animals _____

Common local birds/fish/insects _____

_____

_____

Speech Patterns & Miscellaneous

Note unusual speech patterns, including age and socioeconomic group
of those speaking _____

_____

_____

Gathering places for local citizens, including old-timers and young people _____

_____

Local residents are proud of what aspects of this community? _____

_____

Names of local newspapers/magazines, including contact persons for each _____

_____

Local booksellers _____

_____

Local book distributor _____

_____

Community festivals/fairs/holiday celebrations _____

_____

Names of friends you made during your visit (with phone numbers/ addresses) you may wish to consult later _____

_____

Kind of energy utility (natural gas, electricity, etc.) _____

_____

Note: Nancy Berland grants permission to reproduce this form for personal use but not for publication. For questions, call Nancy at 405-721-2571.

INDEX